PLEASE INSERT into Frederick L. Schuman's book THE COMMONWEALTH OF MAN (Knopf, 1952):

ERRATA	CORRECTION
page 433, lines 21-25 "...the Campaign for World Government established in Chicago in 1937 by the Lloyd family of Winnetka..." page 440, lines 17-19 "In 1946 Mary and Georgia Lloyd, Edith Wynner, Harris Wofford, and a few other Americans evolved the idea of a 'Peoples' Convention.'"	The Campaign for World Government was established in 1937 by Rosika Schwimmer and Lola Maverick Lloyd to promote the establishment of a Federation of Nations, based on a plan first developed by them in 1924 in which the project for a Peoples' World Constitutional Convention was also first formulated. Most variations of the Peoples' Convention idea popularized internationally between 1945 and 1950 derive directly from this original source.

Books by Frederick L. Schuman

EUROPE ON THE EVE

The Crises of Diplomacy, 1933–1939

NIGHT OVER EUROPE

The Diplomacy of Nemesis, 1939–1940

SOVIET POLITICS

At Home and Abroad

THE COMMONWEALTH OF MAN

An Inquiry into Power Politics
and World Government

THE COMMONWEALTH OF MAN

FREDERICK L. SCHUMAN

Woodrow Wilson Professor of Government, Williams College

THE COMMONWEALTH OF MAN

An Inquiry into Power Politics and World Government

NEW YORK · ALFRED · A · KNOPF

1 9 5 2

L.C. CATALOG CARD NUMBER: 52-6424

THIS IS A BORZOI BOOK,
PUBLISHED BY ALFRED A. KNOPF, INC.

Manufactured in the United States of America.
Published simultaneously in Canada by McClelland & Stewart Limited.

FIRST EDITION

TO

MARCIA AND NORMAN

"*Quintilla prudentia regitur orbis!*"

—COUNT AXEL GUSTAFSSON OXIENSTIERNA (1583–1654),
CHANCELLOR OF SWEDEN.

"Ye men of Athens, I perceive that in all things ye are too superstitious. For as I passed by and beheld your devotions, I found an altar with this inscription, TO THE UNKNOWN GOD. Whom therefore ye ignorantly worship, him declare I unto you. God that made the world . . . And hath made of one blood all nations of men for to dwell on all the face of the earth . . . For we are also his offspring."

—SAINT PAUL ON MARS HILL, Acts xvii, 22–8.

PREFACE

This is a book about war and peace. It deals with Man's search for unity and for love and righteousness among the children of God. In its pages I have sought to apply the findings of some of the pioneers of the social sciences to the problem of anarchy and the prospects of order in the human community. I have also sought to reappraise the major World-States of our mortal adventure, the psychopathology of the "Cold War," and the various paths by which people have striven so long, and so often in vain, to find brotherhood and surcease from the killing of men by men.

The blind alleys and the hopeful highways are alike explored. No royal road to salvation is here charted or prescribed. All seekers for easy routes to the goal are unaware of the wastelands to be traversed. But the direction of the journey and the uses and disuses of sundry itineraries are, I trust, here revealed in a new light—not by way of neglecting but by way of assisting many other wayfarers, living or lost, to find a road through the wilderness.

The first summer days of 1952, when these words were written, were glorious days of beauty in the Berkshires. Elsewhere over the earth they were days of local violence, of universal anxiety, and of renewed efforts by devoted men and women, amid manifold discouragements, to banish the shadow of fear. United World Federalists held their Sixth General Assembly in Philadelphia. The World Association of Parliamentarians for World Government issued invitations for a second conference in London for early autumn. Preparations for the celebration of United Nations Day, October 24, proceeded apace. The World Council for the Peoples' World Convention planned a "Preparatory Assembly" for 1953. The World Movement for World Federal Government held an August preparatory conference in Holland in anticipation of the World Congress of WMWFG in 1953. Federal Unionists and the Atlantic Union Committee rejoiced that Estes Kefauver was a Federalist and that Dwight Eisenhower was committed to European Union. Amid much madness, these and other groups—all dealt with in these pages as to their origins and programs—reaffirmed their faith in the rationality of mankind.

But loud voices were raised in denunciation. A special issue (July 1952) of *United Nations World* examined the upsurge of discontent with the U.N. and within the U.S.A. The propagandists of the Scarlet Empire sang hymns of hate against America, screamed of "germ warfare" in Korea, and, as always, equated all proposals for world government with "Wall Street plots." In Washington, Senate Bill 2039, approved by the upper chamber on April 22, prohibited the "display of the flag of the United Nations . . . in a position equal or superior to that of the flag of the United States." Senator John W. Bricker pressed a constitutional amendment—inspired by the U.N. draft covenant of human rights, which he described as a "blueprint for tyranny"—to limit the treaty-making power of the Great Republic. The Senate Appropriations Committee registered alarm at UNESCO (labeled by the "American Flag Committee" as a "subversive association") and sought to ban the use of U.S. funds for "any international agency that directly or indirectly promotes one-world government or world citizenship." Dr. Jaime Torres Bodet, UNESCO's

Director General, pleaded not guilty. In invincible ignorance and fearful wrath, professional patrioteers throughout the land of liberty strove to censor textbooks and to ban from public schools all study of U.N., UNESCO, and other organizations dubbed "atheistic" or "communistic" by the self-appointed saviors of public purity.

Confusion among the worshippers of the tribal gods was further confounded in the America of 1952 by belated doubts as to whether national solvency was compatible with the costs of commitments already incurred to save the Free World from Red Sin. As military expenditures approached $167,000,000 per day, Congress cut Mutual Security authorizations from a requested $7,900,000,000 to $6,447,730,750, and tried to limit arms spending to $46,000,000,000 per year. The Pentagon cried havoc. Taxpayers took aspirin. The maintenance of the proposed levels of sacrifices to Mars (everywhere described as "the price of peace") threatened further inflation, ultimate bankruptcy, and a Garrison State. Their reduction threatened Soviet victory and an American depression.

This dilemma seemed unlikely to be resolved by the political devices of the quadrennial American hurly-burly. Taft proposed to cut taxes fifteen per cent. Eisenhower, while championing "peace through strength," proposed to cut expenditures forty billion dollars. Kefauver declared that neither taxes nor expenditures could be reduced. Truman demanded that both be raised. Harriman opined that Taft was "Stalin's candidate."

Communists remained cynical, Britons apprehensive, and Americans apathetic and hysterical by turns in the face of the continued addiction of Washington policy-makers to what George F. Kennan called "the legalistic-moralistic approach to international problems" and the "dangerous delusions" of total war and total victory. A year of negotiations for a Korean truce resolved all questions save one—but this quite sufficient to make peace improbable. "To agree to forced repatriation [of prisoners]," declared President Truman on May 7, "would be unthinkable . . . and repugnant to the fundamental moral and humanitarian principles which underlie our action in Korea." "There can be no retreat," editorialized the *New York Times* of June 22, 1952. "We believe in liberty and dignity. . . . These compulsions do not leave us a wide latitude of choice. . . . We are in a permanent conflict with a relentless antagonist. . . . We shall not be able to surrender at any other point when right and wrong, good and evil, are arrayed against each other."

Conflicts so defined admit of no termination save through annihilation or exhaustion. Since "perpetual war for perpetual peace," as the late Charles A. Beard termed it, is intolerable, the nihilists continued to toy with annihilation. "Many of the persons most familiar with the awful consequences of an atomic and hydrogen attack and the poverty of defense against it," wrote Edgar Ansel Mowrer on June 18, "are coming to feel that until these super-weapons are done away with or brought under control, life on this planet will never again be safe for anybody. Therefore they are cautiously taking the position that at some point the U.S. administration must compel the USSR to accept universal atomic disarmament by all necessary means, even including violence."

This paradox of power politics in its most pathological form will be with us always, until the Great Society either devours its own sons and daughters or gives them the hope of peace and life through the governance of all the globe. To this issue these chapters are addressed.

Many have helped to make this inquiry possible. My first and major acknowledgment must be to the Foundation for World Government, which granted me a stipend for this purpose and generously permitted me to define the scope and purport of the project as I saw fit. I was thereby enabled last year to take leave for a semester from my academic responsibilities and to pursue my studies of these matters in Western Europe. I am indebted to Clifford C. Dancer for reading a portion of Chapter viii and giving me the benefit of his counsel, and to Stringfellow Barr and Scott Buchanan for encouragement and inspiration. I am grateful to President James

Phinney Baxter III and the Trustees of Williams College for affording me a semester's leave, and to my colleagues, Dr. Fred Greene, E. Drexel Godfrey, Jr., and Walter S. Wilmot, for cheerfully sharing my duties in my absence, in addition to their own work. From the labors of my students in "Political Science 17," an experimental seminar in World Government in the autumn of 1950, I have borrowed freely and hereby give humble homage: to William A. Anderson, Richard E. Chapell, David S. Fischer, Samuel B. Grant, Jr., Burton H. Hall, Joseph P. McElroy, J. Kenneth Moore, Arthur H. Moss, Charles L. Smythe, Jr., Donald F. Vogel, Richard W. Wheeler, and Frederick Wiseman.

Among those abroad who extended many kindnesses and courtesies of great aid in the enterprise I am especially indebted to Patrick Armstrong, George Catlin, Henri Freney, John Fitzgerald, Pierre Hovelaque, F. Elwyn Jones, J. Keith Killby, Mary Lloyd, Alexandre Marc, Gilbert McAllister, R. W. G. Mackay, Franklin Roudybush of the U. S. Consulate in Strasbourg, Noël Salter and Nic M. Athanassiou of the Secretariat of the Council of Europe, Richard P. Taylor of the U. S. Information Service in London, Arnold J. Toynbee, and Henry Usborne.

To the authors and publishers who have graciously given permission to quote from their works, my thanks. In most instances acknowledgment is made on the page on which the quotation appears. In other instances (see Index for the passages used), acknowledgment is hereby made: to Bertrand Russell and the *New York Times Magazine; The New Yorker;* Harold Nicolson and Constable & Co., Ltd.; James Branch Cabell; Arnold J. Toynbee and Oxford University Press; Harvard University Press for the quotations from John U. Nef's *War and Human Progress* and Crane Brinton's *From Many One*, copyrighted respectively 1950 and 1948 by The President and Fellows of Harvard College; D. G. Redmond, Editor of *Current History*, where, in the October issue of 1951, the section entitled "The Disunion of Europe" first appeared as an article under my name; Henry R. Luce and *Time*, Inc.;

David L. Cohn and *The Atlantic Monthly;* Walter Lippmann, for passages from his column; Lawrence Dennis, for excerpts from his weekly analysis, *The Appeal to Reason;* Max Lerner and Simon and Schuster, Inc.; the University of Chicago Press, *Foreign Affairs*, and the Council on Foreign Relations for quotations from George F. Kennan; Herman Finer and the Macmillan Company; Linden A. Mander and Stanford University Press; and Robert M. Hutchins and the University of Denver Press.

The entire manuscript was read by Philip Vaudrin and by Professor V. O. Key, Jr., to both of whom I owe much for many helpful suggestions. I have no doubt that the book would have been further improved if I had been sufficiently openminded to accept all of their advice. My wife lent a hand in gathering data, at home and abroad, and gave me the benefit of her comments on portions of the manuscript. For this, and for much else, I am thankful. To Marcia Taft and to her successor I am deeply appreciative for competent and generous bibliographical, clerical, and stenographic aid. To Dr. Wyllis E. Wright, Ethel Richmond, and Donald E. Cary of the Williams College Library I owe more than they realize.

No person or organization named here or in the following pages is in any respect responsible for the form, content, or conclusions of this analysis. All have contributed to whatever merits it may possess. Its limitations, defects, and possible errors of fact or judgment are all my own handiwork.

This volume is dedicated to my niece and her husband, Mr. and Mrs. Norman E. Sweet, Jr. In their happiness, their ambitions, and their work for days to come, they speak for the cause of youth and the future in a world worthy of the hopes of all the human family. Should this work contribute anything to that cause, it will have served its purpose.

FREDERICK L. SCHUMAN

Williamstown, Massachusetts, July 4, 1952

CONTENTS

THE COMMONWEALTH OF MAN

CHAPTER ONE

THE WAY OF VIOLENCE

1. SUMMER SOLSTICE

Midsummer Day is the great turning point in the sun's career, when, after climbing higher and higher day by day in the sky, the luminary stops and thenceforth retraces his steps down the heavenly road. Such a moment could not but be regarded with anxiety by primitive man so soon as he began to observe and ponder the courses of the great lights across the celestial vault; and having still to learn his own powerlessness in face of the vast cyclic changes of nature, he may have fancied that he could help the sun in his seeming decline—could prop his failing steps and rekindle the sinking flame of the red lamp in his feeble hand. In some such thoughts as these the midsummer festivals of our European peasantry may perhaps have taken their rise.

—SIR JAMES G. FRASER: *The Golden Bough.*[1]

HUMAN BEINGS, being human and therefore blessed or cursed with the gift of imagining both the past and the future, are ever addicted to speculating about the destiny of mankind. This use of the magic of the mind more often than not evokes only a feeble and feckless simian chattering, having no purpose beyond that of enabling men to feel important through identifying themselves with Man. Yet occasionally from the words of prophets flow spiritual insights and some half-plausible mirroring of the inscrutable will of God.

[1] Sir James G. Frazer: *The Golden Bough—A Study in Magic and Religion* (Macmillan; 1940, one-volume abridgment), p. 622.

It now appears to be widely agreed by gossips and prophets and social scientists, and above all by fearful physicists shocked at the uses made of their handiwork, that mankind has reached a parlous pass indeed in the middle years of the twentieth century after Christ. Whether this is so—and, if so, why—is less important than the fact that men believe it to be so. For humans, notoriously, are not moved to action by any objective truth transcending human understanding (if indeed anything of the kind exists), but rather by what they suppose to be true. Those who cry havoc often produce it. And if enough people anticipate disaster, and act accordingly, disaster is what they are apt to get.

What we and our fellows choose to believe about human destiny and about the unending "crisis" of our age plainly admits of no simple statement. Nor is any complex statement likely to be meaningful. There are people and people, living out their lives in joy or grief or boredom or quiet desperation all over the turning earth—and entertaining such varying beliefs and expectations that common denominators are not easy to come by. Yet some clues to the mood of the times may perhaps be had by the device of ignoring for the moment the words of the wise men, and contemplating what people do on a typical day and what they read and hear about the doings of others. The device is faulty, to be sure, perhaps to the point of foolishness. Each day in the life of every woman and man is unique. None is typical. Nobody knows what everybody does—and wouldn't care if he did. What is offered to the public eye and ear, moreover, is the result of fallible guesses as to what people are interested in and what events merit being deemed important for tomorrow. All this granted, our device may yet be enlightening.

Take a day then, at random. Since any day will do, let us choose the longest day of 1951—the first year of the second half of our century. Summer begins in the northern hemisphere at 12.25 a.m. on June 22, Eastern Standard Time, U.S.A. Our spinning planet, tilted askew, silently passes an unseen point on an invisible course and thereby makes the northern night shorter, and the southern night longer, than it has been, or will be again, during our year-long circling of the sun. This cosmic event is precisely predictable, since it is repetitive and, for practical purposes, uniform year after year. What people do during this particular rotation of their earthly home is equally predictable only if we limit ourselves to those recurrent acts which, despite cultural differences, are yet remarkably alike everywhere.

By inference from ourselves, and from the few we see and know to the vast throngs we can neither see nor know, we take it for granted that on our June day all people in the world act much the same with regard to an astonishing number of things. They sleep and wake up. They breathe air, save for the few who breathe water and drown, or breathe earth or fire and die. They eat food, thrice or oftener if they belong to the rich Atlantic communities, less often if they belong to the unprivileged two thirds of the species spread over Asia, Africa, America to the south, and many of the islands of the seas. They drink: water everywhere, milk somewhere, brews of tea and coffee in many climes, juices and distillates, beers and wines, vodkas and whiskies, and all manner of concoctions designed less to quench thirst than to dull unpleasant excitation or to excite pleasant dullness.

Along with all the more complicated organisms, all human creatures perform this day all the animal acts for which we have indelicate four-letter Anglo-Saxon words and dignified polysyllabic Latin names. Most people also labor, producing and selling and buying. Most move to and fro—by foot, horse, or mule, by oxcart, camel, or elephant, by motor car, tramway, train, or plane. Others are immobile in hospitals, asylums, or jails. A few plan or commit theft, murder, or suicide. Some are miserable. Some are happy. The business of marrying and mating and breeding and burying goes on as always. For the most part people on our chosen day are spending most of their time as they have done for days without end: they dress, undress, and bathe; they sweat from toil or play; they curse, or weave dreams of glory; they swindle their neighbors or do them kindnesses; they make love or abstain, talk politics or refrain, and display everywhere, we may guess, the usual proportions of affection, fear, and hate, along with greed, unselfishness, lechery, devotion, skepticism, religiosity, meanness, magnanimity, and all the other attributes judged virtuous or sinful among all the tribes of men.

Is then the world of June 22, 1951, One World? Hardly, despite all the uniformities in the daily routine of the earth-dwellers. Men are not much united by their similarities as organisms or even as producers, consumers, and citizens. Men are sharply divided by their differences in what they believe and expect. The divisions among them, and the frictions and conflicts that are unique rather than repetitive, are everywhere regarded as somehow more significant for the future of the race than the uniformities. Our summer day is the anniversary of wars of hideous destructiveness and terror: ten years earlier Hitler's hosts invaded Russia; one hundred and thirty-six years earlier, with one day's difference, Bonaparte's Grand Army crossed the Niemen on an equally ill-fated mission of slaughter and conquest. Our day is also a day of war. Men are killing men in Korea. The bid for peace, in recognition of defeat, on which Jacob A. Malik is working in New York will be broadcast only on the following evening. It will be acted upon by American policy-makers, in recognition of the unattainability of victory, a week later—with a cessation of killing long deferred.

What else among unique events goes on among men, from the narrow and somewhat neurotic purview of a dweller in eastern North America? A widely distributed pamphlet asserts: "When you see a flash of light brighter than the sun—don't run; there isn't time. Fall flat on your face. *Get down fast!* . . ." [2] But the flash, eagerly awaited by an expectant people, does not occur—yet. Actual events compel more immediate attention. The Giants defeat the Cubs, 9 to 6, in ten innings at Wrigley Field in Chicago. At New London,

[2] Civil Defense Agency of the Commonwealth of Massachusetts: *Protection from the Atomic Bomb* (1950).

Harvard crews win the eighty-sixth regatta with Yale. Pintor defeats Jet Master by a head in the Tremont Stakes. Stocks drop for the fifth day in a row. Broadway offers *Darkness at Noon*, *The Moon Is Blue*, *Guys and Dolls*, and *The Rose Tattoo*. Radio City Music Hall is showing "The Great Caruso" and the RKO chain, "I Was A Communist for the FBI." *The New Yorker* (June 23) opines:

> Until the *Daily Worker* quits running baseball news, we won't be convinced that the Communists really believe the stuff they keep peddling. It would appear that even Communists have an insatiable curiosity about the Giants, and this, of course, gives the whole Communist religion a fuzzy glow. Baseball is capitalism in its gaudiest form, and not even the Giants, although underdogs, can be said to be underprivileged. The gate receipts are enormous, salaries are so high as to be suspect, and there is a rumor that some teams exist not to win games at all but merely to sell players at a profit. The spectacle is utterly degrading, yet the *Worker* reports it straight. (The only factual news in the paper.) . . . How is it possible for a man to follow the fortunes of the ball clubs while engaged in the revolution to overthrow the exploiting class? We withdraw the question.

"All the News That's Fit to Print" on June 22, 1951, as on other days, is largely news of war, diplomacy, politics, and other crimes, follies, and disasters. "U.S. Plane with Forty Vanishes Over West African Jungle." "The House of Representatives, 233 to 160, Passes a Bill Calling for the Biggest Tax Increase in History"—$7,200,000,000, involving a total tax rise of $17,000,000,000 since the outbreak of the Korean War, and an annual tax load of $65,300,000,000. "Thug, Two Passersby, Shot in Battle as Police Foil East 26th Street Hold-up." Archbishop Josef Groesz confesses in Budapest to plotting with the United States' help to overthrow the Hungarian government. Nobody believes the confession. General David G. Barr testifies that America did everything humanly possible to keep Chiang Kai-shek in power in China. Gromyko in Paris says the Western Powers must bear "entire responsibility" for the breakup of the conference of the Deputy Foreign Ministers in the Palais Rose, after seventy-four meetings. Iran wants a U.S. loan. White House and State Department authorize the Export-Import Bank to permit Spain to buy wheat and coal out of the $62,500,000 loan granted by Congress to Franco last year. Charles E. Wilson predicts "industrial miracles that will astonish the world and, I hope, confound our enemies," since we can soon "blast great cities into rubble anywhere in the world."

Also: Congressman Clarence Cannon, seventy-two-year-old Missouri Democrat, inflicts a cut on the lip of Congressman John Phillips, sixty-three-year-old Californian Republican, in a name-calling fist fight in the Capitol corridors. Congressman Taber says Congressman Cannon called Congressman Phillips "a son-of-a-bitch." After treatment by the Capitol physician, the victim returns to the floor to vote on the tax bill. "Argentina Seizes Five Officers in Plot." In Italy, three quarters of a million civil servants strike for higher wages. "New York City's Dope War to Fingerprint 28,000 Workers." Presidents Truman (U.S.A.) and Galo Plaza (Ecuador) pledge that their countries will "remain steadfastly united in the present emergency." Supreme Court Justice Robert H. Jackson rules that eleven convicted Communists must go to jail. U.S. District Court Judge Henry W. Goddard rules that the transfer of Mrs. Ethel Rosenberg, convicted atomic spy, to the Sing Sing death house is not "cruel and inhuman." Plane spotters in twenty-three states hold tests.

United Nations youth experts study delinquency. Psychologist G. M. Gilbert, addressing the Institute on Mental Hygiene Aspects of Civil Defense in Trenton, New Jersey, says we must "combat totalitarianism with the most formidable and most feared weapon: the truth." Psychologist George B. Vetter in New York, speaking on atomic defense, urges "practicing hymns so you'll be prepared—the old hymns are wonderful for calming crowds." Arthur Hays Sulzberger in Lenoxville, Quebec, deplores "too much emphasis on physical survival." The Senate transmits to the President a "compromise resolution" affirming friendship for the Russian people. The Carnegie Endowment for International Peace announces that its new building, to face the U.N. headquarters, will have a frame of reinforced concrete instead of steel "to save war materials."

Addenda: The State Department declares that the "American Peoples Peace Congress," scheduled for Chicago, June 29, "hopes to establish a permanent U.S. phony 'peace' organization," to follow the Communist-line of the "American Peace Crusade," which demands negotiations for peace among China, Russia, France, Britain, and America. The MacArthur hearings in Washington approach their end after Senators take 1,900,000 words of testimony and listen to MacArthur for 21 hours, 10 minutes; to Marshall 27 hours, 42 minutes; and to Acheson 39 hours, 6 minutes. Bitterly the *Chicago Tribune* quotes Senator Kefauver ("The present Administration has given the public nothing to look forward to in foreign affairs for the next thirty years except war and paying for wars") and adds: "We pay and pay, kill and get killed, endlessly. Who can say that this will stop in thirty years? Who can say that it will ever stop, as long as the (Roosevelt-Truman) policy remains in effect?" [3] Bitterly Bernard De Voto, borrowing a text from Lincoln, writes that Senator Robert A. Taft, to the sole end of winning the nomination and election of 1952, "had already allied himself with the foul birds and dirty reptiles, and so stripped from himself the garmenture of integrity and shown that as a leader of the Republican Party he was entirely irresponsible. But he is bare naked now, for his adoption of the anti-Europe, pro-Asiatic war policy shows that . . . he is also fearfully deficient in intelligence." [4]

[3] *The Chicago Daily Tribune* (June 23, 1951).

[4] Bernard De Voto in *Harper's Magazine*, July 1951, p. 51. His text is from Lincoln's letter of October 5, 1863, to Charles D. Drake: "It is easy to conceive that all these shades of opinion, and even more, may be sincerely entertained by honest and truthful men. Yet, all being for the Union, by reason of these differences each will prefer a different way of sustaining the Union. At once, sincerity is questioned and motives are assailed. Actual war coming, blood grows hot and blood is spilled. Thought is forced from

Meanwhile, the papers, as ever, report engagements, marriages, births, and deaths—each event unique for the participant, all events a statistical average for cities, towns, and villages in a Great Society where individuals are mere ciphers on ledgers. Or are they? This day I have recently returned from Western Europe, where individuals are still individuals and where almost no one fears Russia or expects war, to an America where almost everyone expects war and fears Russia. What do we most value? What do we most deplore or regret? Who knows with any certainty? On this same first day of summer my local paper reports a solemn High Mass in the Church of the Incarnation at Blackinton—as a final tribute, preceding burial with full military honors in Southview Cemetery, of Corporal Roland L. Burke, nineteen, of 25 Taft Street, North Adams, Massachusetts, killed in action in Korea on September 11. He was "laid to rest in the free soil he helped to defend. . . ."[5]

Whoever ponders this day's news, or any day's happenings in our troubled times—and imagines, if he can, the uncountable myriads of other human events all over the earth, unrecorded but no less crucial for those to whom they bring ecstasy or heartbreak—must wonder if they have any common meaning and, if so, what it is. And since all meaning is a matter of relating the particular to the general, each observer and participant will find significance in the record, and interrelationships among its separate items, in terms of his own preconceptions regarding Man and God, the world and the universe, and the problems and prospects of humankind. An infinity of meanings is thus available. But infinity is measureless and meaningless. It can fairly be argued, more tangibly, that the midcurrent of events in our time flows through a single muddy channel that seems to broaden and deepen and

---

old channels into confusion. Deception breeds and thrives. Confidence dies and universal suspicion reigns. Each man feels an impulse to kill his neighbor, lest he be killed by him. Revenge and retaliation follow. And all this, as before said, may be found among honest men only. But this is not all. Every foul bird comes abroad and every dirty reptile rises up. . . ."

[5] *The North Adams* (Massachusetts) *Transcript*, June 22, 1951.

grow more turgid and troubled mile by mile and month by month. That channel can be given a name: Anxiety.[6]

This painful quality of experience can never be isolated from other facets of living, for it tinctures, however slightly, every waking hour. In its currently acute and epidemic form it may well be viewed as a product of grave conflicts among values and purposes, each of which by itself might promote peace of mind but all of which, taken together in clashing confusion, beget doubt and tension and anguish. Our anxiety is suffused with rage against evildoers, clouded over with guilt and indecision because we were once told: Resist not evil; love thine enemies; let him who is without sin cast the first stone. Our anxiety is blended with frustrated love, for in our worry we need more than ever a sense of being wanted, and we wonder whether we are loved or even lovable. But our anxiety is basically a neurotic perversion of fear. And the fear, in turn, even though it attaches itself to a bewildering kaleidoscope of private problems and public symbols, is most probably a product of our dim conviction that our common civilization has somehow reached an impasse that threatens us with destruction.

2. THE HOUSE OF FEAR

> Love casts out fear; but conversely fear casts out love. And not only love. Fear also casts out intelligence, casts out goodness, casts out all thought of beauty and truth. What remains is the dumb

[6] W. H. Auden, with a poet's insight, has called our epoch *The Age of Anxiety*. Among the more suggestive commentaries on this theme, see Sigmund Freud: *Civilization and Its Discontents* (Cape and Smith; 1930); Karen Horney: *The Neurotic Personality of Our Time* (Norton; 1937); Erich Fromm: *Escape from Freedom* (Farrar & Rinehart; 1941) and *Man for Himself* (Rinehart; 1947); and Harold D. Lasswell: *World Politics and Personal Insecurity* (McGraw-Hill; 1935). The widespread prevalence in America of an acutely felt need for reassurance is exemplified by the tremendous sales in the years since World War II of books with such comforting titles as *Peace of Mind, Peace of Soul, The Mature Mind, How to Stop Worrying and Start Living, The Anatomy of Happiness*, and so on.

or studiedly jocular desperation of one who is aware of the obscene Presence in the corner of the room and knows that the door is locked, that there aren't any windows. And now the thing bears down on him. He feels a hand on his sleeve, smells a stinking breath, as the executioner's assistant leans almost amorously toward him. "Your turn next, brother. Kindly step this way." And in an instant his quiet terror is transmuted into a frenzy as violent as it is futile. There is no longer a man among his fellow men, no longer a rational being speaking articulately to other rational beings; there is only a lacerated animal, screaming and struggling in the trap. For in the end fear casts out even a man's humanity. And fear, my good friends, fear is the very basis and foundation of modern life. Fear of the much touted technology which, while it raises our standard of living, increases the probability of our violently dying. Fear of the science which takes away with one hand even more than what it so profusely gives with the other. Fear of the demonstrably fatal institutions for which, in our suicidal loyalty, we are ready to kill and die. Fear of the Great Men whom we have raised, by popular acclaim, to a power which they use, inevitably, to murder and enslave us. Fear of the War we don't want and yet do everything we can to bring about.

—ALDOUS HUXLEY: *Ape and Essence.*[7]

So plastic is protoplasm in all its forms that beasts and men, if they must, can learn to live with fear forever in their hearts. The tensions engendered thereby are all but intolerable—and often shatter unstable individuals and even whole communities. The Germans of the Nazi era, reduced to madness by fear of their own phobias, were given to shouting: "Better a terrible end than an endless terror." Such feelings of desperation find voice again in our own time. Yet the mass of men and women, lacking leisure or inclination for morbid absorption in the woes of the world, go about their daily tasks apparently oblivious of preachments of doom.

The detached observer might indeed question the premise that our generation is more anxious and fear-ridden than its

[7] Quoted by permission of Harper & Bros., publishers in 1948 of the novel *Ape and Essence*, by Aldous Huxley, who depicts plausibly the culture pattern that develops among the barbarized survivors of an atomic holocaust.

precursors. The physiologist and psychiatrist can measure fear in an organism. Animal fear is a matter of heartbeat, blood pressure, respiration, perspiration, eye reflexes, and the like. But the sociologist, though he can profitably study statistics of crime, suicide, alcoholism, divorce, psychosomatic diseases, and other illnesses of widespread insecurity and strain, has no infallible yardstick for measuring the prevalence and intensity of fear in an entire society. No one is justified in asserting flatly, on the basis of unchallengeable empirical evidence, that the living sons and daughters of Adam are more afflicted with anxiety than were their departed ancestors. We may here be confronted by something not new but hoary with the dust of centuries—i.e., the fact that each generation deems its own troubles more painful, its worries more agonizing, its crises more crucial, and its decisions more decisive than any that have gone before.

Be it further recalled, before we crown Fear as king of our epoch, that all of us—save dumb animals and the happy people of folk-cultures not yet disposed to question ancient answers to the puzzles of Man and Nature and Divinity—share some measure of universal apprehension, by virtue of the very nature of ourselves and our relationship to the cosmos. Earth is fair, yet frightening. Life is good, yet baffling. Who are we? Why? Can we ever know our brothers? Or ourselves? Erich Fromm comments on these eternal mysteries as a common source of "existential anxiety":

> We are alone, put into this world at an accidental time and place, and forced out of it again accidentally and against our will. Our existence is beset by contradictions, not only those we can resolve but those inherent in our human situation. Man is part of nature, subject to physical laws and unable to change them, yet he transcends the rest of nature. He is set apart, and in being apart, he is homeless, yet chained to the home he shares with all creatures. Being aware of himself, he realizes his powerlessness and the limitations of his existence. He realizes his own end: death. Never is he free from the dichotomy of his existence. He cannot rid himself of his mind even if he should want to; he

cannot rid himself of his body as long as he is alive, and his body makes him want to be alive. We are beset by conflicting desires; we have to make decisions before we have acquired wisdom. . . . If we dispense with all comforting props, then indeed we look into an abyss of aloneness and conflict which makes us anxious.[8]

These fears we share with others in many times and places. There is none the less a sense in which our particular anxieties, albeit admitting of no measure for purposes of comparison, would appear to be more acute and disturbing than any others of which we have record, at least since the Wars of Religion. The fact is attested to by the quality and mood of our literature—in which "the novel as nightmare"[9] has become the norm—of our æsthetic vagaries, of our intellectual gyrations and, above all, of our demagogic politics, where "freedom from fear" is the great goal, forever unattainable, and where anxious salesmen of panic vie with one another in seeing who can frighten the largest number of anxious buyers of panic. These phenomena are ubiquitous throughout the Western world. They afflict the Eastern realms as well, possibly to a greater degree beneath the silence imposed by the high priests of ideological orthodoxy. They are most advanced, visible, and malignant in America: the wealthiest, most productive, most powerful, and (therefore, one might falsely assume) most secure of the major communities of today's world.

The sources of these fears, subjective or objective, rational or neurotic, are doubtless deeply imbedded in the very fabric of the way of life we call "modern civilization," and are both cause and effect of the "culture crisis" of our age. Confidence in "progress," which seemed beneficently inevitable and interminable to our great-grandparents, has waned almost to the vanishing-point. All now perceive that few are happier or more virtuous or more blessed with a sense of direction than

[8] Erich Fromm: "The Age of Anxiety," *Bennington College Alumni Quarterly*, Vol. II, No. 3 (1950), pp. 24–5.

[9] H. Stuart Hughes: *An Essay for Our Times* (Alfred A. Knopf; 1950), pp. 37–58.

their ancestors, despite the uninterrupted "advance" of science and technology. Disillusionment with dreams once widely cherished has marched apace with corroding skepticism. Both together have conspired with cynicism in the gray twilight to thrust their stilettos into the body of religious conviction. The victim is grievously hurt, if not mortally injured. Faith, art, and science no longer appear royal roads to health, beauty, and truth, but only trivia, or devices of escape, or merely means to make a living, sans inspiration and joy, with their fruits subtly corrupted to the service of evil.

Explanations of this malaise are cheap and abundant, for we belong to a curious species whose members must forever be explaining all that gives them pause, often to no purpose save further confusion. Among the intellectuals, for whom this exercise is a professional duty, the economists seek causes in the instability of the business system; the sociologists and psychologists in "cultural lag" and in social mobility and breakdown; the clergymen in secularism, hedonism, and apathy; the philosophers in as many hypotheses as there are philosophers. There may be no valid explanation, or none with operational utility, just as there may be no answers to the endless questions posed by our shared frustrations. The notions that all puzzles can be resolved, and all problems solved, may be shabby relics of the nineteenth and eighteenth centuries—a suspicion that is itself further evidence of the poignancy of our misfortune.

But there is at least one aspect of disorder which all can agree is global in its spatial dimension, and quite possibly primary in any order of priorities, however much savants may disagree as to what is cause and what is effect and what relationships may reasonably be assumed to exist between this and other attributes of chaos. This aspect has to do with the recurrent demise of our hopes that the national communities of men, comprising a now-worldwide society, can somehow or other find ways of living together on the same planet without indulging periodically in orgies of mass murder and devastation. The hopes are old. Their frustrations have never been more bitterly felt than in our own time, when so much has been promised and so little fulfilled. Consider three voices out of a noisy Babel—each proceeding from different premises to different conclusions, but agreeing that our aspirations for a viable international order have been betrayed.

Nathaniel Peffer, writing in a "learned" journal, because editors of "popular" journals tend to eschew truths that are too discouraging, wrote in 1948:

> Somehow, in ways and for reasons not clear even to those who have lived through the period and tried to analyse its moving forces, we seem to have lost two wars, we no less than our enemies. I do not mean this only in the obvious and conventional sense that victor and vanquished alike have suffered impoverishment, destruction and human sacrifice. I mean that the ends of the wars have not been gained, that on the contrary we, no less than our enemies, have retrogressed, that our own outlook, as well as the world's outlook, is darker than before 1914 or even 1939. We as the victors have escaped subjugation and enjoyed the emotional satisfaction of exacting retribution from the Germans and Japanese, but in all else we have lost. We and the world are worse off for our victory. We have not even the assurance of a transient peace, to say nothing of a long truce, as after Waterloo and the Congress of Vienna. On all the evidence, judged by historical precedents, we are now in the state of prelude to war, analogous to the years 1912 and 1937. . . . There is more than this or we should be on familiar ground. There is also the conflict of social philosophies. . . . There is something else, related but deeper and more lasting in its impact, something that strikes closer to the foundation of modern society. It concerns the principle and method of the conduct of human relations. Here, too, there is conflict—the most dangerous of our time. In this the world is worse off than before, and in this conflict the officially victorious nations, or, rather, the democratic nations among them, not only have not won, but may be said to be losing.[1]

Harry Elmer Barnes, two years later:

> Those who can remember "the good old days" before 1914 in-

[1] Nathaniel Peffer: "Democracy Losing by Default," *The Political Science Quarterly* (September 1948), pp. 321 f.

evitably look back to those times with a very definite and justifiable feeling of nostalgia. There was no income tax before 1913, and that levied in the early days after the Amendment of 1913 was little more than nominal. All kinds of taxes were relatively low. We had only a token national debt of around a billion dollars which could have been paid off in a year without causing even a ripple in national finance. Inflation was unheard of here. Ours was a libertarian country in which the Four Freedoms flourished, at least for the white inhabitants. There was little or no witch-hunting and few of the symptoms and operations of the police state which has been developing so drastically here during the last decade. Not until our intervention in the first World War had there been sufficient invasions of individual liberties to call forth the formation of such organizations as the American Civil Liberties Union. Libertarianism was also dominant in Western Europe. . . . Enlightened citizens of the Western World were then filled with buoyant hope for a bright future of humanity. . . . Unfortunately, there are relatively few persons today who recall those happy times. . . . The great majority have known only a world ravaged by war, depressions, international intrigue and meddling, vast debts and crushing taxation, the encroachments of the police state, and the control of public opinion and government by ruthless and irresponsible propaganda.[2]

Bertrand Russell, warning that all may be lost and that we had best seek the consolations of philosophy, writes more recently:

There is only too much reason to fear that Western civilization, if not the whole world, is likely in the near future to go through a period of immense sorrow and suffering and pain—a period during which, if we are not careful to remember them, the things that we are attempting to preserve may be forgotten in bitterness and poverty and disorder. Courage, hope, and unshakable conviction will be necessary if we are to emerge from the dark time spiritually undamaged. . . . The fall of Rome was another such time, and in that time, as now, varying moods of despair, escape, and robust faith were exemplified in the writings

[2] Harry Elmer Barnes: *The Struggle Against the Historical Blackout* (Stonewood, Cooperstown, N.Y.: privately printed; 1950, 7th edition), pp. 1–3.

of leading men. . . . Boethius, who represents the very last blossoming of Roman civilization, was a figure of use to our age. . . . The sages of our time have a similar duty to perform. It is their duty to posterity to crystallize the achievements, the hopes and the ideals which have made our time great—to study them with monumental simplicity, so they may shine like a beacon light through the coming darkness.[3]

Advice to renew our faith in the verities, to refrain henceforth from involvement in foreign quarrels, to devote our energies to winning the peace (if any) is advice more easily given than taken. But the central circumstance in our multitude of troubles is plain enough. "Opinion polls which have been completed in recent years," observe the authors of a recent study of the goals of political science, "leave no doubt that anxiety concerning international instabilities represents the public's chief worry—a concern which exceeds that arising from any other problem."[4] Expectation of the inevitability or imminence of World War III is widespread, with almost everyone taking it for granted that the next holocaust will involve the atomic incineration of many or most of the major cities of men, and will quite possibly leave little but small groups of demented survivors living in savagery amid the ruins.

The most generalized answer to the question of how and why our culture finds itself confronted with such a prospect—and what ought to be done about it—would seem to run somewhat as follows. The Great Society is a congeries of disparate communities, each of which is possessed of "sovereignty" and all of which, therefore, live in "anarchy." Under anarchy, in Thomas Hobbes's immortal phrase, life is "poor,

[3] Bertrand Russell: "If We Are to Survive This Dark Time—" *The New York Times Magazine* (September 3, 1950), p. 5.

[4] *Goals for Political Science*, Report of the Committee for the Advancement of Teaching, American Political Science Association (William Sloane; 1951), p. 44, citing, as further confirmation, a Gallup public opinion poll published May 5, 1950. See also Robert K. Merton: "The Self-fulfilling Prophecy," *Antioch Review* (Summer 1948), and Harold D. Lasswell: " 'Inevitable' War—A Problem in the Control of Long-range Expectations," *World Politics* (October 1949).

solitary, nasty, brutish, and short." The sole cure for anarchy, we are assured by many voices (including Hobbes's), is government. The remedy for world anarchy is thus widely held to be "world government." Whether this familiar formula is sound or senseless, and, if sound, to what degree and with what implications, is the prime object of our inquiry. Yet the inquiry, if it is to be more than an empty rephrasing of formulas, must recapitulate and, so far as feasible, reappraise the elements of the problem of violence in the relations among sovereignties.

---

3. OLD WINE IN NEW BOTTLES

> In all times, kings, and persons of sovereign authority, because of their independence, are in continual jeolousies, and in the state and posture of gladiators; having their weapons pointing, and their eyes fixed on one another; that is, their forts, garrisons and guns upon the frontiers of their kingdoms; and continual spies upon their neighbors; which is a posture of war. . . . The notions of right and wrong, justice and injustice, have there no place. Where there is no common power, there is no law: where no law, no injustice. Force and fraud are in war the two cardinal virtues. . . . It is consequent also to the same condition that there be no propriety, no dominion, no "mine" and "thine" distinct; but only that to be every man's, that he can get; and for so long as he can keep it.
>
> —THOMAS HOBBES: *Leviathan* (1651).

AN INTELLIGENT interplanetary traveler is always a useful companion in any effort to comprehend human affairs. Literary license permits us to assume that our voyager through space, while possessed of as sharp an eye and as clever a brain as Man, is fairly free of men's vices and stupidities. He brings to the human scene the godlike perspective of a never-never land where prejudices, if they exist at all, are so different from our own that they do not distort the traveler's earthly observations. He thus sees clearly, through the eternities and infinities of the cosmos, what we see not at all—or only through a glass, darkly.

A bright visitor arrives from, let us say, Saturn. No matter that Saturn sustains no life and that to be *à la mode* our migrant should really come from a satellite of Sirius or from a remote moon in the solar system of Antares. As he contemplates thoughtfully the human adventure on Planet Earth, he is at once impressed with the fact that the earth-dwellers, for reasons not immediately obvious, do not live and have never lived "together" in one world-embracing community, but always live in separate clans or tribes or kingdoms or nations or empires. These herds or bands of the extant Hominidæ, however, do not live alone, content and secure unto themselves, but are forever jostling one another in confused relationships of trade or travel or conflict. Our Saturnite, as he considers reflectively the whole gamut of these contacts through terrestrial space and time, notes particularly a curious fact—or one at any rate curious on Saturn where, by hypothesis, all is for the best on the best of possible planets. This is the fact of war.

The various gangs of earthlings, he soon perceives, indulge, and have ever indulged, in periodic excitements and excursions in the course of which they murder one another with enthusiasm, rape one another's wives and daughters, starve or strangle one another's children, and steal or burn one another's property. All the while they protest solemnly that what they do is done with the utmost reluctance and in the face of the most extreme provocation and, in the last analysis, only for the good of all.

Should our Saturnite be puzzled by this conduct of the earthmen, he might resolve his puzzlement in sundry ways. He may conclude that the earthmen, by their very nature and despite all their protestations, enjoy killing one another and therefore do so gladly. Or he may conclude, taking the protestations seriously, that men loathe killing other men but yet do so for the purpose of penalizing sin and vindicating virtue—men being seemingly divisible into the two categories of Good and Bad. Or he may decide, on third thought, that the whole business is a kind of unforeseen consequence of a wholly unplanned circumstance—namely, the propensity of the earthmen to divide themselves into groups, each geographically circumscribed, each with its own language and lifeways, each pushing and shoving other groups in the same neighborhood. Within each group, moreover (and this might strike our visitor as the heart of the matter), each individual is somehow driven from within to seek sympathy and a sense of oneness with his fellows, for these Hominids are terrified of loneliness. And this hunger in their hearts, it turns out, can most easily be sated through the game of joining together to rob and kill the members of alien groups and to resist like efforts on the part of neighbors similarly disposed.

Leaving open the question of which explanation, among these and others unmentioned, our celestial voyager might at last accept as most nearly true, we may yet pause to consider—while he wings his way homeward through the void—the drift and import of his third line of thought. Men evidently live in groups because the miseries of so doing are less, and the joys of so doing are greater, than those of living apart. Fearful of aloneness, and physically feeble against the other mammalian carnivores (including other humans united for the hunt), men clump themselves together for safety, food, and warmth. One type of grouping, amid a great multiplicity, has a unique character in terms of its meaning in men's lives—for its value is not to be found directly in creature-comforts or erotic gratifications or philoprogenitive satisfactions or nutritional endeavors or spiritual salvation. This grouping is universal among all people who learn to read and write and live in cities. It has no real counterpart, save by loose analogy, among the primitives who lack these skills and are thus both unlettered and uncivilized. This grouping is called the "State."

What we choose to believe, or happen to believe, about the State as a ubiquitous institution of civilized peoples colors completely, and shapes inexorably, what we believe about might and right, war and peace, international enmity and world government. We may here defer this portion of our search—not so much because of the improbability that anything new can be said on so well-worn a topic but rather because it is more useful for present purposes to reconsider what typically happens in the relations among States than to examine the relations between men within States. The two sets of relationships, to be sure, cannot be sharply sundered without tearing apart the fabric we wish to describe. Our procedure is yet permissible, for the particular relations between men with which we are here concerned can most readily be approached by observing the relations among States. These in turn can be depicted with reasonable adequacy by reference to a fairly simple and repetitive pattern, despite the fervid attempts of politicians and political scientists to render them fearfully complicated.[5]

Whenever two or more States, each "sovereign" and "independent" of others, confront one another across landways or seaways familiar to all, their relations will tend to be dominated by a competitive quest for power and by calculations of relative power. This familiar design, observable in all systems of States, from the earliest we know about to the system in which we find ourselves today, can scarcely be attributed to the circumstance that all statesmen by nature crave power (they do of course—otherwise they would not be

[5] For example, Robert Strausz-Hupé and Stefan T. Possony in their general college text, *International Relations in the Age of the Conflict between Democracy and Dictatorship* (McGraw-Hill; 1950), suggest (pp. 179–92) with the aid of charts and equations that in a hypothetical system of 6 States, with symbols for 4 types of "social action," 3 types of "power relationships," 7 types of "coefficients for Q relationships," and so on, it is possible to list 240 types of international relationships on a single array. "It is clear that international relations can be analyzed in this manner by *several dozen* arrays. . . . It can be seen that the problem is by no means simple. . . ." In the actual system of States "the total number of their *possible* relations is 240^{9900} or about $10^{23,564}$"—which figure, if written out, would, it transpires, "cover about 12 typewritten pages."

statesmen) or to the supposition that some States thirst after power and others do not. The clue to the pattern lies rather in the fact that in such systems of independent sovereignties, power is the price of continued independence. Unless it be a buffer between rivals who checkmate one another, any State lacking power to prevent others from imposing their power upon it will almost inevitably lose whatever power it has, and ultimately its freedom to act as a sovereign. The most effective assurance against any such calamity—for the loss of independence through alien subjugation is almost invariably deemed calamitous by the losers—is to contain, restrain, reduce and, if possible, extinguish the power of other States to inflict such a fate upon one's own.

From these elementary premises flow all the other apprehensions, expectations, and courses of action which are the warp and woof of inter-State relations or international politics. For the sake of clarity in delineating the traditional schema of these relations, let us neglect for now the pressures and interests within States which often disturb or pervert the classic pattern of politicial contacts among them. The essence of these contacts is rivalry for power. Power is a function of two or more variables, since its meaning is the capacity of one being to impose its will on another. Power is therefore always a relative, and never an absolute, quantity. Power moreover is local, since the efficacy of its exercise diminishes swiftly with distance from the center of strength.

The means available to States in their use and abuse of power among themselves are more limited than the ways of men as they compete with one another within States. When one man obeys another, or otherwise yields to another's will, he does so for one of three motives, or some combination thereof. He may be moved by fear of the probable risks of resistance—e.g., punishment, loss, pain, or death—if the power at the disposal of the power-holders vastly exceeds his own. He may be moved by loyalty—i.e., by old habits of deference, by deeply felt affirmative emotions toward the symbols of authority, by new and favorable responses to the *credenda* and *miranda* of propaganda. Or he may be moved by a rational calculation of advantages, corporeal or spiritual, to be derived from subordination. Every exercise of power among men involves force (long called the *ultima ratio regum̄*), or love, or benefits, or all three in subtle and complex harmonies. And it may be cogently argued that these three devices to command obedience encompass the totality of the weapons of power, as well as the beginning, the middle, and the end of the entire political process in all its contexts and aspects.

What is striking in the process as it is carried on by the members of a system of States is that appeals to loyalty or to some calculus of material indulgences and deprivations are of little efficacy—far less so than is usual within States—in inducing the condition of mind and the course of conduct sought to be fostered. Separate and sovereign States are relatively lacking in common symbols of value and purpose. If they shared such symbols to an emotionally gratifying degree, they would very likely cease to be sovereign and separate, and would become merged in a larger polity. The manipulation of such symbols, however wise and masterly the manipulators may be, is therefore at best a feeble device for the changing of attitudes and, at worst, a waste of words. Trading in loaves and fishes, in the spoils and perquisites of patronage, in greed and gain and loss, also leaves much to be desired as a means for the pursuit of power among States. Much diplomacy, obviously, is a business of bargaining over material goods: provinces, subjects, waterways, markets, and money from time immemorial; and, more recently, all the tangled issues of tariffs, quotas, subsidies, embargoes, exchange rates, and the like. Yet bargaining capacity in the international arena, like the potency of propaganda, is less a product of the artistry of the practitioners than of the "prestige" enjoyed by their States. And prestige among States, albeit occasionally the concomitant of a reputation for honorable dealing, is chiefly a function of power in the primitive form of physical force, coupled with the will and skill to use it to compel obedience.

The "power" that all wise statesmen seek carefully to conserve, shrewdly to enhance, and judiciously to expand to the point of weakening or destroying rival Powers is, therefore, neither a metaphysical entity nor a palimpsest of subtleties but a thing, at bottom, brutally stark. Power is military might—i.e., organized capacity to fight other Powers successfully by use of arms. This ability, on countless bloody fields of battle, has forever been decisive, or has been commonly deemed decisive, in determining the orders of priority in influence and in the allocation of satisfactions among States. This being so, or assumed to be so, the same capacity, as imagined prior to its testing in action, is more than likely to be decisive in the nonviolent bargaining known as "negotiation." Diplomatic demands unsupported by armed power are unattainable. Irresistible armed power requires no diplomacy to serve its purposes. Between these extremes, diplomacy has its necessary functions to perform, ideally buttressed by latent military might and, in turn when need be, directing the use of armed force toward the attainment of political objectives, with commitments and the power to fulfill them being kept as nearly in balance as possible.

Since fraud and favors are thus inseparable from force, which in the ultimate instance is usually decisive, the pursuit of power by States easily becomes not a means to other ends but an end in itself. If, in the famous phrase of General Carl von Clausewitz, war is diplomacy (i.e., policy) continued by other means, diplomacy is war pursued by other means. The objective in both contexts is the accumulation and aggrandizement of fighting capacity, for the loss of which the State may perish at the hands of its enemies and by the winning of which the State may thwart or destroy its enemies. The stakes of diplomacy, over which statesmen are moved to haggle and risk battle, thus become in themselves the components of fighting power, since these are the things that matter most. In consequence the basic "cause" of war, paradoxically, turns out to be the rivalry among sovereigns for control of the elements which are regarded as crucial for the waging of war. This condition of affairs is implicit and quite inescapable in every system of sovereignties in which each Power, for its own safety, seeks to coerce its neighbors and avoid being coerced by them.[6]

The quest for power under these circumstances of rivalry is almost never a self-limiting enterprise. Each Power, unless frustrated by superior power mobilized against it, tends to expand its power to the utmost, and by it to subjugate all others, in a ceaseless search for full security. Costs are reckoned as of little worth when the issue is assumed to be safety and survival. Thus Pericles, in summoning his fellow Athenians to war with Sparta, could say without being reproached:

> You perhaps think that your empire extends only over your allies; I will declare to you the truth. The visible field of action has two parts, land and sea. In the whole of one of these you are completely supreme, not merely as far as you use it at present, but also to what further extent you may think fit: in fine, your naval resources are such that your vessels may go where they please, without the king or any other nation on earth being able to stop them. So that although you may think it a great privation to lose the use of your lands and houses, still you must see that this power is something widely different; and instead of fretting on their account, you should really regard them in the light of the gardens and other accessories that embellish a great fortune, and as, in comparison, of little moment. . . . Remember, too, that if your country has the greatest name in all the

[6] Amid the vast literature on "power politics," the following general analyses, apart from those cited elsewhere, are particularly relevant and stimulating: Gabriel A. Almond: *The American People and Foreign Policy* (Harcourt, Brace; 1950); Henry Noel Brailsford: *Olives of Endless Age—Being a Study of This Distracted World and Its Need of Unity* (Harper; 1928); E. H. Carr: *Conditions of Peace* (Macmillan; 1945); Lionel Gelber: *Reprieve from War* (Macmillan; 1950); R. G. Hawtrey: *Economic Aspects of Sovereignty* (Longmans; 1930); Harold D. Lasswell: *The World Revolution of Our Time* (Stanford University Press; 1951); Hans J. Morgenthau: *Politics among Nations* (Alfred A. Knopf; 1948); and Georg Schwarzenberger: *Power Politics—A Study of International Society* (Praeger; 1951, 2nd edition).

world, it is because she never bent before disaster; because she has expended more life and effort in war than any other city, and has won for herself a power greater than any hitherto known, the memory of which will descend to the latest posterity; even if now, in obedience to the general law of decay, we should ever be forced to yield, still it will be remembered that we held rule over more Hellenes than any other Hellenic state, that we sustained the greatest wars against their united or separate powers, and inhabited a city unrivaled by any other in resources or magnitude. . . . Hatred and unpopularity at the moment have fallen to the lot of all who have aspired to rule others; but where odium must be incurred, true wisdom incurs it for the highest objects. Hatred also is short-lived; but that which makes the splendor of the present and the glory of the future remains forever unforgotten.[7]

"Imperialism," a modern term of opprobrium, is a name for the process by which a State, driven by ambition or by fear of foreign foes or by irresistible opportunities for aggrandizement, successfully subdues rivals poorer in power than itself. At any given moment in any system of States, some will be relatively content or "satiated" with the prevailing distribution of power, and therefore concerned to maintain the status quo, while others, unsatiated, will seek to subvert it to their own advantage. The former are customarily those who have won the last war and seized upon the spoils of victory, while the latter have lost, suffering the deprivations of defeat. But in this uneasy striving for ascendancy there can be no permanence or continuity in the alleged roles of "aggressor" States and "peace-loving" States, since interests and aspirations constantly change with the shifting vicissitudes of the contest for power. The goal itself has no limits, for each loss of power (unless fatal) is an incentive to new striving and each gain (unless total) but a steppingstone for fresh endeavors.

Thus Pyrrhus, King of Epirus, was (according to Plutarch) tricked by his adviser, Cineas, into conceding that if

[7] Thucydides: *The Peloponnesian War*, Book II, Chapter vii (Random House [Modern Library, Crawley translation]; 1934), pp. 117 and 119.

he should conquer Rome, this success could lead only to the subjugation of all Italy; and, so much gained, Sicily, Carthage, and Libya would be opened to attack.

"But," asked Cineas, "when we have conquered all, what are we to do then?" "Why, then, my friend," said Pyrrhus, laughing, "we will take our ease, and drink and be merry." Cineas, having brought him thus far, replied: "And what hinders us from drinking and taking our ease now, when we have already those things in our hands at which we propose to arrive through seas of blood, through infinite toils and dangers, through innumerable calamities which we must both cause and suffer?" This discourse of Cineas gave Pyrrhus pain, but produced no change in his plan.

And thus Cecil Rhodes, having built an empire in Africa, hankered after "these stars that you see overhead at night, these vast worlds which we can never reach. I would annex the planets if I could. I often think of that. It makes me sad to see them so clear and so far away." [8]

That such vaulting ambitions are beyond realization is less significant for our analysis than the fact that they are inevitably engendered by the very character of the competition for power among States. In this restless striving—so long as none conquers all and some survive as independent sovereignties—there can be no enduring peace, despite the prevailing delusions of the twentieth century that peace is possible through the defeat of the wicked by the virtuous, or by the organization of "collective security" against aggressors. The process here described is as timeless and constant as the pyramids of Egypt—and indeed long antedates their building. That we carry it on into an age in which it has become self-defeating should not cause us to forget, in our agonizing over problems made insoluble by our habits, that the game of power is as old as States and that its ineluctable consequences are always of the same nature, despite local and temporal differences in the nature of their effects on men's for-

[8] Quoted, p. 193, in Hans J. Morgenthau: *Scientific Man vs. Power Politics* (University of Chicago Press; 1946).

tunes and minds. The central consequence was never better put than by Alexander Hamilton in No. 6 of *The Federalist Papers:*

> If these States should either be wholly disunited, or only united in partial confederacy, a man must be far gone in Utopian speculations, who can seriously doubt that these subdivisions into which they might be thrown, would have frequent and violent contests with each other. To presume a want of motives for such contests, as an argument against their existence, would be to forget that men are ambitious, vindictive, and rapacious. To look for a continuation of harmony between a number of independent unconnected sovereignties, situated in the same neighborhood, would be to disregard the uniform course of human events, and to set at defiance the accumulated experience of ages. The causes of hostility among nations are innumerable. There are some which have a general and almost constant operation upon the collective bodies of society. Of this description are the love of power, or the desire of pre-eminence and dominion—the jealousy of power, or the desire of equality and safety. . . . But notwithstanding the concurring testimony of experience, in this particular, there are still to be found visionary, or designing men, who stand ready to advocate the paradox of perpetual peace between the States, though dismembered and alienated from each other.

4. THE SCALES OF FORCE

Ponderous and uncertain is that relation between pressure and resistance which constitutes the balance of power. The arch of peace is mortised by no iron tenons; the monoliths of which it is composed are joined by no cement. A swarm of summer bees upon the architrave, a runnel of April water through some hidden crevice, will cause a millimeter of displacement, will set these monoliths stirring against each other, unheard, unseen—

nor can the fragile fingers of man then stay the rush and rumble of destruction.

—Harold Nicolson: *Public Faces.*[9]

From the long experience of our species with States and systems of States, and with the fortunes and misfortunes of kings and captains in their quest for power, it is evident that each congeries of sovereignties tends to be self-perpetuating—and this for reasons which, though unmistakably embodied in decisions and acts of men, seem to be so mechanical in their operation as to be almost independent of human wills. In the civilizations of which we have knowledge, communities made up of separate sovereignties do indeed appear to have an identical terminus in their travel through time—namely, the subjugation of lesser Powers by the greatest Power, and the ensuing unification of all into one. What is at first glance surprising is that this process is often long delayed, and sometimes, as up to now in our own constellation of Powers, never takes place at all save in the dubious and dangerous shape of polarization into two major centers of influence. Whatever their final fate, all the systems of States which have existed in ages past have preserved their characters as conglomerates of "independent" entities during many centuries.

This continuity in the dispersal of power among a number of political rivals is to be explained by reference to an ancient principle and practice of statecraft, commonly known in our own times as the "balance of power." Every State in a system, precisely because it is a State in a system, seeks to extend its power over all others in its quest for security or empire. But all other States have an equal interest in resisting such endeavors, for the preservation of sovereignty against the forcible imposition of external control is the *sine qua non* of all statesmanship. Weaker Powers therefore find it frequently advantageous, and sometimes imperative for political sur-

[9] This novel by Harold Nicolson, first published in 1932 and reprinted by Penguin Books in 1944, depicts with exceptional wit and skill an imaginary world crisis of June 1939, precipitated by British invention of an atomic bomb.

vival, to combine against stronger Powers in order to prevent the strongest from acquiring such a preponderance as to leave all others helpless.

This elementary counsel of prudence has at times been forgotten, as in the epochs of Philip and Alexander of Macedon, of the non-Roman precursors of the Cæsars, and again in the European system of the 1930's. The penalty of such neglect has ever been either the permanent conquest of all by one, or a belated and extravagant outpouring of blood and treasure in liberating the conquered and casting down by force of arms the aspirant to universal hegemony. When power-holders and policy-makers have acted with foresight, they have seldom hesitated to unite in alliances and coalitions against any Power so formidable as to imperil the independence of all the rest. Contrary to popular impression, the objective of a wisely conceived balance-of-power policy is not to "preserve peace," since war may be, and usually is, necessary to maintain the equilibrium. Nor is the goal the restraint of the vicious by the virtuous. Such judgments are devoid of meaning in any universal contest for predominance.

Two centuries ago David Hume pointed out that the principle of the balance of power is probably as old as inter-State relations:

> It is a question, whether the *idea* of the balance of power be owing entirely to modern policy, or whether the *phrase* only has been invented in the later ages. It is certain that Xenophon, in his Institution of Cyrus, represents the combination of the Asiatic powers to have arisen from a jealousy of the increasing force of the Medes and Persians; and though that elegant composition should be supposed altogether a romance, this sentiment, ascribed by the author to the Eastern princes, is at least a proof of the prevailing notion of ancient times.
>
> In all the politics of Greece, the anxiety, with regard to the balance of power, is apparent, and is expressly pointed out to us, even by the ancient historians. Thucydides represents the league which was formed against Athens, and which produced the Peloponnesian war, as entirely owing to this principle. And after the

decline of Athens, when the Thebans and Lacedemonians disputed for sovereignty, we find that the Athenians (as well as many other Republics) always threw themselves into the lighter scale, and endeavored to preserve the balance. They supported Thebes against Sparta, till the great victory gained by Epaminondas at Leuctra; after which they immediately went over to the conquered, from generosity, as they pretended, but in reality from their jealousy of the conquerors. Whoever will read Demosthenes's oration for the Megalopolitans, may see the utmost refinements on this principle that ever entered into the head of a Venetian or English speculatist.[1]

In the same essay Hume observes that while the concept of the balance was too much ignored by the rivals of Rome, to their ultimate ruination, the principle was not unknown:

> The only prince we meet with in the Roman history, who seems to have understood the balance of power, is Hiero, King of Syracuse. Though the ally of Rome, he sent assistance to the Carthaginians during the war of the auxiliaries; "Esteeming it requisite," says Polybius, "both in order to retain his dominions in Sicily, and to preserve the Roman friendship, that Carthage should be safe; lest by its fall the remaining power should be able, without control or opposition, to execute every purpose and undertaking. And here he acted with great wisdom and prudence: For that is never, on any account, to be overlooked; nor ought such a force ever to be thrown into one hand, as to incapacitate the neighboring States from defending their rights against it." Here is the aim of modern politics pointed out in express terms.

In the midst of another contest by arms in a later system of States temporarily threatened with the subjection of all to one, Thomas Jefferson commented:

> We especially ought to pray that the powers of Europe may be so poised and counterpoised among themselves, that their own security may require the presence of all their forces at home, leaving the other quarters of the globe in undisturbed

[1] David Hume (1711–76): "Of the Balance of Power" (1751) in *Essays and Treatises* (Edinburgh: 1825), Vol. I, pp. 331 f.

tranquility. . . . [1812] Surely none of us wishes to see Bonaparte conquer Russia, and lay thus at his feet the whole continent of Europe. This done, England would be but a breakfast; and, although I am free from the visionary fears which the votaries of England have affected to entertain, because I believe he cannot effect the conquest of Europe; yet put all Europe into his hands, and he might spare such a force to be sent in British ships, as I would as leave not have to encounter, when I see how much trouble a handful of British soldiers in Canada has given us. No. It cannot be to our interest that all Europe should be reduced to a single monarchy. . . . [1814] For my part, I wish that all nations may recover and retain their independence; that those which are overgrown may not advance beyond safe measures of power, that a salutary balance may be ever maintained among nations, and that our peace, commerce, and friendship, may be sought and cultivated by all. [1815][2]

Another classic statement of the principle was penned by Sir Eyre Crowe in his famous Memorandum of January 1, 1907:

The first interest of all countries is the preservation of national independence. It follows that England, more than any other, non-insular power, has a direct and positive interest in the maintenance of the independence of nations, and therefore must be the natural enemy of any country threatening the independence of others and the natural protector of weaker communities. History shows that the changes threatening the independence of this or that nation have generally arisen, at least in part, out of the momentary predominance of a neighboring State at once militarily powerful, economically efficient and ambitious to extend its frontiers or spread its influence, the danger being directly proportionate to the degree of its power and efficacy and to the spontaneity or "inevitableness" of its ambitions. The only check on the abuse of political predominance derived from such a position has always consisted in the opposition of an equally formidable rival or of a combination of several countries forming leagues of defence. The equilibrium established by such a grouping of forces is technically known as the balance

[2] Quoted in Hans J. Morgenthau: *In Defense of the National Interest* (Alfred A. Knopf; 1951), pp. 20–1.

of power and it has become almost a historical truism to identify England's secular policy with the maintenance of this balance by throwing her weight now in this scale and now in that, but ever on the side opposed to the political dictatorship of the strongest single State or group at a given time.[3]

The process of so balancing and harmonizing forces and interests that none will establish an intolerable domination over all, and each will co-exist with the others in rough parity, is of the essence of all politics, at least where power is shared among equals. In this large sense a dynamic balance of power, delicately attuned to nuances of influence and adroitly modified to meet changing circumstances, is the presupposition of all civic order and stable government.[4] Within States all parties to the process are normally united by some consensus of shared symbols and values, in terms of which differences can be reconciled without violence. But between and among States in a system of States no such consensus exists, or at least none of sufficient efficacy. Neither are there convenient devices available—elections, referenda, polls, parliamentary votes, and the like—to measure accurately the relative strength of competitors and the shifts of influence in the dimension of time.

It follows that the preservation of the balance in inter-State affairs is invariably a highly uncertain and hazardous business of guessing about matters that, more often than not, are imponderable and unpredictable—for they embrace every

[3] *British Documents on the Origins of the War* (London; 1928), Vol. III, p. 403, quoted in George Schwarzenberger: *Power Politics* (London: Cape; 1941, 1st edition), pp. 117–18, as part of an excellent survey of the forms of power politics. For a further analysis of the balance, with numerous references to sources, see Quincy Wright: *A Study of War* (University of Chicago Press; 1942), Vol. II, pp. 743–66, and for a briefer treatment, with quotations from Frederick the Great, Sir Robert Walpole, and Vattel, see F. L. Schuman: *International Politics—The Destiny of the Western State System* (McGraw-Hill; 1948, 4th edition), pp. 80–4.

[4] Among more recent books, the most suggestive and incisive single-volume treatment of group tactics and pressure politics as they operate within the democratic frame of reference is the work of my erstwhile colleague, now of Columbia University, David B. Truman: *The Governmental Process—Political Interests and Public Opinion* (Alfred A. Knopf; 1951).

factor in national life, internal and external, changing and static, affecting the potency or impotence of each State and the total equipoise of force among all. In sharp contrast, moreover, to the usual mixed ingredients of balance and compromise among groups within a State ruled by a government, the equilibrium that is striven for among sovereignties in the international arena—or that emerges, unsought, out of their rivalries and clashes—is exclusively a function, in the last resort, of fighting strength. Far from simplifying the problem of forecasting the interplay of the elements of power, this common denominator by itself admits of little precise measurement, whether it be further analyzed into its alleged component parts or considered as a total to be weighed against the fighting strength of other States. Only the experimental method of putting the issue to a practical demonstration—i.e., ordeal by battle—is conclusive in validating or discrediting prior estimates and assumptions.

In the making of guesses before the event, mistakes are literally innumerable. Would-be conquerors easily persuade themselves that the power they have succeeded in amassing will give them preponderance over their rivals and intended victims. They therefore resort to the test of force—a decision never taken by a rational statesman or even a mad one save on the premise of such preponderance—and frequently discover that the enemy coalition is able in the end to mobilize decisive superiority in military might. Members of "Grand Alliances," conversely, often overestimate their ability to "deter" a prospective foe through convincing demonstrations of superior force and sometimes, in the face of opportunities for bargaining, incur risks of war which prove disastrous.

Precise measurement of the changing balance would, hypothetically, obviate these perils and indeed make war itself unnecessary, since a game whose outcome is known in advance need never be played. But the hypothesis is dubious. No such measurement is possible. Were it otherwise, pugilists, wrestlers, and fencers; chess-players, card-experts, and golfers; and coaches, managers, and athletes in all sporting contests between teams would have no professions. Inter-State politics resembles such games of chance and skill, save that no one is permitted to win the championship or pennant, the rules are more obscure and less humane, and the roles of the fortuitous and the unforeseeable in determining the outcome are even greater. Every so-called "calculated risk" therefore means, most of the time, an incalculable risk. The balance is thus preserved as much by killing men and burning their houses over their heads as by menacing or cajoling them through the more subtle practices of propaganda and diplomacy.

---

5. THE PRIESTS OF BAAL

> Ferdinand of Melphé to his son: "Cesario, you must now put aside Branlon and the fine dreams of your youth, and your rights as a private person to any special happiness, or indeed to any particular virtue." "Why?" said Cesario, drily. "But why on earth, my dear sir, need I be paying to iniquity any such large and expensive tribute?" "Because, my poor boy, you are one of those luckless persons out of whom accident has made a king. So you must learn to lie, and to steal, and to kill—yet always judiciously, and always for your people's profit—because each of these vices is needful to the beneficent ruler. It would be more pleasant, as beyond doubt it would be more edifying, if all kingdoms did not remain dependent upon the wise dishonesties and the thrifty crimes of their overlords; but, thus far, mankind has not invented any more efficient method of restraining its own fond imbecilities. We kings must needs work with the tools at hand."
>
> —BRANCH CABELL: *The King Was in His Counting House.*[5]

[5] This novel of the Renaissance is subtitled *A Comedy of Common Sense*, and was published by Farrar & Rinehart, 1938, with whose permission this passage is here quoted. It flows from the same pen, then signing its author's name James Branch Cabell, which wrote *Jurgen*, *Figures of Earth*, and other novels of the life of Manuel.

Cesare Borgia was duke, archbishop, cardinal, and bastard son of a Pope. By his contemporaries and by posterity he was commonly and rightfully described as a swaggering swashbuckler, unscrupulous adventurer, ferocious tyrant, treacherous intriguer, cruel conqueror, and great statesman. When he was slain on March 12, 1507, while besieging the castle of a rebel count, those who learned of it doubtless pondered over the relationship, if any, between this life and death and the problem of justice in the universe. Death is the wages of sin—in the after-life, perhaps. But here? Is virtue merely its own reward, and a liability in politics and war? If victory and power go to those who are wicked, and the mob fawns upon them and praises their goodness to the skies, do they thereby cease to be wicked and become righteous?

One view of such questions—and a view not to be ignored in any effort to fathom the dynamics of inter-State relations —is suggested by W. Somerset Maugham at the close of his delightful novel, *Then and Now*, dealing with an amorous episode of trickery and frustration in the youth of a famous man. He fancies the man, one Niccolò Machiavelli, saying of the dead hero:

> In this world it is only necessary to seize power and hold it and the means you have used will be judged honorable and will be praised by all. If Cesare Borgia is regarded as a scoundrel it is only because he didn't succeed. . . . You say that he suffered the just punishment of his crimes. He was destroyed not by his misdeeds, but by circumstances over which he had no control. His wickedness was an irrelevant accident. In this world of sin and sorrow if virtue triumphs over vice, it is not because it is virtuous, but because it has better and bigger guns; if honesty prevails over double-dealing, it is not because it is honest, but because it has a stronger army more ably led; and if good overcomes evil, it is not because it is good, but because it has a well-lined purse. It is well to have right on our side, but it is madness to forget that unless we have might as well it will avail us nothing. We must be-

lieve that God loves men of good will, but there is no evidence to show that He will save fools from the result of their folly.[6]

It is permissible to accept or reject such judgments. What is not justified, among reasonable beings possessed of talent for analysis and penetration, is the assumption that it is within the capacity of men to make right rather than might the test of statecraft in a system of competing sovereigns. Whoever does so, possessing power, must lose it. Whoever, keeping power, speaks of goodness as his guide is guilty of hypocrisy or self-deception. The point is not that power is necessarily conducive to evil. Power is neutral, beyond good and evil, a mere means that can be used for either. The point is that in the quest for power, particularly when it becomes an end in itself to be pursued with singleminded devotion, those who would have and hold this prize cannot be bound by the standards of conduct we take for granted in interpersonal relations and in most intergroup relations within ordered societies.

The immorality or amorality of high politics and diplomacy has little to do with the virtues or vices of particular politicians, diplomats, peoples, social systems, ideologies, or religious faiths. It arises from the fact that in the rivalry among sovereignties the immediate criteria of success or failure, and the ultimate determinants of political survival or extinction, have no demonstrable relation to the ethical or unethical qualities of behavior. Whatever preserves and enhances power must be cherished. Whatever leads to the enfeeblement or loss of power must be avoided. Other definitions of value have no relevance to the stakes of the game, or have at best a tangential one. In systems of States, power readily plays the roles of creator, protector, redeemer, and destroyer. But these, let us not forget, are synonyms for divinity. When power becomes god, worshippers soon see that their deity is a jealous god who will have no other gods be-

[6] From *Then and Now*, a novel by W. Somerset Maugham (Doubleday; 1946), pp. 273, 277–8, quoted by permission of the publishers.

fore him. Truth and goodness are then servants or victims, never masters, of the godhead.

These propositions, one might suppose, need only be restated to be recognized as valid beyond debate. Yet so blind are many men to the reality of power, and so sensitive are others to the demands of a morality inapplicable to statecraft, that stormy disputes have raged for endless generations over matters self-evident to Cain and Abel, if not to Adam and Eve. Since the cinquecento these contentions have largely swirled and eddied about the writings—*The Prince, Discourses on Livy, The Art of War, The History of Florence*, and so on—of the renowned diplomat of the Renaissance already named above.

Niccolò Machiavelli, born in Florence, May 5, 1469, served the Republic long and honorably after the fall of the Medici in 1494. Following the Medici restoration in 1512, he took unhappy refuge on a farm. Here for fifteen years in rustic exile he cogitated on history and diplomacy, life and politics, and put into manuscript much wisdom, all the while yearning for a chance to return to the service of his native city. In 1527 a new Republican triumph fanned his hopes to new fire, but before he learned of the rejection of his plea, his own bright flame flickered out in death.

That the Florentine, by virtue of the words he wrote during his lonely years of enforced retirement, should have ever since set all the world by the ears is less a proof of his genius (though he was undoubtedly a genius) than an evidence that modern mankind wants to eat its cake and have it too, and is outraged when anyone points out, with clarity and eloquence and unanswerable logic, that this cannot be done, and that choices must sometimes be made. The argument can neither be refuted, since it is true, nor ignored, since it cuts to the core of the dilemma of inter-State politics, where men find glory in pursuing power, feel shame for the price that power exacts, and spend centuries explaining how expediency and morality can or can not be reconciled.

Machiavelli is scarcely, as some assert, the "founder of political science." After a millennium of sterile scholasticism, he simply revived—albeit he was by no means unique in this among his contemporaries—an idea taken for granted by Plato and Aristotle, Herodotus and Polybius, Plutarch and Cicero: that political truth might better be arrived at by observing the behavior of man than by spinning out syllogisms in which words mean only other words, untested by the evidence of experience. Neither is Machiavelli the father of cynicism. Let Antisthenes and Diogenes receive credit where credit is due. The strange merit or demerit of the Florentine is that he undertook, from a rich knowledge derived as much from practice as from books, to describe the nature of the game of power and to prescribe the rules that the seekers after power must follow if they would acquire and retain this treasure. His exposition was judged so shocking by later generations that his very name was equated with the Devil or "Old Nick." This evaluation is not at all a tempered judgment of Machiavelli as man, diplomat, or author. It is rather testimony to the anguish of the men and statesmen who have been too candidly reminded—with consequent injury to their pride and purpose in rationalizing, by reference to "moral" principles, acts unjustified save in the imperatives of power—that the conquest and rentention of authority require qualities quite different from those appropriate to the pursuit of virtue by theologians, philosophers, and ordinary citizens.

The passionate and sensitive son of Florence has thus become the symbol of the painful paradox confronting all those who know that they ought to love and trust one another, and also know that trust and love may be self-defeating in contests for power among sovereigns. The prince who would preserve and enhance his power must copy the lion and the fox.

Nothing is so natural or so common as the thirst for conquest, and when men can satisfy it, they deserve praise rather than censure. But when they are not equal to the enterprise, disgrace is the inevitable consequence. . . . The Prince who contributes toward the advancement of another Power, ruins his own. . . . It is safer to be feared than be loved, for it may truly be affirmed of mankind in general, that they are ungrateful, fickle, timid, dissembling, and self-interested. . . . Men sooner forget the death of their relations than the loss of their patrimony. . . . A prudent Prince cannot and ought not to keep his word, except when he can do it without injury to himself. . . .[7]

That these sentiments seem sinister and shabby attests to the unwillingness of modern man to accept the implications of politics in the system of States in which he finds himself. He continues to act upon Machiavellian precepts, because he must. He continues to protest that the precepts are monstrous or immoral or nonexistent. Voltaire, who encouraged the young Frederick the Great to write an anti-Machiavellian tract, slyly commented in his *Memoirs:* "If Machiavelli had had a prince for disciple, the first thing he would have recommended that he do would have been to write a book against Machiavellianism." Indignation against the doctrine of the Florentine is futile so long as politics among nations are shaped by the rules of anarchy. Such indignation can be creative only in the degree to which it contributes to a revolutionary alteration of inter-State relations.

The moralistic storm that has so long thundered about Machiavelli is a product of misunderstanding or confusion. The political problem he posed is all-important, though he clarified it only by implication and sought no more in the way of its solution than the unification of Italy. To the question of whether morals and politics are separable, the best answer would seem to be that they are inevitably separate, and often contradictory, whenever politics consist in a striving for ascendancy among separate political units that are subordinate to no higher authority and share no common values that seem more vital than the stakes of diplomacy and war. To the question of whether the end ever justifies the means, we

[7] These random but representative excerpts are taken from the Modern Library version (Random House; 1940), of *The Prince and the Discourses*, with an admirable Introduction by Max Lerner.

may well reply that here as everywhere the means habitually employed determine the ultimate moral quality of the end they serve. If the sovereign State in its dealings with others can escape extinction and realize its purposes only by the habitual practice of deceit, intrigue, and mass murder, then the true ethical nature of the State stands revealed in indecent nakedness. But this is anticipatory. And in any case it is not Machiavelli's argument.

His ethical thesis is that most men are evil (whether by nature or because they live by institutions and practices that foster vice, he does not say), and that a prince, unless he chooses to be an ex-prince or a martyr, must learn to do necessary evil to maintain his place. As George Santayana puts it: "Machiavelli was not thinking of the saints; and like Thrasymachus and Callicles in Plato he thought it a matter of course, if not a point of honor, that at least a prince should prefer to be occasionally wicked rather than to be worsted and die; and he seemed to assume (what Thrasymachus proclaimed loudly) that it is better to be a wicked prince than not to be a prince at all." [8] But this view does not stem, as Santayana suggests, from any assumption that "whatever is done is right," or from any attempt to base morals on the will to live and dominate.

The matter is rather more simple, as Count D'Entrèves has contended.[9] Machiavelli is not quarreling with anyone

[8] George Santayana: *Dominations and Powers* (Scribner; 1951), p. 209. See also such other recent commentaries as H. Butterfield: *The Statecraft of Machiavelli* (London: Bell); J. H. Whitfield: *Machiavelli* (Oxford: Blackwell; 1947); and A. H. Gilbert: *Machiavelli's Prince and Its Forerunners* (Durham, North Carolina: Duke University Press; 1938). James Burnham's *The Machiavellians: Defenders of Freedom* (Day; 1943) is a sympathetic running commentary on Machiavelli, Mosca, Sorel, Michels, and Pareto.

[9] See Count Alessandro P. D'Entrèves's admirable article, "Immortal Machiavelli," in *Measure* (a critical quarterly published by the Henry Regnery Co., Chicago), December 1950, pp. 34–46, and Robert M. Hutchins's comment, pp. 46–8, in which the Chancellor reaffirms Machiavelli's "badness" and concludes: "The world today is full, as the world has always been, of political 'realists,' who hold the Thrasymachus-Machiavelli view of human nature and who use it to justify complete political amorality. Let us by all means look the fiend in the face; but let us not forget that he is a fiend."

about the nature of good and evil, nor advocating that any man seek power or do wrong. But the business of a prince (if men insist on having princes) is to be a prince, and in dealing with other princes and his subjects to act in the service of his principality—virtuously if he can, wickedly if he must. This indeed is his duty, imposed by realities. But Machiavelli does not confuse evil with good, nor even make a virtue of necessity. He writes, not with hypocrisy but with the melancholy regret of a sincerely virtuous man:

> If men were all good, this precept would not be a good one. . . . A Prince who wishes to maintain the State is often forced to do evil. . . . It is necessary for a Prince, who wishes to maintain himself, to learn not to be good. . . . It cannot be called virtue to kill one's fellow citizens, betray one's friends, be without faith, without pity, without religion. Such means may gain an empire but not glory.
>
> These courses are very cruel, and against all Christian and indeed all humane manner of living. And every man ought to avoid them, and desire rather to live a private man, than reign, so much to the ruin of mankind. Yet he that will not use that way of good, if he will preserve himself, must enter into this evil.[1]

So long as statesmen, with the support and applause of their fellow citizens, worship power more than they cherish virtue, and so long as the two values are in conflict —as they are, of necessity, in every system of rival States—so long will the precepts of the Florentine be applicable to the practice of politics. Whoever would make them obsolete must find means to change men into angels, with no need at all of government; or else must find a way so to change the structure of power in the Great Society that competition among sovereigns for control of the means of violence is brought to an end.

[1] Quoted by Count D'Entrèves, *loc. cit.* The first paragraph is from *Il Principe* and the second from the *Discorsi*.

6. THE ALTARS OF MARS

> In looking over any State to form a judgment on it, it presents itself in two lights: the external and the internal. The first, that relation which it bears in point of friendship or enmity to other States. The second, that relation which its component parts, the governing and the governed, bear to each other. The first part of the external view of all States, their relations as friends, makes so trifling a figure in history that I am very sorry to say it affords me but little matter on which to expatiate. The good offices done by one nation to its neighbor; the support given in the public distress; the relief afforded in general calamity; the protection granted in emergent danger; the mutual return of kindness and stability, would afford a very ample and very pleasing subject for history. But, alas! all the history of all times, concerning all nations, does not afford matter enough to fill ten pages, though it should be spun out by the wire-drawing amplification of Guicciardini himself. The glaring side is that of enmity. War is a matter which fills all history, and consequently the only, or almost the only, view in which we can see the external of political society is in a hostile shape; and the only actions, to which we have always seen, and still see, all of them intent, are such as tend to the destruction of one another.
>
> —EDMUND BURKE: *A Vindication of Natural Society.*

WAR is at once the cause and consequence of competition for power among rival sovereigns, and thus the ultimate shape of politics within all systems of independent States. This hypothesis has been so often presented in recent years, particularly by writers desirous of establishing a case for world government, that it is no longer unfamiliar.[2] In this instance familiarity need not breed contempt. When tested against the experience of mankind, the hypothesis would seem to be true. As with all truths about human affairs, the

[2] Among the better-known works devoted to "proving" this hypothesis are Emery Reves: *The Anatomy of Peace* (Harper; 1945); Mortimer J. Adler: *How to Think about War and Peace* (Simon & Schuster; 1944); and Cord Meyer: *Peace or Anarchy* (Boston: Little, Brown; 1947).

validity of our generalization is relative not absolute, partial and not complete. All war is violent, but not all violence is war. Men's addiction to violence, as we shall see shortly, has roots far deeper than those embedded in the dispersion of power among many polities. It finds expression in sundry private ways having little in common with war—if war be envisaged as the clash of organized "political" groups armed for slaughter and destruction in the service of "public" purposes. Even in this narrower sense, war often erupts in contexts evidently having nothing to do with strife between States. Class wars, religious wars, race wars, and many civil wars all have their matrix in relations between groups other than sovereign entities, although such contests become frequently enmeshed in the feuds among sovereignties, and may well represent a kind of imitation, in other intergroup rivalries, of habits of violence originating in contacts among States.

All this granted, it is still plausible in the light of the record to accept the view that war is primarily a form of conduct indulged in wherever a number of contiguous States co-exist with no higher power above them. Whenever men have lived under an effective common authority, politics has proceeded with a minimum of violence, and human wills have been imposed upon, or resisted by, other wills through means other than organized killing and devastation. Whenever men have lived under several separate authorities, each exercising sovereignty, they have from time to time waged war upon one another. This dichotomy does not provide an "Open, Sesame" to universal peace, as has been so long and so widely assumed. Doubts on this score will be explored in due course. What is not doubtful is the historical authenticity of our initial proposition. Under the postulated condition of a geographical fragmentation of sovereign power among diverse units, war is a recurrent experience, a social institution, and a way of life—frequently deplored but always accepted in all past times as part of the natural order of things.

Before turning to the considerations that may be adduced on behalf of the contention that in our own time, by virtue of allegedly peculiar and unprecedented conditions of human fortunes, the way of war is obsolete, it will be well to notice that just as our primary hypothesis denies that the will to war stems from vice and the will to peace from virtue, so also it denies that the former stems from "tyranny" and the latter from "democracy." This common American belief, while it has counterparts abroad and precedents of great antiquity, is chiefly the contribution made to semantic confusion and popular bewilderment by Woodrow Wilson, who was doubtless sincere but unquestionably mistaken in his eloquent espousal of this ideal.[3] Its reiteration by Western spokesmen during World War II and the ensuing "Cold War" does not make it any less false.

The fact is that during the past century (and during other centuries in other times and places) democracies have resorted to armed hostilities more frequently than autocratic and totalitarian States.[4] All of Oceania, almost all of Africa, and much of Asia were conquered by the forces of Western "democracies," not by those of Eastern "tyrannies." The wealth and power of the Atlantic citadels of freedom were in an earlier epoch built up in no small measure by piracy, the slave traffic, the commerce in opium, and the butchery and exploitation of native peoples whose goods were seized and whose lands were annexed. Even the great contemporary drama of American defense of the "Free World" against Communist aggression scarcely demonstrates the superior devotion of democrats to pacific procedures.

To argue that the domestic habits and institutions of States

[3] In almost all his major addresses of 1917–18 Woodrow Wilson depicted World War I as a moral and ideological battle between "democracies" and "autocracies," with the Allied coalition conducting a crusade against "autocracy," "militarism," and "secret diplomacy" for the sake of "ending war" and "making the world safe for democracy." The supposition that democracies are more pacific than autocracies is also to be found in the writings of Immanuel Kant, Paul S. Reinsch, Eduard Beneš, Clarence K. Streit, and even Machiavelli (*Discorsi*, Chap. x, p. 59). Error does not become truth, however, through its compounding by high authorities.

[4] See Quincy Wright: *A Study of War*, *passim*, and especially the elaborate tables of wars in the appendices of Vol. I and pp. 839–48 of Vol. II.

bear no relation to the disposition of their policy-makers to resort to military violence abroad would be manifestly absurd. But to affirm any positive correlation between democracy and reluctance to make war, or between autocracy and eagerness to make war, is to ignore or deny the data of experience. More persuasive is the hypothesis that in an age of mass nationalism statesmen responsive to public clamor are likely to be more bellivolent than those acknowledging no such responsibility, for the former must somehow satisfy the expectations of citizens stirred by demagogues to martial fervor. The point was well put, with a corollary, a generation ago by Thorstein Veblen:

> Any politician who succeeds in embroiling his country in a war, however nefarious, becomes a popular hero and is reputed a wise and righteous statesman, at least for the time being. Illustrative instances need perhaps not, and indeed cannot gracefully, be named; most popular heroes and reputed statesmen belong in this class. . . . Since the ethical values involved in any given international contest are substantially of the nature of after-thought or accessory, they may safely be left on one side in any endeavor to understand or account for any given outbreak of hostilities. The moral indignation of both parties to the quarrel is to be taken for granted, as being the statesman's chief and necessary ways and means of bringing any war-like enterprise to a head and floating it to a creditable finish. It is a precipitate of the partisan animosity that inspires both parties and holds them to their duty of self-sacrifice and devastation, and at its best will chiefly serve as a cloak of self-righteousness to extenuate any exceptionally profligate excursions in the conduct of hostilities.[5]

The *modus operandi* of this process in its opening stages has never been better described than by Mark Twain (under the spell of the events of 1898) in *The Mysterious Stranger*. The scene is Vienna in 1590. Satan is talking to the narrator, Theo Fischer:

[5] Thorstein Veblen: *An Inquiry into the Nature of Peace* (Huebsch; 1919), pp. 22–3.

"I know your race. It is made up of sheep. It is governed by minorities, seldom or never by majorities. It suppresses its feelings and its beliefs and follows the handful that makes the most noise. Sometimes the noisy handful is right, sometimes wrong; but no matter; the crowd follows it. The vast majority of the race, whether savage or civilized, are secretly kind-hearted and shrink from inflicting pain but in the presence of the aggressive and pitiless minority they don't dare to assert themselves." . . .

I did not like to hear our race called sheep, and said I did not think they were.

"Still, it is true, Lamb," said Satan. "Look at you in war—what mutton you are, and how ridiculous!"

"In war? How?"

"There has never been a just one, never an honorable one—on the part of the instigator of the war. I can see a million years ahead, and this rule will never change in so many as half a dozen instances. The loud little handful—as usual—will shout for the war. The pulpit will—warily and cautiously—object—at first. The great dull hulk of the nation will rub its sleepy eyes and try to make out why there should be a war and will say, earnestly and indignantly, 'It is unjust and dishonorable and there is no necessity for it.' Then the handful will shout louder. A few fair men on the other side will argue and reason against the war with speech and pen, and at first will have a hearing and be applauded; but it will not last long; those others will outshout them, and presently the anti-war audiences will thin out and lose popularity. Before long you will see this curious thing: the speakers stoned from the platform and free speech strangled by hordes of furious men who in their secret hearts are still at one with those stoned speakers—as earlier—but do not dare to say so. And now, the whole nation—pulpit and all—will take up the war-cry and shout itself hoarse, and mob any honest man who ventures to open his mouth; and presently such mouths will cease to open. Next the statesmen will invent cheap lies putting the blame upon the nation that is attacked, and every man will be glad of those conscience-soothing falsities, and will diligently study them and refuse to examine any refutations of them; and thus he will by and by convince himself that the war is just and will thank God for the better sleep he enjoys after this process of grotesque self-deception." [6]

War is a habit that men enjoy, as they enjoy drunkenness, gluttony, fornication, gambling, and crime. Its vast superiority over all other forms of sin is that it embraces all the vices and casts over them the thrilling shadow of danger and the glittering cloak of honor, thereby making them "heroic" or at least permissible. This is so because all one's fellows, sharing vicariously in the experience of war, glorify and indulge those who bear the brunt of battle. From the dawn of human time, a few eccentric spirits have always protested that war is immoral or irreligious or insane. But it could scarcely have been supposed that such protests would have had any appreciable effect on an institution so pleasurable and profitable to the masses of men. And indeed no effect is visible, unless it be a negative one suggested by the fact that widespread and indignant denunciations of war have commonly been followed by armed struggles of unprecedented scope and ferocity.

This exciting social practice, we are now told on every hand by sensitive, intelligent, and sincerely troubled souls, has become incompatible with the survival of twentieth-century culture, if not of the human race itself. This opinion is accepted even by America's popular war-leader, General Douglas MacArthur: "Convention after convention has been entered into designed to humanize war and bring it under the control of rules dictated by the highest human ideals. Yet each war becomes increasingly savage as the means for mass killing are further developed. You cannot control war; you can only abolish it. Those who shrug this off as idealistic are the real enemies of peace—the real warmongers." [7] The hypothesis that war will abolish civilization

[6] From the *Collected Works of Mark Twain* (Harper; 1906). On the same point, see Alexander Hamilton in *The Federalist Papers*, No. 6.

[7] Address of General Douglas MacArthur to the Massachusetts Legislature, July 25, 1951.

unless civilization abolishes war cannot be tested save experimentally. Since the two major tests of our time, while impressive, were yet not wholly conclusive, a third would seem to be in order. But the third will be novel—with nuclear weapons on both sides. Some experiments can be performed only once. Most people, even as they feverishly prepare for the final test—in the name, as always, of "preserving peace" —appear to have their warlike ardor somewhat diluted by doubt. The chief sources of the doubt, and the bases of the hypotheses, are well-enough known to need only a mention, for our purpose here.

Science and technology have made war so destructive of life and property as to raise grave questions of national survival. Rivers of gore in the first world war of our century became seas of blood in the second, with the advent of indiscriminate bombing (dignified by the adjective "strategic"), unrestricted destruction of merchant ships, adroit utilization for slaughter of thousands of new gadgets from laboratories and assembly lines, and the highly efficient refinements of human charnelhouses operated by methods of mass production. All this pales into insignificance before the fascinating prospects of atomic warfare, in which the military objective of inducing the enemy to yield is to be achieved, if possible, by vaporizing all his major cities overnight and converting their inhabitants into well-cooked radioactive meat. That the rural survivors would continue to enjoy very much in the way of "civilization" is, in all conscience, to be doubted.[8]

[8] The literature of science in warfare is too voluminous to be touched upon here. The best one-volume survey of developments during World War II is James Phinney Baxter, 3rd: *Scientists Against Time* (Boston: Little, Brown; 1946). Those who write about the Bomb are roughly divisible into groups which hold that atomic weapons will be decisive; e.g., Bernard Brodie, editor: *The Absolute Weapon* (Harcourt, Brace; 1946), or indecisive; e.g., Patrick Blackett: *Fear, War, and the Bomb* (McGraw-Hill, 1949); intolerable; e.g., Dexter Masters and Katherine Way, editors: *One World or None* (McGraw-Hill; 1946) and David Bradley: *No Place to Hide* (Boston: Little, Brown; 1948), or tolerable; e.g., R. E. Lapp: *Must We Hide?* (Addison Wesley; 1949) and Vannevar Bush: *Modern Arms and Free Men* (Simon & Schuster; 1949). See also William L. Laurence: *The Hell Bomb* (Alfred A. Knopf; 1949). Dr. Alexander D. Mebane, in the supplement to his remarkable brochure, *Whither Must I Fly?* (mimeographed, February 1949)

Inseparable from these developments are other changes no less disturbing: from small professional armies to the nation-in-arms; from localized warfare to global hostilities; from "limited" war, directed toward practicable objectives, to "total" war, waged for unattainable goals; and from political contests, fought for territory, markets, and other components of power or wealth, to "holy wars" or spiritual "crusades," fought in the name of creeds and cults for the sake of forcibly converting or exterminating unbelievers. Modern man's very efforts to suppress war have aggravated and compounded the evil. The Wilsonian slogan that "any war anywhere is everybody's business" has evolved into the fantasy of "collective security," by which is meant in practice, as will be shown later in these pages, not the "abolition of war" or even the "punishment of aggressors," but the global renunciation of neutrality and the attempted universalization of every clash of arms. All these circumstances, coupled with the worldwide bipolarization of power in our system of States, do indeed offer the most somber of prospects and the most tenuous of hopes for the morrow. As John U. Nef has written, in the conclusion of his richly perceptive and brilliant study, *War and Human Progress* (Cambridge, Massachusetts: Harvard University Press; 1950, pp. 412–14):

The only justification for war is the defense of a culture worth defending, and the states of the modern world have less and less to defend beyond their material comforts, in spite of the claims of some to represent fresh concepts of civilization.

---

accuses Dr. Bush of attempted deception in implying that atom bombs can be stopped and of "naïve and primitive militarism," "narrow crudity," and "reckless fanaticism." While I do not fully share this unfavorable judgment by an able chemist and brilliant political and psychological commentator, Dr. Mebane's broader, albeit even more unkind, conclusion (p. 24b) is worth quoting as a portent: "This paranoid absurdity successfully passes as the responsible utterance of a scientist and a democrat, simply because it is festooned with piously 'democratic' verbiage. Bush's success in winning general acclaim for his contemptible production is indeed an omen of grave import. To me it signifies nothing less than that the American people are now prepared to accept—providing only that it is *called* 'democracy'—a paranoid totalitarianism fundamentally indistinguishable in spirit from that now prevailing in the U.S.S.R."

The new weapons have made nonsense of defensive war. Peoples have been left without any means of defending except by destroying others, and the destruction is almost certain to be mutual. . . . Our inquiry shows that in the past there have been limits to the process—the historical cycle—toward greater and greater destruction. Eventually a point has been reached where wars ceased to beget war, where the willingness of men to kill and destroy diminished. Like the human capacity to love, the human capacity to fear and to hate is not boundless. But, as the material and intellectual restraints imposed by Western civilization upon war have broken down, one after another, the limits have become much less narrow than they were in the era of the Napoleonic wars, less narrow even than in the era of the religious wars. . . .

War is now even less a separate problem than in earlier times; it is part of the total problem of modern civilization. The seriousness of wars can be mitigated, therefore, only by the growth of a common community of understanding relating to life as a whole, such as existed to some extent among the peoples of Europe in the age of limited wars during the late 17th and much of the 18th Centuries, such as existed still earlier and on a broader basis in the 12th and 13th Centuries when wars among the Christian peoples were few and relatively inconsequential. This community of understanding can no longer be confined, as it then could be, to the Western peoples, for the only community that can preserve Western civilization is a world community, in which both individuals and regions, with their cultures, are given an opportunity to develop their special talents and genius under general law.

No such community exists. Meanwhile, preparation for war has ceased to be a sane instrument of national policy and become a mad means, fraught with the menace of irremediable catastrophe for all, of serving the greed for gain or the lust for power of frightened and irresponsible oligarchies, each terrified at the threats of destruction hurled against it by its major ideological foe abroad. Hans J. Morgenthau observes: "War is no longer, as it once was, a rational instrument of foreign policy, the continuation of diplomacy by other means. In centuries past, resort to wars could be defended as a means to an end. . . . The total war of our age has fundamentally altered the traditional relationship between political means and military means. Today war has become an instrument of universal destruction, an instrument which destroys the victim with the vanquished."[9] Lawrence Dennis adds a more heretical comment:

> To evaluate a given war or plans for one, it is necessary to have clearly in mind the ends to which the war is a means. Here the trouble now is that the publicly stated ends of our elite are not their real ends. The cold war and the war we are preparing for cannot be considered rational means to publicly stated ends, such as our national security, our freedom, world peace, or the containing of Communism. But the war we are waging and preparing to wage would seem to serve the real ends of our managerial bureaucracies, at least for the short run. And, in the long run, we are all dead anyway. The major propaganda thesis of Washington and its Western satellites is that our war plans and moves aim at the prevention of war. This is nonsense. They aim at the prevention of a depression or a deflation. How to use war to prevent deflation without bringing on a total war between the world's only two remaining big powers, the U.S. and the U.S.S.R., is the real problem, not Communism. Neither Washington nor Moscow really wants World War III now, soon, or ever. But can they avoid it, using war of a limited sort, as a means as they are now doing? We doubt it.[1]

The sword of Damocles hanging over contemporary civilization may be no less fatal even if global atomic hostilities never break out. The appalling waste and ruination of the wealth of mankind which it is the professional soldier's business to bring about, always in the name of preserving "peace" and "freedom," can in the long run be wholly disruptive of civilized life though no guns go off and no bombs fall. All that is needed to produce the result is for the great leviathans and behemoths to devote such a large proportion of their re-

[9] "The Foreign Policy of the United States," *The Political Quarterly* (London: January-March, 1951).

[1] *The Appeal to Reason, A Private Weekly Analysis*, by Lawrence Dennis, No. 261 (March 24, 1951).

sources to armaments as to leave no choice but to use them or to face impoverishment and social disintegration.

The Soviet federal budget for 1950 provided for "defense" expenditures (i.e., those acknowledged as such) of 79,400,000,000 rubles out of a total of 427,900,000,000 rubles, with the latter figure including, of course, in the completely socialized Soviet economy virtually all the counterparts of "private" investments in industry and agriculture under a regime of free enterprise. In 1951 the Soviet budget, totaling 457,900,000,000 rubles, provided 96,376,000,000 for "defense"—the largest figure since 1945; and the budget for 1952 provided for that purpose 113,800,000,000 rubles out of a total of 476,900,000,000. If Soviet citizens, regimented by their self-appointed and self-perpetuating rulers in spurious "peace" campaigns, had no effective means either of comprehending, or of protesting against, this huge sacrifice of their national toil and substance to the Moloch of armaments, they were none the less impoverished thereby. The far more modest sums that Western European governments, under American prodding, were spending on arms in the interest of "security" were already disrupting the hard-won recovery of their national economies, thanks to shortages, inflation, and diversion of goods and services away from productive activities to the work of destruction—with resultant Cabinet crises, strikes, and growing popular apathy or bitterness.

In the America of 1951 a comparable process was already far advanced, behind the deceptive façade of an arms boom. By July, current arms-spending was running at an annual rate of $35 billion with goals set for a rate of $50 billion a year by January 1952, and $65 billion by July 1952. By this time the gross national product was expected to reach $345 billion. Some 20 per cent of total national production would then be devoted to armament, compared with 6 per cent in 1949 and 11 per cent in 1951, while an "inflationary gap" of 15 to 20 billion dollars would develop, representing the spread between a scarcity of nondefense goods available for purchase and an abundance of cash at the disposal of consumers.[2] Forced to choose between runaway inflation and a crushing burden of taxation, America's elected leaders contrived to inflict large measures of both evils on the citizenry of the Republic, even as corporation executives, bureaucrats, corruptionists, and blatherskites waxed fat. All was held justified and indeed imperative for survival, in view of the Red Menace, despite the few who agreed with General MacArthur (Boston, July 25, 1951) that "talk of imminent threat to our national security through the application of external force is pure nonsense." Unheeded were such lonely warning voices as that (February 26, 1951) of Walter Lippmann:

> The temptation may become irresistible to embrace the hallucination that the third world war could be fought, won and finished and that after that the world would be happy again. The third world war can be fought. There is no prospect whatsoever that it could be finished. Nothing is so certain, no prophecy is so sure, as that once the third world war started it would spread like a prairie fire and would become an uncontrollable, inconclusive, interminable complex of civil and international wars. . . . To raise the level of armaments too high, to subject the country to an intolerable strain, is to make the great military mistake which has ruined so many other nations. It is to arm past the point of no return. It is to create armaments that are so heavy to bear that they must be used in the hope of getting rid of the burden. Wars that are inspired not by self-defense or by clear policy but by internal pressures and irrational hopes invariably end in ruin and disaster.

The most striking aspect of the grim game in which all mankind was here engaged is not that the astronomical outpourings of riches for war were everywhere depicted as essential for "peace"—a form of self-delusion that is age-old—but that no security whatever was being purchased by colossal spending for "security." On the contrary, the more that mountains of guns, tanks, planes, and bombs were piled up

[2] Mid-Year Report of the President's Council of Economic Advisers, *The New York Times* (July 24, 1951).

on both sides, the nearer did all shreds and tatters of safety approach the vanishing-point. And, indeed, under technological and political conditions rendering all calculations of relative military might more and more meaningless, it is probable, despite hints to the contrary on the part of general staffs and war ministries, that no demonstrable relationship whatever prevailed between the estimated requirements, pecuniary, material, and human, of "national defense" and any increment of effective fighting-power supposedly thus acquired.

Warlords asked for all they could get, and often referred coyly, as proof of their moderation, to initial intentions of asking for twice or thrice as much. Legislators voted like automatons, being deprived of any capacity for independent judgment by fear of defeat, awe of brass, and patriotic fervor for the general welfare and the common defense. Congressmen sometimes sought to induce generals to raise their pleas for funds and to spend more than the military saw any way of spending. Neither group had any accurate knowledge of, or even impressive guesses about, the relationship of ends and means, nor could anyone anywhere know or say—or even dare question the ignorance of others. In the atomic age war is assuredly obsolete, in the sense that no statesman or commander can anticipate its course or consequences, even within the widest possible margins of error. "Preparedness," always a snare, is now a delusion. Thus, except in the minds of those who are mentally "out of this world," there can be no articulated military doctrine, no trustworthy strategic program, and therefore no rational conception at all of what weapons, ships, planes, and men are needed where and when to do what. Convictions to the contrary, carefully publicized in Washington and Moscow, are likely to be found by the test of events to be but the shadowy wraiths of which nightmares are made.

The demise of military science need not here be elaborated. When he died, Max Werner was working on a book that, had it been completed, would probably have supplied definitive documentation. Lacking this, the inquiring student can yet learn much by studying carefully the "strategy" of the Korean War, on both sides, and the published transcripts of Congressional hearings on the North Atlantic Treaty (May 1949), *Assignment of Ground Forces to Duty in the European Area* (February–March, 1951), the MacArthur dismissal (May–June, 1951), and above all the "Battle of the Pentagon" in 1949, in which the Navy, equipped with blueprints for aircraft carriers, was defeated by the Air Force, armed with blueprints for B-36's. Summer of 1951 found Senator Henry Cabot Lodge, Jr.—backed by Earle Cox, Jr., National Commander of the American Legion, and inferentially by Air Secretary Thomas K. Finletter—demanding an Air Force of 150 groups and 1,800,000 men, to cost $96 billion within three years, while Secretaries Acheson and Marshall insisted on $25 billion more for the same period, to make Europe defensible. The Air Force was meanwhile reported to be asking $40 billion annually, out of a proposed arms budget of $70 billion, with the Army and Navy to split the remainder. This violation of the concept of "balanced forces"—another masterpiece of political mythology—threatened new battles after a brief period of "peace" in the Pentagon, achieved, wrote Hanson W. Baldwin, by "inter-service log-rolling and back-scratching. . . . Some officers declare that each service has used inflated and exaggerated estimates of Communist strength, first to be on the safe side, and second, to support in the Pentagon and in Congress their own service estimates of their needs." [3]

In such a century as we live in, it is not wholly fortuitous that the world's most distinguished living historian, on the basis of the most meticulous and convincing research, should

[3] *The New York Times* (July 24, 1951). See also editorials in *The Chicago Tribune:* "Military Megalomania" (July 16, 1951), "Militarism Run Riot" (July 25, 1951), and "All Is Confusion" (July 30, 1951). The inability of Congress, as now organized and functioning, to arrive at or apply any independent and informed judgment of the nation's military needs is shown quite clearly, even if cautiously, by Elias Huzar in *The Purse and the Sword: Control of the Army by Congress through Military Appropriations,* 1933–50 (Ithaca: Cornell University Press; 1950).

have come to the conclusion that "war has proved to have been the proximate cause of the breakdown of every civilization which is known for certain to have broken down. . . . There have been other sinister institutions with which Mankind has afflicted itself during its Age of Civilization: Slavery . . . Caste, the Conflict of Classes, Economic Injustice, and many other social symptoms of the nemesis of Original Sin. . . . [Yet] War stands out among the rest as Man's principal engine of social and spiritual self-defeat during a period of his history which he is now beginning to be able to see in perspective." The writer of these words, Arnold J. Toynbee, although not despairing of the abolition of war through the voluntary collaboration of "peace-loving peoples," was at pains to argue, with massive evidence, in his monumental *A Study of History* that "progress" promoted by militarism is a mirage and that now, as in past eras, the way of war is not only, in the final event, utterly destructive of civilized life but is self-perpetuating in its grip on men's minds and in its disintegrating effects on human communities, even when they appear to have gained peace through victory:

> The truth seems to be that a sword which has once drunk blood cannot be permanently restrained from drinking blood again, any more than a tiger who has once tasted human flesh can be prevented from becoming a man-eater from that time onwards. The man-eating tiger is, no doubt, a tiger doomed to death; if he escapes the bullet he will die of the mange. Yet, even if the tiger could foresee his doom, he would probably be unable to subdue the devouring appetite which his first taste of man-meat has awakened in his maw; and so it is with a society that has once sought salvation through the sword. . . . Time is, indeed, working against these unhappy empire-builders from the outset; for sword-blades are foundations that never settle. Exposed or buried, these blood-stained weapons still retain their sinister charge of *karma;* and this means that they cannot really turn into inanimate foundation-stones, but must ever be stirring—like the dragon's-tooth seed that they are—to spring to the surface again in a fresh crop of slaying and dying gladiators. Under its serene mask of effortless supremacy the Œcumenical

Peace of a universal state is fighting, all the time, a desperate losing battle against an unexorcized demon of Violence in its own bosom.[4]

If the "Savior with the Sword" brings not salvation but doom, and if our own civilization is in truth menaced with death through militarism and war, then the will to survival might be expected to be sufficiently aroused by fear to discover somehow the road to safety and life. This expectation may prove to be as false in our time as in similar times gone by. But still many men and women throughout our world are eagerly and earnestly striving to find the way and to rear structures of peace which will weather the storm and protect the earthlings from their ever-present temptation to drown themselves in the blood of their brothers. The paths are divergent. The designs for the unbuilt mansion are many. But almost all have this in common: that the seekers of security take for granted as a premise or goal, and endeavor to bring into being as a living reality, the unity of humankind in one all-embracing community and polity. The nature and genesis of this conception, and the obstacles in the way of its realization, would thus seem to deserve exploration before we consider the various highways toward peace, and the plans of those who hope to come to journey's end and there build the Temple of Man.

[4] This quotation is from pp. 157–8, and the preceding one is from the author's Preface in Arnold J. Toynbee: *War and Civilization* (Oxford University Press; 1950, edited by Albert V. Fowler), consisting of selections from *A Study of History*. John U. Nef, in *War and Human Progress*, quoted above, arrives independently at a similar conclusion on the basis of the data of medieval and modern European economic history.

CHAPTER TWO

THE VISION OF MAN

1. THE HUMAN FAMILY

> . . . this goodly frame, the earth, seems to me a sterile promontory; this most excellent canopy, the air, look you, this brave o'erhanging firmament, this majestical roof fretted with golden fire, why, it appears no other thing to me but a foul and pestilent congregation of vapours. What a piece of work is a man! how noble in reason! how infinite in faculty! in form, in moving, how express and admirable! in action how like an angel! in apprehension how like a god! the beauty of the world! the paragon of animals! And yet, to me, what is this quintessence of dust?
>
> —WILLIAM SHAKESPEARE: *Hamlet*, Act II, Scene ii.

IN THE "City of Light"—beloved and blessed by gods and men for many centuries past—the visitor who walks westward from the Eiffel Tower across the Pont d'Iena, and upward through the Trocadero Gardens, comes upon the Palais de Chaillot, a new semicircular building of majestic proportions, housing two large museums. In the northern wing are reproductions of many of the noblest façades, tombs, and monuments of medieval France. In the southern wing is the *Musée de l'Homme*, whose curator, M. Paul Rivet, is also a Deputy, a Socialist, a member of the International Council of the European Movement, and a participant in other activities looking toward the establishment of a government for all men.

Whether the good Curator became an anthropologist because he believed in the unity of mankind, or came to this belief because of his research in anthropology, only he can say. The museum over which he presides is a hugely impressive visual demonstration of diversity in community, and unity in diversity, among all kinds and breeds of men. Differences in culture are strikingly revealed in admirable ethnographic exhibits of costumes and customs from all ends of the earth. Similarities and identities in the animal structure of Man are no less apparent in the displays given over to physical anthropology. Skulls and skeletons, to be sure, vary greatly. Here are exhibited bones of giants and dwarfs, of "Nordics" and "Alpines," of dawn-men and half-men, of Chinese, Amerindians, and Europeans, and row on row of skulls: of idiots, apes, and troglodytes, and of geniuses including, rather incredibly, those of Saint Simon and Descartes. Here are shown all the variables of human skin-color, hair-texture, and facial angles, along with the protean shapes of lips, noses, ears, and breasts. Pictures, models, and charts reveal extremes of difference—perhaps, to us, most curious in the Hottentots, Pygmies, and Bushmen. A nude plaster image of the "Hottentot Venus," who died in Paris in 1838, reveals, among other charms, the huge buttocks of these African peoples whose women vaguely resemble the "Aurignacian figurines" of prehistoric Europe.

Beneath all the diversities of sizes and shapes, however, it is plain that all living men are of one species, have a common origin, and are divided but slightly into "races" whose members resemble one another far more than they differ. That all men are brothers has been affirmed for ages in legend and folklore and in the sacred scriptures of the higher religions. What was an ancient faith and hope, stemming from man's humanity to man, has become a scientific fact since the advent of the evolutionary postulate and the development of human biology into the "Science of Man." The patient labors, over the past century, of the anatomists, physiologists, geologists, and archæologists who have contributed to this result cannot here be reviewed—nor, happily, need they be for our purposes.[1] A résumé of their most widely accepted conclusions is enough.

All the earthmen now alive, and all their ancestors for at least fifty thousand years, including the vanished race of the Cro-Magnons, are of the species Homo sapiens. All have the same general morphology and the same number of bones, muscles, viscera, sense organs, nerve cells, and all other components of our mortal frame. To say that all living men and women are of one "species" is to say that all may mate, if so they choose, regardless of origin and background—be it Tierra del Fuego, Woonsocket, Pyongyang, Timbuctu, or Oslo—and produce fertile offspring. Lions and tigers can be persuaded to beget young in zoos, and horses and asses in fields or barns, but all such progeny are as sterile as mules—since the parents, though of the same genus, are of different species, to employ the nomenclature in use since Charles Linnæus published his *Systema Naturæ* in 1759.[2] Homo sapiens occupies a definite place as a single species amid the vast proliferation of life forms on the flowering planet.

The biological unity of mankind is affirmed no less vividly by the hypotheses of human evolution. No true mammals emerged, so far as the record of the rocks attests, until

[1] Among the more useful recent surveys of these findings are Roy Chapman Andrews: *Meet Your Ancestors* (Viking; 1945); L. C. Dunn and Th. Dobzhansky: *Heredity, Race, and Society* (New American Library [Mentor Books]; 1946); E. Adamson Hoebel: *Man in the Primitive World* (McGraw-Hill; 1949); Earnest Albert Hooton: *Up from the Ape* (Macmillan; 1947); William Howells: *Mankind So Far* (Doubleday; 1944); Ralph Linton: *The Study of Man* (Appleton-Century; 1936); and George R. Stewart: *Man—An Autobiography* (Random House; 1946).

[2] R. Ruggles Gates in *Human Ancestry from a Genetical Point of View* (Cambridge, Massachusetts: Harvard University Press; 1948) argues that extant mankind consists of one "genus," divided into five "species." This contention, however, is not a denial of acknowledged biological facts but rather an effort, apparently unsuccessful to date, to change accepted zoological nomenclature. A more hopeful, though still controversial approach to the problem of the varieties or "subspecies" of men is to be found in William C. Boyd: *Genetics and the Races of Men* (Boston: Little, Brown; 1950).

seventy million years ago. The life experience of more or less manlike mammals is limited to the last million years of these seventy million revolutions of our globe around its star. And in these million years our own species has lived, probably, but a mere fifty thousand years (though apparently older fossils of our kind are being found), and has developed "civilizations," as a strange and precarious way of life, only during the most recent seven or eight millennia.

As "civilized" beings, we are still children of the sunrise. But our ultimate ancestors among the Metazoa crawled out of the primal slime an eternity ago. The intervening stages of change and growth are by no means simple, even if we limit ourselves to what is known, amid much still unknown, from the record of calcified bones. The earliest Primates, and presumably the progenitors of all succeeding Primates, were the insect-eating tree-shrews or Tarsioids, whose age as an "Order" is roughly sixty million years. From their loins in successive mutations, and from the loins of the mutants, emerged in weird and complex ways the lemur, loris, and tarsius; the New World and Old World monkeys; Parapithecus, a monkey-like ape, and Propilopithecus, the first true ape, as the probable ancestors of all the later apes; the four living species of anthropoids—gibbon, orangutan, chimpanzee, and gorilla; the extinct South African man-apes: Plesianthropus, Paranthropus, Australopithecus, and other types; the Asiatic ape-men christened Pithecanthropus Erectus (Java) and Pithecanthropus Pekinensis (China); the dubious dawn-man of Piltdown (Eoanthropus Dawsoni); the long lost and buried Neanderthalers, struggling for survival against the hairy mammoth, the woolly rhinocerus, the saber-toothed tiger, and the glaciers; and at last (though perhaps not finally, and possibly not quite as the glorious culmination our vanity leads us to imagine), Homo sapiens, making his first entry in the aftermath of the most recent glacial epoch as Cro-Magnon Man, long expired but still of our species, and then—ourselves, all of us everywhere over the earth.

We now number, according to the best estimate of the World Health Organization, some 2,377,400,000 souls as of 1949 or, as of the time these words are written, at least two and one-half billion people. The capacity of humans to produce more humans—no longer held in check, as before the Industrial Revolution, by periodical famine and pestilence and chronic disease, and not yet held in check, save in a few areas, by contraception—has itself become a disturbing human problem. For it makes a mockery of much of the work of all who strive for the good life in the good society. So abundantly do we breed as to give birth to some two hundred thousand new babies each day. The majority die in infancy or childhood, since most of mankind—save for the five hundred million privileged peoples on both shores of the North Atlantic—still lives in squalor and poverty and sickness. The black, brown, and yellow babies face grave prospects compared to the whites.

These colors suggest that the species is not one, after all. Yet so it is, regardless. "Race" is much more a myth, and a means of reassuring the insecure that they are superior to inferiors, than it is a scientific basis for classifying peoples. Men differ, to be sure, in biologically inherited traits, as well as in characteristics acquired from their cultures. And they can be broadly grouped by reference to such traits—for example, as Mongoloids with straight hair, Negroids with woolly hair, and Caucasians with wavy or curly hair. But no such categories, whether based on hair type or skin color or skull shape or any single trait whatever, or even any combination of traits, afford any meaningful knowledge of heredity differences among humans. Individual variations within families and larger groups inside of any postulated "racial" category are greater than the differences between "typical" or average types in any one category and their counterparts in other categories. Peoples called Mongoloids may have skins that are yellow, brown, red, or white; short heads or long heads (e.g., the Eskimos); all possible blood types; all possible brain sizes —which, within our species, has nothing to do with intelligence; all possible degrees of cleverness or stupidity, little of which is hereditary in any case; all possible nose shapes, lip sizes, facial angles, and the like. So also with Negroids, although most woolly-haired peoples have dark skins and heavy lips. And so with the Caucasian, though wavy locks commonly go with pale skin, abundant body-hair, and thin lips —in which respects most "white" men resemble the apes more closely than do "yellow" men or "black" men.

But the essentially unreal problem of "race" as a biological phenomenon need not here detain us. Anthropologists and psychologists have shown conclusively that so-called "racial" attitudes and characteristics which set people apart from, and often against, one another are not at all products of heredity but are products of culture—i.e., of social environment and status, of learning, of adaptation, of insecurities and fears and aggressions.[3] The hate and horror of "racial" prejudice, discrimination, and persecution spring from sources that have no necessary connection with "race" as a loose label for physical differences among men. Visible variations due to the genes are not so distributed as to make possible any neat divisions of our kind into clear-cut "breeds" or "subspecies." Only the members of isolated and long-inbred groups tend to conform to standard physical prototypes. Men and women have long bred domestic plants and animals "true to type," but seldom men and women. Among the Pharaohs, brothers married sisters and begot generations of children looking more and more alike. But most humans, from the earliest beginnings of culture, have obeyed universal taboos against such inbreeding and have sought mates outside the ranks of blood relatives.

Many of our ancestors, moreover, have traveled and migrated and mingled and coupled in love one with another on so lusty and promiscuous a scale that no "pure" stocks remain, if indeed there ever were any save among little groups

[3] See, for example, Abram Kardiner and Lionel Ovesey: *The Mark of Oppression—A Psychosocial Study of the American Negro* (Norton; 1951), Gunnar Myrdal: *An American Dilemma* (Harper; 1947), and Ruth Benedict: *Race—Science and Politics* (Modern Age; 1940).

of out-of-the-way savages. Even were such classifications feasible and significant, they would in no way qualify the conclusion that we are all of one species. The only "race" that is one and indivisible is the human race.

Yet the biological unity of all men has never led them to any cultural unity—were this to be deemed desirable, which is doubtful—or to any political unity, even in an era when many contend that political unity is imperative. Human nature in politics and in society is, quite obviously, something more than a result of the fusion of chromosomes in sperm and ovum. Man is born of woman, and his make-up and potentialities as an organism are doubtless fixed by his heredity, immediate and remote, and by the age-old experiences, built into his brain and bones, of a long line of animal ancestors stretching back to the amœba. But what comes of his potentialities in any given case is shaped by interaction with environment. And the most decisive component of his environment, without which he would perish in infancy and never become human in childhood, is other people. Personality—whether looked at as a universal common to all men or viewed as a variable between and within particular groups—is always the product of contacts between people. No one is alone, or can ever be alone. This elemental fact might be supposed to bind all men together. That it has never yet done so suggests the need for a reconsideration of those qualities of the human spirit which keep men apart and often move them to slay their fellows.

---

2. THE PSYCHE AND THE TOTEM-GODS

And Cain talked with Abel his brother: and it came to pass, when they were in the field, that Cain rose up against Abel his brother, and slew him. And the Lord said unto Cain, Where is Abel thy brother? And he said, I know not: Am I my brother's keeper? And he said, What hast thou done? the voice of thy brother's blood crieth unto me from the ground. And now art thou cursed from the earth, which has opened her mouth to receive thy brother's blood from thy hand. . . . And the Lord set a Mark upon Cain, lest any finding him should kill him.

—GENESIS iv, 8–15.

You are now soldiers. . . . To many of you, this transition is probably shocking. When you analyze it, the prospect of being a soldier is shocking. You are in the army to learn to kill. That is a shocking thing to do. It is not in agreement with our religious and educational training. But you will find that there are times when it is justifiable. Whether as an individual or a nation, there comes a time, when it is a question of "Kill or be killed!"

—BRIGADIER GEN. FRANK C. MCCONNELL, UNITED STATES ARMY.[4]

IN THEIR ANATOMY and physiology men startlingly resemble the anthropoid apes, their cousins and closest relatives among the living Primates. Yet the differences between them might well be deemed more significant by apes and men alike. All the anthropoids, save the gorilla, live in the trees, where they are relatively safe from four-footed beasts of prey. For so feeble a mammal to live on the ground, amid wolves and bears and the big cats, requires slyness, shrewdness, and trickery for survival and involves great courage and great fear. The apes have one-pound brains. The ape-men of ancient days had two-pound brains. Three pounds of brains fill the skulls of Homo neanderthalensis and Homo sapiens. Men always (but apes never) use fire, including apparently the Java ape-men and even the man-ape, Australopithecus. Men use tools and weapons. Except when taught by men, apes do not—or do so to a very limited degree. Men use language to transmit experience. Apes, like other lower animals, merely utter sounds expressive of emotions.[5] Men's capacity for fear

[4] Orientation talk to recruits at Fort Jackson, reprinted in *Freedom and Union* (January 1951), p. 20.

[5] All such distinctions reflect differences in degree rather than differences in time. Karl von Frisch in his fascinating study of *Bees: Their Vision, Chemical Senses, and Language* (Ithaca: Cornell University Press; 1950) has shown that these insects have a "dance-language" whereby they can communicate to one another the location, direction, and distance of food supplies.

and rage and love, including erotic prowess, far exceeds that of the apes. These characteristics, we may assume, aided survival in the forest primeval, and enabled those who possessed them in greatest abundance to live and procreate while those less well-endowed died young. Last, although far from least, all the apes—and all the Primates before them, save the age-old insect-eating Tarsioids—are vegetarians. Man is a carnivore.

Unless they eat carion, meat-eaters must kill in order to eat. That this killing is man's Original Sin has been asserted or implied by some of his major prophets, among them Gautama Buddha, Leo Tolstoy, George Bernard Shaw, and Mahatma Gandhi, and by many religiously inspired "vegetarians." Whatever the merits of this view may be, the odd fact remains that the Hominidæ, who somehow at some far time began eating flesh, became the only mammals given to killing and eating their own kind, and this long before Homo sapiens appeared. Available data indicate that the Java and Peking ape-men killed and cooked and ate one another, or, to give them the benefit of doubt, ate other hominids very like themselves. Cannibalism is widespread among primitive peoples. It is not altogether fanciful to suppose, though the evidence is fragmentary, that man as he became civilized renounced the eating of his fellows but retained the habit of killing them, with the meat burned or buried rather than chewed and swallowed. This indeed remains one of his major vocations in the twentieth century after Christ. No other species kills its own kind for the sheer joy of killing. . . .

In our present state of knowledge, this approach to the problem of why men kill men can hardly be fruitfully pursued. Something more relevant may perhaps be said in terms of the work of scholars who have devoted their lives to the study of organic behavior, human cultures, and personality as a social concept. Man is a beast of prey—the most ferocious and destructive among all the carnivores. But this truism tells us little about his psychic nature and motivations. To review here the gigantic, bewildering and, on the whole, inconclusive literature of olden times and of our own time on these matters, from the busy pens of poets and scientists, is impossible. To contribute anything new is difficult. But, whatever the risks of brevity and simplification, a few findings and plausible hypotheses are in need of re-emphasis if any light is to be thrown on the phenomena of disunity and conflict among the members of the human family.

All living protoplasm exhibits the quality of responsiveness to stimulation. Human genius, at its best, is no more than a highly exaggerated form of protoplasmic irritability. All efforts at fathoming the minds of men which have neglected the organic postulate have arrived at nothing that is usable for the advancement of knowledge or the amelioration of human fortunes. John B. Watson demonstrated that man's "instinctive" or inborn responses, aside from a multiplicity of simple reflexes, are very few. The human organism in infancy reacts with "fear" (i.e., physiological changes promoting withdrawal or flight) to loud noises, pain, and loss of support; with "rage" (i.e., aggressive approach and preparations for fighting) to constraint of bodily movements; and with "love," or affectionate approach, to petting and to satisfaction of hunger. In later life each response becomes attached to, and can be evoked by, a great variety of situations and circumstances having no relation to the original stimuli except that of association in time and space with one or another of the initial signals.

Ivan Pavlov (1849–1936) and his immortal dogs explored the ways by which responses can be "conditioned." The classic formula is familiar: sight or smell of food evokes salivation; food plus sound of bell evokes salivation; sound of bell, without food, evokes salivation after the two stimuli have been presented together many times. Bell "means" food, for the meaning of all meaning is that elements of experience are apprehended and responded to as if they were other elements of experience with which they may or may not have a necessary or logical connection. Since Man has some ten billion nerve cells through which links are established between stimuli and responses, he "learns" more rapidly than less well-equipped organisms, and builds up a vast repertory of conditioned responses to a huge multiplicity of substitute stimuli.[6]

The physiology of these and related processes of interaction between organism and environment has been studied and described in detail by specialists. Suffice it to say that the very stuff of all life is a substance always in a state of unstable equilibrium, and that its metabolism, motility, and general behavior, as Walter B. Cannon has shown in *The Wisdom of the Body* (1932), constitute an elaborate set of devices to maintain a dynamic balance or "homeostasis" in the face of disturbances from within and without. We need not here linger over the mechanics of the matter, involving the sense organs and afferent neurones; the hypothalamus in the "old brain," which is both the seat of "emotions" and the activator of the cortex of the "new brain"; the efferent neurones to muscles and glands; and all the complex physics and chemistry of living. All social scientists could probably do worse than to follow the example of C. Reinold Noyes, who makes these findings the point of departure for his fascinating and monumental two-volume work, *Economic Man.* A single sample will suggest the approach:

> Loud sounds, probably bright light, and perhaps any strong somatic stimulus produce the "alert" (*i.e.*, opening eyes, pricking up ears and turning of head); these when very strong and sudden, produce the "fear" reaction which may include "escape"; loss of equilibrium or support also produces the "fear" reaction, without "escape" but probably with "forced grasping" in primates; restraint and constraint of movement or posture produce the "rage" reaction, including "attack"; injury by external causes produces "pain" reactions, including "withdrawal" or even "escape." Translating these into terms of our original analysis, we may assume that the necessities of homeostasis in

[6] See Ivan Pavlov: *Lectures on Conditioned Reflexes* (International Publishers; 1928); John B. Watson: *Behaviorism* (Norton; 1924); Norbert Weiner: *Cybernetics* (Wiley; 1948); and Walter Lippmann: *Public Opinion* (Penguin Books; 1946).

general include also freedom from strong external stimuli of any kind, freedom from the loss of equilibrium or support; freedom from constraint or restraint of movement or posture (bodily freedom); and freedom from external injury. Variation from homeostasis in any of these respects leads to stereotyped and automatic behavior patterns suited generally to restore homeostasis—patterns which are analogous in every respect to the types of behavior produced by internal wants.[7]

All these things are common to men and beasts. Men differ from beasts in that they develop "culture"—i.e., a complex totality of learned or socially acquired responses, distinct from "instinctive" or biologically inherited responses, constituting for every human being, in Melville J. Herskovits's phrase, "the man-made part of the environment."[8] Without embracing, or quarreling over, any crude materialism, mechanicsm, or determinism, we may yet agree that the device by which all learning takes place, and all acquisition of the habits, skills, and values of any culture proceeds, is the conditioned response, by which each new element of experience is integrated into the whole repertory of experiences through identification with, definition by reference to, and differentiation from, earlier elements of experience. This is not merely the principle on which dictionaries and encyclopedias are compiled, but the principle of all living and learning.

"Inference," the name often given to this process, is "logical," correct, and operationally useful when the identification, definitions, and differentiations between A and B correspond to the actual, objective similarities and distinctions between A and B. When B is mistaken for A and responded

[7] Pp. 75–6, C. Reinold Noyes: *Economic Man in Relation to His Natural Environment* (Columbia University Press; 1948). This invaluable work of 1,400 pages is the most notable and suggestive recent attempt to survey the latest findings of physiological psychology, to synthesize several of the social sciences, and to apply the results to a fresh exploration of economic behavior and, by implication and extension of the method, to political and all other "social behavior" as well. A suggestive review is H. T. Poffenberger's "The Physiology of Economic Man," *The Political Science Quarterly* (September 1950), pp. 321–34.

[8] M. J. Herskovits: *Man and His Works—The Science of Cultural Anthropology* (Alfred A. Knopf; 1948), p. 17.

to as if it were A when in fact it is not A, then the organism, like Pavlov's unfortunate canine after the removal of the food, is a victim of "nonlogical" inferences or "stereotypes" that are bound to lead him astray. Trial-and-error fumbling and "monkeying" are in this case preferable as devices of comprehension, adaptation, and solution of problems, for they often "work," while mistaken inferences never work—as has been discovered by rats in mazes, by apes with puzzle-boxes, and by scientists in laboratories.

Non-logical inference, untested by experimentation, is the perpetual curse of the time-binding and word-using animal called Man. Words are abstractions, easily divorced from the things they are meant to symbolize, and readily transferred to things they never originally signified at all. The two-valued logic of Aristotle has confounded the resultant confusion, which has been resolved only in the exact sciences. Here a multivalued logic prevails, and all symbols are constantly tested and rechecked against direct sensory experience, preferably measured with mathematical precision, and are therefore never far removed from their meanings. The efforts of the late Count Alfred Korzybski and of like-minded investigators to evolve a non-Aristotelian logic and a science of "general semantics," whereby words and the things they signify can be kept in correspondence and human responses can be kept attuned with reality, offers ultimate hope that illogicality, nonrationality, and irrationality may be appreciably reduced among men.

Meanwhile, the befuddlements born of these errors—magic, superstition, prejudice, some varieties of "philosophy," and all varieties of aberrations—are with us always, nowhere more so than in politics, where abstract words, such as "justice," "liberty," "freedom," "peace," and "welfare," are habitually transferred by the verbal skills of politicians from things and situations they once meant to situations and things they never meant, and cannot mean. The affirmative or negative emotional responses thus manipulated are the essence of political behavior, in democracies and dictatorships alike

—with the former, however, still tolerating (though within ever-narrowing limits in the 1950's) the corrective criticisms and redefinitions through which some correlation may yet be preserved between names and things named. In the absence of such aids to truth, nonlogical inference in the sphere of public symbols, when systematically propounded by propagandists and demagogues monopolizing the media of communication, leads in the direction of George Orwell's *1984*, where "War Is Peace, Freedom Is Slavery, Ignorance Is Strength."

Thus far in our journey we have been traveling through fairly accessible terrain, well charted, and easily seen and traversed. We have an answer to the question of why X slays Y in war: X's physiological response of "love," through elaborate conditioning, has been transferred from the original stimuli evoking it to the symbols of his State, while his physiological responses of "fear" and "rage" have been attached to the symbols of Y's State, at the same time that a comparable process has been operative across the frontier—so that X and Y, if their leaders demand this, are in patriotic duty bound to try to kill one another because of the respective political signals to which their organisms have been exposed. We also have a solution to the problem of the conditions under which such killing could in all probability be avoided: the love, fear, and rage-responses of both X and Y and all their fellows must be reconditioned so as to be elicited by the same symbols, not by different symbols—in which case their States will cease to be foes and become allies against some third State or, conceivably, will merge their identities into a single State with a shared symbol-system and a common government. The answers are correct enough, however difficult their practical application may prove to be. But something tells us that we have still not got the whole answer, for X and Y are not machines or dogs but men, shaped by their pedigrees and by their cultures, yet with powers of choice and with secret motives and complex "personalities" that our formulation seems somehow to dismiss.

Where shall we go from this crossroad of doubt? It may be useful to re-examine the ways in which all of us "grow up." Consider the implications of the complete helplessness in babyhood, and the prolonged and troubled childhood, of Homo sapiens, compared with all other species. In all the cultures of men the human infant, if it is to live, must have all its needs fulfilled by parents or other attendants. At first all is loving care and there are no problems. The universe is as safe and sleepy a place, almost, as the mother's womb before the terrifying experience of birth. The baby slowly acquires awareness of itself and of the environment, and of the distinction between the two, the hard way: by denial of its wants, or delay in their gratification or fulfillment in exchange for performance as part of the conditioning process known as "bringing up" children. The world becomes alarming.

The love and protection of mamma, papa, siblings, or their surrogates is now consciously and desperately required, as the child begins to walk and talk and gets involved in scrapes and quarrels and in heartbreaking and frightening frustrations engendered by discrepancies between its expectations and the facts of life, including the will of others. One must learn to "be good" or be punished. Habits, beliefs, and values are sternly and affectionately inculcated. Parents become hateful as well as lovable. Worst of all is dread of, or experience of, loss of love—"separation anxiety" or, as Karen Horney calls it, the "basic anxiety" of not being wanted. To be left alone, especially in the dark, is to face nameless terrors. To be forbidden to do this and commanded to do that inevitably evokes anger and worry, fear and guilt, all the more painful if suppressed.

Such a miserable life would scarcely be worth living except for love and for the adolescent transfer of emotional responses from members of the family to the all-embracing symbols of God and Fatherland, Church and State. These transcend petty personal woes and afford a new status and a new security in the great community—providing that one conforms in belief, word, and act to the expectations of others. Fear and hate of brothers or neighbors wane, along with panic at the increasingly obvious fallibility of parents, when all together love the Lord and the King (or their equivalents) and hate and fear only the Devil and the alien enemy who threaten the common home of all. Religious and political beliefs—i.e., response patterns transferred from immediate and intimate persons and objects to distant and abstract symbols, all the more awe-inspiring by virtue of their misty remoteness—bring reassurance through a sense of "belonging" and of being wanted. If and when the beliefs later break down under the impact of individual skepticism or social disaster, the result is a new and more acute anxiety, called by Emile Durkheim "anomie." In the words of Sebastian de Grazia:

> A political community exists among men who regard each other as brothers. But they will not think of themselves as a brotherhood until they have and avow filial love and faith for their ruler and for their God. If they have no faith in their rulers or if they allow opposing directives to sway them from the commandment of love for their fellowmen, they have no political community; they have anomie.[9]

We are here approaching more closely to a workable formulation of the problem of union and disunion among men. A vital ingredient is still lacking, however—and a most baffling one. We now enter upon *terra incognita*, where the going is rough and night threatens to close in upon us. Men's acts are no doubt the fruit of the beliefs they have been conditioned to accept within their culture—modified, or sometimes rejected, by their hearts and heads in the light of

[9] Sebastian de Grazia: *The Political Community—A Study of Anomie* (University of Chicago Press; 1948), p. 189. This admirable, though widely misunderstood, reformulation of the genesis and breakdown of belief-systems will repay careful reading. See also the stimulating books of Harold D. Lasswell, particularly *Psychopathology and Politics* (University of Chicago Press; 1930) and the series of suggestive volumes by Karen Horney, beginning with *The Neurotic Personality of Our Time* (Norton; 1937) and *New Ways in Psychoanalysis* (Norton; 1939).

unique experiences whereby they formulate, rightly or wrongly, their own stereotypes of the world and of themselves. But people do not invariably act in accord with their beliefs. And their avowed beliefs often are transparent justifications of acts that, to others, seem clearly to have been inspired by motives unknown to the actors. Take an extreme case: A man walks down a sunlit street holding an open umbrella. Ask him why. He says he fears rain or sunburn or is testing the umbrella on the way to having it mended. You know that two hours earlier he was hypnotized and ordered to perform precisely this act at this exact time. He knows of the hypnosis, but his "mind" has no awareness of the command given, since he was "unconscious" at the time. He can be brought to understand the true "reason" for his behavior only after his own incredulity and resentment are overcome.

At this point in our explorations we come to bleak and stony roads, skirting uncharted precipices and shadowy wastelands. That many of the motives of men lie buried in secret darkness in some subterranean cavern of forgotten experiences and unknown desires has long been known to seers and priests in the oldest of human cults. But this knowledge as data of science is less than a century old. A young physician in Vienna in the late 1880's found that his colleagues regarded hypnosis as humbug. He worked in France with Doctors Charcot and Janet, who demonstrated that through hypnosis they could both cause and cure, in women as well as men, the symptoms of hysteria. From Dr. Josef Breuer he learned of the case of a young woman who was cured of paralysis by virtue of recalling, under hypnosis, various experiences in nursing a sick father which she had banished from consciousness. The young physician was Sigmund Freud.

The "unconscious mind" is here to stay. To ignore it in any effort to explore motivation is to remain ignorant of what may be by far the larger constituent of the sources of human acts. Explaining it adequately and employing its powers usefully for mental therapy and social analysis are still tasks fraught with immense difficulties and dangers. Out of his work with hypnosis, Freud (1856–1940) evolved psychoanalysis as a technique of free-fantasy verbalizing and of dream interpretation through which the unconscious could be recaptured and the abberative effects on present conduct of suppressed past experiences of pain, shame, or frustration could, in some cases, be reduced or removed. Violent quarrels subsequently developed among Freud, Alfred Adler, and Carl Jung over the theory and practice of the new art. Few practitioners would now pretend that it is an exact science.

The enduring residue of the work of Freud and his successors, including many of his critics and enemies, resides in a new description of the structure and dynamics of personality.[1] The psyche, like the body itself (albeit no valid distinction between psyche and soma is possible), turns out, not surprisingly, to be a system in a state of unstable equilibrium. Its elements, functioning harmoniously in sane and happy people and at war with one another among the miserable and the mad, are three: the "id," or repository of "libido" (instinctual drives)—wholly unconscious, irrational, and ruled solely by the "pleasure principle"; the "ego," or conscious self, rationally governed by the "reality principle" and charged with the task of repressing id-impulses that conflict with the natural and social environment, first with the aid of parental discipline, later through the transfer of the child's ambivalent love-and-hate orientation from parents to social and public authority, and finally through the "internalization" of social controls; and the "super-ego," or seat of conscience, partly conscious, partly unconscious, subject to the "morality principle," and the home of socially acquired restraints and redirections of id-motivated and ego-motivated behavior. Personality is here envisaged as an uneasy balance among potentially contradictory motivations. Unresolved inner conflicts, repressed into the unconscious, beget neuroses as defense mechanisms against tension or anxiety. If the conflict is so severe that defenses against it lead to

[1] See the books and articles of Franz Alexander, Erich Fromm, Abram Kardiner, Karl A. Menninger, and Frederic Wertham.

departures from accepted norms of morality and reality, the victim is psychotic or "insane." [2]

This formulation is in no way incompatible with the postulates of physics and physiology, though few have sought to bridge the gap.[3] Neurotics and psychotics are people whose cortices function poorly in integrating and organizing their response patterns and whose psychic energies are misdirected, wasted, or turned into channels harmful to themselves and to others. Such misfortunes are attributable to inner conflicts and frictions. Confront even so placid an organism as a sheep with conflicting signals in the conditioning of reflexes, so that energy cannot be mobilized in an appropriate way to respond to stimuli, and the animal becomes "neurotic"—which is to say that the thwarted energy, blocked by conflict, begets persisting anxiety which the poor creature discharges in restlessness, rapid breathing, overreaction to other stimuli, exaggerated fear and rage responses, and the like. When reality fails to conform to expectations, and mobilized energy cannot be discharged in a relevant way, the normal organic response is either fear-and-flight or rage-and-fight. Homo sapiens is constantly confronted with such situations in his own society and must repeatedly repress or redirect both types of responses—or become involved in even graver difficulties. Serious study of these matters promotes wonder not at the widespread incidence of mental and emotional disturbances but at the rather astonishingly large number of

[2] The serious student of these matters would be well advised to begin his inquiries by reading *The Basic Writings of Sigmund Freud*, translated and edited, with an Introduction, by Dr. A. A. Brill (Random House [Modern Library]; 1938).

[3] See George Soule: *The Strength of Nations* (Macmillan; 1942). Amid the vast literature on these issues I have been favorably impressed with Dr. Leon J. Saul: *Emotional Maturity* (Philadelphia: Lippincott; 1949), August Aichhorn: *Wayward Youth*, with a foreword by Sigmund Freud (Viking; 1935), Andrew Salter: *Conditioned Reflex Therapy* (Creative Age Press; 1949), Norbert Wiener: *The Human Uses of Human Beings* (Boston: Houghton Mifflin; 1950), Joseph Winter: *A Doctor's Report on Dianetics—Theory and Therapy* (Julian Press; 1951), and the contributions to criminology of Dr. Walter M. Germain of the Police Department of Saginaw, Michigan, notably *Psycho-Truth* and *Subconscious-Evolution*, both published by the Self-Improvement Guild, Saginaw, Michigan.

persons who maintain equanimity and "balance" in facing conflicts of motives which are ever more numerous and severe in our culture.

The Freudian postulate reaffirmed much ancient wisdom, denied or neglected since the Age of Reason. Man's unconscious libidinal motives, held by Freud to be biologically inherited (though this is debatable), are essentially antisocial and destructive. Rational and ethical conduct are hard-won and precarious blessings of late civilization, superimposed upon a blind bestiality of enormous antiquity and durability. The uncontrolled id, argued the good gray doctor, is conducive to murder, incest, and suicide—the crimes of Œdipus—though others contend, among them the late Bronislaw Malinowski, that the "Œdipus complex" is not universal but only a concomitant of cultures where the family is patrilinear, patrilocal, and patriarchal. In any event, fear has been built into our blood and bones, and the ultimate form of fear is self-destruction. So also with lust, which finds its most monstrous expression in incest. And so with rage, among whose murderous manifestations patricide and matricide have commonly been viewed with the greatest horror. Dr. Ernest Jones, best-known British psychoanalyst, comments:

> That man can so readily hate and destroy members of his own species is a prerogative that he shares with no other vertibrate animal, though it is displayed by many of the insects. With those insects, man also has shared the propensity to devour his fellow-creatures. And although he has now for the most part (if by no means altogether, as the last war illustrated) learned to refrain from this logical culmination of killing, it is disconcerting to know that cannibalistic impulses are a regular constituent of the infantile mind and remain one of the most common features of the adult unconscious.
>
> All this signifies that there is in man a permanent capacity for hostility, aggression and cruelty towards his fellow creatures; whether this capacity, mostly dormant, is best described as a propensity, a trend, or an innate instinct is a difficult problem about which there is much discussion. . . . Psychopathology can show that an uncontrollable outburst of aggression in

war as an inherent quality of mankind (thanatos)

the individual is always due to frustration or fear (or, of course, both). . . . What the psychopathologist has to contribute to the understanding of international tension is to point out the significance of aggressions, guilt, and above all anxiety in the unconscious mind, with the effects of these on behavior.[4]

Discord and mutual murder among men are now seen to have sources so deeply embedded in the structure of human personality, in all cultures of all times and places, that the politics of power and the practices of war can only be regarded as superficial and particular manifestations of drives to actions far older than the State itself. Debate goes on as to whether the sadistic, incestuous, and masochistic impulses that psychotherapists uncover again and again in the unconscious minds of multitudes of patients are hereditary or acquired, primary or derivative, "natural" or nurtured. Rage, it is agreed, is an "instinctive" response of the organism, built into its body by the hereditary ferocity needful for survival ever since the first fish and saurians struggled for life. But overt aggression against other humans is widely held to be not part of nature but the product of society's inevitable frustrations of many demands and expectations. War, as one form of aggression, is even more self-evidently a phenomenon of culture. Malinowski denies that there are any biological determinants of war, or that war is possible at low levels of cultural development. He defines war, quite precisely, not as any sporadic or indiscriminate outbreak of violence, but as "an armed contest between two independent political entities, by means of organized military forces, in pursuit of a tribal or national policy." He continues:

> The simplest analysis of human behavior shows that aggression is a *derived* impulse. It arises from the thwarting of one or the other of the basic physiological drives, or else from interference with culturally determined interests, appetites, or desires. When sex, hunger, ambition, or wealth are threatened, aggression occurs. Culture is an adaptive instrumentality which

[4] George W. Kisker (editor): *World Tensions—The Psychopathology of International Relations* (Prentice-Hall; 1951), pp. 61, 67, 69.

transforms and redefines even such biological imperatives as sex, hunger, or the need of protection. The derived and initially amorphous impulse of aggression is even more subject to redefinition in an infinite variety of ways. Human beings fight not because they are biologically impelled but because they are culturally induced, by trophies as in head-hunting, by wealth as in looting, by revenge as in punitive wars, by propaganda as it occurs under modern conditions.[5]

The latent violence of man against man, we are bound to conclude, is as old as Man himself, and has its roots of rage in the very glands and guts of all men everywhere. What is latent becomes overt when the homeostasis of the psyche breaks down under tension and frees the id-impulses from the controls of the ego and the super-ego. The aggression of group against group is a product of culture, stemming from the frustrations and resentments that all cultural restraints engender in the unconscious mind, feeding upon physiologically latent rage, and in turn being sanctioned as permissible manifestations of hostility by the folkways and mores of the culture itself—with remarkably few exceptions, and these controversial. War, as an organized form of such aggressions, is largely a phenonemon of Statehood in literate and urban cultures or civilizations. It has been universal thus far in our long voyage together out of the shadows of prehistory and into the recurrent darkness of Great Societies self-destroyed.

What is hopeful in this process to those concerned with the abolition of war, and what is impressive to all who seek to survey the ways of men, is the fact that from the dawn of civilization, and indeed long before, human societies have striven to control and restrain the addiction of their members to violence. The fact is undeniable. Its implications, and the motives and *modus operandi* of the restraints, are still speculative. But it seems probable that the earliest tribes of men, like most of the primitives still living in preliterate

[5] Bronislaw Malinowski: "War—Past, Present, and Future," in Jesse D. Clarkson and Thomas C. Cochran (editors): *War as a Social Institution* (Columbia University Press; 1941). See also his article, "An Anthropological Analysis of War," in *The American Journal of Sociology* (January 1941).

folk-cultures, put an end, within each group, to incest, killing, and cannibalism through the magic devices of totemism as a widespread system of beliefs, values, and practices.

In its most common form, though the variations are endless, totemism involves the supposition that all the members of the tribe, or of specified groups or "clans" or "sibs" within the tribe, are brothers and sisters (siblings) in the sense of being descendants of a totem-god or sacred animal that must be protected and never harmed, save on the religious-feast days of sacrifice and celebration when the divine beast is slain and eaten as a means of imparting its virtues to its worshipful children. The members of each totem group must abide, under the severest penalties, by two further taboos or prohibitions: none may kill another; none may marry or cohabit with a partner of the same group but must find a mate in a different group. These strange arrangements, found among primitives all over the earth, fascinated the most eloquent and prolific of the earlier English anthropologists, Sir James G. Frazer (1854–1941), who argued that the sacred totem-animal is generally envisaged by savages as the repository of the soul of all the members of each totem group, and may therefore not be killed (save on the day of ritual sacrifice) without jeopardizing the well-being or even life of all.[6] The Australian psychiatrist, Dr. John Bostock, describes totemism on his continent as follows:

> Although unaware of the modern concept of universal brotherhood, the Australian Aboriginal glimpsed the essential

[6] See Sir James G. Frazer: *The Golden Bough—A Study in Magic and Religion* (Macmillan; 1940, one-volume condensation), pp. 688–93: "The killing of the crow [in Western Australia] caused the death of a man of the Crow clan, exactly as, in the case of the sex-totems, the killing of a bat causes the death of a Bat-man or the killing of an owl causes the death of an Owl-woman. Similarly, the killing of his *nagual* causes the death of a Central American Indian, the killing of his bush soul causes the death of a Calabar negro, the killing of his *tamaniu* causes the death of a Banks Islander, and the killing of the animal in which his life is stowed away causes the death of the giant or warlock in the fairy-tale (pp. 689–90)." Sir James's first book (1887) was *Totemism.* His second major work, following the publication of the first two of the twelve volumes of *The Golden Bough*, was *Totemism and Exogamy* (1910). His last book (1937) was entitled *Totemica.*

methods for harnessing the emotions. Sentiments were fostered to such a degree that they became the guiding factor of tribal behavior. Boys and girls were initiated into a totem belief. They were taught to regard themselves as belonging to the fish, oppossum, kangaroo, emu or some other family. Henceforward they must obey the totem law and befriend others who belonged to the same totem group. The strength of these emotional bonds was so strong that it was possible for an individual Aboriginal to traverse the continent in safety, provided he was fortunate enough to encounter only those of his own totem grouping.[7]

Freud's startling hypothesis, set forth in one of his most brilliant and hotly disputed works, *Totem and Taboo*, is a psychological *tour de force* rather than a conclusion derived from evidence, despite its erudite documentation. Yet few who have given thought to the matter would care to deny the possibility of its containing some kernel of truth. He postulates a "primal horde" in which early men lived in polygynous patriarchal family groups, dominated by a stern and jealous father with a plurality of wives and a multiplicity of children. The sons habitually conspire to kill and eat the father, then fight one another to the death for sexual access to the women, and for succession to the father's place. At some point unspecified, and for motives unclear (save for the negative survival-value of such practices for the group), the sons acquire a conscience and feel guilt over such deeds. In the fullness of time they substitute for the actual father a symbolic father, the totem animal, and show respect to their paternity by giving it love and protection—until the coming of the holy day when it is to be slain and eaten as a sacrament. (Be it noted here that all kings and rulers are father-images, and that the initial mystery of Sir James G. Frazer's *The Golden Bough* is the widespread practice of the sacrificial killing of the sacred king.) More important, the sons agree to keep the peace among themselves as brothers and to renounce their desires (now tabooed as "incestuous") for the

[7] Kisker: *ibid.*, pp. 3–4.

wives and daughters of the patriarch. Exogamy thus replaces endogamy. Murder and incest are banned. Cannibalism is renounced. Parents are respected. Brotherhood prevails. In these innovations Freud found the genesis of morality and perhaps of culture itself.

All of this may be fantasy or fact. Proof or disproof can never be conclusive in efforts to reconstruct the behavior of people who lived and died many millennia before the advent of writing. And since that behavior, as we observe it in living cultures, is almost infinitely plastic, no dogmatism is in order as to what was done or not done during the long-lost years of jungle times and the ice age. All that can safely be affirmed is this: the most primitive of living peoples, and most probably the earliest dawn-men of the remote past, reject violence and strive in strange ways to conquer their savagery and achieve peace through brotherhood among themselves. This striving seldom extends to outsiders or aliens. But within each group, fraternity, decency, and order are somehow established. "Totemism" seems to us a curious means to such an end, though we take for granted its modern variant of nationalism, which is also a totemic cult of eagles, lions, bears, cocks, dragons, and other sacred fauna. Nothing beyond this was possible until the first emergence of the ideal of universal brotherhood as an ingredient of the "higher religions."

---

3. MONOTHEISM AND ONE WORLD

"I will divide all the land of the false god among those who are content with living and have labored with their hands, that they may be happy and bless the name of Aton. I will divide all the land among them, for my heart rejoices at the sight of plump children and laughing women and men who labor in the name of Aton without fear or hatred of any." He said also, "The heart of man is dark; I should not have believed this had I not seen it for myself. For so loosened is my own clarity that I do not comprehend the darkness, and when light pours into my heart, I forget all the hearts that are twisted and shadowy. . . . So near to me then is the darkness! It stands beside me in you, Sinuhe. You cast doubts and obstacles in my path—but truth burns like a fire within me. My eyes pierce all barriers as if they were barriers of pure water, and I behold the world that will come after me. In that world is neither hatred nor fear; men share their toil with one another and there are neither rich nor poor among them—all are equal—all can read what I write to them. No man says to another 'Dirty Syrian' or 'miserable Negro.' All are brothers, and war is banished from the world. And seeing this, I feel my strength increase; so great is my joy that my heart is near to bursting." Once more I was persuaded of his madness. . . . Yet his words were a torment, and my heart felt the sting of them, for there was something in me that had matured to receive his message.

—The Pharaoh Ikhnaton to Sinuhe, the physician, in
MIKA WALTARI: *The Egyptian.*[8]

THE ODD CONTRIVANCES of early men, all mixed together with animism, magic, and superstition, to put an end to killing among themselves seem to us gibberish. Yet these devices serve their purpose. One should never expect more from any social belief or practice. If men think themselves brothers by virtue of common descent from a wolf or crocodile or tree or sprite, they will be moved, however nonsensical their belief, to love one another or at least to refrain from mutual murder. But their restraint will apply only among the "children" of a particular sacred ancestor. How from this did men come later to assert that all men everywhere are brothers, that humankind is one, and that all killing of any man by any man is evil?

No answer can be conclusive in our present state of knowl-

[8] The quotation is from pp. 286–7 of the novel, *The Egyptian*, by Mika Waltari, translated by Naomi Walford (Putnam; 1949), by whose permission this passage is here reprinted. This remarkable and exciting fictional reconstruction of life in Egypt in the fourteenth century B.C., cast in the form of the autobiography of Sinuhe the Physician, is an indictment rather than a eulogy of Ikhnaton, but it reflects, I believe accurately, the social and moral vision that inspired the founder of monotheism.

edge. We are here dealing with probabilities, reinforced but feebly by verified facts. Most Western peoples have a ready reply derived from the Jewish and Christian scriptures: God, the Father of all, sought to teach His children to live together in love, using as the vessels of His teaching the Prophets of Israel and His only begotten Son who died on the cross that all might be saved. This answer we may accept as true—as a manifestation of the divine guidance of men and of men's reverence for the divine. But the answer begs the question of the historicity of the vision, save among those so devout as to reject all further inquiry. If the Hebrew seers of long ago derived their wisdom from sources human as well as divine, what were the sources and what do they tell us of the origins and nature of the process whereby men transcended totemism and tribalism and began to cherish the aspiration, still unrealized among us, of the unity and brotherhood of all mankind?

This much is evident: the transition, however caused by secular circumstances, was "religious" in character in that it was a part of men's deepest beliefs about the nature of truth, of justice, and of the heavenly and hellish powers that men had ever been wont to believe controlled their destinies. The change, moreover, is somehow linked to the "Exodus" of the Jews from Egypt, to the charismatic leadership of Moses, and to the holy covenant on Mount Sinai between Israel and Yahweh. The facts of these relationships, and even the time of these events (unrecorded by the Egyptians and recorded by Jews only after the lapse of uncounted centuries) are obscured in a mist of legend not thus far penetrated by modern minds. Yet it is clear that the vision of the fraternity of all men, unquestionably associated with the conception of one God, is far older than the earliest of the Israelites, whose mission was to preserve and transform the dream and to transmit it ultimately to the men of the most recent millennia by way of the faiths of Judaism, Christianity, and Islam. These are the only enduring "higher religions" that are monotheistic. The second two stem from the first. All had their origin in the areas of southwestern Asia once dominated by Egypt.

World government, many of us are prone to suppose, is concomitant with the oneness of humanity under God. It appears more likely that the ideas of one God and of the unity of mankind, in the assumptions and hopes of men who lived and died in ages past, were belated products of world government. In contemplating the tangled complexities of human affairs, where ends become means and means become ends, we have no right to assert, with Marx, that politics is but the mirror of economics, or, with Hegel, that history is but the march of ideas, or, with many a modern thinker, that religion is but the expression of ethical ideals, or of the interests of ruling elites. Yet there is sound historical evidence in support of the view that the religious goal of the unity of all men under God was at the outset a result, rather than a cause, of political and economic unification.

The first "States" appear on the human scene along with the first cultures of men possessed of the art of writing and living in urban, stratified societies. Where and when these attributes of civilization, as distinct from earlier and vastly older folk-cultures, first appeared is still debatable. But the earliest time is not later than seven thousand years ago, and the earliest place is either the valley of the Tigris-Euphrates or the valley of the Nile. In both instances, as in others later, the institution of the State probably emerged out of the conquest of farmers by nomads—at the time when the victors saw more gain for themselves in subjugating and exploiting the vanquished on their lands than in butchering them or dragging them off into slavery. The Sumerians of early Mesopotamia have less to contribute to our inquiry than the Nile-dwellers.

The Sacred River flows from the high marshlands around lakes Victoria Nyanza and Albert in east central Africa northward for almost thirty-five hundred miles into the Mediterranean—first through jungles, swamps, and canyons, then through the Nubian Desert far to the west of the Abyssinian plateau and down a series of cataracts, and finally through the waterless wastes of northeastern Africa to its complex delta. During the final five hundred miles of its course the great waterway, now lacking all tributaries but rising and falling with the seasons, deposits its rich alluvium over a long and narrow basin of great fertility and lush vegetation, flanked on either side by rainless, sun-drenched dunes. Amid the woodlands and meadows of this basin lived primitive men of the Stone Age, dwelling timelessly on the emerald fringes of the silver stream threading its way through the yellow sands. And in this basin their successors, perhaps challenged to inventiveness by the encroachments of the desert, learned to write, establish States, smelt metals, clear forests, irrigate the wilderness, cultivate grain and cattle, build cities, and establish the most enduring of all the civilizations of men.

Following the coalescence of these city-States, strung like gems along the Nile, into a "First Union" or Kingdom some time before 4000 B.C., there ensued some centuries later, after disunity and conquest, a "Second Union" under Menes, uniting the Lower Kingdom around Memphis near the roots of the delta with the Upper Kingdom of Thebes below the first cataract. With this event begin the numbered dynasties. There followed a thousand years, from the thirty-fifth to the twenty-fifth centuries B.C., of the uninterrupted growth of a great creative culture. Life here was relatively secure. Yet survival was constantly menaced by an unpredictable nature, and was ever at the mercy of the river and the sun, twin sources of the crops. Belief in the immortality of the soul is widespread in primitive and civilized cultures alike. In early Egypt it so fascinated the imaginations of men as to control their waking hours and the hopes of their slumbers. To live in the hereafter one must not only merit grace by virtuous living here, but must also, the earliest Egyptians believed, preserve intact after death the body from which the soul has fled. Hence the mummification of the departed and the erection of sturdy tombs, including the giant pyramids of Giza, reared by the Pharaohs of the IVth Dynasty as resting-places to endure for all time.

In the pantheon of Egyptian polytheism were many gods of sundry shapes and powers, rising and falling in prestige through the centuries and often merging one with another. Only the most popular and enduring deities need concern us. One was Ra the hawk-headed sun-god, early personified at Heliopolis (whose kings created the First Union), later pictured as a falcon or "sun of righteousness with healing in his wings," often identified with the great god Ptah of Memphis, and ultimately envisaged as the protector of the realm, the support of the Pharaoh, and the sovereign ruler of all the gods. Min, the local god of Koptos and phallic giver of fertility, evolved into Amon ("the Hidden One"), god of Thebes, who became a nationwide divinity with the establishment of the Theban XIIth Dynasty. During the XVIIIth Dynasty Amon merged with Ra as Amon-Ra, King of the Gods.

Best loved, longest-lived, and most widely worshipped in later times and in far places was Osiris, the nature god of the waters and grain, held to be the offspring of the earth-god and the sky-goddess. Osiris was believed to have married his sister, Isis, and to have ruled as an earthly monarch, rescuing the first Egyptians from cannibalism and savagery by bringing them religion and law, the cultivation of cereals and grapes, and the secrets of wine and beer. Murdered by his brother Set and cast in a coffer into the Nile, his body, say the legends, is sought in the delta swamps by Isis, who there gives birth to Horus (mother-and-child depictions in Egyptian art strongly suggest the Christian Madonna). The coffer floats out to sea and comes to rest at Byblos on the Syrian coast, whence Isis recovers it.

Here the tale is variable, as are all such tales. Set finds the body, tears it to bits, and scatters them in the marshes. Isis recovers the members, all save the sex organs, which have been eaten by the fish. Isis makes a sacred phallic image to replace what is lost. The pieces of Osiris are buried at various points, so each may become a holy place. But, more plausibly, Isis, after many vicissitudes, induces Ra and other deities to help her put the mangled parts together, to convert the body into the first mummy, and then to revive the dead God. He is henceforth Lord of the Underworld and Ruler of the Dead. Osiris is thus the Resurrection and the Life, symbol of the divine triumph of immortality over death.[9]

These beliefs, as they grew and changed in the ancient Egyptian mind, were early suffused with lofty ethical precepts as can be shown from the pyramid texts, the Book of the Dead, and other records of vast antiquity. They tended slowly toward a kind of universalism or unitarianism, with the aggrandizement of the kingdom. Egypt became a military empire in the long process of expelling the invading Asiatic horsemen known as the Hyksos, or "Shepherd Kings," who ruled the land as Pharaohs of the XVIth Dynasty. Thebes became a vast metropolis under the XVIIIth Dynasty. Thutmose III (1501–1447 B.C.) conquered western Asia. Egyptian rule was extended from the northern Syria and the Euphrates to the fourth cataract of the Nile in the far southland of Kush. Various deities, including Ptah of Memphis and Amon of Thebes, were now thought of as "world-gods." In the splendid days of Amenhotep III (1411–1375 B.C.) the sun-god Ra was beginning to be praised as the "Creator of All," the benevolent Lord of all men everywhere, and sometimes as the "Sole God."[1]

[9] The tale is told by Plutarch, Diodorus Siculus, and other classical writers. For details, see the literature on the religion of ancient Egypt. Sir James G. Frazer offers a full and fascinating summary and interpretation in *The Golden Bough* (one-volume abridgment), pp. 362–85.

[1] See James H. Breasted: *The Dawn of Conscience* (Scribners; 1933). This remarkable interpretation of the ethical history of early Egypt, and of the significance of Ikhnaton, by America's most famous Egyptologist is widely accepted by many other authorities. It should be noted, however, that in matters so uncertain and obscure, some scholars come to different conclusions. William Foxwell Albright argues, for example, in *From the Stone Age to Christianity—Monotheism and the Historical Process* (Baltimore: Johns Hopkins Press; 1948, 2nd edition), that Ikhnaton could not have played the role here suggested but must have been a tool of others (pp. 165 f.), since he was not older than twenty-eight when he died, and his mummy reveals a misshapen skull and other evidence of pathology.

When Amenhotep III died in 1375 B.C., he was succeeded by his son, Amenhotep IV, child of Queen Tiy and husband of Nofretete. If this woman of exalted dignity and loveliness was "every inch a queen," her royal consort was assuredly the most remarkable and most tragic of all the Pharaohs. The young prince was inexperienced, a "dreamer," an addict of theology and philosophy, possibly an epileptic. His portrait-mask reveals a sensitive face, strong of chin, broad of nose and brow, with heavy lips and the eyes of a mystic. He and his queen had seven daughters, but no sons. It was the strange destiny of this ruler, sometimes called "the first individual in history," to effect, temporarily, a religious revolution almost at the cost of losing his empire, to suppress polytheism, and to establish the first recorded cult and creed dedicated to the worship of one God for all men.

The God of Amenhotep (the name means "pleasing to Amon") was not Amon, whose wealthy and powerful priesthood dominated the imperial capital of Thebes and held vast estates elsewhere throughout the land. Neither did he deem Ptah or Thoth or Osiris worthy of his vision, which told him that all heat, all light, and all life came from the blazing orb of day. Ra the sun-god he also rejected as but another manifestation of narrow parochialism and meaningless idolatry. On the principle that a good god is the noblest work of man, the King fashioned himself a deity he named "Aton," from the old name for the disk of the sun. Yet here was no worship of the sun as such, nor yet any traffic with ape-headed or bull-faced or manlike statues. Aton was a personal God only in the sense of being the common father of all men and of all life and a beneficent protector of all living things. But he was a spirit, eternal, all-pervasive, all-seeing, and symbolized by, yet not incarnate in, the sun.

Many religious prophets, however, have been pathological and died young. Albright contends (p. 195), with more assurance than would seem to be warranted by the established facts, that the Exodus took place in 1290 B.C.—*i.e.*, sixty-eight years after the death of Ikhnaton. If, as now seems to be generally conceded, it occurred at any time after, rather than before, Ikhnaton's reign, the hypothesis here suggested is still plausible.

The symbol and the sign of Aton was the sun's bright face with streaming rays, each with a human hand at its end, reaching down to earth. Of Aton no graven image could be made, nor was any magic practiced in his worship. To honor his deity the Pharaoh renamed himself "Ikhnaton," meaning "Aton is content."

The world's first iconoclast and first founder of a world religion located his new temple to Aton in the Garden of Amon, which his father had laid out between the Temples of Karnak and Luxor. Thebes was called "the City of the Brightness of Aton." But here the spirit of the old order was too somber for Ikhnaton. He soon decided that his God of empire and of all men should have his own cities, one in each of the three major divisions of the imperium: Egypt, Asia, and Nubia. All three were founded. The Egyptian shrine was established at the site of modern Tell el 'Amarna, 300 miles down the river from Thebes and 160 miles above the delta. Here, between the shore and cliffs to the east, Ikhnaton had his followers build a magnificent metropolis named "Akhetaton," or "Horizon of Aton." It at once became his capital, the center of the new religion and the matrix of a great artistic renaissance, marked by a new and superb plasticity, realism, and movement in incredibly beautiful works of painting and sculpture. On the carved walls in the cliff-tombs of the nobles near Akhetaton have been found in our time such hymns and teachings as have come down to us to disclose the spirit and purport of the world's first monotheistic faith.

Here is no gloomy guilt-ridden cult of sinners, confessing their shortcomings and begging forgiveness (any such conception would have been wholly un-Egyptian), but a creed of joy and delight in nature and in all the glory of the world. Here too is devotion to "Maat"—i.e., truth, justice, righteousness. "O living Aton," declares the Royal Hymn, "who wast the beginning of Life! . . . When Thou shinest as Aton by day, Thou drivest away the darkness. When Thou sendest forth Thy rays the Two Lands are in daily festivity. . . . Every highway is open. . . . The fish in the river leap up before Thee. Thy rays are in the midst of the great green sea. . . . Creator of the germ in woman, who makest seed into men, making alive the son in the body of his mother, soothing him that he may not weep, nurse even in the womb, giver of birth to sustain alive everyone that He maketh. . . . How manifold are Thy works! They are hidden before men, O sole God, beside whom there is no other. Thou settest every man in his place. Thou suppliest their necessities. Everyone has his food, and his days are reckoned. . . . How benevolent are Thy designs, O Lord of Eternity! . . .[2]

Every universalism exalts men's spirits by uniting them with other men and with their image of God. But every universalism that has thus far appeared among men has also exacted from its disciples a ghastly toll in tears and blood and ultimate failure. For such faiths, by their nature, drive the faithful into efforts to impose their beliefs and values on others. Such efforts encounter resistance, which is equated with wickedness or ignorance, and must be suppressed as devil-worship or sin. The bringers of liberty and life thus become bearers of hatred and violence. The Great Society which is to be made one is then racked and wrecked by the frightful miseries of persecutions, purges, crusades, and holy wars in which there are no victors. So it is in the world of the 1950's. So it was with the wars of religion, and with the first coming of Islam and Christianity, and with the dawn of Judaism. And so it was in the very beginning with the monotheism of Aton—as proof, if proof be needed, that men cannot achieve righteousness when they are god-driven and drunk with their beliefs.

The priests of Amon fought Ikhnaton. He therefore sought to make Aton the sole lawful God, to dispossess the older priesthoods, to ban the worship of the ancient deities, to efface literally from the tombs and temples all mention of

[2] See the hymns and prayers in *The Dawn of Conscience*, pp. 281–300, translated by James Henry Breasted, reprinted in "Ikhnaton," *Encyclopædia Britannica*, 14th edition, Vol. XII, pp. 78–9.

Amon and other divine fictions, and even any reference to "gods" in the plural. All the vested interests of conservatism were outraged. We may surmise that the masses of peasants, serfs, and slaves were less pleased by Pharaoh's social reforms than grieved or moved to fury by his abolition of the comforting Osiris, who promised life eternal, and by his waging of war on all the other familiar folk-gods who were close to men's hearts. While Ikhnaton elaborated his gospel, the Empire fell apart. Hittites from the north, rebel kings in Syria, and Habiri or Semitic nomads from the Arabian desert all placed the provinces beyond Sinai in such peril that not even Egypt's greatest commanders were hopeful of saving the realm. People, priests, and soldiers resisted the way of the idol-smashers. Mob rioting and mass killings spattered with blood the steps of the temples and the streets of the cities, though Ikhnaton condemned all violence and would have nothing to do with war.

How the end came we do not know. We know only that Ikhnaton departed this earthly life in 1358 B.C. and that the son-in-law who succeeded to the throne was Tutenkhaton—who soon appeased the priests and changed his name to Tutenkhamon. Within six years he died and was entombed at Thebes in a glittering, treasure-filled sepulcher not to be found and opened for three millennia. The High Priest Eie followed him briefly before the crown passed to the warrior, Horenheb, who restored order and defeated the Hittites. After Horenheb ruled Rameses I, founder of the XIXth Dynasty, and then Rameses II, who was to reign for sixty-seven years—and make a peace with the Hittites in a treaty (1280 B.C.) of alliance, outlawry of war, extradition, and collective security against aggression and revolution: the first treaty whose full text is preserved to us.

The passing of Ikhnaton was followed by black reaction, with Amon and all the old gods restored. Aton was condemned. The mystic Pharaoh's very name was expunged from the records and reviled as "the criminal of Akhetaton." His capital was abandoned to the jackals. On the back of the gold-and-silver chair in the tomb of Tutenkhamon, between the graceful reliefs of Ikhnaton's daughter, and her husband, still appears the sacred sign of Aton. But the new God was dead. The pathetic and fanatic effort to make his faith triumphant had reduced Egypt to ruin.[3]

The lost vision of Ikhnaton, purified and infused with an even holier passion for righteousness, was handed down to later ages by the Hebrews—but precisely when and how and why, we can only surmise. These originally obscure nomads, perhaps of the tribes of the Habiri, had filtered into Palestine from the desert. Some of them had evidently become mercenaries, laborers, and slaves of the Egyptians. Ages later their scribes wrote that under the guidance of Noah and of Abraham, Isaac, and Jacob they had, while still in Palestine, become worshippers of the one true God. This may permissibly be doubted. What is less doubtful is that they were led out of Egypt and into the wilderness on their way back to the "Promised Land" sometime after the reign of Ikhnaton. Their leader is depicted in the Scriptures as Moses the Levite, a foundling reared by a Princess of Egypt. His recorded story begins with his killing of an Egyptian. There are grounds for inferring that at the end he himself was slain by rebellious followers. Between these lethal events—and this is his glory—he is depicted as leading "his" people out of bondage and inducing them to worship a strange god with whom they make a covenant. The confused narrative in the Old Testament is, of course, part of the oldest dated Hebrew manuscript of these writings, the Massoretic text, compiled in the early tenth century A.D. from oral traditions and now-lost older writings, the earliest of which seems to date from the ninth century B.C.—i.e., many centuries after the happenings recounted. The tales told are no more contemporary or credible than the story of Osiris.

The puzzles here posed are fascinating but insoluble. Of Moses's God we know more than of Moses. "And God spoke

[3] See Tutenkhamon's lament, as translated by Breasted, *The Dawn of Conscience*, p. 306.

unto Moses and said unto him: I am the Lord, and I appeared unto Abraham, unto Isaac, and unto Jacob . . . but by the name of Jehovah was I not known to them." This name in the King James version is a late Greek and medieval corruption of YHWH with the vowels of "Adhonay," Hebrew for "Lord." The consonants signify "Yahweh," a local Midianite deity of whom Moses learned from Jethro while tarrying south of Palestine. Yaweh was assuredly one god among many and was almost certainly a volcano-god to begin with—earlier destroying Sodom and Gomorrah with "brimstone and fire," appearing to Moses in a "burning bush," raining hail and fire on the Egyptians, bringing lightning and thunder and darkness, leading the escaping Hebrews "by day in a pillar of cloud and by night in a pillar of fire," and finally speaking to Moses on Mount Sinai amid smoke and flame and earthquake. He is pictured as performing miracles to convince Moses and the Hebrews, who were clearly skeptics and backsliders into polytheism, that He is the one true God, the Lord of Abraham, Isaac, and Jacob, and a jealous divinity whose first command, before the Ten Commandments, is: "Thou shalt have no other gods before me."

It is conceivable that Moses was an Egyptian noble and a follower of Ikhnaton who, fleeing from the wrath of the triumphant priests of Thebes, made himself the leader of a despised minority people. These he led out of Egypt and converted, or reconverted, to monotheism, through the worship not of Aton but of a borrowed and more terrifying deity, identified with the original tribal god of the Jews. The evidence and inferences, such as they are, in support of this hypothesis, along with its psychic implications, were presented by Sigmund Freud in his last and (to many) most shocking book, *Moses and Monotheism.* Certain it is that the name "Moses" is Egyptian, not Hebrew; that he was said to have possessed "all the wisdom of the Egyptians"; that Hebrew polytheism died a slow death; that some of the Hebrew psalms remarkably resemble the hymns to Aton; and that circumcision and the taboo on pork were Egyptian practices for a thousand years before their adoption by the Jews.

Egypt came, if only ephemerally, to the conception of One God, before whom all men were brothers, because the Pharaohs ruled most of the world the Egyptians knew, and came close to making all of it One World. Israel came to One God through spiritual torment, bred of weakness and bondage, and through a tortured quest for righteousness almost unique among the earth-dwellers. Whether Yahweh antedated or came after Aton, he remained, for a long time after Moses, the provincial tribal deity of a "chosen people," imbued with a fierce and intolerant nationalism.[4]

"For thou art an holy people unto the Lord thy God, and the Lord has chosen thee to be a peculiar people unto himself, above all the nations that are upon the earth" (Deut. xiv, 2). Not until Isaiah does God say to his servants: "It is too slight a thing for your being my servant that I should but raise up the tribe of Jacob and restore the survivors of Israel; so I will make you a light of the nations, that My salvation may reach to the ends of the earth." Only slowly with the passing centuries did the Lord God of Israel come to resemble—among the late Hebrew prophets and, still later, the first Christians and Moslems—Ikhnaton's dream of a loving and universal God of all mankind.

It may well be that Aton died in the hearts of men because no god, other than tribal divinities enshrouded in mysticism and magic, can serve any State—such is the nature of politics among men. Jehovah has perhaps lived so long because the Israelites, from 586 B.C., when the Babylonians took Jerusalem, until only yesterday, have had no State. Amos, Isaiah, and Jeremiah warned them of old to put righteousness, the dignity of man, and love of mankind above earthly power. "My kingdom," said Jesus of Nazareth, "is not of this world."

[4] See Hans Kohn: *The Idea of Nationalism* (Macmillan; 1945), pp. 27–62, "Israel and Hellas: From Tribalism to Universalism." See also the suggestive article, "Monotheism and the Sense of Reality," by Dr. Leonard R. Sillman in *The International Journal of Psychoanalysis*, Vol. XXX, Part 2 (1949), pp. 2–9.

And again: "The kingdom of God is within you." No people obliged to wage war against others can translate into reality its visions of the brotherhood of Man, and the fatherhood of God, however exalted these may be—least of all when war is waged in the name of God against the Infidels. Such dreamers, if possessed of formidable military might, have occasionally, as we shall see, achieved some secular facsimile of their heavenly vision. But we shall not grasp the meaning of such deeds until we reconsider the final way, thus far, by which men have put an end to killing among themselves.

---

4. ESCAPE FROM SIN

> Although war is so cruel a business that it befits beasts and not men, so frantic that poets feign it is sent with evil purpose by the Furies, so pestilential that it brings with it a general blight upon morals, so iniquitous that it is usually conducted by the worst bandits, so impious that it has no accord with Christ, yet our popes, neglecting all their other concerns, make it their only task. Here you will see feeble old men assuming the strength of youth, not shocked by the expense or tired out by the labor, not at all discouraged, if only they may upset laws, religion, peace, and all humane usages, and turn them heels over head. Learned sycophants will be found who will give to this manifest madness the names of zeal, piety, and fortitude, devising a way whereby it is possible for the man to whip out his sword, stick it into the guts of his brother, and nonetheless dwell in that supreme charity which, according to Christ's precept, a Christian owes to his neighbor.
>
> —DESIDERIUS ERASMUS: *Moriæ Encomium* or *The Praise of Folly*. Section xxxiii.

IF ALL MEN everywhere would willingly accept the worship of the same God; if all would praise Him in similar ways and lead their lives in accord with His precepts; if all would see that they are all brethren by virtue of their common creation, judgment, and possible salvation by one Heavenly Father; then the fraternity of totem-groups derived from ancestral ghosts, and the comradeship of national tribes derived from shared adoration of tribal deities, would *ipso facto* give way to the brotherhood of all men. People have dreamed of this glory for at least three and a half millennia, which is half the life span of the cultures called "civilizations"—and have translated it, over and again, into prophecies of the coming of an "Anointed One" or "Messiah" who would accomplish this miracle. Never yet has the dream been fulfilled, save in localized and transitory "world-States" among peoples isolated from other peoples in outer darkness.

This perpetual defeat of a heavenly vision must move the thoughtful observer either to dismiss the aspiration as one of Man's chronic follies or to suspect that certain peculiar features of men's life together have repeatedly put the vision beyond realization. The first conclusion is wholly unacceptable to almost everyone in the twentieth century after Christ. Consider then the problem posed by the second.

Men conquer their own savagery first by totemism, later by the adoration of tribal or national divinities, and ultimately by the worship of One God for all men. The third step , however, has usually had the paradoxical result of promoting religious persecution and warfare on a hideous scale, thus redoubling the savagery it is intended to abolish. Virtually all polytheisms are tolerant of others, but those who believe in the One True God invariably strive to suppress those who do not. The third step also—as another paradox—has always thus far reflected the power of particular groups of men, sooner or later organized as imperial conquerors, to impose their will on other and less powerful groups. Such power has occasionally succeeded, and often failed, in bringing large numbers of peoples of diverse beliefs and values under a common rule. In no instance to date has it turned the trick of bringing all men under common rule.

The sources of these contradictions and failures admit of

a multiplicity of explanations. One among them merits our particular attention: It is that large communities of men achieve peace and brotherhood among themselves not by replacing hatred and fear with love—a biological and psychological impossibility in all cultures, save for a handful of exalted psychoneurotics, commonly revered as saints and martyrs—but by transmuting their fears and hates of one another into shared fears and hates directed against alien enemies and domestic scapegoats. One of the oldest rules of practical politics is that war abroad, provided the war is popular and not disastrous in its course and outcome, promotes peace at home. Conversely, peace at home begets the capacity to wage efficient war abroad. On the basis of all available evidence, collective fitness to wage war has ever been the prime incentive for the establishment, via "the State," of order, law, justice, and effective administration within the in-group, whether it be a tribe, a nation, or an empire.

The symbols by whose magic men live together in peace are "religious" and "political." The two categories are so mingled as to be inseparable throughout the larger part of the human adventure. These symbols are emotionally potent and socially efficacious in the measure to which they direct men's organic responses into common courses through which human energies flow in similar directions. If all the members of a community love, respect, obey, or worship the same ruler or the same gods or God; if all fear strangers from without or heretics within who refuse to acknowledge the authority of the sacred king or his surrogates; if all hate the same enemies and the same traitors—then all are brothers and the community is a living and functioning reality. The elements of hate and fear in the formula are as necessary as the ingredient of love—if not more so, in view of their greater biological and social antiquity. A community with no foreign foes to detest, and no local pariahs to scorn or persecute, would scarcely be a community at all, or at least would bear little resemblance to any of the "States" of literate cultures. There is no evidence that any such community has ever existed among "civilized" peoples outside the imaginations of priests and prophets.

The somewhat startling political import of these considerations, assuming them to be valid, can best be appreciated after we pause to relate them, however tentatively, to the hypotheses of personality and motivation already described. Man is the beast of prey that devours his fellows when his feral nature is uncontrolled by social restraints. But Man as a social being is all kindliness, sympathy, and self-sacrifice. Within each group virtue flourishes and each man is, more or less, his neighbor's brother and even his brother's keeper. Bestiality is subordinated to sociality. The animal is politicalized. But seldom does this process proceed to the point where social virtues and ethical values become the consistent determinants of collective behavior between separated groups sundered by diversities of interests, symbols, and beliefs. Within the in-group, morality prevails. Between the in-group and out-groups, the law of the jungle prevails—or, at best, the code of an eye for an eye, a tooth for a tooth.

Mutual aid, in Kropotkin's phrase, has survival value. But its value is for particular species or societies engaged in a life-and-death struggle with others. Never has mankind as a whole achieved an ethic as broad as humanity and as applicable to inter-group relationships as to interpersonal relationships within groups. Always aggregations of men, bound together in fellowship, have tended to treat alien aggregations as strangers or foes who may legitimately be cheated, despoiled, or slain. To rob or murder the enemies of one's tribe or clan is not only not unethical, but is affirmatively virtuous.

Albert K. Weinberg, in his notable study of one of the major ideological rationalizations of American aggrandizement, shrewdly observes:

> The difference between individual and international morality is like nothing so much as the difference between Alice's every-day world and the world she discovered when she penetrated the looking-glass. . . . She prophesied that though the

books would be something like our books their words would go the wrong way. . . . Now in the romantic world of nationalism the books of morality are something like those of individual morality in that they have approximately the same major premises. . . . But the really important point in morality is less a general premise than the specific conclusion drawn from it. In individual morality, imperfect as is its common application, premises lead most often to a conclusion dictating self-restraint or even self-sacrifice. . . . But in international morality these premises ordinarily go the wrong way: they lead not to the conclusion of self-sacrifice but to the conclusion of self-aggrandizement.

Mirabile dictu, the altruism of international morality leads to an aggrandizement which usually requires the contraction of some other party. The inverted character of international morality is most striking in the ideology supporting territorial expansion. It is just as true that national policies in general, though showing various degrees of prudent moderation, tend to be self-aggrandizing in some sense. This is not to say as does Ludwig Gumplowicz that "egotism is the only directive of the actions of states and peoples." Rather it is to say that moral ideology as directive is altruistic in premise and selfish in conclusion. Lewis Carroll does not tell what ideology caused the Red Queen to say to the bewildered Alice: "I don't know what you mean by *your* way; all the ways about here belong to *me*." But if this Queen was a typical nationalist, her moral justification of this pretentious claim was certainly the fulfillment of the Red Queen's Burden or some other lofty ideal commended by a Kipling poet laureate.[5]

While this moral ambiguity is characteristic of the behavior of many social groups, it is manifested most strikingly in the conduct of those who act in the name of the State. Edmund Burke's postulate that the principles of true politics are but those of individual morals enlarged has received recognition more in the breach than in the observance. Cavour once remarked: "If we did for ourselves what we do for our country, what rascals we should all be!"

[5] Albert K. Weinberg: *Manifest Destiny* (Baltimore: Johns Hopkins Press; 1935), pp. 5–6.

The heart of the problem of social ethics lies in the role of conscience. That conscience is a product of social interaction is self-evident. What is not so obvious is its significance in the dynamics of personality and in social action. Conscience is not only the basis of tolerable life among members of communities but the device whereby each individual becomes socialized, and thus achieves peace with himself as well as with his fellows. Most men attain self-realization by making the standards of conduct prevalent in their culture an integral part of themselves. In this fashion antisocial impulses are sublimated and redirected into channels that not only are acceptable to the community but also become constructive forces of æsthetic endeavor or social amelioration. Humanism and humanitarianism are both collateral consequences of this remolding of antisocial propensities through the pressure of socially acquired restraints.

But in the course of this process—if we may revert to Freudian terminology—the potentially destructive id-drives and the self-seeking ego-drives are in no sense eradicated or absorbed into an all-sovereign super-ego. The equilibrium among conflicting elements in each personality is never wholly stable. The individual is never totally socialized, nor can any community, even in periods of rapid breakdown, ever become a mere mass of completely unsocialized individuals. Man can never lose himself utterly in the group, however desperately he strives to do so—i.e., he can never destroy the animal impulses and become a transfigured being consisting solely of a socialized self motivated only by conscience. Neither can he ever sunder himself from the group and retire into feral isolation—i.e., he can never quite lose his ego and super-ego and become altogether a self-less and conscienceless beast. Each personality is the microcosm of which society is the macrocosm. Within the community, traditional ethical standards control the criteria of morality. Within the personality, the super-ego controls the ego and the ego controls the id. In the interrelationship among these shifting variables lies the riddle of social order and the tragic mystery of the "soul," which forever baffles the animal that is half-beast and half-god.

But the gist of the matter in hand is this: when destructive drives dominate the ego, they may find release in unethical, "egotistical" behavior on the part of the individual toward his fellows, or in comparable conduct on the part of the whole group toward enemy groups. In the first solution, conscience protests. The individual escapes from the conflict between id and ego through the ascendancy of his antisocial impulses, only to confront a new conflict, between ego and super-ego. This may produce what the psychoanalysts are fond of calling a "narcissistic neurosis." If this danger be averted, the self is faced with one still more serious: that resulting from conflicts between the ego and the external social environment. Such conflict may lead to criminality or to psychosis. But in the second solution of the problem (i.e., collective immorality against alien or enemy groups), no such risks are run. Society does not restrain or penalize those who are serving the purposes of society as a whole. Conscience, moreover, normally inhibits the individual from committing anti-social acts. But when all are acting together in pursuit of a shared purpose—however "immoral" it may be by external standards, or even by the highest ethics of the group itself—the "still, small voice" is either silent, or is advising non-participation (which is lonely and hazardous), or, most commonly, is urging ardent support of the group endeavor, which is readily equated with some loftier moral aim.[6]

The man who robs and kills his neighbor cannot easily justify this to himself, and still less to society, by posing as the defender of ideals. He feels personal guilt unless he follows the example of Robin Hood and shares with the poor what he takes from the rich. But if he steals and slays impersonally at the expense of the members of an alien community, in

[6] Some aspects of this process, though presented and evaluated in different contexts, are cogently discussed by Reinhold Niebuhr in *Moral Man and Immoral Society* (Scribner; 1932), and by T. V. Smith in *Beyond Conscience* (McGraw-Hill; 1934).

co-operation with many like-minded people of his own group, all the wrongdoers together find it simple to justify their conduct and even to suppose it glorious. Whatever serves society is typically envisaged as just and virtuous, whether the "society" be a gang of thieves, a political party, a social class, a religious sect, or a nation-State. Individual evil done to other individuals does not serve society. But collective evil against other collectivities is altruism, self-sacrifice, and heroism in the eyes of all the sinners. Under these circumstances vice may be enjoyed with impunity, tensions may be relieved, aggressions may be discharged, id-drives may be gratified, all without guilt—provided only that the victims are sufficiently removed from the aggressors, by diversities of religion, race, class, party, language, or nationality, to obviate the danger of a confusion of symbols and values.

In this spirit Nietzsche praised war for affording the joys of "cold-blooded murder with a good conscience." In this spirit Goebbels once defended Nazi Jew-baiting by saying: "To be Christian means: love thy neighbor as thyself. My neighbor is my racial comrade. If I love him I must hate his enemies. Who thinks German must despise the Jews. The one implies the other." And in this spirit the leaders of Italian Fascism, in their War Code, inspired their armed followers in East Africa to pillage and kill Ethiopians:

> The march of armed Blackshirts beyond the frontiers of the Fatherland is the fulfillment of human justice and the victory of civilization. . . . BELIEVE, OBEY, FIGHT is no sooner said than done under the Fascist regime. . . . At the first cracking of rifles the Blackshirts will see a mighty figure of the Duce. They will see him enthroned on the background of the sky behind the enemy, like a gigantic vision in a heroic dream of war. This will be the spiritual reality, meaning that the Blackshirts are terrible and splendid, ready to smash all resistance, bombs in hand, daggers between their teeth with a sovereign disdain for danger in their hearts.[7]

[7] *Paris Herald,* September 18, 1935. The preceding quotation is from P. J. Goebbels: *Mjolnir* (Munich: Eher; 1931). For an interesting commentary

The age-old quest of decent and reasoning men for an ethics broader than the in-group may usefully be regarded as a double problem: that of reducing within every community the volume of insecurities, tensions, and aggressions seeking destructive release, and of achieving a symbolism and value-system sufficiently universal to make possible universal fellowship through uniformity of emotional identifications. However variously expressed, this in truth has been the mission of all universalists, social reformers, prophets of righteousness, and preachers of God. Never once in the seventy centuries of civilization has the hope been realized and the vision fulfilled in any Great Society or Universal Polity embracing all mankind. We dare not say that this cannot be or will never be. But we are obliged to say that this nemesis will almost surely continue to pursue human destiny so long as men are as much beasts as gods and so long as communities of men can achieve identity and effectiveness and brotherhood only, or chiefly, through focusing fear and hate against other communities of men.

This evil spell is the more irresistible for the fact that populous and powerful societies, in all the designs for living thus far developed among humans, are governed by a favored few who rule over unprivileged or less privileged multitudes. The few may be priests or nobles, militarists or merchants, plutocrats or commissars, managers or mandarins. The many may consist of slaves or serfs, burghers or wage-earners, citizen-commoners or collective farmers. "Rule" may mean cruel exploitation, inspired leadership, or benevolent protection. Yet the pattern of power is everywhere the same, regardless of whether the elite is hereditary, appointive, or elective, or whether the prevailing ideology is Confucianism, Capitalism, Communism, or what not. Every elite is unsafe. Every mass is prone to envy and hatred of superiors. To deflect the resentments of the multitudes away from those

---

on such phenomena of infantilism, bestiality, primitivism, and decadence, see Dr. Leonard R. Sillman: "Psychiatric and Social Processes," *The International Journal of Psychoanalysis*, Vol. XXIX, Part 2 (1948), pp. 1–5.

who rule them and against foreign foes and domestic pariahs has ever been the most efficacious means of maintaining the loyalty of masses toward elites, preserving the social order against subversion or revolution, and reinforcing the bonds of shared emotion without which no community can function.

All of this has always meant—and, conditions remaining the same, must ever mean—that the way of love, of voluntary co-operation, of a kindly and conscious broadening of men's sympathies, loyalties, and interests to embrace ever-wider areas of the human community (and, in aspiration, all mankind) is a way that never approaches the goal, despite the wishful thinking of poets and priests, historians and prophets. The way of violence of State against State and people against people, bloody with the gore of battle and afire with the flame of war, has on occasion eventuated in the conquest of all members of a system of States by one, and led to a "World-State" of greater or lesser duration, within which some approximation to universal peace through universal brotherhood has been achieved. Never yet have the Word and the Pen by themselves produced this result. The Sword, despite Arnold J. Toynbee's doubts (see p. 58), has sometimes sufficed, when wielded with wisdom and purpose.

To say this is heartbreaking or outrageous to the noble spirits who seek the unity of humanity through universal love. Yet to say this is not to express a preference, but to state a fact. And unless our quest for peace is grounded upon the facts of Man's nature in society and culture—and upon the facts of faith and of power and of politics in all its shapes, as these phases of experience reveal themselves to us in Man's long striving—then our Research Magnificent will begin in a fog of fiction and end in a cloudland of myths, without anywhere touching the actual lives of men.

CHAPTER THREE

PEACE BY CONQUEST

1. UNIVERSAL STATES

> Once let us subdue this people, and those neighbors of theirs who hold the land of Pelops, the Phrygians, and we shall extend the Persian territory as far as God's heaven reaches. The sun will then shine on no land beyond our borders; for I will pass through Europe from one end to the other and with your aid make of all the lands which it contains one country. For thus, if what I hear be true, affairs stand. The nations whereof I have spoken, once swept away, there is no city, no country, left in all the world which will venture so much as to withstand us in arms, By this cause, then, shall we bring all mankind under our yoke, alike those who are guilty and those who are innocent of doing us wrong.
>
> —Xerxes, King of Persia, as quoted by HERODOTUS, Book VII, Chapter viii.

BETWEEN the memories of mundane experience and the creative imaginations of artists, as both are brought to bear on the problem of the actual or possible geographic scope of government among men, a wide chasm yawns. Contemporary science-fiction writers picture realms whose authority embraces all the planets and the solar systems of the farthest stars. Many philosophers and poets through the ages have written of structures of power embracing all terrestrial mankind. None has ever existed. Local tribes, city-States, feudal suzerainties, principalities, protectorates, federations, nations, empires—these and their variants are the usual names given in our language to the only units of political power that have in fact come into being in the actual cultures of Homo sapiens. Of these, the most extensive and enduring of the "empires" have most closely approached the ideal of a global commonwealth. They would thus seem to merit more attention than they have received from the modern protagonists of world government. Even a cursory survey of their genesis, their lifeways, and their decline would require several volumes thicker than this. A glance at the record, albeit superficial and exasperating, may be not wholly unprofitable.

An initial truth must be emphasized, for it has been obscured or denied by a generation of universalists who are sickened of violence and persuaded that men can somehow build in the future (and therefore must have somehow built in the past) wide and all-embracing polities through rational agreement and voluntary collaboration. These things too may come to pass, if the ways of men are changed. The point to be stressed is that no imperium of days gone by has ever been created in this fashion. Every empire has been a product of victorious wars of conquest. Every union or federation of hitherto independent States has been the fruit of fear of alien enemies and of a shared desire to be prepared for possible wars in which all expect to share a common fate.

In all the human record, there are no exceptions to these sweeping statements. The most extensive aggregations of power in our own time conform fully to the rule. The United States of America, originally united in war against the British Crown, formed a more perfect union to escape the evils of domestic anarchy and foreign aggression and became a continental, and then a world, Power by vanquishing and despoiling Amerindians, Frenchmen, Britons, Spaniards, Mexicans, Spaniards and, in the current generation, Germans, Italians, and Japanese, to say nothing of Africans, Polynesians, and Caribbeans who found themselves unwilling participants in the process. The British Commonwealth and

Empire, belatedly converted into a co-operative association of self-governing Dominions, had its genesis in piracy, conquest, and exploitation of aborigines, and countless wars against colonial rivals and European pretenders to hegemony. The vast domain of Soviet Muscovy, as is well known, is exclusively a product of military imperialism on the part of the Kremlin against successive victims unable to offer effective resistance. These simple facts have nothing to do with motives or morals, or with real or fancied designs for world domination. To confuse these latter matters with the verities of armed aggrandizement is to mistake shadow for substance. Crane Brinton's comment on the broader issue is apposite:

> Purely for purposes of analysis, one may distinguish between two different ways of achieving the union of separate political units into a single one. There is the process in which a single unit conquers or tricks other units into defeat and absorption; thus unit A will swallow units B, C, D, and so on to produce a greater unit A. This I shall call the method of imperialism. And there is the process by which a number of units get together voluntarily and agree to merge themselves in a larger whole; thus A, B, C, and D will unite to form E. This I shall call the method of federalism. Now imperialism and federalism are in these senses mere abstract polar concepts, useful to us in ordering our thought, but by no means accurate descriptions of how political units do get integrated. Pure force or pure consent, pure imperialism or pure federalism, simply do not exist on this planet. The conqueror always finds among the conquered some who had been won to his cause in advance. To use the language of our own times, there have always been quislings. Nor does the best of federal unions evolve from unanimous consent and without frustrations. It would clearly be an exaggeration to say that when at long last the State of Rhode Island and Providence Plantation deigned to join our federal union force was required to bring her in; but I think we can say that at least force of circumstances was necessary to that end.[1]

[1] Crane Brinton: *From Many One* (Cambridge, Massachusetts: Harvard University Press; 1948), pp. 20–1.

Among the major imperia of historic time—all created initially by conquest—a number would seem to be deserving, by virtue of their impressive scope and persistence, of being described as "World-States" or "universal empires." It further appears that the time and manner of emergence of these political structures bear some relationship to the observable development of the chief literate cultures or "civilizations" of mankind—at least if any credence is to be attached to attempts to evolve a "science of history," meaning here a comparative morphology and phylogeny of civilized cultures. This enterprise is old. Suggestive contributions have been made to the endeavor by Saint Augustine, Jacques Bossuet, Giovanni Batista Vico, Georg Wilhelm Hegel, August Compte, H. T. Buckle, Karl Marx, Brooks Adams, and, of late, by Pitirim A. Sorokin. Lack of space requires that we here limit our inquiry to two other investigators, usually deemed more influential in our own time than the rest.

Of these particular adventures in the "meaning" of history, the earlier is embodied in *Der Untergang Des Abendslands* of Oswald Spengler (1880–1936), much of which was written before World War I. These twenty-five weighty chapters may well prove to be as exciting reading in 1965 or 1955 as they were in 1945 or 1925—albeit more convincing perhaps in the later years, since the only test of prophecy is fulfillment. That portion of the complex thesis of the once obscure German *Hochschullehrer* which is relevant to our inquiry comes to this:

Every literate culture passes through comparable periods or "seasons" of growth and decay in the "political" sphere—from tribalism to feudalism ("spring"), from feudalism to absolutism ("summer"), from absolutism to democracy ("autumn"), and from democracy to Cæsarism ("winter")—with the last phase characterized by the "victory of force-politics over money, increasing primitiveness of political forms, inward decline of the nations into a formless population, and constitution thereof as an Imperium of gradually-increasing crudity of despotism," culminating in a "World-State" that finally dissolves and is overwhelmed by barbarians.[2] In Spengler's words—which will here remain undefined, except to note that "civilization" in his vocabulary means not "literate culture" but the final form of such cultures:

> Here, then, I lay it down that *Imperialism,* of which petrifacts such as the Egyptian empire, the Roman, the Chinese, the Indian may continue to exist for hundreds or thousands of years—dead bodies, amorphous and dispirited masses of men, scrap-material from a great history—is to be taken as the typical symbol of the passing away. Imperialism is Civilization unadulterated. In this phenomenal form the destiny of the West is now irrevocably set. The energy of culture-man is directed inwards, that of civilization-man outwards. And thus I see in Cecil Rhodes the first man of a new age. He stands for the political style of a far-ranging, Western, Teutonic and especially German future, and his phrase "expansion is everything" is the Napoleonic reassertion of the indwelling tendency of *every* Civilization that has fully ripened—Roman, Arab or Chinese. It is not a matter of choice—it is not the conscious will of individuals, or even that of whole classes or peoples that decides. The expansive tendency is a doom, something dæmonic and immense, which grips, forces into service, and uses up the late mankind of the world-city stage, willy-nilly, aware or unaware. Life is the process of effecting possibilities, and for the brain-man there are *only extensive* possibilities. Hard as the half-developed Socialism of today is fighting against expansion, one day it will become arch-expansionist with all the vehemence of destiny. Here the form-language of politics, as the direct intellectual expression of a certain type of humanity, touches on a deep metaphysical problem—on the fact, affirmed in the grant of unconditional validity to the causality-principle, that *the soul is the complement of its extension.*[3]

Spengler's strength and weakness, and his exciting capacity to reinterpret the past, are illustrated by his comment that "the idea of a Ruler whose writ should run throughout the whole historical world, whose Destiny should be that of all

[2] Table Three, "Contemporary Political Epochs," at end of Vol. I of *The Decline of the West,* by Oswald Spengler, translated by Charles Francis Atkinson (Alfred A. Knopf; 1929).

[3] Spengler: ibid., Introduction, Vol. I, pp. 36–7.

mankind, has taken visible shape in, so far, three instances—firstly, in the conception of the Pharaoh as Horus; secondly, in the great Chinese imagining of the Ruler of the Middle, whose domain is *Tien-hia*, everything lying below the heavens; and, thirdly, in early Gothic times. In 962 Otto the Great, answering to the deep mystical sense and yearning for historical and spacial infinity that was sweeping through the world of those days, conceived the idea of the 'Holy Roman Empire, German by Nation.'"[4] Pharaoh as the god-king, a thousand years and more before Ikhnaton, is doubtless the first adumbration of the idea of universal dominion. But the symbolism of medieval emperors and Popes, as we shall see and as Spengler himself recognizes elsewhere, was but the late echo of a "World-State" of vastly greater antiquity. Be this as it may, no one can think fruitfully about world government without taking into full account the Spenglerian hypothesis in all its rich and provocative detail. That few proponents of the cause have done so is a judgment on them rather than on Spengler, whose analyses of our prospects and possibilities is quite likely to outlast their own.

More erudite, gracious, and brilliant (for all its basic Spenglerian pessimism and mysticism) is the contribution of Arnold J. Toynbee in his tremendously learned and inspiring *Study of History*, of which the final three volumes, of nine, should appear soon after the publication of this work. Toynbee comes close to fulfilling the cultural anthropologist's dream—not yet fulfilled by any anthropologist—of achieving a comparative study of the literate cultures of mankind. Of these, apart from the "abortive" and the "arrested" civilizations, he identifies twenty-one, beginning with the Egyptiac and ending with the "Western." In his listing, two—the Yucatec and Mexican—are envisaged as fusing to produce the "Central American," and another two—the Iranic and Arabic—as merging to create the Islamic, while two others—the Japanese and the Russian—are conceived to be offshoots,

[4] Spengler: ibid., Vol. II, p. 373; see also H. Stuart Hughes: *Oswald Spengler—A Critical Estimate* (Scribner; 1952).

respectively, of the "Far Eastern" and the "Orthodox Christian." Most of the fully developed civilizations are asserted to have evolved a "Universal State," after a "Time of Troubles" and prior to a period of "Universal Peace," each achieved by a "creative minority," transmuted through degeneration into a "dominant minority." Instances cited are the "New Empire" of the Egyptians, the T'sin and Han Empires of China, the "Empire of Sumer and Akkad" of the Sumerians, the Mongol and Manchu Empires of the "Far Easterners," the Roman Empire of the Hellenes, the Ottoman and the Muscovite Empires of the "Orthodox Christians"—and for the "Western," to date, nothing.[5]

Professor Toynbee's full exposition of "Universal States" will appear in the volumes not yet available as these pages are written. His broad conception of these phenomena of culture is nevertheless clear enough from the volumes of the *Study* already published. Late cultures typically exhibit an obsession with militarism and "geographical expansion coinciding with deterioration of quality" (p. 191). Some—i.e., the Hindu, the Far Eastern in China, and the Orthodox Christian in the Near East—have had a "Universal State" imposed upon them by alien invaders, in these cases, respectively, the Mongols and later the British, the Mongols and the Manchus, and the Ottomans (pp. 383ff.). In all, the dominant idea is either that of a Universal Law or a Universal Deity (pp. 497ff.).[6] Ordinarily the ruling elite, now uncreative and oppressive as a "dominant" minority, establishes the imperium through the military conquest of neighboring peo-

[5] See the table following p. 565 of D. C. Sommerville's one-volume abridgment of Arnold J. Toynbee's *A Study of History* (Oxford University Press; 1947).

[6] Page references in this paragraph are to the one-volume abridgment. Serious students should read the three thousand pages of the original six-volume work, published by Oxford University Press, 1934 (the first three volumes) and 1939 (the second three volumes). In April 1951, in Chatham House, Professor Toynbee told me of his expectation that the remaining three volumes would be ready to go to press in 1952. I can only hope that he may find it in his heart to forgive this wholly inadequate résumé of his thesis—justified as to its defects only by considerations of space and by widespread familiarity with the works of the master in their original form.

ples who have lost their will and capacity to preserve independence.

The Universal State, if blessed by fortune, prolongs the Indian summer of the culture and gives peace to a vast congeries of communities. But since its advent is *per se* an aspect of decay, it can postpone but never prevent the ultimate disintegration and suicide of the civilization that brought it into being. Each civilized culture is destined, although not so inexorably as in the Spenglerian cosmology, to suffer breakdown through the "Nemesis of Creativity" and then, usually, to go to pieces under the impact of the "Schism in the Soul," in the course of which the "internal proletariat" and/or the "external proletariat" finally tear the old fabric to bits. The last creation of the "dominant minority" is the Universal State; of the internal proletariat, the universal church; and of the external proletariat, the barbarian warbands that in the end inherit the wreckage. In our contemporary Western civilization, Toynbee suggests, we lack fertility in establishing universal States and churches, but are formidably productive in breeding barbarians within the ranks of our most "civilized" peoples.

Of disputation over the validity of the conclusions of Spengler and Toynbee there is no end, even as we grow weary of seeking to comprehend the place, if any, of our "time of troubles" in the larger scheme of events. The two theses have obvious parallels, though their respective intellectual sources make it clear that they were arrived at independently. Spengler views cultures as organisms. Toynbee denies they are such. Spengler so narrows our choices as to leave us none save to do what is necessary ("inevitable," if we do it) or to do nothing and perish. Toynbee salvages volition. Spengler sees the coming holiness as nothing more than the "Second Religiousness" of every dying culture wherein the masses flee reality in mighty piety while the conquerors slay and burn and do battle for the spoil of the world. Toynbee sees hope of our salvation in a return to God. Many other divergencies are apparent. Yet they are less striking than the similarities. Both writers are agreed that the World-State is the last political form of every late civilization as the only alternative to chaos—and that we in our own tragic harvest-time will either attain to some approximation of this pattern of power or experience the early demise of our culture through mutual murder and suicide.

There is no sure test of truth in grappling with such issues as these. Yet a theory of history which purports to foretell the future, as well as read the past, can be judged in part by what happens with the lapse of time. So impressive, in retrospect, were Spengler's prophecies that in 1940 Edwin Franden Dakin published a little volume of excerpts and commentaries, *Today and Destiny* (Knopf), which was well received and is even more "contemporary" reading in the 1950's. Toynbee, too, has been appropriately honored by the abridgment already noted and by a book of excerpts: *War and Civilization* (Oxford University Press; 1948). Both thinkers may have been unduly under the spell, as some critics have contended, of the life cycle of Græco-Roman civilization.[7] Each may have, as T. V. Smith once put it, "bitten off more than he can chew in any finite time. . . . The cosmic cud is indeed at least one size too large for any mortal denture."[8] It is nevertheless the case that no one sensitively concerned with human fortunes in the second half of our century can read either Spengler or Toynbee without suspecting that each, in his own involved way, long ago hit upon some vitally important truths regarding the meaning of past times and of our time.

Our inquiry here is much more modest. World-States or universal empires—however they may be fitted into, or left

[7] Paul Sweezy in "Signs of the Times," *The Nation* (October 19, 1946), makes this point in an attempted Marxist "refutation" of Toynbee, wherein he finds salvation in "socialism." This view I find unconvincing, partly because of what "socialism" has become, in Russia and elsewhere, and partly because Spengler forecast with uncanny accuracy what it would become.

[8] T. V. Smith: "Toynbee, Pro and Con," a review of *The Pattern of the Past*, by Pieter Geyl, Arnold J. Toynbee, and Pitirin A. Sorokin (Boston: Beacon Press; 1949) in *The New York Times Book Review* (October 16, 1949), p. 3.

out of, philosophies of history—have from time to time come into being and have clearly constituted the closest imitations of "world government" which mankind has thus far experienced. Of these constructs, we know much about some and something about all. Does our knowledge tell us anything regarding the apparent preconditions of success and durability in efforts to bring diverse peoples and nations under a common rule?

Politics is no science, but a body of skills and arts in the governance of men. Its most devout practitioners, excepting the madmen who now and then acquire power and use it solely for destruction, are concerned with order and growth—that is to say, with restraining the savagery of men against men, and minimizing violence in human affairs, through the promotion of justice and of practices of creative co-operation. Politics, we are all disposed to believe, has no other purpose, or ought not to have any other. Those who practice it for other ends (and they are many) betray themselves and mankind. The "order" and "growth" that are striven for—the living and dynamic homeostasis of the body social—may be a vision of equity, a mask for exploitation, a dream of human dignity and joy, or, most commonly, the devices whereby a community may most effectively defend itself against hostile communities or may most effectively subdue them. Whatever its imperatives and attributes, the work of government endures only as the governed are persuaded that they derive benefits therefrom, or are helpless to alter their lot, or are better off with all their burdens than they could possibly hope to be if government vanished into thin air. In the World-States or universal empires more men and women in wider lands and for longer spans of time have enjoyed orderly and fruitful lives than has been the case under any other forms of power.

The prerequisites of stability and development in the Great Societies (and hypothetically in the World Society of days to come, if we are capable of its creation) are not in essence different from their prerequisites in all lesser polities.

There must be a fund of common symbols in terms of which the loves, hates, and fears of men, as they find public expression, are evoked, mobilized, and discharged in similar ways. Without such a shared "ideology" or "belief-system," no government is possible. There must be procedures for "enforcing law" efficiently on those who break it. Rules without sanctions are futile. Men can live in order only when their propensities toward anarchy are restricted by arrangements offering reasonable expectation that malefactors will be held in check. There must be ways for altering in peaceful fashion through moderation, compromise, and balance the distribution of influence and of indulgences and deprivations among groups of men. No status quo is static. Power-holders who forbid change sooner or later lose power, for no one has yet discovered, from Plato to Franco, how change can be prevented in the ever-shifting aspirations and relationships of human beings. There must, finally, be a self-conscious and self-confident corps of rulers—whether it be a caste or class, a nobility or priesthood, a bureaucracy or intelligensia—whose profession it is to popularize symbols, maintain law and order, and facilitate nonviolent change to the end that the commonwealth may prosper.

These are the preconditions of all government, and therefore of world government: Myth—to win men's minds and touch their hearts; Authority—to impose common rules of conduct and keep the community secure; Adaptation—to meet men's expectations and demands with flexibility enough to avoid both rigor mortis or violent convulsions in the body politic; and Elite—to command popular respect, to supply talent for the tasks of rulership, and give meaning and direction to men's lives together. All are interwoven in the tapestry of power. If one breaks, the rest are loosened. If all remain in place, the fabric holds and those who enjoy its protection prosper and increase. The problem of government, in a time-worn phrase, is the reconciliation of Authority and Liberty. But in the terms here preferred the enterprise is one of keeping men content, or at least acquiescent and indisposed to violence against their fellows, by providing them with shared beliefs and purposes, by convincing them that lawlessness is at once sinful and hazardous, by persuading them that their changing hopes are not in vain, and by imbuing them with loyalty toward their rulers. How these operations have been contrived in several of the World-States or universal empires of the past and present will be our concern in the balance of this chapter and the next, on the assumption that global government is impossible without these devices and that past experience in using them is the only safe guide to their future use on a broader stage and for larger goals.

---

2. THE SACRED EMPIRE

> The whole commonwealth of the world is governed by one good ruler, and every member of that commonwealth may turn to one common center, from which all receive their due rights. Everywhere your rule is equitable. Every order that you give is instantly obeyed. You have but to decree a thing and it is done. Yours is a world-wide Empire, distinguished by the fact that your subjects are all free men. The whole world keeps holiday; the age-long curse of war has been put aside; mankind turns to enjoy happiness. Strife has been stilled, leaving only the emulation of cities, each anxious to be the most beautiful and the most fair. Every city is full of gymnastic schools, fountains and porticos, temples, factories and schools of learning. The whole earth is decked with beauty like a garden.
>
> —ÆLIUS ARISTIDES TO ANTONINUS PIUS.[9]

THE TEMPLE is thronged with the local populace, mingled with strangers and dignitaries. Amid suitable pageantry, following celebration of the sacrament, a high priest places a

[9] The writer was a philosopher of Asia Minor who traveled to Rome in A.D. 143. His words are addressed to the Emperor Antoninus Pius, A.D. 138–61, successor of Hadrian and precursor of Marcus Aurelius. They are here quoted from the paraphrase by Lawrence Waddy: *Pax Romana and World Peace* (Norton; 1950), pp. 133–4.

crown upon the head of a mighty monarch, just as he rises from prayer. The crowds, led by men who know what words must be said on so memorable an occasion, shouts: "To Charles, the Augustus, crowned by God, great and pacific Emperor of the Romans, life and victory!" The donor of the crown is Pope Leo III. The recipient is the King of the Franks, later to be known as Karl der Grosse, or Charlemagne. The place is the Church of St. Peter in Rome. The time is Christmas Day in the Year of Our Lord 800.

The ruler thus honored was a Christian barbarian who thirty-two years earlier, as eldest son of Pepin III, had inherited the broad lands then named Austrasia, Neustria, and Aquitaine. He had married the daughter of the King of the Lombards, abandoned her in favor of Hildegarde of Suabia (mother of his three legitimate sons), taken two later wives, and lustily spawned sundry bastards by five mistresses. Wine, women, and war were his life, along with a not inconsiderable interest in learning and lawmaking. By the turn of the century he was ruler of most of Western Europe, having *seriatim* crushed Aquitainian and Gascon rebels; invaded North Italy and made himself Lombard King; annexed Bavaria and, later and temporarily, the Byzantine provinces of Venetia and Dalmatia; got himself named a "Patrician of Rome"; waged annual war on the pagan Saxons, 4,500 of whom he captured and butchered in a single day at Verden—after which Chief Widukind submitted to baptism; forcibly compelled the Avars in Hungary to accept the true faith; fought the Arabs and the Basques in northern Spain, where the fall of Roland at Roncesvaux became a heroic legend; and sided with the Papacy against the image-worshippers of Constantinople.

As for the Pope who crowned him Emperor, Leo had been elected in 795, but was none too secure on the Holy See. He was accused of perjury and adultery, savagely beaten by his enemies, and allegedly deprived of his tongue and eyes—which organs, however, were miraculously restored. Charles came to Rome to do justice between the Pope and his foes. These worthies finally accepted Leo's solemn oath of innocence two days before Christmas. The coronation in St. Peter's was scarcely a surprise to the King, though he is depicted as unaware and unwilling by his biographer Einhard. Two of his court theologians, Anghilbert and Alquin, prophesied the event some months in advance. But Charles was too wise to use his new title as a weapon for disputing the mastery of all Christendom with the Cæsar of the East. After a brief naval war in the Adriatic, he gave up the Byzantine provinces he had claimed. The two "Roman Emperors" henceforth recognized each other as equals. The World-State was thus restored, but by "realists" able to accept the partition of the globe. But they were unable, as events turned out, to preserve the Western restoration beyond the lives of the restorers in anything like the form Leo and Charles had envisaged.

The Yuletide ceremony in St. Peter's has a symbolic significance far broader than the symbolism of the scene itself. The vision of a world imperium here embodied in the crowning of prince by priest was far older than Christianity. A thousand years earlier (200 B.C.) the original Romans, victorious over Carthage, were already laying the foundations of the universal empire that was to eclipse the Alexandrine World-State of a time still more remote. A thousand years later (A.D. 1800) the same "empire," albeit now but the ghost of a memory and fated to fade away within another six years, was still nominally in existence as a State. This version of the dream, though it can rightly be regarded as having "come true" for but a fraction of this long period, thus spanned much of the lifetimes of two civilizations: the Græco-Roman and our own, Hellenic and Western, or, in Spengler's terminology, "Appolinian" and "Faustian."

Other and older versions had budded in men's minds and come to flower in far-away cultures. We must limit ourselves for the moment to those lying nearest to us in space and time. Charles the Great, by the very title put upon him by the Holy Father, was conscious of the continuity, tenuous as it was, between his works of peace through conquest and those of the original Augustus. Whether he perceived a longer continuity with Alexander the god-king is less certain. But in retrospect we see the links that bind all these efforts into a common striving, by differing devices, toward a similar goal.

The Alexandrian Empire was a fusion of the glory that was Greece, then long past its zenith, with the "Achæmenian" Empire of the Persians—who, having subdued all Asia Minor, Syria, Babylon (538 B.C.), and Egypt (525 B.C.), had vainly sought under Xerxes to conquer the Hellenic cities in the early fifth century. At the age of twenty, in 336 B.C., Alexander became King of Macedonia and overlord of Greece through the death of his father Philip at the hands of an assassin. After brutally crushing rebellion in the Greek city of Thebes, the young prince led his phalanxes to the conquest of Persia. He won battle after battle in Asia Minor. By way of Tyre and Jerusalem, he entered Egypt in 332 to found the most famous of the many "Alexandrias" and to visit the Oasis of Amon far west of Memphis.

A year later he crushed the armies of Darius III, Persian "King of Kings," at Arbela north of Babylon and then went on to Susa and Persepolis. The vanquished monarch perished at the hands of his own fleeing soldiery. Alexander pressed on to far horizons in an unbelievable seven-year Odyssey of adventure and exploration—reaching the south shore of the Caspian in 330, moving east and south and then north through Bactria by way of Kabul and Samarcand, descending into India through Khyber Pass, defeating the war-elephants of King Porus on the Upper Indus, and refraining from pushing on to the Ganges—who knows how far beyond? —only because his troops refused to follow.

By land across southern Iran and by sea up the Persian gulf, his forces returned to the West. In 324 he was back at Susa, undisputed ruler of the largest empire thus far forged by the sword. After much violence, murder, and heavy drinking, he died of a fever at Babylon in 323 B.C., aged thirty-three. His immense imperium speedily fell apart, though much of his work endured in the lives and beliefs of men. Save for

Italy to the far west and the States of India and China to the farther east, he had "conquered the world" as it was then known.

The ways whereby this realm was ruled were to persist throughout its parts long after its disintegration, and were to influence generations still unborn. The elite of this military empire consisted of Macedonian generals and Greek commanders and governors, left behind to control arms and revenues in the subjugated provinces as the armies moved on. Alexander likewise founded some seventy cities, each a Greek colony, a center of Hellenism, and a focal point of authority—and each with a council, popular assembly, and magistrates. The Alexandrian system was not a rigid rule of naked force, despite the magic of military invincibility which sometimes leads to this result. It was kept flexible by respecting local customs, by giving each people such an image of authority, albeit now incarnate in the conqueror, as they had previously been most accustomed to, and by other and stranger devices and ideas soon to be noted.

That Alexander was a military genius all concede. That he was a political philosopher-king on Plato's model, but more imaginative than Plato, blessed with the gift of command, and unencumbered by reverence for tradition, many have overlooked—no doubt because verbalizers judge more by the word than by the deed. He left few words and no really adequate account of his deeds outside of his practice of the arts of war. Yet there is a near-miracle here, and a portent for a long posterity. Alexander faced a problem many men and statesmen have confronted but few have understood: the discrepancy, even the contradiction, between the needs of men in a Great Society and the parochial stereotypes inherited from a dead past as their own ideological equipment for dealing with the living present. He grasped the problem and solved it—not by logic or religion or ancestor-worship, but by a daring trial-and-error grappling with the realities of human experience as perceived by an extraordinarily acute and sensitive mind. The impression conveyed by the chroniclers that the solution was ephemeral and therefore vain is unwarranted. The creative method of the solution, if not its substance, will be applicable to government so long as men are in need of being governed.

Alexander's problem was this: he was born into a world wholly dominated by the political theory and practice of the small Greek city-state, but imperatively requiring a practice and theory of government appropriate to One World. His tutor, Aristotle, never saw the problem, nor had Plato or Socrates earlier. All of them equated the city with the State and never posed the question of the unity of the Greeks, much less of mankind. Alexander did not permit Aristotle's lessons to control his practical decisions. The teacher had nothing to teach regarding the issue of uniting divers peoples into a great commonwealth. Alexander perceived that his enemies, the Persians, had a partial answer in Zoroastrianism, whose converts held that the supreme deity or Lord of Good, Ahura-Mazda, was ever at war with Ahriman, Lord of Evil, and (more significantly) that the King was the divinely inspired embodiment of Mazda's justice and a kind of living law. He saw that the Egyptians, who made their Pharaoh a god, had another part of the answer. Had he gone on into India and China he would doubtless have seen more things relevant to his dilemma.

The sword with which he cut this Gordian Knot was no crude weapon of violence but a subtle instrument, delicately attuned to the varying expectations of men. He did not—because he could not, nor could anyone—expand the Greek *polis* into a multilingual and many-cultured empire. His passion for founding new cities had other motives. Neither did he blindly import Oriental despotism into Greece. In his own Macedonia he remained, like his father before him, a quasi-constitutional monarch. In Greece he was willing to be deemed a god, but not an autocrat. In Asia he borrowed from the "King of Kings" the role of divinely inspired autocrat, though taking care to deal with his vanquished Persian enemies as equals and to recruit them into his armies and civil service. In Africa, he was pleased to be god-king. In the synthesis, he was less concerned with being "all things to all men" than with uniting all men in a new commonwealth.

The fragmentary records of this achievement, as they have come down to us, reveal political genius at work, even as the genius was seemingly preoccupied by his fantastic journey into Asia. In his brief stop at the shrine of Amon, he seems to have let it be known that he had exchanged greetings with the deity (Zeus to the Greeks) who had called him "son," invested him with the royalty of Ra and of Horus, reserved for him "the empire of the world," and assigned him the divine task of "holding all countries and all religions" and unifying all peoples by his arms. Alexander in Egypt, says Plutarch, declared that God was in truth "the common Father of us all."

In Persia he allowed his beaten foes to kiss him and thus treated them as kinsmen, a privilege accorded to his own Macedonians only when they protested. He not only married a Persian noble's daughter, Roxanne, in 327 B.C., but officiated at a great mass wedding at Susa in 324 of Macedonian-Greek bridegrooms and Persian brides. In all of this he departed widely from Aristotle's precept: "Treat Greeks as free men, but barbarians as slaves." Neither did he accept, save as an initial means, the old advice of Isocrates to King Philip to unite Greece by a Pan-Hellenic crusade against Asia. He is said to have planned organized mass migrations of Europeans into Asia and Asiatics into Europe. His principle, said historians of later days, was "*homonoia*" (oneness of mind and heart) between victors and vanquished, partnership in empire, "peace and mutual fellowship among all men," and the transformation of humanity into "one polity" wherein "all men are one people."

Plutarch, writing of these matters four centuries later under the spell of a myth that was coming to life in a new matrix, was probably not far from wrong in commenting:

The much admired *Republic* of Zeno, the founder of the Stoic sect, may be summed up in this one main principle: that all the inhabitants of this world of ours should not live differentiated by their respective rules of justice into separate cities and communities but that we should consider all men to be of one community and one order common to all. . . . This Zeno wrote, giving shape to a dream or, as it were, a shadowy picture of a well-ordered and philosophic commonwealth: but it was Alexander who gave effect to the idea. For Alexander did not follow Aristotle's advice to treat the Greeks as if he were their leader, and other peoples as if he were their master; to have regard for the Greeks as for friends and kindred, but to conduct himself toward other peoples as though they were plants or animals; for to do so would have been to cumber his leadership with numerous battles and banishments and festering seditions. But as he believed that he came as a heaven-sent governor to all, and as a mediator for the whole world, those whom he could not persuade to unite with him he conquered by force of arms, and he brought together into one body all men everywhere, uniting and mixing in one great loving-cup, as it were, men's lives, their characters, their marriages, their very habits of life. He bade them all consider as their fatherland the whole inhabited earth, as their stronghold and protection his camp, as akin to them all good men, and as foreigners only the wicked; they should not distinguish between Grecian and foreigner by Grecian cloak and targe or scimitar and jacket; but the distinguishing mark of the Grecian should be seen in virtue and that of the foreigner in iniquity; clothing and food, marriage and manner of life they should regard as common to all, being blended into one by ties of blood and children.[1]

This credo, though reflecting the yearning of men's hearts, took no firm root in men's minds in Alexander's own brief

[1] Plutarch: *Moralia* (translated by Frank Cole Babbitt, Loeb Classical Library), Vol. IV, pp. 397–9, from *De Fortuna Alexandri.* See Hans Kohn's comments in *The Idea of Nationalism,* pp. 58–60. See also Plutarch: *Life of Alexander;* Mason Hammond: *City-State and World-State in Greek and Roman Political Theory until Augustus* (Cambridge, Massachusetts: Harvard University Press; 1951), pp. 16–53; Charles Alexander Robinson: *Alexander the Great* (Dutton; 1947); W. W. Tarn: *Alexander the Great and the Unity of Mankind* (Cambridge University Press; 1948); Ulrich Wilcken: *Alexander the Great* (Dial; 1932); and Benjamin Wheeler: *Alexander the Great* (Putnam; 1911).

time. His empire reverted to an anarchic system of separate sovereignties after his demise. But we are dealing here with no transitory flash of insight, but rather with a dream that has never since lost its fascination, coupled as it is with the inspiring image of a beardless, god-like youth who led his warriors to the conquest of the earth. No matter that Alexander in an age of beards insisted upon shaving; that vindictive savagery and insane rage were ingredients of his character; and that he perhaps died young because he could not endure the thought of growing old. In Europe, Asia, and Africa he is still revered as a hero. His bold imaginings were to be almost realized centuries later, under a strange witchery of necessity, destiny, or *Fortuna*, by another people whose gravity and severe practicality left them no time for dreaming.

The story of the grandeur that was Rome is familiar, though each generation since must retell it and reinterpret it. At a ford in the River Tiber, where primitive Latins and Etruscans traded goods and blows, a city grew some centuries before Alexander's birth. At the time of the god-king's death the Romans, having long since expelled their Etruscan kings and established a Republic (510 B.C.), were masters of most of Italy. Their government comprised a Senate, chosen by and in turn choosing two annually elected Consuls, dominated by the "patrician" class of bluebloods or (later) plutocrats; an Assembly of citizens, representing the "plebeians," with its Tribunes of the People to insure the rule of law; Magistrates or, as we should say, Ministers directing the public services and responsible to the Senate; occasional "dictators" entrusted with supreme authority in times of crisis; and a gradually growing body of skilled citizen-soldiers and expert administrators. Whole libraries are devoted to telling how this Republic fought and finally destroyed Carthage in three frightful conflicts spread over 118 years; conquered Macedonia and the Greek leagues of cities; fought off German and African barbarians; took Asia Minor; fell into social convulsions and civil wars; subdued Gaul and invaded Germany and Britain; and, by the time of the death of Julius Cæsar (44 B.C.) had already become, with no one in particular having willed this result, a World-State, because the legions were now invincible and no other Power remained in the West to challenge Rome's mastery of mankind.

Here again, as in Alexander's time and in our own, the ways and beliefs of small outmoded political units, rendered obsolete by the emergence of a Great Society, were ill-suited to the service of human needs in a vast commonwealth. The task of adjustment (unlike our own) was hugely simplified by the disappearance of the previous system of sovereign States under the irresistible impact of one conquering Power. Yet this Power—in respect of Myth, Authority, Adaptation, and Elite—was still a city, now summoned to rule a world. The solution of the problem ultimately involved the painful displacement of a sturdy and frugal Republic of freemen by a gaudy Despotism—tempered, to be sure, by wisdom, moderation, and assassination, yet doomed, by its rulers' growing obsession with money and militarism, to sink into final ruin. The great Gibbon attributes the decline and fall to "barbarism and religion," a judgment we must judge as superficial, despite Gibbon's other profundities of description and analysis. Seas of tears and of ink (and, long ago, of blood) have been spilled in deploring the transition from Republic to Imperium. The fact remains that the Roman solution gave Western mankind "world government" for a longer time, over a wider area, and over more numerous and prosperous populations that it has ever known before or since.

If the outcome seems to us in many of its aspects full of crudity and cruelty, we should perhaps do well to remind ourselves that we, the people of Christendom in the twentieth century after Christ, have in somber fact fostered more madness, sadism, and grossness, all in the name of our illusions and hypocrisies, than the most degenerate Roman could ever have supposed possible. Nothing in our own time requires any alteration of Gibbon's conclusions of a century and a half ago:

If a man were called to fix the period in the history of the world, during which the condition of the human race was most happy and prosperous, he would, without hesitation, name that which elapsed from the death of Domitian to the accession of Commodus. The vast extent of the Roman empire was governed by absolute power, under the guidance of virtue and wisdom. The armies were restrained by the firm but gentle hand of four successive emperors, whose characters and authority commanded involuntary respect. The forms of the civil administration were carefully preserved by Nerva, Trajan, Hadrian, and the Antonines, who delighted in the image of liberty, and were pleased with considering themselves as the accountable ministers of the laws. Such princes deserved the honor of restoring the republic had the Romans of their days been capable of enjoying a rational freedom. [2]

[2] Edward Gibbon: *The Decline and Fall of the Roman Empire* (Random House Modern Library), Vol. I, p. 70. Crane Brinton in *From Many One*, pp. 24–5, comments on this passage: "To our Victorian forefathers, secure in peace, Gibbon's ideal on earth seemed stodgy, unaspiring, not nearly so interesting to contemplate as exciting ages like those of the *Chansons de Roland* or the *Morte d'Arthur*, when knighthood was in flower. I am not so sure but that in 1948 we are more inclined to agree with Gibbon. At any rate, the years he chose, 96 A.D. to 180 A.D., mark the nearest to 'one world' at peace we Westerners have ever seen realized in institutions on this earth. It is true that toward the North and East barbaric groups of German, Slavic, and Hunnic stocks were constantly pressing upon the *cordon sanitaire* held against them by the Roman Legions. It is true that slavery, suffering, and all the rest of the tale of human woes is no briefer here than at any other time in human history. It may well be true that Antonine Rome was already a state in decline, a society that had failed to resolve fundamental social and economic tensions which must at least be mitigated if a society is to endure. Nevertheless, Antonine Rome did preserve international peace for a longer time and over a greater area than any other political organization Western Man has ever set up. The Roman Empire at its height was our greatest Western international society."

Lawrence Waddy, in his *Pax Romana and World Peace*, observes (pp. 3–4): "Roman history, after the generation of Julius Cæsar, is not the story of political experiments in miniature, such as the brief city states made; nor is it concerned with a balance of power between nations, like so much later European history; nor with the fluctuating strength and weakness of rival Empires, such as forms the background to the history of the Near East in the centuries before Christ. We are justified in saying that the Roman Empire was an experiment in world government. Rome combined in her citizen

For all students of world government the *modus operandi* of the Roman Imperium is worthy of more than the passing notice that can here be given to it. A few clues may be helpful. Here was a community of perhaps one hundred million souls at its zenith, of whom only some five million were citizens in Augustus's time. Caracalla's edict of A.D. 212 made virtually every freeman a citizen—as a means of adding to the tax-rolls. During the great days, however, almost one half of this populace consisted of slaves. Of the free, the mass were poor plebs; i.e., proletarians or tenant farmers on the great *latifundia*. The elite was a fusion of old patrician families, new nobles, and a fluctuating group of urban capitalists, merchants, entrepreneurs, bureaucrats, and generals. The balance comprised small farmers, small businessmen, and intellectuals—doubtless less numerous, proportionately, than in our own Western societies, since a community without science and technology (and Rome had little of either in our modern sense, using slave labor instead) cannot sustain great numbers of secondary or tertiary producers or members of the service trades. But no theory of "class conflict" will explain Rome and its problems, any more than they will explain America and its problems two millennia later.

The central problem was not "economic" or "social," but political in the narrowest sense. Seldom in the later centuries was Roman politics a game of power between classes or other economic groups. Slave rebellions were rare. When they took place, as in the uprising led by Spartacus, 73–1 B.C., they were ruthlessly suppressed. Six thousand of Spartacus's followers were crucified along the Appian Way. Proletarian and

---

body almost as many peoples, though not as many races, as the United Nations. She evolved such a flexible system that a native of Spain or Gaul could reach the position of Emperor at Rome by peaceful means. In the best age of her Empire she seemed to have made the *Pax Romana* a working instrument of prosperity, with racial prejudices sinking into oblivion. It was not a world-wide Empire. Other civilizations existed, for example in China and South America, the one known to enterprising Roman traders, the other quite unknown. Nevertheless, it was more than just a neat pun when Roman writers boasted that their *urbs* (city) was being turned into *orbis* (a world), and *vice versa*."

agrarian unrest was unimportant, save in so far as persistent exploitation and degradation of the "lower" classes in any society make for sullen anger or apathy—qualities scarcely conducive to "loyalty" or to useful participation in community life. Just as many aristocrats, businessmen, and politicians came to live off the spoil and tribute of the East, rather than by their own enterprise, so many less favored in the capital and other centers became parasitic and lived by publicly supported "Bread and Circuses." The quarrel of "little business" with "big business," if modern terms may be allowed, was often real, but never politically decisive. Rome had few problems of international relations, since in a World-State there are none, and only occasional problems of defense, when the power of the outer barbarians was underestimated. All these challenges to political ingenuity could be met if (and only if) a single overwhelming puzzle could be solved: how to organize decision-making and administration on an imperial scale in a world governed by a city-State republic.

Rome's tangled constitutional history is beyond our present purview. Only the transition to the final shape of power need here be noted. Julius Cæsar, named dictator for life, was stabbed to death on the Ides of March, 44 B.C., because many Senators rightly believed that he was enough enamored of Oriental despotism and the example of Alexander to contemplate kingship. But the Republic could hardly be preserved, save as an empty form, when the Senate charged with its protection had become a body filled with self-seeking opportunists and cowardly corruptionists. Cicero, the most eloquent defender of Republican virtue, championed the old constitution in the face of a new civil war and thus incurred the wrath of Marcus Antonius, Æmilius Lepidus, and Julius's nephew, Octavian. All three joined forces in 43 B.C. as the "Second Triumvirate," legalized by the Senate as an extraordinary commission for the "reorganization of the commonwealth." Their first act, in the tradition of Sulla, was to order a proscription; i.e., slaughter, of their enemies, among whom (over Octavian's objection) Cicero was the foremost to be liquidated. His severed hands and head were indecently displayed in the Forum. Such acts, and many that ensued, seem to us an odd way to prepare for the establishment of world government. But the will of the gods is inscrutable—and our contemporary proponents of One World, wedded like Cicero to constitutionalism, have not as yet found any better way that works.

The triumvirs divided the Roman world among themselves. But Octavian got the Senate to eject Lepidus from North Africa and order his banishment in 36 B.C., and then, in 32, to depose Marcus Antonius from his command in the East. Here Cæsar's friend had divorced Octavian's sister, Octavia, and lingered long and luxuriously in amorous dalliance (and in Oriental dreams of empire) with Cleopatra, Queen of Egypt. Antony's fleet was destroyed at Actium (September, 31 B.C.) by the ships-of-war of Octavian. Antony's legions were besieged a year later in Alexandria. He took his life, falsely thinking Cleopatra dead. His paramour, having failed to seduce Octavian, followed suit. The victor returned to his triumph in Rome—and then relinquished his extraordinary powers and sought to restore the constitution.

But public law, however ancient and revered, wields no spell over men who believe their needs require fresh departures. Its magic can do no more than enclose new gifts in old wrappings. Octavian, so he wrote, "handed over the Republic to the control of the Senate and people of Rome." But people and Senate, longing for order, could conceive of no control of men's passions save through the prestige and leadership of Octavian. Cicero in his *De Republica* had written of the ideal of a constitutional President of a free Republic. But the ideal presupposes that men still are responsible enough to merit freedom, and that constitutions reflect the facts of power. As practical people, the wise men of Rome accepted the facts, however ugly, and, in deference to their antimonarchism and their nostalgia for a past gone beyond recall, clothed the realities in the seemly garments of tradition. It is easy to sneer at the pretense across the vista of twenty centuries. But men cannot live without making believe that things are nearer their heart's desire than they can ever possibly be. This has been the way, and the only way leading to success, of all of our own great empire-builders: British, American, and Russian alike.

The Roman solution was ingenious. Octavian induced the Senate to elect him to the consulship (31 B.C.), and held it for eight years. In 27 B.C. he offered to resign all his offices. The Senate refused and, in gratitude for the "compromise" now achieved, conferred upon him a new title. After considering "Romulus," the Senators (or he) hit upon "Augustus," an adjective thus far kept for the gods. His official name, henceforth, was Imperator Cæsar Augustus. Only the second name was a family name, though it was destined to become a title of sovereignty in many lands and times for centuries thereafter. The third name was honorary. He preferred "Octavianus." The first meant, merely, commander of the armies or holder of a military imperium—which word, in turn, originally meant no more than the authority of any holder of a Roman public office, carefully defined by law. Outside of Rome, throughout the widespread provinces, he assumed the familiar powers of "Proconsul," but concentrated in a single hand, as Pompey had once done before him, the diverse authorities of men of old who had advanced from ministerial posts in Rome to become generals and governors on the frontiers. This authority, declared by the Senate in 23 B.C. to be applicable to Italy and Rome as well as the provinces, and to be a *maius imperium* or "superior power," meant that its holder could command and, if need be, could supersede governors possessed of ordinary proconsular powers.

Having conciliated the Senate, which he controlled effectively through patronage and through selectively reducing its members from more than a thousand to six hundred, Octavian "Augustus" proceded to appease the plebs. As a patrician, he could not become a "Tribune," but he took unto himself the *tribunicia potestas* or "tribune's power" and used it to champion the underlings. Since his actual authority was informal, rather than legalized, he came also to be called "princeps"—which then did not in the least signify what we now associate with the word "Prince," but meant merely "leading man" or "first citizen," applicable to many honored public figures.

In A.D. 14, when Augustus, at the age of seventy-six, reconciled himself to death in the presence of his good wife Livia—leaving the succession, after many disappointed hopes, to his stepson Tiberius—he is said to have asked: "Have I played my part well in the comedy of life?" Enough has been said to suggest the answer. A genius in semantics, he was therefore a genius in politics, since men live by words rather than by the realities words so often conceal. He chose his words well to give men what they wanted under the delusion that they were getting what they supposed they wanted. The restorer of the Republic had in fact made Rome an absolute monarchy. Apart from Tacitus and Suetonius, few suspected what had happened. Virgil celebrated the apparent triumph of the old Rome in one of the great epic poems of the ages. But the "principate" was now established, with the Senate its obedient servant and the people grateful for order, prosperity, and entertainment. Such a beneficent ruler, men readily perceived, had divine attributes, like the Pharaohs and Alexander. Augustus was *Divi Filius*—meaning not son of god, but "son of the deified Julius." In the East he was adored as a divinity, and throughout the realm Emperor-worship was at first encouraged and later required.

The secret, then, of the world government of Rome was simplicity itself: concentration of Authority to make decisions in a single hand, supported by a loyal Elite, an effective army, and a talent for Adaptation through moderation and compromise—with the totality glorified by a Myth that led people to assume that they were still free citizens of a Republic, blessed with the leadership of a godlike statesman. We may judge the devices of politics, as intellectuals are wont to do, by their consistency, sincerity, or conformity to some preconceived ideal. Or we may judge them, as common men always do in judging world government or local government or any government, by the pragmatic test of results. The devices of Imperial Rome, in modern parlance, "worked" and "delivered the goods." The goals were materialistic, perhaps ignoble (though it ill becomes us to say so), unconcerned with spiritual salvation, holy wars, or ethical crusades. What men wanted was peace, prosperity, and a happy life.

These objectives were largely attained in what Pliny the Elder called "the immeasurable majesty of the *Pax Romana*." Did this way of life involve cruelties and injustices and frustrations? So has every way of life ever known among men. Did the Great Society finally disintegrate and vanish? So have all the artifacts of mankind from the beginning of time and, most probably, to the end. The Roman Empire was for centuries the most successful experiment of Western humankind in achieving peace and plenty and happy living through world government. Today's generation will do amazingly well if it achieves half as much for half as long.[3]

The lives of the Emperors and the fortunes of the people in later times we must leave to the historians. The Romans never evolved representative institutions on an imperial scale, nor did they ever approach federalism save in the single matter of citizenship. Roman citizenship was extended to individuals (e.g., non-Roman veterans of the armies) and to whole communities in such wise as to make it a cherished privilege and to convert subjugated peoples and infiltrating barbarians to loyalty to the World-State. This loyalty was a blend of local love for a man's city or immediate countryside,

[3] To my mind, one of the most astute and provocative evaluations of the civilization of imperial Rome (though classical scholars may not agree) is to be found in H. G. Wells: *The Outline of History* (Garden City Publishing Co.; 1940, one-volume edition), pp. 481–501, written as only Wells could write, with all his essentially post-Victorian hopes, regrets, and dreams. In the brief account attempted in the pages of the present section, I have largely relied, apart from standard historical and biographical reference-works, on the writings of Gibbon, Hammond, and Waddy previously cited and upon Leon P. Homo: *Roman Political Institutions* (Alfred A. Knopf; 1929); James Bryce: *The Holy Roman Empire* (Macmillan; 1914); and David Jayne Hill: *A History of Diplomacy in the International Development of Europe* (Longmans; 1924, 3 vols.).

whether Italian or provincial, with pride in the great imperium, marred by no such intermediate allegiance to provinces or "nations" as has afflicted our own world. Provincials were admitted to the Roman Senate and even to the office of Emperor. All rejoiced in the protection of the Roman legions, the convenience of Roman roads and shipping lines, and the justice of Roman Law, codified in its classic form under Justinian, Emperor of the East, in the sixth century A.D.

This autocracy strikes us as a strange structure. The god-kings were neither hereditary nor elective. Emperors commonly chose and trained their successors, often of their families, sometimes adopted. The legitimacy of the imperial title in each case depended, in theory, on the sanction of the Senate and in fact, in later days, on the approval of the household troops or Prætorian Guard, established by Augustus. When men fell to fighting over the succession, as Gibbon puts it, "the Romans combatted only for the choice of masters. Under the standard of a popular candidate for empire, a few enlisted from affection, some from fear, many from interest, none from principle."[4] Degenerate Emperors, reveling in Oriental fanfare and debauchery, wasted men and means. Caligula, Augustus's great-grandson (A.D. 37–41), was a monster; Nero (54–68), a great-great-grandson, a murderer of his mother and wife and of early Christians, among other victims; Elagabalus (218–22) a sun-worshipper and half-mad voluptuary.

But these and others of their ilk were murdered. The convulsions their lives and deaths occasioned scarcely affected the peace and prosperity of the Empire, whose various peoples continued to enjoy safety and justice under prefects, judges, and commanders who were, on the whole, honest, just, and able. More numerous among the Emperors than accidents and perverts were statesmen acclaimed as "Great"– e.g., Tiberius (14–37), despite his unpopularity; Claudius (41–54), who conquered Britain and accepted his role as a god; Ves-

[4] Gibbon: ibid., Vol. I, p. 104.

pasian (69–79) and his sons Titus (79–81) and Domitian (81–96); Trajan (98–117), who expanded the frontiers to their greatest territorial extent; Hadrian (117–38) the builder; the humane philosopher Marcus Aurelius (161–80); Septimius Severus (193–211); Aurelian (270–75), who restored unity after a generation of barbarian invasions, vain wars in the Orient, and internal chaos; Diocletian (284–305), who converted the Emperorship into an Asiatic despotism, with diadems and robes, and divided its powers among colleagues; Constantine the Great (312–37) who made Christianity the state religion and built an Eastern Capital at Constantinople; and perhaps Theodosius (382–95).

Here we are already in the shadows wherein the Roman world government is in process of collapsing from inner decay and displaying its impotence to the astonished and reluctant barbarians. The long death-agony was marked by the defeat and killing of the Emperor Valens at Adrianople at the hands of the Visigoths (378), the sacking of Rome by the hordes of Alaric (410); the repetition of the tragedy at the hands of the Vandals (455); and at last the abdication of the last Western Emperor, Romulus Augustus, in favor of Odoacer, barbarian warlord, in 476.

Long before this dark time and for earlier generations, life after life, the men and women of ancient Rome enjoyed security and plenty. They celebrated "the increasing splendor of the cities, the beautiful face of the country, cultivated and adorned like an immense garden; and the long festival of peace, which was enjoyed by so many nations, forgetful of their ancient animosities, and delivered from apprehension of future danger." [5] For more than two centuries in the happy times, most of Western mankind was free of fear and want and knew no violence of men against men, apart from the killing of criminals and scapegoats, the occasional assassination of Emperors, and the skirmishing with barbarians on the

[5] Ibid., Vol. I, p. 50, quoting an unnamed ancient writer, but referring in a footnote to Pliny, Aristides, and Tertullian for similar comments.

frontiers. Here the Christian precept, finally adopted by Rome and never since so fully realized, came closest to fulfillment: "Peace on earth, good will to men!"

So dear is this memory that it captured and held men's minds far beyond any limits of space and time known to the ancient Cæsars. The vision lived on for a thousand years in the Eastern Empire and was then inherited by the Grand Dukes of Muscovy. In the West its attempted resurrection, A.D. 800, was followed by the dissolution of Charlemagne's barbarian realm and by dreary centuries of feudal chaos. Otto the Saxon was crowned "Roman Emperor" by the Pope in A.D. 962—and thereafter the "Holy Roman Empire of the German Nation" preserved in Western Christendom the recollection of the only world government ever known to European mankind.

Since this curious polity was all Myth, and had no Authority, no Elite, and no mode of Adaptation save happenstance, we need only sketch its outlines. While Popes and Emperors struggled against one another for power, the "Empire" displayed some semblance of a functioning structure under the House of Hohenstaufen, whose best-remembered rulers were Frederick Barbarossa (c.1123–90) and his grandson, Frederick II (1194–1250). Both monarchs, having failed to give life to a dream vaguely symbolizing something men can never forget, were depicted in legend (with the tale first told of Frederick II and later attached to his grandfather) as sitting after death in a cave before a stone table around which their beards had grown, waiting for the magic moment when they might return to the world and restore the golden age of peace. The office of "Emperor" later became elective. A College of electors, consisting of the Princes of the German States, chose its occupants. After 1273, however, the honor went invariably to the reigning monarch of the House of Hapsburg—whose actual influence in world affairs had little to do with the shadowy title but much to do with concrete possessions in Austria, Spain, and the Low Countries.

The later history of this spectral imperium is tedious and meaningless, for Western mankind had come to worship not One God or One King in One World but a great diversity of tribal deities equated with national patriotism. The old aspiration found its most poignant expression in what James Bryce called its "epitaph"—the political essay, *De Monarchia*, of Dante Alighieri, written in 1309 by the immortal author of the *Divine Comedy*, when the popes were French captives at Avignon and no Emperor had come to anarchic Italy for five decades. Dante evidently hoped, though subsequent events were to prove him wrong, that Henry VII might somehow restore peace if he and his foes could be persuaded by argument to see truth. Dante's "truth" was a scholastic echo of the wisdom of Alexander and of the Cæsars:

> Temporal Monarchy, or, as men call it, the Empire, is the government of one prince above all men in time, or in those things and over those things which are measured by time. . . . Now it is plain that the whole human race is ordered to gain some end, as has been before shown. There must, therefore, be one to guide and govern, and the proper title for this office is Monarch or Emperor. And so it is plain that Monarchy or the Empire is necessary for the welfare of the world. . . . This the Philosopher [Aristotle] saw when he said: "The world is not intended to be disposed in evil order; in a multitude of rulers there is evil, therefore let there be one prince." . . . Oh, race of mankind! What storms must toss thee, what losses must thou endure, what shipwrecks must buffet thee, as long as thou, a beast of many heads, strivest after contrary things! Thou art sick in both thy faculties of understanding; thou are sick in thy affections. Unanswerable reasons fail to heal thy higher understanding; the very sight of experience convinces not thy lower understanding; not even the sweetness of divine persuasion charms thy affections, when it breathes unto thee through the music of the Holy Spirit: "Behold how good and how pleasant it is for brethren to dwell together in unity!"

Such words had no power to influence men's acts, now more and more determined by the precepts to which Machiavelli was to give expression two centuries later. Yet so precious was the dream that the ghostly "Empire" persisted, through many vicissitudes, for half a millennium after Dante. Its demise was sudden and undramatic. The last "Roman Emperor" was Francis II who, as Emperor of Austria, was Francis I (1792–1835). He perceived that the Napoleonic conquest of Central Europe and the establishment by the French Emperor of the "Confederation of the Rhine" meant that the sacred crown must either disappear altogether or pass from the House of Hapsburg to the House of Bonaparte. In 1805 he abdicated the imperial title. Neither Napoleon nor anyone else thought it worth perpetuating. The "Holy Roman Empire," so long in dying, was now dead. A rose-colored memory of a vanished past and an iridescent hope of a distant future, both symbolized by this mystical polity, were henceforth to take shape (as indeed had long since been the case) in the drifting clouds of other skies. The Cæsars of old are long since dust. But Cæsarism as a possible way to world unity and peace is with us always, since it is the only way thus far contrived that has ever, in fact, come near to achieving political order for mankind.

3. THE REALMS OF THE HORSEMEN

> In Xanadu did Kubla Khan a stately pleasure-dome decree: where Alph, the sacred river ran through caverns measureless to man down to a sunless sea. So twice five miles of fertile ground with walls and towers were girdled round; and here were gardens bright with sinuous rills, where blossomed many an incense-bearing tree; and here were forests ancient as the hills, enfolding sunny spots of greenery. . . . Five miles meandering with a mazy motion through wood and dale the sacred river ran, then reached the caverns measureless to man, and sank in tumult to a lifeless ocean; and 'mid this tumult Kubla heard from far ancestral voices prophesying war! . . .
>
> —SAMUEL TAYLOR COLERIDGE: *Kubla Khan.*

HARUN AL RASHID or "Aaron the Just" (A.D. 763–809) was Caliph of Bagdad when Charlemagne ruled the West from his capital at Aachen. The two monarchs exchanged gifts and greetings. The actual sovereign of the East and inheritor of another World-State of impressive size and splendor was not the Empress Irene of Byzantium (whom Charles once considered marrying) or her successor, Nicephorus, but the fabulous Prince of the *Arabian Nights*, who invaded the lands of the Byzantines eight times, defeated them in battle, and compelled them to pay tribute. His famous threat to the defiant Emperor was made good: "In the name of the most merciful God, Harun al Rashid, commander of the faithful, to Nicephorus, the Roman dog. I have read thy letter, O thou son of an unbelieving mother. Thou shalt not hear, thou shalt behold, my reply." The miserable Nicephorus was later (811) defeated and slain by the pagan Bulgarians, whose Emperor Krum made a drinking cup of the Eastern Cæsar's skull.

The Caliph or Successor of the Prophet, fifth ruler of the Abbasid line, vanquished Romans and Khazars and cultivated all the arts and sciences, particularly algebra, astronomy, medicine, and Greek philosophy, all then almost unknown in the barbarous Christian West. Nine times Harun went on a pilgrimage to Mecca. Many times he visited his many provinces, extending from Egypt to Central Asia. He heeded the grievances of the poor and humble. He ordered the execution of the family of the Barmecides, who brought him to power, when he became suspicious of their purposes. His capital was the center of a magnificent system of administration, and a shining center of luxury and learning. A century later the historian Abul Feda, describing the reception of a Byzantine ambassador in Bagdad, wrote of an officialdom gorgeously apparelled and glittering with gold and gems; of rubies and pearls splashed about like rice at royal weddings; of seven thousand eunuchs at the court, four thousand white and three thousand black; of superb ornamentation on barges in the Tigris; and, in the palace, of 22,000 carpets, 38,000 tapestries, clever mechanisms of silver and gold, and a hundred trained lions, each with a keeper.[6]

This is a glimpse at the way of life of the holders of power in a succession of World-States in the Near and Far Orient during the centuries following the original "fall of Rome." To review their rise and decline in detail would be fascinating, but would inordinately multiply these pages. A sketch of the major instances may serve to suggest novel ways whereby world government and world peace through conquest have been attained. All the empires we are here concerned with were the creations of peoples who were originally barbarian nomads, converted to "civilized" ways by contacts with old and sophisticated cultures and destined to unify and reanimate their fragments in the times of their decay. The armed hosts who carved out these empires were primarily forces of warriors on horseback. Cavalry and war-chariots seem first to have been used by the ancient Assyrians, whose far-flung military state (1100–612 B.C.) rapidly collapsed and vanished by virtue of their too-obsessive preoccupation with warmaking. More than a thousand years later the herdsmen and hunters of the Asiatic deserts and the vast steppes of Eurasia became the first peoples to make armed horsemen the chief weapons of conquest and the tools of power over immense territories, encompassing at times most of civilized humankind.

The first of these empires was the creation of Semitic peoples who, within a single generation, were transformed from primitive tribesmen into rulers of much of the world by the miraculous impact upon men of a new religion. Born in Mecca about 570, Mohammed, founder of Islam, was a poor

[6] Quoted in Gibbon: ibid., Vol. III, p. 231; cf. pp. 234–41. In the remainder of this section I have not deemed it needful to cite authorities, since the historical literature of Islam, the Mongols, and the Ottomans is vast, varied, and readily accessible to most scholars. The relevant portions and the references in the unabridged version of Toynbee's *A Study of History* are useful. Popularized and romanticized (but on the whole accurate) accounts of some of these matters are to be found in the books of Harold Lamb—*Genghis Khan, Tamerlane, The Crusades, The March of Muscovy*, and so on—issued by various publishers during the past twenty-five years.

and illiterate herdsman, tending sheep and camels, until he became servant and then husband of Kadija, widow of a wealthy tradesman. At the age of forty he declared that he had received from an angel a revelation of God. He was familiar with the God of the Jews, the God of the Christians, and the many gods of the Arab tribes. Abraham, Moses, and Jesus, said he, had all been divine teachers, but now "God is Allah, and Mohammed is his Prophet!" After death men's souls will suffer in hell if they reject Allah and do evil, and rejoice in heaven if they do good and see the light. Every Moslem is the brother of every other. None is superior to another. Even slaves are Allah's servants, to be treated with fraternal kindness. Idolatry is sin. Sacrifices to divinity are evil. Priests are agents of the devil. (Islam has no professional priesthood.) Allah is a God of righteousness, and all righteous believers shall be saved. Those who lose their lives in extending the true faith shall be blessed with life eternal in a paradise where all are equal and each enjoys forever the most exquisite of earthly delights.

These and other teachings Mohammed spun out at first to a smallish company, comprising his good friend Abu Bekr, Ali his adopted son, and his dear Kadija—and, following her death, Ayesha and, later, Safiyya the Jewess, Mary the Egyptian, and other wives and concubines, along with the children of his harem and a slowly growing number of disciples. At fifty he had made no great impression in Mecca, where most were hostile to his monotheism and iconoclasm. He was now invited by converts to come northward to Medina and rule the city in the name of God. After long and cautious preparation, he escaped from enemies who plotted his murder, outdistanced his pursuers in a long flight (the Hegira) over the desert, and reached Medina in September 622.

Inconclusive wars ensued with Mecca. When Hebrews and Christians denied that Allah was their God or that Mohammed was a Prophet, he became incensed, preached Allah as a God of Islam rather than of all men, and on occasion put Israelites to the sword. By 629 he was master of Mecca, and by 632, when he died, King of all Arabia. He left no sons. At the death of little Ibrahim, Mary's boy, he had wept bitterly and smoothed the sand over the grave, saying: "This eases the afflicted heart. Though it neither profits nor injures the dead, yet it is a comfort to the living. . . ."

Unlike Ikhnaton, who was born of royalty, and Jesus of Nazareth, who never claimed or attained earthly power, though mocked on the cross as "King of the Jews," Mohammed made his faith the basis of a worldly empire. In 628 he had summoned the Cæsar Heraclius, King Kavadh of Persia, and the Chinese Emperor Tai-tsung to accept Allah. The first was contemptuous, the second insolent, and the third respectful but unconvinced. First Abu Bekr and then, upon his death, (634), Omar, Mohammed's brother-in-law, assumed the title of Caliph. They undertook the fantastic task of conquering the world in the name of Allah. To the infidels two choices were offered at swordpoint as alternatives to death: pay tribute, or accept Islam. In 636 the Arab horsemen cut to pieces the legions of Heraclius along the Yarmuk, near the Jordan, and soon took Damascus and Antioch. A year later they beat and slew King Rustam of Persia at Kacessia on the Euphrates.

The "Saracens," as they came to be known to the Greeks, brought a message of unity, equality, and salvation which won them many converts, not only among the Semitic tribesmen but among masses of the urban poor, including goodly numbers who had been Christians, Jews, or Zoroastrians. They also brought ever-growing clouds of armed horsemen who swept all foes before them. By 656, when Caliph Othman died by murder, the hosts of the Crescent ruled all Persia, Armenia, Syria, and Egypt, and were pushing northward and westward. The fourth Caliph, Ali Ben Abu Talib, "Lion of God" and husband of Fatima, the prophet's daughter, was slain in turn in 661 in a confused, intrafamily civil war in Medina, though the Koran forbids Moslems to kill Moslems. The Shiite Moslems (e.g., the Persians) have ever since contended that Ali's hereditary right to the Caliphate is an article of faith and have cherished as martyrs his son, Hasan, and his brother, Husein, both of whom also died by violence. The orthodox Sunnites (e.g., the Turks) deny all of this and regard Ali as a usurper. This schism in Islam bears little resemblance to the theological hair-splittings and once ferocious persecutions between Catholics and Protestants. But it reveals an early and persistent weakness in the Moslem system of power: the combination of unlimited autocracy with the absence of any fixed rules of succession.

The Arabic Empire, despite symptoms of confusion and corruption at its center, continued to expand until contained by superior force at its peripheries. Contrary to contemporary Christian opinion, the faith that at the outset united its peoples and drove them forward in an effort to win the world was not imposed by force, but made its way by its own appeal among communities lying far beyond any lands ever controlled by the commanders and administrators of the Caliph—e.g., in the terminology of today's political units, Pakistan (the most populous of Moslem communities), Afghanistan, Soviet Central Asia, Sinkiang, parts of East Africa, much of Southeast Asia, and Indonesia. The coming to the Caliphate of Muawiya (661–80) marked the beginning of the Omayyad dynasty, under whose rulers Arab armies swept over North Africa, invaded Spain in 711, crossed the Pyrenees, and met defeat at Tours (732) at the hands of the Frankish war-host of Charles Martel. They then retired to Spain, most of which remained under Moorish rule for the next seven centuries. In the east, the Omayyads also failed to destroy the Byzantine Empire, being beaten by the Greeks under Emperor Leo the Isaurian in their naval assault on Constantinople in 717. Despite these checks, here was a universal State of majestic scope.

In the middle years of the eighth century this realm stretched from the Pyrenees to Transoxiana and the Indus, and from the Caucasus and Taurus mountains to the Indian Ocean and the wastes of the Sahara. Peace, order, and the loving care of art and science were its earmarks under successive Caliphs: Yazid, Marwan, Abdalmalik, Walid, Omar, and Hisham. But the white banner of the Omayyads at last went down in battle and murder before the black standard (in mourning for Hasan and Husein) of the Abbas family, which held with the Shiites. In 749, under Abul Abbas, first of the Abbasid Caliphs, the Omayyads were defeated in civil war, hunted down and slain, and, so far as was possible, effaced from the memories of men—save that a survivor, grandson of Hisham, escaped to found the Omayyad dynasty in Cordova in a henceforth independent Moslem Spain.

After much disorder and killing, Abul's successor, Mansur, established his ascendancy and moved his capital from Damascus to the new city of Bagdad on the Tigris, which became a scintillating metropolis. The Abbasids soon broke with the more fanatical Shiites and, like their predecessors, championed Islamic orthodoxy. But they represented the triumph of non-Arab elements in the empire. Their dynasty endured for five hundred years. Its last reigning member surrendered Bagdad to Hulagu the Mongol, brother of Kubla Khan, in 1258—and was butchered, with his sons and relatives, by these demonic invaders from farther east. The title of Caliph was later tossed about among local Moslem potentates and assumed by many, including finally the Ottoman Sultans—following whose political demise the office was formally abolished in A.D. 1924. The Caliphate as a symbol of central authority in Islam thus came to a prosaic end, after a tumultuous and dazzling history of almost thirteen centuries.

If we seek to distill, from the chronicles and later histories, the essence of the wine of power in the Arabic Universal State, we are impressed, as we must be in contemplating all of Man's political artifacts during the creative periods of his literate cultures, with an apparent discrepancy of appalling and incomprehensible proportions between what men believe and do as citizens and what they do and believe as thinkers, writers, scientists, artists, farmers, artisans, and merchants. So great is the paradox as to render most difficult, at first sight, the establishment of any demonstrable correlation between the tasks of "government" and the works of "society."

The Saracen Empire wass originally the creation of nomadic tribes, united by a magnificent Myth that brought peace to men's souls by inspiring them with ardor for war. Authority was concentrated in an unlimited despotism, tempered by intrigue and assassination—the usual means in such systems for achieving change in the distribution of power and perquisites. The Elite was a weird mixture of warriors, nobles, merchants—and, incredibly, slaves. The Abbasids bought captives from central Asia, mainly Turks, and trained the best of them to be commanders, governors, and collectors of tribute and taxes. Effective power at Bagdad passed from the Caliphs to the Turkish guards and mayors of the palace. Our very word "slave" owes its origin to the habit of the Caliphs of Cordova of maintaining a bodyguard largely composed of captives sold to them by the Franks, who in turn met the demands of this market in living manflesh by making raids across the eastern marches and dragging off barbarians whose language and culture were Slavic. In Arabic Egypt the Mamelukes were, to begin with, the slave-soldiers of Saladin's dynasty. By the mid-thirteenth century these "slaves" were ruling the land, buying new slaves abroad, and defeating the Mongols in Syria.

It is inconceivable to most contemporary Westerners, with their worship of "freedom," that any such scheme of governance could spell anything other than oppression, violence, and unrelieved darkness. What emerged, in fact, was a series of great universities—Cordova, Cairo, Kufa, Bagdad, Basra, and elsewhere; the invention of modern mathematics, particularly algebra, spherical trigonometry, optics, and the new astronomy; the advent of modern chemistry and medicine, scientific agriculture, and the manufacture of paper; and an enchanting new beauty in architecture, ornament, and storytelling. A millennium ago, even in the opinion of the more enlightened Christians, the greatest living scientist was Avicenna (Ibnsina), "Prince of Physicians" (980–1037), who was born in Bokhara, while the greatest philosopher was Averroes of Cordova (1126–98), who recast Aristotle in a fashion conducive to scientific research.

The paradox here posed is not wholly insoluble. Men—even in hitherto "decadent" cultures—produce works of beauty, truth, and goodness when they enjoy the dignity and the opportunity for self-expression afforded by ordered security and some sense of sharing in a great collective endeavor. Whether their governors are despots or democrats is less important than whether their rulers give them peace, leave them in peace, and encourage them to believe that they are creative participants in a *Pax Œcumenica.* In these respects autocrats have perhaps made a better record, on the whole, than demagogues. Rulers may murder one another and wage incessant warfare on far frontiers. What matters is peace of mind at home and order among men within the far-flung imperium. This was the gift of the Pharaohs of Egypt, the Cæsars of Rome, the Caliphs of Bagdad, and the later Khans of Tartary and Sultans of Constantinople. This is the offering of all universal empires, although its cultural fruits occasionally flourish in contexts lacking any World-State and resembling, in our foggy retrospections, a kind of anarchy—as among, for example, the Greek cities of the fifth century B.C., the Italian cities of the Renaissance, and the Western nation-States between the fifteenth and twentieth centuries A.D. Give people peace, whatever the means or the matrix, and they will cultivate virtue and science, harmony and rhythm, form and color, self-respect and the joy of life. Give them incessant or endlessly recurring war and they will revert to brutes.

The later World-States of the Far and Near East, also forged by nomad swords and maintained by despotism and violence, afforded peace to many men for many centuries by methods that to us, with our stereotypes of "democracy" and the "rule of law," are beyond understanding. In the eleventh century the Seljuk clan of Turks, bursting out of the steppes of Central Asia, overran and reunified the world of Islam. Already Moslems of the Sunnite persuasion, they became rulers of the vast Central Asian realm of Khorezm (or Khorasam, Charismia, Qarizm—no standardized English spelling is available for this remote and long-lost land), east and south of the Caspian and Aral seas and embracing most of the territories we call Turkestan, Afghanistan, and Iran. Under Alp Arslan the Turkish cavalry beat down the Byzantines at Manzikert (1071) and occupied most of Asia Minor. The Seljuks became "protectors"; i.e., masters, of the Abbasid Caliphs of Bagdad. It was against this Seljuk Islam that the Crusaders waged war. This successor-State of the early Caliphate was in part displaced, albeit later to be revived in a new form, by another universal empire created by other horsemen out of Asia, who became the most formidable and feared conquerors of all time.

. . .

World government as a functioning reality of global power, rather than as a circumscribed empire or an aspiration of dreamers, was once upon a time virtually achieved, with the ensuing *Pax Orbis* enduring for at least as many centuries as ancient Rome enjoyed. This most extraordinary of all military and political creations was the work of primitive cattlemen and horse-riders, living on meat and mare's milk and moving their tents on oxcarts over the trackless prairies with the seasons. These Mongols or Tartars first learned war by rebelling against the Chin rulers of Cathay (northern China) in the twelfth century. A certain Yesukai the Valiant, Khan of the Yakka, son of the Blue Wolf, and member of the Clan of the Gray-eyed Men, became parent of a baby boy in the year 1162. The child was called Temugin, after the name of a tribal leader whom the father, chieftain of forty thousand tents, had defeated and enslaved. His later names and titles were Jenghis Kha Khan, "Heavenly Ruler," "Master of Thrones and Crowns," and "Emperor of All Men."

Since these designations were less rhetorical than realistic, it is plain that we are here in the presence of the most remarkable of empires in the whole journey of humankind from petty tribes and tiny towns toward a World-State. The tale of its establishment and governance is less a record of political or religious genius than of the sudden emergence and long perpetuation of an invincible military machine. Mounted archers and lancers were organized into troops of 10, squadrons of 100, regiments of 1,000, and tumans or divisions of 10,000, grouped by threes into self-sufficient armies commanded by able strategists. Against the Mongol light and heavy cavalry no force in Christendom and few forces in Islam could hold. Jenghis first took over the Uighurs of the Tarim Basin in Sinkiang, north of Tibet, and then defeated the Chin Empire and occupied Pekin (1215). When he sent emissaries to Samarcand, capital of Khorezm, the authorities there were so imprudent as to put the Mongol envoys to death.

In the year 1219 a vast host of Tartar horsemen, commanded by Subotai and Chepe, descended from the northlands and smashed the Khoresmian Empire to bits. Adventurous squadrons of this ever-victorious cavalry went on to the Persian Gulf, the Caspian, and the wild passes of the Caucasus, beyond which they roamed the steppes of the Don. Mitislav the Daring, Prince of Kiev—center of the earliest Russian State—also slew the Mongol envoys and went out at the head of eighty thousand warriors to meet the foe. "You have killed our envoys," warned the Mongol leaders. "Well, as you wish for war you shall have it. We have done you no harm. God is impartial. He will decide our quarrel." In June of 1223, on the River Kalka, north of the Sea of Azov, the Prince's army was ground to pieces. He and his vassals were taken and crushed to death beneath heavy timbers. The Mongols raided the Crimea. From Jenghis's capital, Karakorum, "City of the Black Sands" between Lake Baikal and the Gobi Desert, orders went out to return. The horsemen turned homeward, following now the broad steppe stretching from the Dnieper to Mongolia, skirting the Black Sea, the Caspian, the Aral Sea, and Lake Balkash. Europe was panic-stricken by this apparition. Fear was the greater for lack of all knowledge of the sources and nature of the Mongol miracle. "Only God knows," wrote an old Russian chronicler, "whence they came and whither they went."

When Jenghis joined the ghosts of his fathers in 1227, he ruled all lands and peoples, north to south, from Siberia to the Persian Gulf, the Indus, the towering mountains of northern Tibet, and the valley of the Yellow River and, east to west, from Sakhalin and Korea to the Tigris, the Don, and the middle Volga. This was already the most extensive world-State of all time, though its expansion was just begun. No "message" or myth accompanied the conquering horsemen. Their leaders were pagan polytheists and shamanists with no idea of "saving" or uniting the world, and quite innocent of any Messianic mission. Complete religious toleration and freedom of trade and travel prevailed throughout this empire. Nothing was demanded of the conquered save payment of tribute, abstention from local warfare, and acknowledgment of the authority of the Great Khan. The crudities of nomad rule were softened by the influence of Yeliu Chutsai, a Chinese sage and statesman employed by Jenghis and his successors, and much concerned with art and learning.

What followed the passing of Jenghis was even more improbable than what had gone before. An assembly of chiefs elected his third son, Ogdai, to succeed him as Khan (1227–42). In the sequel, under Ogdai and those who came after, all of China, including Tibet and the southland of the Sung Emperors, was subjugated, along with Burma and Syria and what was left of Persia. Ogdai's nephew, Batu the Splendid, resumed war against the West, leading his riders to the Volga; taking Vladimir, north of Moscow; compelling Alexander Nevski, Prince of Novgorod, to pay tribute; and destroying Kiev in December of 1240. The following year found Batu and Subotai doing battle in East Europe with a mixed Christian host led by Kings Boleslas of Poland, Wenceslas of Bohemia, Mieceslas of Galicia, Henry of Silesia, Bela of Hungary, sundry German men-at-arms, and French Knights Templar. All were beaten and most were slain. The invaders had a system of espionage, intelligence, and communications undreamed of in Christian Europe, an army invincible by virtue of superior mobility, weapons, and strategy, and commanders who had no peers. At Liegnitz in Silesia (April 9, 1241) and at Mohi in Hungary, near the River Sajo and the dark hills of Tokay (c. April 27, 1241), the warriors who followed the Mongol battle-standard with its nine yak-tails annihilated the enemy forces arrayed against them and established their dominion over East Central Europe and everything southward to the Adriatic.

The problem of why the Mongols did not overrun all Europe in the mid-thirteenth century bears a fascinating resemblance to the problem of why their ultimate successors did not overrun all Europe in the mid-twentieth century. Unlike the Saracens before them and the Ottoman Turks after them, the Mongols were never defeated by European arms. The soldiers of the Khan were not "contained" or "deterred" by atomic bombs, nor by any transatlantic support of Western Christendom, nor by any fatuous effort to organize the "defense" of Europe against a Power so formidable that all defenses crumbled before its forces. The Mongols nevertheless paused and then turned back. The contention that their armies could operate effectively only on the prairies is unconvincing in view of their record in eastern Germany, the Magyar hill-country, and a hundred other fields of blood all over the deserts, highlands, and valleys of Eurasia. Perhaps their leaders saw no point in an indefinite extension of their power, with all its attendant and arduous tasks of administration and exploitation—so long as it was obvious that no military threat from the West could be mounted against them. Their conclusion was reinforced by anxiety regarding the structure of power in their own imperium. Ogdai Khan died in 1242. His unvanquished armies withdrew from Hungary, Rumania, Bohemia, Silesia, and Poland. But the Mongol yoke remained fastened on all of Russia for almost two and a half centuries (A.D. 1240–1480).

The limits of the empire here began to take shape, since

even the most limitless World-States have always, thus far, had frontiers beyond which it has not been profitable to go. Some years later, in 1260, one of Jenghis's grandsons and a brother of Kubla, the Hulagu who took Bagdad and established the Ilkhan Dynasty in Persia, found his road to Africa blocked. His troops were beaten at Ain Jalut in Syria (September 3, 1260) by the forces of Kotuz, Mameluke Sultan of Egypt. Mongol policy-makers abandoned the Levant, though obliging the Seljuk Turks in Anatolia to pay them tribute, and left India, for the present, to its own devices. Mangu had become Great Khan in 1251 and named his brother, Kubla, ruler of China. In 1260, Mangu having died, Kubla was elected Great Khan and transferred his capital to Pekin, where he ruled until his death in 1294. This extraordinary monarch of most of the earth met with failure in his expeditions against Japan, Cochin-China, and Java. Yet he commanded a realm extending from Poland to Korea and from the valleys of the Ob and the Yenisei to Arabia, the Punjab, and Indo-China.

In the west (Russia) Kubla Khan's Mongol agents were the men of the Kipchak Empire or "Golden Horde" with its capital at Sarai on the lower Volga. In the southwest his agents were the officials of Hulagu's Iranian-Turkish realm. Other tributaries ruled other areas of this imperium. Taken all in all, it encompassed something like one half of the land surface of the planet (more than this if the then unknown Americas are omitted from the reckoning) and embraced in a single domain—though population statistics for these times are vague—something like two thirds of the human race.

Since nothing before or after has even remotely approached this enterprise in world government, it would be instructive to describe its framework in terms of Myth, Authority, Adaptation, and Elite. Unfortunately the Mongols left few records. Indian, Chinese, and European accounts are either fragmentary or are expressions of horror—save among later Westerners who became familiar with Rusticiano's version of *The Travels of Marco Polo*. This gentleman-adventurer of Venice roamed Eurasia with his father, Nicolo, and his uncle, Maffeo, and tarried sixteen years at the court of Kubla Khan, serving him well on many missions. If we limit ourselves to what is known with some certainty, we may say this:

The Mongols had no "ideology" or "way of life" for export, and treated all others with indifference or amused respect or contempt. Kubla invited disciples of various faiths, including the Christian, and asked the Polos to bring him oil from the lamp in the Holy Sepulcher in Jerusalem. Tolerance in religion and lack of racial pride are obvious assets of all empire-builders. They may also be a source of weakness. The Eastern Mongols in the fullness of time were "absorbed" by China and embraced Confucianism or Buddhism, while their Western confreres adopted Islam—thereby contributing to ultimate political disintegration. The power of the Khans to command obedience was exclusively a function of the fact that armed resistance was futile. But slaughter for the joy of killing was seldom part of Mongol culture. Those who submitted had peace. In administration and adaptation the Mongols showed wisdom in respecting local customs, permitting regional potentates to collect their tribute (e.g., the Grand Dukes of Muscovy in the fourteenth century), and organizing efficient methods of postal communication, military conscription, tax collection, coinage, and census taking. The Mongol ruling class first consisted of the progeny of the herdsmen who had become warriors and then governors whose writ no man dared defy without risking death. Later many able men of sundry races and creeds were recruited into a new elite in a vast melting-pot of peoples, among whom the *Pax Mongolica* brought security and fruitful freedom of commerce from the Baltic to Burma.

The slow dissolution of this most titanic of all empires was a gradual and disorderly process. Great provinces or Khanates became autonomous and then independent of Pekin. In western Turkestan a descendant of Jenghis, Timur the Lame (Tamerlane), assumed the title of Great Khan in 1369 and sought to restore the unity of old. His frightful armies exacted tribute from Egypt, decimated and subjugated the Golden Horde, destroyed the age-old irrigation works of Mesopotamia, and smashed the Ottoman Turks, whose Sultan Bayezid I was made captive at Angora in 1402 and exhibited in a cage. But here was a destroyer, not a builder. The memory of his hideous atrocities in Persia and the Punjab remained fresh until they were many times multiplied by Western Christians in the twentieth century. After his death in 1405 nothing endured of his work save the ruin he had wrought. His body, say the chroniclers, was preserved in musk and rosewater, swathed in linen, and sent in an ebony coffin to Samarcand, where his now empty tomb still stands.

A century later one of his descendants, Baber (c. 1530) having fled Samarcand and established his power in Kabul, sought to reclaim the Punjab. In the course of this endeavor he conquered most of India and made himself "Emperor of Hindustan" (Kaisar-i-Hind) and founder of the Mogul (Mongol) Dynasty, which lasted until the eighteenth century and was succeeded by the British Raj. His grandson, Akbar (1556–1605), was the most brilliant, tolerant, and humane ruler of any empire of his time. In China the Mongols had given way to the Ming Dynasty in 1368. In Russia, long under the Mongol darkness, the Muscovite Grand Duke, Ivan the Great, succeeded in discontinuing tribute to the Golden Horde in 1480, though the Tartars and Turks of the Crimea were still able to sack and burn Moscow as late as 1571. In our own day what remains of the Mongol conquests? All else is dust, but these live still: scattered Tartar communities throughout Russia and the Orient; the Soviet satellite of Outer Mongolia; the "Gypsies" of Europe who seem originally to have fled from the Near East before the Mongol horsemen—and the mighty legend of the nomad Cæsars who were the "Emperors of All Men."

• • •

The third and most recent of the major World-States founded by riders out of Asia was the Ottoman Empire. Among the Moslems of Khorezm who fled before Jenghis Khan in the early thirteenth century was a little band of a few thousand souls who wandered somewhat aimlessly around the Near East, seeking a place to settle or a way of returning home. Storytellers relate that in 1227 when they were crossing the Euphrates on their way back to Turkestan their leader was drowned and some of them decided to remain under his son, Ertoghrul, who succeeded in securing lands near Angora in Anatolia from the Seljuk Sultan Ala-ue-din. When Ertoghrul died in 1288, aged ninety, he was succeeded as tribal chieftain by his son Osman (or Othman), from whose name the group became known as the Osmanli or Ottoman Turks. Osman remained loyal to the Seljuk Sultan in the face of new Mongol incursions, and increased his lands thereby. But he finally declared the independence of his people and ruled them as a sovereign monarch until his demise in 1326, by which time he had added greatly to his holdings through waging successful war on the Byzantines.

This realm grew in the usual way, though its final form as a would-be universal empire was highly unusual. Osman's younger son, Orkhan, succeeded to the crown (1326–59) and made his older brother his "Grand Vizier." His armies and those of his son, Murad I (1359–89), drove the Byzantines from all of Asia Minor, subdued most of the now-broken Seljuk principalities, crossed into the Balkans, and left the Eastern Roman Empire little more than the city of Constantinople. The Sultans married the daughters of the Byzantine Cæsar and maintained cordial relations with them, while cheerfully taking over their cities and provinces. The Ottoman capital was moved to Adrianople in 1367. Ottoman control of the Balkans was secured at the battle of Kossovo (August 27, 1389) where the King of Serbia lost his life as well as his army of one hundred thousand Serbs, Rumanians, and Hungarians—and Murad was assassinated in the aftermath of victory by a Serb leader who came to offer submission. His son Bayezid I (1389–1403) took the throne and promptly ordered the execution of his own brother. A younger brother had already been put to death by the father for plotting a double parricide with the son of Emperor John Palæologus. Bayezid perished as a captive of Tamerlane, whose Mongols almost destroyed the Osmanli realm. Mohammed I restored, and Murad II (1421–51) added to, what had been lost.

The heirs of Osman became monarchs of a World-State and a formidable menace to Christian Europe after Mohammed (II) the Conqueror (1451–81) took Constantinople and made it his capital. The Roman walls of the ancient city of Constantine, still standing in large part today with their scores of large and small towers and their overgrown moats and crumbling gates, had withstood all sieges for a thousand years, and kept the metropolis of the Eastern Empire secure against attack by land. Byzantine sea-power was a guarantee against the danger of submission through starvation. (The butchery and plunder perpetrated by the Western adventurers of the Fourth Crusade, who took the city in 1204, were made possible only by the superiority of the Venetian navy.) Sultan Mohammed, already master of Epirus, Macedonia, most of Serbia, Bulgaria, and Thrace, opened his assault from the European side with much artillery and a great preponderance of numbers. On May 29, 1453, the walls were breached. Constantine Palæologus, last Roman Cæsar of the East, was slain. Amid massacre and looting, the great Basilica of St. Sofia was plundered and then converted into a mosque. Mohammed later took all of Serbia, Bosnia, Albania, the Crimea, and even Otranto in South Italy in a vain effort to reach Rome.

Allah forfend that we should tarry here over the tangled vicissitudes of his successors. The annals of this empire offer a weird pageant of parricide, fratricide, pretenders, rebellions, intrigues, corruption, and frequent succession to the Sultanate through murder and civil war—all in all, a most untidy way of establishing world government. But so long as the Turkish armies were superior to their foes, as was the case throughout a vast area for some centuries, the realm continued to expand, maintained internal stability of a kind, and even attained distinction in commerce, administration, art, architecture, and learning. Selim the Grim (1512–20), son of Bayezid II, wrote poetry, conquered Egypt, and bought the title of Caliph of Islam from the last Abassid, living under the guardianship of the Mamelukes. By the time of Suleiman the Magnificent (1520–66), who symbolizes the zenith of the empire, the Sultans ruled all the lands from Austria and Poland southeastward to Mesopotamia and Arabia and thence westward through Egypt across North Africa. The Hungarians were crushed at Mohacs (1526), and Vienna was unsuccessfully besieged in 1529—and again as late as 1683. Sulieman took Bagdad, accepted an alliance with Francis I against Charles V, and expanded the Turkish navy. This fleet, however, was badly beaten at Lepanto in 1571, in the reign of Selim the Sot, by Don Juan of Austria, commanding the combined fleets of Venice, Spain, and the Pope in the "Holy League."

The causes of the decay of governments, including world government, and of the fall of empires, including universal empires, have long intrigued men and scholars, with no general solution emerging (save *à la* Spengler or *à la* Toynbee) and often with no specific answer agreed upon by the authorities in any given case. It is easy to attribute the slow decline of the Ottomans to their peculiar political and military arrangements, to be noted presently. Yet in fact they flourished until the external might of Russia and the internal pressures of Greek, Balkan, and Arab nationalisms reduced the realm to ruin. The "sick man of Europe" would almost surely have expired in the nineteenth century save for British support against the Tsardom, dictated by considerations of strategy and *Realpolitik*. In the aftermath of defeat in World War I, and of the postwar defeat of the Greeks and the Allies by the "New Turkey" of Mustapha Kemal's nationalists at

Angora, Mohammed VI fled to Malta in November 1922. The Sultanate and the Caliphate were soon afterwards abolished. The end came not tragically but miserably. Here, nevertheless, was a World-State, which for all its weirdness had been a long-lived imperium, uniting many peoples under a common rule for many centuries and somehow achieving great things in arts and letters no less than in war and politics. Even the most hostile of Christian skeptics will concur in this judgment if he will but go to fabulous Istanbul and visit at twilight the Blue Mosque of Sultan Ahmed, with its six minarets, or the mosque and tomb of the Magnificent Suleiman.

The features most strange, to Orient and Occident alike, of the Ottoman system of power in its heyday were these: The ruler was an unlimited Autocrat, but also a common soldier and often a slave or the son of a slave. With no fixed rules of succession, power often passed by murder. This State long remained a nomad army on the move. Authority was shared between fighters and the *ulema* or religious class of theologians, educators, and judges. The chief administrators or viziers were also warriors. The imperial *divan* or cabinet consisted of seven viziers or pashas with three horsetails. Each *vilayet* or province was governed by a pasha with two horsetails, and each district or *sanjak* of a province by a pasha with one horsetail. All public offices tended to be sold to the highest bidder. The army consisted of a feudal cavalry, a motley group of volunteers, and the highly trained and disciplined infantry corps of the Janissaries or slaves of the palace (established by Orkhan and bloodily suppressed in 1826), who were recruited by the kidnapping of Christian children into a kind of highly privileged monastic order or secret society, converted to Islam and sworn to celibacy. Formidable in battle, they finally became, like other imperial guards, masters of their master.

In no other World-State have slaves been made generals, governors, and despots. As early as the thirteenth century a Persian commentator observed: "From the days of Adam down to the present day no slave bought at a price has ever become king except among the Turks; and among the sayings of Afrasyab, who was king of the Turks, and was extraordinarily wise and learned, was his dictum that the Turk is like a pearl in its shell at the bottom of the sea, which only becomes valuable when it leaves the sea and adorns the diadems of kings and the ears of brides." [7] Toynbee points out that the training of slaves as warriors and rulers has precedents in other nomadic empires—the Parthian, the Abbasid, the Mameluke—but quotes Lybyer to show that the Ottomans carried this system to its acme:

> Grandly disregarding the fabric of fundamental customs which is called "human nature," and those religious and social prejudices which are thought to be almost as deep as life itself, the Ottoman system took children forever from parents, discouraged family cares among its members through their most active years, allowed them no certain hold upon property, gave them no definite promise that their sons and daughters would profit by their success and sacrifice, raised and lowered them with no regard for ancestry or previous distinction, taught them a strange law, ethics and religion, and ever kept them conscious of a sword raised above their heads which might put an end at any moment to a brilliant career along a matchless path of human glory.[8]

To the obvious question—how could such a system work? —the only answer is that it did, amazingly and for centuries on end. Give men a mission, give the conquered peace, and maintain a war-machine that can expand or at least defend the frontiers, and seemingly any system will work. We currently fancy that there must be better ways to establish world government on more secure foundations. There may be. But the way of conquest—whether followed by the Roman method of granting the vanquished citizenship in an empire

[7] Quoted by Sir Dennison Ross in H. G. Wells: *The Outline of History*, p. 703.

[8] Albert H. Lybyer: *The Government of the Ottoman Empire in the Time of Suleiman the Magnificent* (Cambridge, Massachusetts: Harvard University Press; 1913), pp. 57–8.

disguised as a republic, or by the Mongol method of leaving them alone so long as they submitted and paid tribute, or by the curious Turkish method of recruiting an elite from slaves—is the only method a benighted humankind has ever found to be effective, to date, in giving political reality to the Commonwealth of Man.

4. THE DISUNION OF EUROPE

> To regard a tribe or a state as a sort of personality is a very old disposition of the human mind. The Bible abounds in such personifications. . . . And while such tribal persons as "Israel" or "Tyre" did represent a certain community of blood, a certain uniformity of type, and a homogeneity of interest, the European powers which arose in the 17th and 18th Centuries were entirely fictitious unities. . . . Aristotle said that man is a political animal, but in our modern sense of the word politics, which now covers world-politics, he is nothing of the sort. He has still the instincts of the family tribe, and beyond that he has a disposition to attach himself and his family to something larger, to a tribe, a city, a nation, or a state. . . . As the idea of Christianity as a world brotherhood of men sank into discredit because of its fatal entanglement with priestcraft and the Papacy on the one hand and with the authority of princes on the other, and the age of faith passed into our present age of doubt and disbelief, men shifted the reference of their lives from the kingdom of God and the brotherhood of mankind to these apparently more living realities, France and England, Holy Russia, Spain, Prussia, which were at least embodied in active Courts, which maintained laws, exerted power through armies and navies, waved flags with a compelling solemnity and were self-assertive and insatiably greedy in an entirely human and understandable fashion.
>
> —H. G. WELLS.[9]

THE ROMANTIC medieval exercises in devout ferocity known as "the Crusades" have bemused men during all succeeding

[9] *The Outline of History*, pp. 836–8.

centuries. The stories and legends of the time have been oft retold. The mixed motives of the participants, and the place of their deeds in the larger picture of the development of Christendom, have long been sources of wonder. To add to, or even recapitulate, these accounts is needless. But a few features of these adventures in bellivolent religiosity may be noted, as prologue to an argument.

Michael VII and his successor as Cæsar of Byzantium, Alexius Comnenus, both appealed to the Pope of Rome for aid against the Seljuk Turks. Gregory VII (1073–85), busy with cleansing and reanimating the Church and quarreling with the Emperor over the investiture of bishops, gave no apt reply. But Urban II (1089–99) summoned all the faithful to unite in rescuing the Holy Sepulcher from Islam. Peter the Hermit, shoeless and shirtless, riding a donkey and carrying a cross, addressed great throngs with a like message and persuaded thousands to set forth for the Holy Land. Far short of arrival, these ardent simplefolk, self-betrayed by their hopes, were lost, scattered, or massacred. But the organized men-at-arms of the First Crusade, recruited from all over the West and largely led by Norman knights, defeated the Turks in Asia Minor and succeeded in taking Jerusalem (July 15, 1099).

A Second Crusade in 1147 eventuated in a German war against the pagan Wends and in the founding of the Kingdom of Portugal, but did not extend the Christian holdings in the Levant. Crusades invariably beget countercrusades. The Third Crusade was set off by the preaching of a Jehad or Holy War of Islam against Christ on the part of Sultan Saladin of Egypt. His troops retook Jerusalem in 1187. Two years later the Christian knights, led by Emperor Frederick Barbarossa, the King of France, and Richard the Lionhearted, smote the foe, saved Antioch, but failed to regain the Sacred City. The fighters of the Fouth Crusade took Byzantium in 1204 and set up a Latin Emperor on the Eastern Cæsar's throne for the next half-century, while the Roman and Greek Churches were temporarily reunited by violence.

The cynical Frederick II regained Jerusalem in the Sixth Crusade (1229), but by negotiation, rather than by war, and at a time when he himself had been excommunicated by Innocent III, who proclaimed a crusade against the crusading Emperor. Jerusalem was lost again in 1244 and not regained by Christian arms until 1918. Other crusades, tragic, comic, and innumerable, were without enduring results.

By and large these expeditions, like much other "Christian" conduct, strike us as a strange way to serve the cause of the Prince of Peace. One of Peter the Hermit's "people's armies" began its holy work with a butchery of Jews in the Rhineland. All robbed, raped, and slew fellow Christians on their way. The first liberators of Jerusalem literally waded through blood, sobbing with joy and kneeling in prayer at the Sepulcher amid rivers of gore. After another slaughter, this time of Greek Christians, Constantinople was looted. As Toynbee remarks of the Crusaders, "their practical efficiency was surprisingly higher than the general level of their culture. It was as remarkable that they should have reached Jerusalem as it is that their descendants should have reached the North Pole and the stratosphere. It is still more remarkable that, nevertheless, they should have remained in other respects the barbarians that they manifestly were." [1]

Yet this West European Christendom exhibited a species of unity eight centuries ago which it had never known after the breakup of Charlemagne's empire, and has never known since. Neither Pope nor Emperor ever ruled any European World-State. Yet a deeper communion of faith and purpose inspired the Western peoples and found living expression in the Crusades as a joint enterprise of all. There were later, if less impressive, warlike incarnations of such solidarity—as, in vain, against the Mongols and, successfully, againt the Ottoman Turks—and always a rich efflorescence of the basic

[1] Arnold J. Toynbee in *The Observer* (London) (April 29, 1951), reviewing the first of the planned three-volume work by Steven Runciman: *A History of the Crusades* (Cambridge University Press; 1951). For an excellent brief account, see Richard A. Newhall: *The Crusades* (Holt [Berkshire Studies in European History]; 1927).

oneness of the Western civilization in the works of all Europeans in the arts, letters, and sciences. Yet this Great Society, unlike its counterparts in the Egyptian, Hellenic-Iranian, Græco-Roman, Arabic, Turkish, and Chinese "worlds," was never to attain any semblance of a persisting common rulership or effective universal empire. This indeed has remained its distinguishing political characteristic down to our own time, when it has been overshadowed by the non-European colossi of East and West.

The many and complex sources of this disunity we cannot here consider, save to notice that the great ecclesiastical schism of the Reformation, followed by hideous and devastating wars of religion, put an end forever to the spiritual bases of possible atonement, while the emergence of the rival national monarchies and the slow growth of ethnocentric national patriotism destroyed such psychopolitical foundations of union as might otherwise have developed. A free and voluntary federation of the European nation-States has been talked about for centuries, but has never yet been realized in any workable fashion. The present-day "Council of Europe" is the closest approach to such union, but the gap between aspiration and reality is by no means bridged.[2]

Union by the sword of a conqueror has long remained a hypothetical alternative. Various aspirants have sought to achieve it. Had any succeeded for any term of time longer than a few years, the divers cults and creeds of the Continent could doubtless have been smelted together into some enduring unity-in-diversity, as has repeatedly happened elsewhere. But all such ventures have been shipwrecked in the end by the politics of the balance of power, and broken on the rocks of nationalistic resistance to every attempt to establish a single European imperium.

The early effort of the House of Hapsburg under Charles V and Philip II came to grief under circumstances prophetic of the fate of later martial enterprises. Bourbon France was

[2] See pages 458f. below, and the present writer's "The Council of Europe," *The American Political Science Review* (September 1951).

similarly contained and restricted by successive coalitions. Napoleon I came closer to the goal. He could proclaim in 1810 that "a new order of things now guides the universe" and, a year later, that "the present epoch carries us back to the time of Charlemagne." In Nietzsche's words, he "wanted *one* Europe, which was to be mistress of the world."[3] This was not to be, nor was Hohenzollern Germany a century later any more successful in uniting the Continent by conquest. Adolf Hitler as pseudo-Cæsar came nearest of any to the target in his "racial" empire of lunacy and extermination. But, like Bonaparte, he was too weak to conquer Britain and too fearful, ambitious, and unwise to leave Russia at peace.

What emerged from these failures was the familiar Western system of separate sovereignties, maintaining an uneasy equipoise among themselves by war, and by diplomacy registering the results of past wars and preparations for future wars. In its political structure this system was less a community than an aggregation of States, vaguely bound together by the habitual rituals of diplomatic intercourse and the loose rules of a "law of nations." This so-called "international community," "family," or "society" of nations, or *Völkerrechtsgemeinschaft*, lacking any common ideology or ruling class, employed a disorderly method, and ultimately a self-destructive method, of maintaining order through the accommodation of the interests and demands of its members one to another and each with all. As Georg Schwarzenberger puts it:

> Through the mirror of international law, we can observe the development of the international society from its revolutionary starting-point, the break-up of the Christian Commonwealth of the Middle Ages. In little more than four centuries the *Civitas Christiana* has gradually covered the whole world with the framework of a universal society. This result was achieved at the price of the elimination of the spiritual values

[3] The quotations are taken from "Napoleon and the Age of Nationalism" by Hans Kohn in *The Journal of Modern History* (March 1950).

common to the former Christian community, and its transformation from a community into a society.[4]

Among the more interesting illusions engendered by the experiences of men in this society were the "Concert of Europe" and the *Pax Britannica*, both products of the fabulous century of "progress" between Waterloo and Sarajevo. The Napoleonic debacle ended in the establishment of a system of five roughly equal Powers, with a now chastened and safely reactionary France admitted to the victors' company in 1818. The "Quadruple Alliance" of Britain, Prussia, Russia, and Austria—embodied in the Treaty of Paris of 1815 and sanctified by the mystical instrument of the "Holy Alliance" devised by Alexander I—became the Quintuple Alliance, dedicated to maintaining the status quo and suppressing liberal or national revolutions through collective measures against aggression or subversion. Under the guidance of Metternich, the members held periodical diplomatic congresses in Vienna (1814–15), Aix-la-Chapelle (1818), Troppau (1820), Laibach (1821), and Verona (1822). Austrian armies were authorized to suppress a mildly liberal revolution in Naples in 1821. French armies did likewise in Spain in 1823. So far so good.

Vague talk of joint intervention to restore Spanish America to the rule of Bourbon absolutism in Madrid led to British resistance, based on sound commercial calculations, and to the Monroe Doctrine of 1923, based on equally sound considerations of *Realpolitik*. Canning's famous statement that he had "called the New World into being to redress the balance of the Old" was inaccurate. Yet American and British opposition to the "Concert," followed by Anglo-French-Russian intervention on behalf of revolution in the Greek rebellion against Turkey, caused the music-makers to fall into cacophony amid the discords of divergent national interests. In the European liberal revolutions of 1830 and the more extensive upheavals of 1848 there were no collective inter-

[4] Georg Schwarzenberger: *Power Politics* (London: Jonathan Cape; 1941, 1st edition), p. 42.

ventions. The Crimean War (1854–6) rendered the Concert non-existent. At the outbreak of the Franco-Prussian War, Count Beust of Austria exclaimed: "I cannot find Europe." The phantom re-appeared in the Congress of Berlin (1878) and in later Congresses called to adjust the policies of the "Great Powers" in dealing with the "Eastern Question," the partition of Africa, and the problems posed by the impacts of Western imperialisms on China. But the Concert was no longer European, and its task was no longer one of promoting European unity but one of postponing and preparing worldwide war.

The image of the *Pax Britannica* turns out, upon critical examination, to be equally unsubstantial. In its usual form, taken over in our time by some Americans, it held that Britain in the nineteenth century preserved "world peace" by virtue of industrial domination of markets, mercantile domination of the seas, financial domination of foreign investments, and naval domination of global politics. In fact there was no *Pax*. During the century in question, apart from innumerable contests between lesser States, colonial wars, and civil wars (of which the two bloodiest on record were fought in China and America), there were conflicts in arms between Russia and the Western Powers, France and Austria, Prussia and Austria, France and Prussia, France and China, America and Spain, and Japan and Russia.

All these hostilities, to be sure, were limited and local, not total and general. In so far as British policy contributed to this relatively happy result, it did so through maintaining naval superiority, avoiding entangling alliances, assuming no commitments beyond British power to fulfill them, abstaining from interventions in other peoples' wars save when vital British interests were at stake (and not always then), and scrupulously eschewing all moral crusading against "aggression" or "lawlessness" or ideological "sin." Opinions will differ as to whether the changed conditions of the early twentieth century made possible a continuation of this policy of nonintervention, isolationist neutrality, self-seeking tolerance, and prudent moderation. But no good purpose is served by having the policy itself, with its pragmatic means and purely practical ends, misunderstood by contemporary Britons or by their would-be American epigoni.

In our own generation the traditional European system of States has passed away, even though no political unification of Europe has been achieved. The system became obsolete when men outgrew its limits and found them more and more intolerable rather than conducive to faith, hope, and charity. Veblen called attention long ago to an important aspect of this age-old process:

> Patriotism is evidently a spirit of particularism, of aliency and animosity between contrasted groups of persons; it lives on invidious comparison, and works out in mutual hindrance and jealousy between nations. It commonly goes the length of hindering intercourse and obstructing traffic that would patently serve the material and cultural well-being of both nationalities; and not infrequently, indeed normally, it eventuates in competitive damage to both.
>
> All this holds true in the world of modern civilization, at the same time that the modern civilized scheme of life is, notoriously, of a cosmopolitan character, both in its cultural requirements and in its economic structure. Modern culture is drawn on too large a scale, is of too complex and multiform a character, requires the cooperation of too many and various lines of inquiry, experience and insight to admit of its being confined within national frontiers, except at the cost of insufferable crippling and retardation.[5]

But Europe found in unity no answer to its problem. So deep had become its disunity that the ultimate answer was not union, but abdication and partition.

The passing of Europe as the political center of our world stems from the fact that shifts of population, industrial productivity, and national power, under the influence of the spreading "industrial revolution," brought about a condition

[5] Thorstein Veblen: *An Inquiry into the Nature of Peace and the Terms of Its Perpetuation* (Huebsch; 1919), pp. 38–9.

of affairs in which it was no longer possible for the European "Great Powers" to maintain, unaided, any balance among themselves, as they were able to do in the seventeenth, eighteenth and nineteenth centuries. By 1914 Germany dominated the Continent. The Hohenzollern bid for hegemony could not be checked by the Anglo-French-Russian coalition, even with Japan and Italy added to it. Only American intervention in World War I prevented a German unification of Europe—and contributed to the destruction of one of the traditional "Great Powers," Austria-Hungary. Twenty years later Germany, now allied with Italy and Japan, again dominated the Continent. The West yielded Eastern Europe to Hitler at Munich in 1938, hoping that Germany and Russia would somehow fall afoul of, and destroy, one another while France and Britain remained at peace. The hope proved fatuous, while the surrender ended all possibility of restoring the European system. Western abandonment of Czechoslovakia was to mean, in the end, Muscovite domination of Eastern and Central Europe, though few Westerners foresaw this at the time and still fewer have been able or willing to reconcile themselves to the later *fait accompli*.

Within a year after Munich, Germany and Russia partitioned the East between them. Germany then conquered the Continent. Britain could not, Russia would not, prevent this result. Its perpetuation was made impossible only by American aid to Britain and by the Nazi madness, which drove its victims not only to the organized mass murder of millions of people on a scale unimagined by Tamerlane, but to the fatal folly of invading Russia. Had Germany left Russia alone, there is no reason to suppose that Moscow would have attacked the Reich—or that Britain, even with American aid, could have done so effectively. In this case, the Nazis, had they not been psychotics, might still be ruling a united Western Europe today. Or had Hitler induced Britain and America to make common cause with him against the Soviet Union, Russia would have suffered ultimate dismemberment and the Continent might have endured a long unity under

Nazi hegemony. The policy the Western Powers did in fact pursue—aid to Russia, insistence on German unconditional surrender, and final invasion of the Continent through France—meant inexorably that a triumphant Russia would fill the great vacuum of East Central Europe, Danubia, and Balkania in the wake of the vanquished Reich, since the Powers west of Germany had long since abandoned their influence in this part of the world. The outcome was the consequence neither of Soviet "perfidy" nor of Anglo-American "betrayal" of the Eastern peoples, but simply of the geometry, geography, and dynamics of power.

In the sequel German power was demolished, just as Germany had previously destroyed the power of France and reduced Italy to a satellite. In the process the essentially non-European Russian behemoth played the major role, with the next largest role played by the non-European leviathan of America. Europe therewith became an object, rather than a subject, of diplomacy and war, with decisive power over her fortunes residing in Washington and in Moscow. The non-European super-Powers could either partition the estate or quarrel over it. Churchill, vetoed by Washington in his efforts to restrict the extension of Russian power, and capable of facing realities, preferred partition. Truman, Byrnes, Bevin, Marshall, and Acheson preferred quarreling, and found a ready response in the Kremlin.[6]

As these words are written, the quarrel is unresolved in principle, but actually resolved in practice. A *de facto* partition has been achieved, with West Europe the pensioner of the United States and East Europe the prisoner of Muscovy. America cannot permit Russian control of all Europe, nor can Russia permit American control of the whole. Either Power in full mastery of the Continent could rule the world and destroy the other. A Europe unified by Europeans can, in our century, be only a Europe controlled by the Germans

[6] A suggestive sketch, with a brief but useful bibliography, of the diplomatic and military developments that have brought Europe to its present status is to be found in Hajo Holborn: *The Political Collapse of Europe* (Alfred A. Knopf; 1951).

—a contingency that Americans, Britons, and Russians fought World Wars I and II to prevent. The existing partition must therefore go on indefinitely, or Europe must be neutralized as a buffer zone, or the two giants must clash in arms, utterly destroying European civilization between them. There are no other possibilities. Among things quite impossible are American mobilization of West Europe to "liberate" East Europe, or Russian use of East Europe to "liberate" West Europe, or any effective reconstitution of Europe as an independent Power or group of independent Powers. World power has long since passed to centers outside the Old Continent. Its partition, symbolized by the splitting of Germany, Austria, and the Balkans, means that the West follows Washington and the East follows the Kremlin. Rehabilitation and rearmament of the sundered segments have now become non-European projects pursued for non-European purposes by non-European Powers interested in Europe only as the Rome of old was interested in auxiliaries and mercenaries to help hold the frontiers.

This new configuration in the global distribution of fighting capacity need not doom to destruction the rich culture of the venerated motherland of our common civilization—though the morbid fears and follies (shared by few Europeans) of Russians and Americans may unhappily produce such a tragedy. All that is certain for the next half century is that the European communities will remain disunited, and drawn in their two spheres toward the titans of Orient and Occident. Should either giant Power seize the whole, it will be destroyed by the other. Nevermore in our time will the Continent enjoy the dubious blessings of enduring peace in the wake of unification through conquest. Political prudence and a decent concern for the preservation of the fruitful diversity of the garden of Europa might seem to suggest that the U.S.S.R. and the U.S.A., in their own interests, should carry their quarrel elsewhere. Better yet, they might arrange a truce to a conflict in which neither can win and Europe is certain to lose everything that has hitherto given meaning to the lives of its people and of the people of all the earth. But decency and prudence are unfortunately not qualities conspicuous in the motives and conduct of those so hypnotized by power as to be blinded to the desirability of survival. The actual qualities that characterize each of the present-day candidates for rulership of the earth by arms will be commented upon in the chapter that follows, in an effort to assess their title, if any, to Cæsar's purple.

CHAPTER FOUR

THE NEW CAESARISM

1. THIRD ROME

"The church of ancient Rome fell because of the Apollinarian heresy; as to the Second Rome—the church of Constantinople—it has been hewn by the axes of Ishmaelites, but this Third new Rome—the Holy Apostolic Church, under thy mighty rule, shines throughout the entire world more brightly than the sun. All the Orthodox Christian realms have converged in thine own. Thou art the sole Autocrat of the Universe, the only Cæsar of the Christians. . . . Two Romes have fallen, but the Third stands, and no fourth can ever be. . . ."

—ABBOTT PHILOTHEUS OF PSKOV MONASTERY TO IVAN THE GREAT, GRAND DUKE OF MUSCOVY, C. A.D. 1475.

FEODOR MIHAILOVICH DOSTOEVSKY (1821–81) was arrested as a subversive at the age of twenty-eight and ceremoniously sentenced to die. After the authorities had prepared him and his co-conspirators for the firing squad, the "real" sentence was at the last moment revealed: penal deportation to Siberia. This experience aggravated his epilepsy. In later life he went abroad to escape his creditors, indulged in gambling and licentiousness, and became a conservative Pan-Slavist and Russophile Christian. The most fascinating of all novels, *The Brothers Karamazov* (1880), was the culmination of a literary career that early earned for Dostoevski a place among the immortals. Among his other deathless legacies was a sardonic and moralistic tale of the "world-savers" among the Russian revolutionary intelligentsia. It was written in 1871 and published under the title of *The Devils*, which, in translation, became *The Possessed*.

In its pages he portrays a meeting of radicals who center their discussion around the ideas of one Shigalov:

"Dedicating my energies to the study of the social organization which is in the future to replace the present condition of things, I've come to the conviction that all makers of social systems from ancient times up to the present year have been dreamers, tellers of fairy-tales, fools who contradicted themselves, who understood nothing of natural science and the strange animal called man. Plato, Rousseau, Fourier, columns of aluminium, are only fit for sparrows and not for human society. But, now that we are all at last preparing to act, a new form of social organization is essential. In order to avoid further uncertainty, I propose my own system of world-organization. Here it is." He tapped the notebook. "I wanted to expound my views to the meeting in the most concise form possible, but I see that I should need to add a great many verbal explanations, and so the whole exposition would occupy at least ten evenings, one for each of my chapters." (There was the sound of laugher.) "I must add, besides, that my system is not yet complete." (Laughter again.) "I am perplexed by my own data and my conclusion is a direct contradiction of the original idea with which I start. Starting from unlimited freedom, I arrive at unlimited despotism. I will add, however, that there can be no solution of the social problem but mine."

Shigalov is ridiculed by the younger members of the "society" for his conceit and his admitted "despair." A lame teacher rises to his defense:

"Mr. Shigalov is too modest. I know his book. He suggests as a final solution of the question the division of mankind into two unequal parts. One-tenth enjoys absolute liberty and unbounded power over the other nine-tenths. The others have to give up all individuality and become, so to speak, a herd, and, through boundless submission, will by a series of regenerations attain primeval innocence, something like the Garden of Eden.

They'll have to work however. The measures proposed by the author for depriving nine-tenths of mankind of their freedom and transforming them into a herd through the education of whole generations are very remarkable, founded on the facts of nature and highly logical. One may not agree with some of the deductions, but it would be difficult to doubt the intelligence and knowledge of the author."

Bantering talk follows. Shigalov insists he has a formula for earthly paradise. Lyamshin opines that if he "didn't know what to do with nine-tenths of mankind, I'd take them and blow them up into the air." Shigalov agrees that this might be the "best solution," but since it is impractical we must go on building paradise. Later Verhovensky comments:

"He's written a good thing in that manuscript. He suggests a system of spying. Every member of the society spies on the others, and it's his duty to inform against them. Every one belongs to all and all to every one. All are slaves and equal in their slavery. In extreme cases he advocates slander and murder, but the great thing about it is equality. To begin with, the level of education, science, and talents is lowered. A high level of education and science is only possible for great intellects, and they are not wanted. The great intellects have always seized the power and been despots. Great intellects cannot help being despots and they've always done more harm than good. They will be banished or put to death. Cicero will have his tongue cut out, Copernicus will have his eyes put out, Shakespeare will be stoned, that's Shigalovism. Slaves are bound to be equal. There has never been either freedom for equality without despotism, but in the herd there is bound to be equality. . . .

"Without science we have material enough to go on for a thousand years, but one must have discipline. The one thing wanting in the world is discipline. The thirst for culture is an aristocratic thirst. The moment you have family ties or love you get the desire for property. We will destroy that desire; we'll make use of drunkenness, slander, spying; we'll make use of incredible corruption; we'll stifle every genius in its infancy. We'll reduce all to a common denominator! Complete equality . . . Slaves must have directors. Absolute submission, absolute loss of individuality, but once in thirty years Shigalov would let them have a shock and they would all suddenly begin eating one another up, to a certain point, simply as a precaution against boredom. Boredom is an aristocratic sensation. The Shigalovians will have no desires. Desire and suffering are our lot, but Shigalovism is for the slaves."[1]

These words were written fourscore years ago, in the year of Lenin's birth—and almost half a century before the Russian Revolution of 1917. They may be taken, according to taste, as a prophesy, a caricature, a paradox, or a cry of despair over the fate of Man. Their author, a year before his death, reiterated an older and more exhalted theme in his address at the dedication of the Pushkin Memorial, when he forecast that Holy Russia, dedicated to perfect love and fraternity, would some day "pronounce the final word of the great general harmony, of the final brotherly communion of all nations in accord with the law of the gospel of Christ."

Among past builders of World-States, such Messianic visions were unknown to the early Romans and the Mongols, but have obvious counterparts elsewhere. In our own day, following the Teutonic *Götterdämmerung*, two aspirants for global dominion have emerged, both committed to the salvation of mankind—the one in terms of Dialectical Materialism, Proletarian Revolution, and the Communist Millennium, the other in terms of Democracy, Free Enterprise, and the American Century. As rival heirs of the Cæsars, they are irreconcilable enemies, since the *Pax Orbis* can by definition be ruled by only one Power, not two. In their enmity they may destroy the world and themselves. We are here first concerned with the older Power, whose people have much longer been addicted to mystical dreams of saving the world, and whose rulers inherited Cæsar's crown in a line of succession that, while tenuous, is yet more direct than the American claim.

Any fresh effort to "explain" Russia would be out of order.

[1] From *The Possessed,* by Fyodor Dostoevsky, translated by Constance Garnett (Macmillan; 1931), pp. 376–8 and 391–2.

Loyal American citizens of the 1950's, save for a few scholars and little groups of cranks, have no desire or ability to understand Russia, but only a desire to destroy Russia or to "liberate" Russia or to enjoy the excitements of unending conflict. By the same token loyal Soviet citizens, with no exceptions outside of the prisons and the forced labor camps, have no wish or competence to understand America, but only a wish to undermine or "emancipate" America or to gain the dangerous advantages of an interminable feud. When defamation and destruction are the tests of patriotism, honest efforts at analysis are either forbidden or are futile.[2]

What is germane to our purpose is an effort at assessing the potentialities of the Russian community to assume the role of world conqueror and world ruler played by other States in earlier times. Any attempt, however, to evaluate the qualifications of either Russians or Americans for the part can at best be but a highly tentative speculation. Comparisons of resources, manpower, armaments, productivity, and other ingredients of power have their uses, but are inconclusive since the imponderables in any such equation far outweigh the factors that can be measured. Past analogies may be helpful, but are also imprecise. It need only be noted to prove the

[2] I do not, of course, include in the category of honest efforts at analysis the vast and popular American literature of the 1940's and 1950's designed to prove that the U.S.S.R. is a hell on earth, ruled by devils, nor the correspondingly voluminous literature of opposite import on the Soviet side. Among the more "objective" accounts, for whatever they may be worth, mention may be made of the various books by Edward Hallett Carr, the late Sir Bernard Pares and Sir John Maynard, Isaac Deutscher, Alexander Baykov, and Edward Crankshaw—whose *Russia and the Russians* (Viking; 1948) and *Cracks in the Kremlin Wall* (Viking; 1951) seem to me admirably suggestive analyses, impressionistic but incisive, of the historical and psychological determinants of Soviet conduct. All the authors named are Britishers. Their American counterparts are few: the late Samuel N. Harper, Ronald Thompson, George Vernadsky, John Hazard, Ernest C. Simmons, Ivar Spector, and a scattering of others. My own *Soviet Politics at Home and Abroad* (Alfred A. Knopf; 1946), while still useful, I trust, as a history and evaluation, is now "dated" in that it assumed the possibility, however remote, of an ultimate "liberalization" of the Soviet regime, and supposed that the policy-makers of both Moscow and Washington might conceivably so behave as to avoid the probability of mutual self-destruction. Events have shown this hope and premise to be most dubious, if not altogether false. Most recent Western literature on Russia, and virtually all Soviet literature on America, is the literature of defamation.

point that no contemporary, however well informed, could possibly have guessed that the farmers of Latium in the fourth century B.C. or the nomads of Arabia or Mongolia in the seventh and eleventh centuries A.D. could conceivably have become rulers of the world. Our present knowledge is little better as a basis of prediction. Only future events can judge. A few hints may yet be suggested.

The first thing to notice is that Russia became a Eurasian World-State many centuries before the Messianic gospel of Marxism-Leninism-Stalinism was ever dreamed of. Secretary Acheson recognized that the "enemy," against which Americans were girding themselves for war as a means of preserving peace, was "Russian Imperialism" as well as "Soviet Communism" when he told the House Committee on Foreign Affairs on June 26, 1951, in appealing for $8,500,000,000 to support the Free World against aggression: "It is clear that this process of encroachment and consolidation by which Russia has grown in the last 500 years from the Duchy of Muscovy to a vast empire has got to be stopped." [3] It is indeed the case that the Russian Empire—in this respect comparable to all other imperialisms, past and present—was and is an artifact of conquest and annexation, extending from a center of power and impinging upon and subjugating other peoples originally independent or ruled by weaker adjacent

[3] This statement, followed by an approving editorial of June 28, 1951, "Realism about Russia," led to an interesting series of letters in *The New York Times* by proponents and opponents of the "dismemberment" of Russia, whose "unity" under anti-Communist auspices had been championed officially by the U.S.A. between 1917 and 1922. None of the writers displayed awareness of the fact, which tended to be generally ignored as well by official Washington and by the American press and public, that in order to carve bear meat one must first catch and kill the bear. In the issue of July 29, 1951, appeared a bitter letter by Alexander Kerensky, asserting that if the new "realism" represented American policy, then Comrade Pospelov had been "right in his cynical Moscow speech of January 21," charging that the U.S. was seeking the dismemberment of the Russian realm, despite the State Department's rejoinder then that such statements were lies and libels. For a far broader, more philosophical, and more historical discussion of Russian attitudes and policies toward world government, see the mimeographed documents of the Committee to Frame a World Constitution (University of Chicago; 1946–7), Nos. 105 and 108 (Bernard Guillemin, "Russia and World Federalism") and 146, in four reports (Vera Sandomirsky: "Russian Survey").

States. Like most of their predecessors and current competitors engaged in similar operations, the rulers of Russia frequently cultivated the illusory but pleasing belief that what they had begun might be continued and extended until all the great globe itself should become subject to their sovereignty.

What is peculiar and unique, however, is more revealing of the distinctive traits of national character and conduct than what is common to many peoples. The Muscovite State emerged from the wilderness and gradually extended itself over much of Eurasia under the magic spell upon its people, and the practical influence upon its masters, of two earlier "world empires"—one a glorious phantom, the other a brutal fact. The ghost was Byzantium, Eastern successor of the Roman Empire. The reality was the *Pax Mongolica* and the yoke of the Golden Horde. From the former the early monarchs of Kiev acquired their Christianity in 989 via Vladimir, prince and saint, who married the sister of the Byzantine Cæsar; their written language via Church Slavonic; their standards of beauty in literature and the arts; and a cloudy myth of a universal commonwealth. From the latter the Grand Dukes of Muscovy learned the skills of tax collection, postal communication, military organization, and the art of war. Church and State were all but fused, as in Spain under comparable circumstances, for the hated overlords of both lands were Asiatic pagans. But the most enduring lesson learned by the Muscovites from the Mongols, without which they could never have liberated themselves from the Tartar yoke, was the lesson of discipline and unity through Autocracy. Each became the slave of all. Every one yielded up the externals (but never the inner pride) of his individuality in order that weakness and anarchy might give way to communal strength and collective dedication to the grim but inescapable duties of battle.

To say that the Russians found freedom through tyranny is not a play upon words, nor an expression of contempt, but a literal statement of the relationship between ends and means in a community long living under alien rule and long threatened thereafter by the ambitions of neighbors possessed of superior power. Individual liberty first flourished in England and later in America—i.e., in societies almost immune, by virtue of geography, from serious threats of foreign invasion and subjugation. In communities not so favored, "liberty" becomes a collective goal, capable of realization only through a despotism which forges the sword of independence by compelling every man to subject himself to the symbolic will of all men. Such "freedom" is travesty or hypocrisy in the eyes of Westerners, just as Western "freedom" is an empty abstraction to the masses of Eurasia and Africa whose daily lives for endless generations have given them no tools to grasp its meaning. It is nevertheless true that age-old agony long ago convinced most Russians that freedom from anarchy among themselves and emancipation from the thralldom of outlanders were attainable only through military absolutism. Those in the West who reprove them for not drawing a better—i.e., a "Western"—conclusion from their experience commonly know nothing of any experience save their own, and not enough of that to be able to imagine that the experience of others might be otherwise.

Ivan the Great (1462–1505), "Grand Duke of All Russia," hired Italian architects to build the Kremlin, succeeded in discontinuing tribute to the Khans (1480), and married Zoe, niece of the last Byzantine Cæsar. He borrowed from the lost Byzantium not only a wife but an honor and an emblem of power: the title of "Autocrat" and the double-headed eagle. His formidable and half-mad grandson, Ivan the Terrible (1533–84), took the name of Cæsar or Tsar and wrested Kazan and Astrakhan on the Volga from the Tartars. He later acquired Siberia and opened the way to the migration of Great Russians all across northern Asia to the Pacific. But he failed in his efforts to recover the old lands in the west and south once ruled by Novgorod and Kiev and seized by Swedes, Lithuanians, Germans, Poles, and Turks in Mongol times in the face of the indifference of Sarai, Karakorum, and

Pekin. The quality of Russian life in these formative times may be dimly grasped by recalling that Moscow was once again burned by Tartars and Turks in 1571 and taken and held for two years (1610–12) by the Poles during the "time of troubles." Every evidence of feebleness at the Muscovite center invited attack and subversion from abroad, and led to the seizure of Russian provinces by ever-menacing foes on the frontiers.

All imperialisms justify their aggrandizements by alleging that their victims were the aggressors. In the Russian instance, the allegation has somewhat more foundation in fact than it has ever had in the overseas colonial imperialisms of the Western Powers. Contrary to the irate mumblings of the myth-makers, this circumstance has nothing to do with any qualities of virtue or vice on the part of Great Russians or of their neighbors, invaders, and ultimate victims. Rich lands weakly held by backward peoples and readily accessible to vigorous near-by Powers invite invasion. Such was the condition of the Muscovite estate for some centuries during and after Mongol rule. As has not infrequently happened, external assault—in each major case falling just short of being lethal—generated internal forces of resistance and counterassault which converted the invaders into the invaded and the oppressors into the oppressed.

The dynasty founded by Michael Romanov in 1613 fought to recapture lost provinces and then moved forward to new conquests as a means of protecting what had been regained—and, if possible, fulfilling the ancient dream of universal dominion. Smolensk and Kiev were not rewon until 1667, after savage war with the Polish nobles in the frontier land, or "Ukraine." Peter the Great (1682–1725) was the first Tsar to call himself "Emperor." He was convinced that "Westernization" was the key to success. He visited Europe, shaved beards, beheaded rebels, made the Church an agent of the State, founded the Russian Navy and the Academy of Science, built St. Petersburg as a new "Western" capital, and in twenty years of war against the Swedes established Russian rule over the Ukraine and the Baltic provinces. The price of such victories was ruthless domestic dictatorship, coupled with an expanding military feudalism, and a pattern of aggrandizement abroad that brought new insecurity rather than safety, as other Powers perceived that their interests required action to halt and contain the Russian juggernaut.

Tsarist troops defeated the Great Frederick of Prussia and took Berlin in 1760, but soon withdrew by agreement. Catherine the Great (1762–96), lady of many lovers, snatched the northern shores of the Black Sea from the Turks, made Constantinople her goal, and partitioned Poland in league with Austria and Prussia. This realm continued to expand at the rate of sixty square miles a day for three hundred years. A "Petrine" tradition dictated extroversion and aggrandizement, while an older "Muscovite" exclusiveness urged withdrawal before superior force and isolation from foreign contamination. These two trends in Russian minds have striven for ascendancy ever since, never more so than in the mid-twentieth century, when they have merged in a strange synthesis.

The Marxist inheritors of this imperium are so hypnotized by their own vocabulary as to interpret all events of later times in terms of the conflict of classes. Non-Marxists are often content to eschew interpretation, or to talk vaguely of "nationalism," or to assume naïvely that a community of slaves has been captured by an elite of demons. Consideration of the record will suggest that what happened within this almost endless empire was principally a function of its successes and failures in doing battle with foreign Powers.

The catastrophic breakdown of Napoleon's invasion of Russia brought the armies of the Tsar to Paris and gave Muscovy such prestige that it long dominated Central Europe, and sent its forces to Budapest to suppress revolution in 1849. It is noteworthy, in view of the problems of the 1950's, that Russian armies in Central Europe have never in the past been driven out by violence but have always been withdrawn by agreement among the Powers. Russian defeat by the West in the Crimean War led to retreat abroad and to "reform" at home, expressed most notably in the emancipation of the serfs in 1861. Russian defeat by Japan in 1904–5 led to revolution at home, though none of the parties desirous of change was able to realize its purposes. Many rebels perished or fled abroad in the subsequent reaction. Russian defeat by Germany in 1915–16 evoked the whirlwind that destroyed the Tsardom, demolished the old social order and, following the failure of the forces of middleclass democracy either to win the war or make a peace, brought to power the Bolshevik fanatics who swore by Marx and undertook to "liberate" the world.

The doleful attempt of the Western Powers in 1918–20 to destroy this regime of world-revolutionists through invasion, blockade, and subsidized civil war rallied most Russians to its defense and thus insured its perpetuation. Winston Churchill has often expressed regret that the monster was not "strangled at birth." Its survival was not due to any lack of murderous effort on the part of the would-be killers, with Churchill at their head. But the Allies and the "Whites" were beaten in battle by the Reds. The victors' subsequent decision—ghastly as to means, successful as to ends—to collectivize and industrialize the Russian economy was dictated quite as much by cold calculations of power in foreign affairs as by glowing Marxist visions of Utopia. As often happens in such matters, the visions proved to be illusory and the calculations proved correct. The final defeat, at fearful cost, of the Axis assault of 1941–2 consolidated the new Autocracy and enabled it to extend its power over most of Eastern Europe and well into Western Europe, thereby terrifying Americans, (whose readiness to be terrified we shall examine later) and raising their terror to hysteria when the native disciples of Muscovite Marxism conquered China in 1949, thus restoring, in superficial appearance, the formidable empire of Kubla Khan.

That we are here in the presence of a possible government of all the earth, achieved by infiltration, conversion, and conquest, admits of no doubt. This potential world government rests upon slavery, exploitation, and absolutism, to the horror of the Atlantic communities. Western peoples, shuddering before the new barbarians, forget their own origins; rejoice still in a large measure of personal freedom, social justice, and political democracy; and solemnly resolve to defend their heritage and, if posibble, to destroy the barbarian Power and liberate its victims, for whom Western eyes weep and Western hearts bleed. In a Great Society wedded to the balance of power, some such resolve would have been elicited in any event by the sheer magnitude of the Marxist Moloch, regardless of its words or deeds or the forms and forces of its structure. Yet the strange and frightening aspect of the system of power hit upon by the self-appointed saviors of mankind quickened the determination of foes and prospective victims abroad to resist it to the death in the sacred name of freedom—without, however, furnishing that insight or understanding which are the prerequisites of wisdom and safety in any such attempt to resist global dominion.

The features of Red Muscovy that appear peculiar and alarming to the West, to the point of panic and desperation, are in reality not at all new, and are in some respects evidence of failure, muddling, and weakness, not of victory, planning, and strength. To attribute these evidences of sin to "Marxism" is absurd, even though the sinners call themselves Marxists. For Marxism, since the death and canonization of its founder (1818–83), has become a creed and a cult, like many others before it, of which anyone can make whatever he likes.[4] To equate the new wickedness with "Fascism,"

[4] But see Karl R. Popper's erudite volume, *The Open Society and Its Enemies* (Princeton University Press; 1950) wherein Plato is depicted as the progenitor of all totalitarianism, Hegel is ridiculed, and Marxism in its original form is subjected to a fresh and searching analysis and critique (pp. 274–398). This effort, while provocative and rewarding, will not be wholly persuasive to those who suspect that most such *tours de force* in intellectual history are of the *post hoc ergo propter hoc* variety and tend to ignore the propensity of men to use ideas as weapons, selected from a well-stocked arsenal to serve immediate purposes—which in turn are shaped by cultural experience and have little to do with the ideas themselves or with the original convictions and expectations of those who first developed them.

here Red instead of Black, Brown, or Blue, testifies to similar semantic confusion. The Word is not the object. The late Cæsars of Rome, Berlin, Nanking, Tokyo, and Madrid, moreover, copied many of their devices of governance from the oligarchs of Moscow, not the other way about. Things equal to the same thing are equal to each other—in mathematics, but not in politics. It may even be respectfully suggested that the vast libraries devoted to demonstrating that Stalin betrayed Lenin, or that Lenin betrayed Marx, or that Marx betrayed Democracy represent, for the most part, a waste of ink and paper. Men become what they do. Men do what they feel they must do in the face of each challenge and opportunity, and adapt and adjust their beliefs accordingly. What is felt to be necessary or desirable in conduct is a function of experience through the whole life span and geographical scope of nations and cultures. This, rather than the word-systems of philosophers and ideologists, is the living stuff of politics.

The temptation to "explain" Russia in these terms must be resisted. It is enough to say that the anatomy and physiology of Marxist Muscovy are less products of Messianism or milleniarism, whether in Muscovite or Marxist tense, than of the exigencies of a fierce struggle for survival, waged with words derived from the scriptures of Marx and Engels, but with deeds derived from the memories, bitter and glorious, of the peoples of the endless prairies in their long ordeal in beating back successive invaders and maintaining unity and community against their own anarchic bent. Does a small, self-selected elite rule the mass? Such was the case in the Romanov Tsardom and its precursors. Is the leader apotheosized by sycophants? So it was in St. Petersburg, old Moscow, Byzantium, and Karakorom. Were images carried in processions and bodies of saints revered in Holy Kiev and in the lands of Dimitri Donskoi? So it is also in Red Square and at Lenin's tomb. Intolerant orthodoxy and insistence on unquestioning conformity are older than ancient Novgorod, as are "elections" by acclamation and decisions by unanimity in primitive Slavic assemblies. Secret police, suspicion of foreigners, devious diplomacy, "iron curtains," dreams of overtaking the West, irresponsible blundering, blithe disregard of human dignity, and callous sacrifice of life—all these things and a dozen more have their roots in Petrine and Muscovite and Mongol and Byzantine Russia as crude devices of adaptation and survival in a land of lonely spaces, bitter cold, recurrent famine, rebellion, and massacre, with alien enemies, swarming and merciless, ready to pour in from every point of the compass.

Such reflections are not here designed either to justify odious Soviet conduct or to belittle the many magnificent accomplishments of the Soviet regime. They are intended to suggest that the Muscovites of the twentieth century bear upon their faces, reveal in their behavior, and preserve in the secret places of the heart the multiform imprint of a thousand years of shared experience. During this millennium they came to know strivings and sufferings and "solutions" of problems in human relations of which the relatively secure and happy peoples of North America, only three centuries old as a community and only half a century old as a world Power, can have no conception because they have no equivalents in their own history. The rough talents of the Great Russians and their kinsmen, the Byelorussians and the Ukrainians or "Little Russians," in building a World-State of vast expanse, inhabited by hundreds of peoples of divergent languages and lifeways, have already been demonstrated by the record. Their potentialities, if any, to enlarge this realm to pan-planetary proportions are the outgrowth, as has been the case with all founders of universal empires in distant days, of their own past. A tentative verdict on the future threat or promise of such skills in governance as they have thus acquired can best be rendered after we cast an appraising eye over the broader reaches of the immense realm of which their present rulers are masters.

2. THE MARXIST IMPERIUM

But this was a mere catchword for the multitude, as the authors of the revolution were really to govern. . . . Fear, and the sight of the numbers of the conspirators, closed the mouths of the rest; or if any ventured to rise in opposition, he was presently put to death in some convenient way, and there was neither search for the murderers nor justice to be had against them if suspected; but the people remained motionless, being so thoroughly cowed that men thought themselves lucky to escape violence, even when they held their tongues. An exaggerated belief in the numbers of the conspirators also demoralized the people, rendered helpless by the magnitude of the city, and by their want of intelligence with each other, and being without means of finding out what those numbers really were. For the same reason it was impossible for anyone to open his grief to a neighbor and to concert measures to defend himself, as he would have had to speak either to one whom he did not know, or whom he knew but did not trust. Indeed all the popular party approached each other with suspicion, each thinking his neighbor concerned in what was going on, the conspirators having in their ranks persons whom no one could ever have believed capable of joining an oligarchy; and these it was who made the many so suspicious, and so helped to procure impunity for the few, by confirming the commons in their mistrust of one another.

—THUCYDIDES ON THE EVENTS IN ATHENS IN 412 B.C.

THE PRACTICE of the arts of government—including world government, both for those who wish to achieve it and those who wish to prevent it—presupposes some capacity to forecast the future consequences of the experiences and decisions of men. All history testifies to the inability of most powerholders to attain even a moderate degree of competence in the fulfillment of this task, for the lack of which all human events take on the appearance of destiny or a game of chance or a manifestation of the unknowable will of the gods. In the

1860's and 70's, a red-eyed, grizzled man, always indigent and often ill, pored over books and public records in the library of the British Museum. In 1900 a young lawyer moved, unknown, from Siberia to St. Petersburg to Switzerland, where he lived impecuniously with his devoted wife, conspiring with fellow exiles and scribbling fantastic articles that only a handful of people ever saw. In 1908 an obscure political prisoner in Tiflis walked unbowed, book in hand, between two rows of soldiers who were beating the inmates with rifle-butts. Contrary to all reasonable anticipation, among them the three were to establish a world government. The first was Marx, the second Lenin, and the third Stalin.

By the middle of the twentieth century the realm ruled by their apostles extended from the Elbe and the Danube to Kamchatka and Hainan and from the Arctic ice-floes to the tropic borders of the Middle East and Southern Asia, with more millions of more or less ardent disciples flourishing beyond the frontiers. Apart from converts and missionaries *in partibus infidelium*, and sundry satellites and marches on its periphery, this realm embraced two immense empires, of which the larger territorially was by far the largest on the planet and was third largest in population, while the smaller territorially was yet the second most extensive country in the world, and by far the largest of all in population. The land area under this rulership comprised 13,720,000 square miles, larger than all of Africa and nearly the size of the entire North and South American Continents combined. The populations directly governed by Communists of the Marxist-Leninist-Stalinist persuasion numbered some 750,000,000 souls, or almost one third of the human race. The Empire of Kubla Khan was only slightly greater.

So vast in scope is this latest enterprise in empire-building that it is no cause for wonder that many Americans and some West Europeans should view its size and power with something akin to the terror the Mongols inspired seven centuries ago. The World-State of Communism wields effective authority over twice the combined populations of Western

Europe and the United States, although its total industrial productivity is far less than a third of the United States alone. If the peoples of all North America, South America, and West Europe were to be envisaged as a bloc, the total population of the Communist imperium would still exceed it by a figure larger than the number of people inhabiting Canada and the United States combined.

Quantitative comparisons are easy but misleading. Qualitative comparisons are so difficult as often to be useless in operational terms. Learned monographs and popular books about contemporary Russia, China, and Eastern Europe are innumerable. No single study to date has sought to describe the Marxist empire in its entirety, nor is such an enterprise possible here. The larger common features of the structure of power in this Universal State may nevertheless be suggested without doing violence to the facts.

The Myth consists, as do many myths, of the figure of the bearded prophet; a set of sacred writings, read by few but revered by all; a pantheon of heroes, saints, and martyrs; a theory of the cosmos; and a vision of a millennium by which the faithful flatter themselves that they can predict and control the future. The verbal content of the Myth is sufficiently confused and flexible to enable disciples to give it such concrete interpretations as are needful in each particular situation. The emotional symbols are sufficiently uniform to promote solidarity among converts. The Elite consists of Party members, solemnly inducted into a dedicated brotherhood, carefully recruited, and frequently purged to insure obedient service to the cause. The Elite of the elite comprises a small group among the faithful who have attained to power and privilege by virtue of past imprisonment, present capacity, intrigue, fanaticism, favoritism, genius, or well-timed liquidation of rivals. As among the Saracens, Mongols, and Turks, wealth and ancestry are here of no account. Those best adapted to survival in such a system rise to the top, remain there, and pick their successors. Others languish in outer darkness, are sent to the uranium mines, or get a bullet through the head after publicly confessing their sins. A few flee from terror or intolerance at home to the loneliness of freedom abroad.

Authority here rests neither upon wisdom nor riches, although some of both come to the few who attain to great power. Conspiratorial cleverness, calculated sycophancy, martial prowess, and genuine public service are all capable of elevating humble members of the brotherhood to positions of influence and indulgence. The highest fall swiftly, however, if they fail to read aright the signs of the times and the caprices of their superiors in the hierarchy. Nothing suffices for survival save performance—and performance means conformity to the theological pronouncements of the high priests, plus demonstrated ability to serve their purposes in leading the masses toward salvation. This system of recruiting leadership bears an obvious resemblance to early Islam and, in Western experience, to the Roman Catholic hierarchy and, more specifically, to Ignatius Loyola's Society of Jesus, at least in its initial phase as the arm of the Church in the Counter-Reformation.[5]

It is in the area of Adaptation or accommodation to changing circumstances that this otherwise impressive system of power would seem, on the record thus far, to display its greatest feebleness and fragility. Succession to authority and adjustment to change, in Lenin's original theory of "democratic centralism," were to be achieved through periodical Congresses of delegates, freely chosen by members, who would reformulate the Party line, elect anew the Central Committee answerable to the Congress, and maintained freedom of debate within the ranks until decisions were reached by a

[5] Paul Blanchard in *Communism, Democracy, and Catholic Power* (Boston: Beacon Press; 1951) has spelled out the analogy in some detail, to the indignation of Catholics and Communists alike. As a non-Catholic, anti-Communist, and non-anti-Catholic, I venture here no judgment on the aptness or justification of his comparison—save to note that rival groups which pretend to monopolistic knowledge of the will of God, the nature of the universe, and the terms of man's salvation are inevitably enemies, while the quantity and quality of the indignation displayed in this instance is something of an index of the validity of the comparison.

majority vote—after which all members were pledged to carry out decisions regardless of their personal views. In practice in the U.S.S.R. no All-Union Congress of the Party has met since 1939, though the rules then solemnly adopted required a Congress every three years. The Central Committee has become a self-perpetuating body. Its Politburo has become a little group of oligarchs who secretly determine among themselves who is "in" and who is "out," and what policies shall be executed through the elaborate panoply of Soviet bodies constituting the formal façade of government.[6]

In this order only the orthodox faithful are presumed to possess wisdom and virtue and are alone deemed worthy of decision-making—and this only at the top of the ranks, with all underlings held to undeviating obedience. Nonconformists, protestants, infidels, and skeptics are indiscriminately lumped together as repositories of vice, enemies of the people, and agents of "capitalism" and "imperialism," the double-headed devil of the comrades. With local variations throughout the whole realm, the Parties soon become, on the Russian model, not associations or societies of the faithful, choosing their own programs and leaders, but rigidly disciplined civil armies taking orders from an officer corps responsible only to a Commander-in-Chief and his immediate staff. Under these circumstances co-operation or coalition between Communists and non-Communists as equal partners is virtually impossible, save in the most transitory, opportunistic, and ephemeral terms. The non-Communists must either abandon their identity or integrity, submit to full control or absorption, or rebel at the risk of suppression or exile.

[6] Useful accounts of the relationship between Party and Government in the Soviet system are to be found in Barrington Moore: *Soviet Politics* (Cambridge, Massachusetts: Harvard University Press; 1950); Michael T. Florinsky: *Toward an Understanding of the U.S.S.R.* (Macmillan; 1951, revised edition); Julian Towster: *Political Power in the U.S.S.R.* (Oxford University Press; 1948); Sanuel N. Harper and Ronald Thompson: *The Government of the Soviet Union* (Van Nostrand; 1949, second edition); Andrei Y. Vishinsky: *The Law of the Soviet State* (Macmillan; 1948); and Nathan Leites: *The Operational Code of the Politburo* (McGraw-Hill; 1951). See also James H. Meisel and Edward S. Kozara (editors): *Materials for the Study of the Soviet System* (Ann Arbor: George Wahr; 1951).

Whatever the choice, the result (wherever the Communists possess decisive power) is invariably a monopolizing of authority by the comrades, with all other parties either outlawed or reduced to an entirely subordinate role as "allies" of their masters. The quasicoalition in revolutionary Russia between Bolsheviks and Left Social Revolutionaries lasted barely six months in 1917–18. Ever since the outbreak of the civil war, the C.P. has enjoyed a "monopoly of legality," with the Party sharing public offices, but not effective power, with unorganized non-Party elements via the electoral and parliamentary formula of the "Bloc of Party and Non-Party people." In the European satellites and in Red China, the externals of "coalition" regimes have persisted longer, after the liquidation or absorption of the less-trustworthy co-operating groups. But those surviving entities which "share" public authority with Communists have no illusions as to their function or as to the actual seats of power.

The advantages and defects of these arrangements, with their corollary devices of co-ordination and control, are exemplified in the relations between the central power in the Kremlin and far-flung local centers throughout Eurasia. The Chinese Peoples' Republic is *sui generis*, and not to be subsumed under generalizations valid elsewhere. The complexities and obscurities of Sino-Soviet relations cannot here be explored. Suffice it to say that the Chinese Revolution that finally defeated and cast out the Kuomintang regime and conquered the mainland in 1949 was an indigenous peasant revolt, although it was led by native Marxists looking to Moscow for inspiration and, occasionally, for guidance. Contrary to the views so often expressed by Republican critics of the Truman Administration, and sometimes by Secretary Acheson himself, the fall of Chiang Kai-shek and the triumph of Mao Tse-tung cannot sensibly be attributed in the face of the record to any Muscovite "conspiracy" or any "conquest" of China by "Russian imperialism." The Soviet Union and Communist China do not deal with the States of Outer Mongolia, North Korea, Sinkiang, or Tibet as equals. But they would appear to deal with one another on terms as close to equality as is possible under the peculiar conditions of their contacts.

The thirty-year Treaty of Friendship, Alliance, and Mutual Aid signed by Chou En-lai and Vishinsky in Moscow, February 14, 1950, pledged the parties to immediate military support of one another in the event of renewed aggression by Japan or "any other State which, directly or indirectly, would unite with Japan in acts of aggression." In supplementary accords, Moscow assumed obligations of extending ten-year credits to China, sixty million dollars annually for five years at one per cent interest, for the purchase of Soviet machinery and railway equipment; restoring to China all Manchurian properties acquired from Japanese owners; and returning Port Arthur, Dairen, and the Manchurian Changchun Railway to Chinese control not later than the end of 1952. American efforts to portray these and other arrangements between Peking and Moscow as proof of China's "enslavement" by Russia are understandable in view of bitterness at past defeat, anxiety over future prospects, and the patent advantages of endeavoring (albeit by methods that have thus far insured the failure of the enterprise) to divide the Red giants against one another. Such efforts, however, are likely to remain unimpressive to most Eurasians.

As for the larger image of this World-State, what is most worthy of emphasis, since few Americans seem aware of the fact, is that Communism as a conspiracy of power-seekers has never secured sufficient popular support to essay a successful seizure of power except in the aftermath of war. No Communist regime anywhere has ever been established as a result of winning a majority in a free election. No Communist regime anywhere has come into being as the fruit of revolution in peacetime. Neither has any such regime (with the debatable exception of North Korea) ever been set up in the wake of conquering Communist armies embarked upon military aggression initiated by Communists as a means of spreading the true faith. In each instance thus far extensions of the Red imperium have been due to opportunities created by community disorganization and breakdown in the wake of large-scale armed hostilities or by the catastrophic failures of armed crusades from without to annihilate Communism. Modern war is the matrix of social revolution, of Communist totalitarianism, and of the phenomenal expansion of the Marxist empire.

The "Paris Commune" of 1871, envisaged by Marx as the prototype of the "dictatorship of the proletariat," was a concomitant of the defeat of France by Prussia. The October Revolution of 1917 was the outcome of the defeat of the Tsardom by the Central Powers and the subsequent demoralization of the Kerensky regime under the impact of continued war. The short-lived Bavarian and Hungarian Soviets of 1919 were made possible by social collapse following upon military disaster, while the failure in the same year of the United States, the Allies, and the White Armies to destroy the Bolsheviks of Muscovy by violence consolidated the grip of the victors on most of the Romanov lands. A decade and a half of warfare between China and Japan and among Chinese factions sufficed to deliver the "Middle Kingdom" to Marxism. The debacle of Hitler's invasion of Russia, followed by the downfall of the Nazi Reich and its Pan-European "New Order," and by Russian military occupation of half of the Continent, brought Communists to power in East Berlin, Warsaw, Prague, Budapest, Belgrade, Tirana, and Sofia, and contributed to the conversion of millions of Greeks, Italians, and Frenchmen.

Within the U.S.S.R. proper, 207,000,000 people in the sixteen Soviet Republics are nominally governed through the forms of a federal constitution, guaranteeing autonomy and even a right of secession to the local units, along with civil liberties, free elections, and responsible parliamentary government. Within the framework of these fictions, borrowed from the West and given Mongol-Muscovite meanings in the East, the Politburo, the Central Committee, and the local Party units rule in their multiple roles as self-perpetuating oligarchs, managers, agitators, ardent disciples, and devoted slaves of the dictators—subject at any time to demotion, expulsion, or liquidation for incompetence or transgressions from orthodoxy, and privileged to advancement toward top posts in the hierarchy for signal achievements and effective adulation of their masters.

Soviet relations with the so-called "People's Democracies" are based upon another set of fictions—i.e., the "national independence" and "sovereignty" of the satellites. Treaties of military alliance were signed with Czechoslovakia (December 12, 1943), Yugoslavia (April 12, 1945, denounced by Moscow September 28, 1949) Poland (April 21, 1945), Hungary (February 18, 1948), and with other allies at other times. With minor variations, these instruments provide, as in Article 2 of the Treaty with Bulgaria of March 18, 1948, that:

> In the event that one of the High Contracting Parties shall become involved in military operations against Germany, attempting to revive its aggressive policy, or with any other State whatsoever which may directly or in any other manner whatsoever join Germany in its policy of aggression, then the other High Contracting Party will give promptly to the Contracting Party involved in military operations all military and other assistance with all the means at its disposal.

The Third or Communist International of 1919, once dubbed the "General Staff of the World Revolution," was dissolved on May 22, 1943. But on October 5, 1947, the Communist Information Bureau, or Cominform, was established with headquarters in Belgrade (later in Bucharest), as a co-ordinating agency of the Communist Parties of nine European countries, including Italy and France, and as a propaganda weapon of Soviet foreign policy in its struggle "against American imperialism, its English and French Allies, and the right-wing Socialists." The Communist "answer" to the Marshall Plan was the creation in January 1949, of the Council of Mutual Economic Aid (Comecon), to co-ordinate economic plans of the satellites, promote trade among them, and pursue common policies of economic "defense" (or "aggression") against the West.[7]

Beneath such garments, the naked realities of power display a wholly different shape and structure, remarkably symmetrical in all the satellite States. Ministries of Foreign Affairs, Foreign Trade, and Interior or State Security are almost invariably held by Communists. Deputy Ministers in all Ministries are usually agents of the Minister of State Security and members of the Political Police, each with a local staff of secret informers and supervisors. The Soviet Ministry of State Security, or M.V.D., in turn maintains in the corresponding satellite Ministries liaison agents who engage in political-intelligence work and transmit orders from the Politburo. Effective Communist control of policy-making is thus assured, since each local legislature (as in the U.S.S.R.) is in practice the agent of the executive, not its equal as in the U.S.A., nor its principal as in parliamentary regimes. While each government exchanges diplomats with Moscow and with other satellites, each Party does likewise. Party representatives are often unknown to the diplomats, but enjoy superior authority in all important decisions. The Parties are rigidly controlled from the Kremlin through the Cominform and through more informal devices of discipline.[8] Soviet economic and military missions, commercial agreements, joint trading-companies, and occasional appointments of Soviet leaders to key posts in other capitals (e.g., Marshal Konstantin Rokossovsky as Polish Minister of De-

[7] See C. Alexandrowicz, "Comecon," in *World Affairs* (London: January, 1950), pp. 35–47.

[8] For obvious reasons most of these arrangements are nowhere acknowledged or admitted, and therefore never described, by Communists. Anti-Communist accounts of them are often incomplete, distorted, or otherwise unreliable. But see Bedrich Bruegel: "Methods of Soviet Domination in Satellite States," *International Affairs* (London: January 1951), pp. 32–7, and the best over-all survey of the whole area—Hugh Seton-Watson: *The East European Revolution* (London: Methuen; 1950). Amid the voluminous and highly controversial literature dealing with the Communist conquest of China, two of the more useful studies are Robert Payne: *Mao Tse-Tung, Ruler of Red China* (Henry Schuman; 1950) and Benjamin Schwartz: *Chinese Communism and the Rise of Mao* (Cambridge, Massachusetts: Harvard University Press; 1951).

fense in 1950) complete this novel design for the effective subordination of "allies" to the will of Mother Russia.

The transition in each satellite to this pattern of power involved purges and treason trials along with doctrinal modifications of the original theory of "People's Democracy" in the direction of more orthodox (i.e., Russian) Leninism. The major necessary changes were effected in Rumania and Bulgaria in 1945–6 and in Hungary and Poland in 1947–8. As for Czechoslovakia, the eleven non-Communist Ministers in the cabinet resigned, February 20, 1948, in protest against political misuse of the police force by Communist Vaclaw Nosek, Minister of the Interior. Through Communist Premier Klement Gottwald and local "action committees," the C.P., seeing in these and related developments evidence of an "American conspiracy" and "reactionary plots" for an anti-Communist putsch, compelled President Beneš to appoint "reliable" successors in a new Cabinet, completely controlled by "loyal" Communists. Jan Masaryk died on March 10, allegedly by suicide, and was succeeded as Foreign Minister by Communist Vladimir Clementis. Under a new constitution a single slate of Communist-approved candidates for parliament was "elected" by 89.3 per cent of the votes cast. Beneš resigned on June 7 (he died on September 3) and was replaced in the Presidency by Gottwald, with Anton Zapotocky as new Premier, amid purges of dissidents and flights of political fugitives abroad. Two years later Clementis himself was moved to confess political error and was demoted from his office.[9]

If the Czechoslovak case illustrates the axiom that the Communist rulers of one third of the world are addicted, at least under the conditions of cold war, to total intolerance of non-Communists in public posts (save when they blindly

[9] A bibliography of these developments cannot here be attempted. But see the articles, with references, on the satellite countries in the *New International Year Book* (Funk & Wagnalls) for the years 1945–52; Seton-Watson, ibid.; and H. Gordon Skilling, "People's Democracy, The Proletarian Dictatorship and the Czechoslovak Path to Socialism," *The American Slavic and East European Review* (April 1951).

follow Communist leadership), the Yugoslav instance demonstrates that Communists are themselves subject to excommunication if they question the Kremlin's will or seek to assert the slightest degree of independence. On June 28, 1948, the Cominform expelled from the *sanctum sanctorum* the Yugoslav Communist Party, accusing its leadership of ideological errors, "pursuing an unfriendly policy towards the Soviet Union," and subjecting Soviet agents and citizens in Yugoslavia to police surveillance. In the customary billingsgate of the comrades, the Belgrade brethren were accused of "slanderous propaganda," "counterrevolutionary Trotskyism," "exaggerated ambition, megalomania, and conceit," "adventurism," "opportunism," "anti-Marxism," "Bonapartism," "idolatry," and love for "capitalists" and "kulaks." Belgrade replied with accusations of "tyranny," "aggressive nationalism," "provocative acts," "Fascism," "imperialism," and other semantic labels to damn the sinners who accused the Yugoslav comrades of sin.

Moscow and its puppets called for a revolution to overthrow Tito and, when none materialized, subjected Yugoslavia to an economic boycott and threats of "liberation." Original accusations that Tito had granted military and air bases to the "Anglo-American imperialists" had apparently no foundation in fact, but—as so often happens in such situations—the chimera that was dreaded ultimately became a reality to be feared as the menaced regime sought aid from the West. The concrete causes and propagandistic complexities of this quarrel need not concern us.[1] It is enough to notice that Marshal Tito and his comrades were staunch Marxists and Leninists, though obviously no longer Stalinists. They were not heretics but schismatics. Their unforgivable crime was to persist in domestic and foreign policies that had been

[1] See Hamilton Fish Armstrong: *Tito and Goliath* (Macmillan; 1951); Stephen Clissold: *Whirlwind—Marshal Tito's Rise to Power* (Philosophical Library; 1950); Josef Korbel: *Tito's Communism* (University of Denver Press; 1951); Leigh White: *Balkan Cæsar* (Scribner; 1951); and *Yugoslavia and Peace: A Study of Cominform Accusations,* published by the National Peace Council (London: 1951) as a Report of the N.P.C. Delegation to Yugoslavia, September 1950.

vetoed by the men of Moscow. The latter falsely assumed that on the Adriatic, as along the Danube, the Vistula, and the Oder, the will of the Politburo could be enforced as law regardless of local conditions and yearnings for "self-determination" on the peripheries of the Communist empire.

The rulers of the Marxist World-State here became the victims of the Mongol-Muscovite-Romanov tradition they had unwittingly inherited. Absolute obedience to a central absolutism makes for unity and strength, providing the area of command is narrowly defined and the will of rulers can be enforced by invincible power immediately applied against dissidents. The Great Khans for a time observed the first condition and enjoyed the second. The contemporary men of the Kremlin know nothing of the first, for they can envisage obedience only in terms of total subjection. They dare not put the second to a test, despite the overwhelming military force at their disposal in Europe, for such a step might involve them in the catastrophe of total war with America. They know, moreover, from the age-old history of Muscovy, that the people they rule fight like heroes when Holy Russia is attacked by alien invaders, but disintegrate in apathy when summoned by their government to sacrifice blood and treasure in adventures inaugurated by their masters. In Yugoslavia, Greece, Iran, Korea, and elsewhere, the Kremlin leaders are therefore obliged to equivocate, retreat, bargain, and wait with remorseless patience—but never to "compromise," since their experience contains no equivalents of this Western concept.

What answer then can be given to the question of the capacity of modern Muscovy to conquer and rule all the earth? On the affirmative side are the elements of great faith, self-sacrifice to the point of masochism, political ingenuity, military imagination, and a talent for fulfilling the wants of simple men. Despite current American impressions to the contrary, the *Pax Sovietica* does not maintain itself only by terror or by invincibility in arms within the area of its control.

No World-State can endure longer than a few wasted years by such means alone. Neither does the Marxist imperium persist merely by giving "peace" to its subject peoples. It serves the needs of men and women, from the Oder to the China Sea, by giving them a "Socialist" vision of a more abundant life and making them participants in its projected realization—free, in principle if not always in practice, of the fetters of racial and national prejudices; free of the private exploitation of men by men for personal profit; free (relatively) of private graft and public corruption; free of feudalism, illiteracy, and old superstitions; and free, by way of communal economic and social planning, of the loneliness of that paralyzing isolation and fatalism that often spring from the corroding conviction that no one can do anything effective to serve society or to make himself a creative participant in the common tasks of mankind.

These gains in Man's striving for unity, brotherhood, and justice have been bought at a cost that is appalling and abominable to the peoples of the Atlantic communities. The price is tyranny, regimentation, ruthlessness, deception, persecution, exploitation of the powerless by the powerful, and recurrent denials of human dignity and autonomy in a hundred ways—not for the sake of personal riches but for public power and for the vindication of the faith as its high priests and dogmatists conceive its imperatives.

This cost is intolerable to Western peoples, most of whom would fight to the death rather than submit to the monster, so long as they enjoy some semblance of individual freedom in thinking, talking, writing, voting, working, and loving as they please. The cost has no meaning to most Asiatic, Middle Eastern, and African peoples, few of whom have ever known these pleasures, and most of whom, for time out of mind, have never experienced anything other than exploitation, regimentation, and tyranny. Their choice between "democracy" and "totalitarianism" is simple. They know nothing of the former save as an empty and alien word. The latter has for centuries been the essence of their daily lives, in the forms of native feudalism, imposed colonialism, and the white man's contempt for the "inferior" races.

The market for Marxist Messianism of the Muscovite variety is hereby delimited. Its limits, happily, are not worldwide. They nevertheless encompass, potentially, such a proportion of mankind as to bring justifiable alarm to the carriers of the "white man's burden," who have found no viable means thus far to undo the consequences of past follies when invincible power was theirs to command. In a new time, when all peoples of darker pigmentation are rebelling against the past and acquiring the power to make their revolt effective, Britons gracefully retreat, Dutchmen reluctantly withdraw before superior force, Frenchmen fight a losing battle to maintain the status quo, and Americans grapple fearfully with issues they scarcely comprehend. The gospel of the "Third Rome" will remain nonsensical and abhorrent to the peoples of Western Europe and the Americas. The same gospel, with its promise (and partial performance) of racial equality, "social justice," fervent faith, and factories, schools, hospitals, and circuses, will continue to exercise an enormous fascination over the darker brethren of the earth, whom the vicissitudes of history have long subjected to a destiny they resent.

Barring some miraculous reorientation of Western attitudes and policies, the "message" of Red Moscow will continue to win converts among the underprivileged. The same "message" will continue to have no appeal whatever to the vast majority of peoples in the North Atlantic communities. Those who rule the Scarlet Empire in the name of this message are unlikely to face breakdown or rebellion among those who have accepted it as a cult and as a way to a better life, despite its concomitants of frustration, bitterness, subjugation, and death in the land of its origin.[2] The fragility

[2] See *Tensions within the Soviet Union* (82nd Congress, first session, Senate Document #41), prepared at the request of Senator Alexander Wiley by the Legislative Reference Service of the Library of Congress (Washington, D.C.: U.S. Government Printing Office; 1951), with useful references to recent literature on this theme.

and possible sources of disintegration of Soviet monolithism will persist, and may well produce new schisms and conflicts. But any early collapse of the system from within is wholly improbable. In the absence of the successful military conquest of Western Europe and the Americas by the armies of the Kremlin (and nothing is less likely) the Marxist World-State will, by the very nature of its gospel, be limited to "backward" peoples and "undeveloped" areas. This barbarian kingdom may yet become more extensive than anyone now imagines. But it can never become global unless the Western peoples, demented by fear, prefer suicide to survival.

3. AMERICAN CENTURY

> In the field of national policy, the fundamental trouble with America has been, and is, that whereas their nation became in the 20th Century the most powerful and the most vital nation in the world, nevertheless Americans were unable to accommodate themselves spiritually and practically to that fact. Hence they have failed to play their part as a world power—a failure which has had disastrous consequences for themselves and for all mankind. And the cure is this: to accept whole-heartedly our duty and our opportunity as the most powerful and vital nation in the world and in consequence to exert upon the world the full impact of our influence, for such purposes as we see fit and by such means as we see fit.
>
> —HENRY R. LUCE, 1941.[3]

[3] This remarkable essay, *The American Century*, by Henry R. Luce, first published in *Life* in February 1941, was subsequently issued in book form (Farrar & Rinehart; 1941), with comments by Dorothy Thompson, John Chamberlain, Quincy Howe, Robert G. Spivack, and Robert E. Sherwood. The passage quoted appeared on pp. 22–3 of the book. While the author and all of the commentators, in one fashion or another, anticipated the future global role of the United States, none of them exhibited any awareness of the possibility that the destiny of the century might in part be shaped by Russians as well as by Americans.

FROM TIME TO TIME in the course of human events a single community—usually hitherto obscure, isolated from the main currents of civilization, and possessed of no predictable talents for world mastery—has come to dominate most of mankind and to build thereby some facsimile of world government. Such was the destiny of Persia in the sixth century B.C., of Macedonia in the fourth century B.C., of Rome later, and subsequently of Islam, the Mongols, and the Muscovites. In our own century such a community has once more emerged. For all of its Continental majesty, it embraces only one tenth of the land surface of the planet. Its people number only one sixteenth of the world's population. But they possess almost one half of all the manufacturing capacity of the globe. They have achieved material riches beyond the dreams of Midas. They have evolved an economy so fabulously productive that its continued function at full capacity (despite the paralysis of the Great Depression) has enabled and indeed required them since 1914 to give away goods abroad, in the name of charity, lend-lease, "loans," investments, and reconstruction, to the value of more than one hundred billion dollars.

Such a supercolossus of technology and productivity might have been expected long since to "rule the world." That America, until lately, has essayed no such role is attributable to the peculiar geographical and historical conditions under which its people, all unwittingly, arrived at their present position of potential global predominance. Those who believe that wine-drinking is wicked seldom become connoisseurs of rare vintages. Those who regard power as evil seldom acquire skill in its use. They lack knowledge of its sources and nature, its possibilities and limitations, its abuses, its pathology, and its decay. The American tradition, derived from the epoch of the Enlightenment and the Age of Reason, holds domestic political power to be suspect as the enemy of private enterprise and the matrix of tyranny, and condemns international *Realpolitik* as a game of trickery and violence to which only benighted foreigners are addicted.

Such attitudes, and the experiences of the lost past which have fostered them, leave Americans ill equipped to discharge effectively, or even to perceive clearly, the puzzling responsibilities of global power which have so recently been thrust upon them.

During the long armistice between World Wars, and again since 1945, the observable consequences of these defects of preparedness have been confusion and frustration of national purposes in world affairs—sometimes of such proportions as to suggest that no affirmative purposes were capable of formulation beyond the level of semantic devices promoting reassurance and a conviction of tribal virtue. Old stereotypes furnish little guidance in grappling with new problems. The three "sacred principles" of American foreign policy were, in old days, Isolationism, the Monroe Doctrine, and the Open Door. The first, in effect, asserted that Americans should do business in Europe but not play power politics in Europe. The second declared that Europeans might do business in the Americas but must not play power politics in the American hemisphere. The third enjoined all nations to do business in Asia but to renounce power politics in the Orient. All have long since become obsolete.

A generation ago most Americans fancied that they could have "peace" and "plenty"—i.e., a minimum of political infringement upon their private lives from domestic or alien sources, and a maximum of prosperity under free-enterprise capitalism—by "avoiding foreign entanglements" and professing indifference to power struggles in the outer world. With the wild aberration often displayed by those unskilled in adapting old ways to new challenges, most Americans in the 1950's fancy that they can have peace and plenty by refashioning all the world according to their heart's desire. The common emotional denominator of the earlier attitude was the negative gospel of Isolationism. The denominator of the current attitude is the negative gospel of anti-Communism.

The Leviathan that once sought safety by fleeing from any responsibility for shaping the world society now seeks safety by reaching out for a monopoly of responsibility. Isolationism failed because it assumed that America was impotent to influence men and events abroad. It thereby helped to engender forms of power in other communities whose rulers refused to leave America alone. Anti-Communism seems likely to fail no less completely, to the degree to which it assumes that America is omnipotent to influence men and events abroad and to the extent to which American methods of fighting the Red Menace, particularly among "backward" peoples, frequently manufacture Communists more rapidly than agents of the Kremlin could ever hope to do.

This recurrent experience of failure stems in part from a national incapacity to assess correctly American power in the world arena and to formulate attainable objectives to be striven for through the wise use of that power. As for the larger picture, the hypothesis may be ventured that the American dilemma of our time, in both its internal and external manifestations, springs essentially from the reluctance of the business elite to adapt itself to the inescapable conditions of success, and in the end of survival, under the circumstances of the twentieth century. Ever since Appomattox, at least, the rulers of America have for the most part been businessmen—sharing power, when politically necessary, with organized farmers, organized labor, and occasionally other groups. Business, quite understandably, has by and large assumed that its interests could best be furthered by preserving a free market for private enterprise in America, with governmental functions kept to a minimum, and by relying upon government abroad only for the purposes of reducing foreign competition in the domestic markets through tariffs, promoting American exports, and protecting American investments.

This assumption was pragmatically sound under the conditions of the late nineteenth and early twentieth centuries. It ceased to be operationally effective as soon as the instabilities and maladjustments of the national economy produced recurrent paralysis, stagnation, and mass unemployment, while simultaneously the instabilities and maladjustments of the international community produced World Wars in which America was reluctantly involved. The former development generated politically effective demands for governmental intervention to restore and maintain full employment and full production. The latter development generated military imperatives calling for public regimentation of business enterprise for the sake of total victory in total war. Most businessmen resented and resisted the New Deal (without being politically able, however, to thwart its major purposes) despite the revival of business opportunities which it promoted. Most businessmen, with some dissenters among them, welcomed war in 1917 and 1941. Federal spending to meet the needs of war meant an assured market and handsome profits for most major corporations, with workers and farmers sharing copiously in the new prosperity. Despite the irritations of "bureaucracy" and "red tape," selling to public purchasing-agencies is easier and often more lucrative than selling to private customers in the competition of the marketplace.

Only those who foolishly profess to the wisdom of Solomon will undertake with any assurance to tell American businessmen what they should have done other than what they did. It is at least arguable, however, that intelligent devotion to the free-enterprise system would have dictated approbation of the New Deal devices to save capitalism, along with opposition to involvement in foreign wars, regardless of their probable outcome, since modern war and the preservation of a free-market economy are incompatible. What most members of the American business-community in fact did was to oppose, tooth and nail and almost always in vain, the programs and policies of the New Deal and Fair Deal—and to welcome the advent of a war economy.

Capitalism can prosper and endure only through the avoidance of disastrous crises. The goal is attainable only through wise and timely governmental intervention in the economy to maintain stability and to promote the expansion of markets. War can be avoided, in the long run, only by replacing anarchy with order in the Great Society. With few exceptions, American businessmen have opposed public policies of social security and economic stabilization and have failed to support policies offering any reasonable hope of a viable world order. The businessmen's formula for prosperity in both postwar epochs was to sponsor a return to *laissez faire*. The current businessmen's formula for peace is to make America militarily omnipotent all over the planet. Neither of these objectives deserves to be regarded as even remotely possible of attainment. Each, moreover, is the negation of the other. Further failure and frustration would thus seem to be probable.

Meanwhile, the American commonwealth muddles and drifts in the direction of total militarism and a garrison State, amid facile rationalizations of "saving civilization from Communism"—an enterprise in which Hitler, Mussolini, and Hirohito might have succeeded a decade ago had Americans been sensible enough, by their later standards of judgment, to have fought World War II on the "right" side instead of the "wrong" side. These developments not only involve a steady erosion of civil liberties and democratic processes, but make the "free enterprise" system increasingly dependent upon public spending for armaments and foreign aid as a means of maintaining full employment and production. The short-run effects of these aberrations are highly advantageous to business, and to labor and agriculture as well. The long-run effects, should the process go on indefinitely, appear well calculated to liquidate most of the values and practices of competitive capitalism and representative democracy.

The contemporary spectacle of American politics reflects these attitudes and preferences, along with the contradictions and paradoxes they entail. The surface pattern of partisan rivalry and bipartisan collaboration is familiar enough. Herblock in *The Washington Post* portrayed it accurately in December 1947 in a cartoon entitled "Preview of 1948"—and, we may add, of 1952. Here the Democratic Donkey and the Republican Elephant, garbed as small boys, scribbled madly on placards, with the former writing "I'm more anti-Communist than everybody in the whole world put together, that's what!" while the latter wrote: "I'm a hundred trillion times more anti-Communist than anybody! So there! Too!"

The Democratic "ins" retained the support of many farmers, most workers, and a segment of big and small business, by sponsoring colossal public spending both at home and abroad. The Republican "outs," representing most of the business community, were politically emasculated by their determination to oppose "welfare" spending at home while championing Cold War spending abroad and denouncing the Administration for being insufficiently anti-Communist and insufficiently ardent in fighting Red Sin all over the world. An electorate by now fully conditioned to look to Washington for loaves and fishes could reasonably be expected to prefer, indefinitely, those who favor huge expenditures both at home and abroad over those who favor spending abroad but not at home. The failure of the national leadership of the Republican Party is a mirror of the inability, thus far, of the American business-community to accept the realities and requirements of our times and to further, effectively, its own interests and purposes. Rational solicitude for the salvation of American capitalism would have dictated full acceptance of the "Welfare State," and energetic efforts to end the Cold War.

Since any such reorientation of attitudes would appear to be all but inconceivable in the 1950's and beyond, it is a fair conclusion that America must continue for years to come to have its public policy, economic structure, and mass attitudes determined less by an affirmative sense of national destiny than by a hypnotic fixation on the Politburo in the Kremlin. Since the men of Moscow have no desire to perpetuate American capitalism and democracy, they may be expected to act in such a fashion as to encourage Americans to destroy their own heritage. Yet the ultimate alternative, as must be obvious even in darkest Muscovy, cannot be an American Socialism or an American Communism but only an American

Fascism, in which Big Business and Big Government merge for the more effective pursuit of profit and power through "total diplomacy" and total war. The extent to which this process is a concomitant of something resembling a national nervous breakdown can best be examined after we glance at the imposing outer structure of global power built up by Americans in the middle years of the twentieth century.[4]

4. THE SHAPE OF ATLANTIS

> When a nation, at any given period of history, bears the responsibility for the military security and the economic stability of a geographical zone, that nation is in fact—whether it wants it or not—the head of an empire. From then on it does not serve any purpose, moral or otherwise, to deny the facts and pretend that business is as usual. Because then the geographical zone, lacking a center of attraction and gravity, will start to disintegrate. The problem of how to manage an empire, given the condition of the time and the political stature of the various states, must solemnly be faced, not minimized. Ancient Rome solved it in its way, and later Victorian Great Britain in another way. The American Republic has to have the creative imagination to adapt the realities of imperial responsibility to a group of democracies.
>
> —J. J. SERVAN SCHREIBER.[5]

[4] Apart from other references following, the matters dealt with in this and the subsequent sections of the present chapter are in some measure illumined by Henry Steele Commager: *The American Mind* (New Haven, Connecticut: Yale University Press; 1950); James McGregor Burns: *Congress on Trial* (Harper; 1949); Seymour E. Harris (editor): *Saving American Capitalism* (Alfred A. Knopf; 1948); H. H. Wilson: *Congress—Corruption and Compromise* (Rinehart; 1951); Howard S. Ellis: *The Economics of Freedom* (Harper; 1950); Lucius D. Clay: *Decision in Germany* (Doubleday; 1950): William B. Wilcox: *Star of Empire—A Study of Britain as a World Power, 1485–1945* (Alfred A. Knopf; 1950); Robert A. Brady: *Crisis in Britain* (Berkeley: University of California Press; 1950); Keith Hutchison: *The Decline and Fall of British Capitalism* (Scribner; 1950); and F. A. Voight: *Pax Britannica* (London: Constable; 1949).

[5] This quotation is taken from an article in *The New York Herald Tribune* of October 1, 1950, in which the distinguished French commentator sought to suggest the inadequacy of the machinery of the North Atlantic alliance as developed up to that time.

THE SOMEWHAT equivocal comments offered in the preceding section may suggest some respects in which contemporary America, for all its prodigious achievements in production, welfare, and warfare, might be deemed to have fallen short of matching these accomplishments in the area of global politics. Since no world government is possible without responsible and prudent statesmanship, America's qualifications for the task of rearing any such structure may appear to some to be doubtful. It is nevertheless a fact that by 1952 the United States, in the face of Communist challenge and aggression, had assumed "leadership" of the "Free World" in organizing, subsidizing, and arming a far-flung imperium of enormous expanse. Its acknowledged purposes were to "contain" the enemy by building up "positions of strength," to oblige him to come to terms acceptable to America or, if need be, in the event of further contumacious defiance, to defeat and destroy him in World War III.

The bonds or tentacles of this empire, with highly variable degrees of tensile strength, stretched from the Far East and Australasia over all the vast Pacific, embraced both the American continents and all the Atlantic, and encompassed most of Western Europe, the Mediterranean, Turkey, the Arab States (more dubiously) and as much of Africa as could be regarded as securely held by its European colonial rulers. A reckoning in 1948 of American possessions, bases, trust territories, occupied lands, and protectorates (leaving out of account the European continent, Africa, China, and S.E. Asia) indicated that some ten million square miles of earth outside United States proper and some two hundred and fifty million people enjoyed the support, subsidy, or protection of Washington. Guarantees and subventions to Greece and Turkey in 1947, and the conclusion of the Atlantic Pact in 1949, followed by the creation and arming of the "North Atlantic Treaty Organization" (NATO), added another one million square miles and almost two hundred million people, all of which taken together, and added unto the land and populace of the U.S.A. itself, comprised a realm larger than the enemy's by a million square miles and inhabited by some six hundred million people, including all of the wealthiest and most productve national communities on the planet.

To term this bloc an "empire," however, is to misuse language and to confuse the nature of this phenomenon (which is quite confused enough), as well as to offend its founders, who are all eloquent in latter-day professions of "anti-imperialism." Only in the vaguest sense are the lands and peoples here grouped together ruled from Washington. The totality bears little resemblance to the Alexandrine, Roman, Saracen, Mongol, Ottoman, or Muscovite-Marxist realms. The relations among its parts suggest at times the Athenian Empire of ancient Hellas and at other times the Holy Roman Empire of medieval Europe, but even these comparisons are scarcely helpful. The new entity bears no resemblance to a federation, despite the pleas of those who would prefer to make it one, nor yet to an imperial commonwealth on the British model. What has here come into being, without any anterior plan or purpose applicable to the whole, is a system of interpenetrating and overlapping circles of colonies, bases, and protectorates; pensioners, mercenaries, and auxiliaries; dependencies, subject peoples, and allies. All are united uneasily by one leadership under a crazy-quilt of intergovernmental agreements, of which the chief instruments, regional in scope and highly variable in the commitments assumed, give to the entirety the appearance of a Great Coalition or Grand Alliance designed to afford its members mutual protection against a common foe.

This structure is protean and bewildering. In these characteristics lie great strengths and grave weaknesses, with policy-makers sometimes uncertain as to which is which. The system is so intricate that no one has yet undertaken to describe and analyze its details in any single volume, nor does the task seem promising. The salient features of its history, forms, and problems will here be outlined on the assumption that a lengthy exposition would not alter fundamentally such tentative conclusions as a brief survey may suggest.

The oldest element in the American "empire" is Latin America. The prediction of Alexander Hamilton that the United States would ultimately be able to organize both continents into "a great American system, superior to the control of all trans-Atlantic force or influence and able to dictate the terms of connection between the Old and the New Worlds" found later expression in the Monroe Doctrine of 1823, in frequently extravagant formulations of "Manifest Destiny," and in a long and bitter history of Latin resentment at "Yankee Imperialism." The latter phenomenon was associated with the Mexican War of 1846–8; the conquest of Cuba, Puerto Rico, and the Philippines from Spain in 1898;[6] the "taking" of Panama in 1903; Theodore Roosevelt's "police power" doctrine; "dollar diplomacy"; and repeated interventions of U.S. troops in Mexico, Haiti, the Dominican Republic, Nicaragua, and elsewhere during the Taft, Wilson, and Coolidge Administrations. Only with the advent of the Hoover-Stimson-Roosevelt-Hull-Welles "Good Neighbor Policy" did the dark image of a Latin America coerced and exploited by the "Colossus of the North" give way to the more pleasant conception of a hemisphere of equal sovereignties co-operating for the common good.

To separate shadow from substance in this vision would carry us far afield. Rhetoric has often been more impressive than reality in inter-American relations. Bolivar's dream of a Great Federation had no enduring results. "Pan-Americanism" came to birth feebly as a loose nonmilitary and nonpolitical method of settling disputes and promoting trade at the First Inter-American Conference in Washington in 1889–90. The ensuing "Pan-American Union" was neither a "union" in any usual sense of the word nor has it ever be-

[6] See the editorial in *The Nation* of May 5, 1898, "Yellow Journalism," commenting on the irresponsible clamoring of the Hearst press for war and conquest—reprinted in the issue of August 25, 1951, on the occasion of the death of William Randolph Hearst, whose papers had for half a century epitomized "jingoism," "imperialism," and xenophobia. See also Walter Millis: *The Martial Spirit*, 1931.

come "Pan-American," since Canada has no part in it. The complex arrangements established in subsequent accords seemed sometimes empty verbiage, sometimes formulæ of fruitful collaboration, and sometimes a façade for the domination of twenty Latin Republics by the United States. In World War I seven of the Republics, including Argentina, Chile, Colombia, and Mexico, remained neutral. But in World War II all followed Washington's leadership, including at the very end a reluctant Argentina. This progression towards common policies, lately come to full harvest save for the recalcitrance of the quasi-Fascist Peronistas of Buenos Aires, was the fruit of patient diplomacy and cajolery over a goodly span of years.

A bare calendar with a minimum of entries may serve to suggest the sequence. In 1936 an "Inter-American Conference for the Maintenance of Peace" gathered in Argentina and reached accord on a common policy of "neutrality" in the face of impending European and Asiatic hostilities. In 1938, with war around the corner, the Eighth International Conference of American States agreed in Lima on a "Declaration," vaguely pledging "Continental solidarity," "collaboration," and loose "consultation" in the face of real or imagined perils. In 1939, immediately after the Nazi invasion of Poland, the Foreign Ministers assembled in Panama and, inspired by Sumner Welles, undertook to set up, contrary to all accepted international law, a "neutrality zone" or "chastity belt" extending far over the high seas, within which they proposed to ban all belligerent acts by non-American nations. Berlin, London, and Paris all repudiated this fantasy, and the first naval battle of World War II was fought off Montevideo. In the summer of 1940 at Havana the Foreign Ministers, eying the possible consequences of the German conquest of France and the Netherlands, "continentalized" the Monroe Doctrine by banning the transfer of any territory from one non-American Power to another. In February and March, 1945, in Mexico City, the "Act of Chapultepec" reiterated the principles of nonintervention, consultation, and solidarity, and urged agreement on collective sanctions against aggression.

An Inter-American Defense Conference at Rio in August 1947 drew up the Inter-American Treaty of Reciprocal Assistance (the "Act of Petropolis"), whereby any attack on an American State "shall be considered as an attack against all the American States" (Art. 3)—but "no State shall be required to use armed force without its consent" (Art. 20). In April 1948 in Bogotá the Ninth International Conference of American States, interrupted by much local bloodshed, concocted a species of new "Anti-Comintern Pact" for collaboration in suppressing subversive activities, and established the "Organization of American States," described as a regional agency within the United Nations under Arts. 51 and 52 of the U.N. Charter. An OAS Charter of 112 articles provided for plenary Conferences, interim Meetings of Ministers of Foreign Affairs, an Advisory Defense Committee, a Council of the Organization with its seat in Washington, an Inter-American Economic and Social Council, an Inter-American Council of Jurists, an Inter-American Cultural Council, and the old Pan-American Union, now the Secretariat of the OAS.

On June 24, 1950, within twenty-four hours after the U.S. (and U.N.) decision, the OAS Council adopted a resolution declaring its firm adherence to the policy of resisting aggression in Korea. The Fourth Meeting of Consultation of Ministers of Foreign Affairs of American States resolved, in Washington in March 1951, on new solidarity to repel aggression, charged the Inter-American Defense Board with "military planning for the common defense," pledged joint efforts to combat "the subversive activities of international Communism," and evaded in mellifluous words the issue of whether Latin-American producers of raw materials needed by the United States and Western Europe should or should not charge all the traffic would bear and should or should not be deemed entitled to as many dollars of U.S. aid as they could squeeze out of the donor in hard bargaining.

All of this may strike the reader as a kind of Wonderland, dreamed up only to reaffirm pleasant platitudes and afford employment to bureaucrats, with no relationship to any of the instruments of effective imperial power previously reviewed in these pages. Such an impression would be only partially correct. Many earnest and devoted men and women have long labored to promote Pan-American solidarity in terms meaningful to ordinary people. Their efforts on behalf of human dignity and welfare have not been fruitless, despite much circumambient pretense and hypocrisy.

The Pan-American system does not conform to any past pattern of empire-building, for there is in it no obvious force to command obedience from inferiors. Nor does it approximate, even remotely, the vision of federalists, since there is no common citizenship, no parliament, no laws, no cabinet, no courts, and no army—only a ceaseless reiteration of the sacred sovereignty of the member States. Nor is this merely an "alliance." The labyrinthian machinery of the OAS testifies to the self-restraint of Washington and to the possibilities of eliciting a large measure of assent through eloquent equivocation and interminable consultations where commands would evoke only resentment. Power is often most effective when exercised by indirection and compromise. "It is always interesting," comments the London *Economist* (April 14, 1951), "to watch the United States, so fervent a champion of rigid moral principles in other international gatherings, carefully picking its way among the dubious characters who appear at Pan-American meetings and emerging triumphant at the end with compromises of the kind which are traditionally supposed to delight only cynical European diplomats."

The U.S.A. has here evolved a design for power in dealing with subordinate "allies" which has numerous merits. The special circumstances of its efficacy may not admit of its successful long-run extension to other areas of American influence. Latin-American communities are essentially "colonial" in the sense that exported raw materials are exchanged for imported manufactures and capital in societies where, for the most part save in post-revolutionary Mexico (and some observers would question the exception), illiterate and impoverished masses are ruled by an elite of feudal landowners and wealthy entrepreneurs. Washington has made peace with these rulers by joining them, bribing them, and arming them rather than by fighting them. Such a course involves hazards. If linked with efforts to improve mass welfare, it alienates the elites of property and money whose privileges depend (or so they suppose) on keeping the multitudes ignorant, poor, and obedient. If coupled with opposition to change in the distribution of wealth and power, it risks ultimate danger of fostering revolutionary movements whose leadership will assuredly be anti-Yankee and possibly pro-Communist. Yet the short-run advantages of the course embarked upon are plain enough, and in our age we tend to proceed on the assumption that in the long run, as Lord Keynes once observed, we shall all be dead.[7]

What is striking, albeit infrequently recognized, is that these slowly emerging patterns of relationships between a Great Power and lesser sovereignties have been lately extended (with ultimate results still unpredictable) to America's relationships with other sovereignties in Europe and Asia. The extension touches both the social sympathies of America's proconsuls abroad and the formulæ embodied in treaties among governments. To regard the entire Atlantic and Pacific system of "security" as a mere projection of the Pan-American system would be an exaggeration. Yet the Pan-American prescription has clearly exercised a dominant influence on Washington policy-makers in dealing with

[7] A suggestive brief survey of these developments is to be found in Arthur P. Whitaker, "Development of American Regionalism," *International Conciliation Pamphlets* (No. 469, March 1951), Carnegie Endowment for International Peace, New York. For current developments see *Annals of the O.A.S.*, published quarterly since 1949 by the Department of International Law and Organization, Pan-American Union, Washington, D.C.

transoceanic allies. In December 1947, Senator Arthur Vandenburg of Michigan piloted the Rio Treaty or "Act of Petropolis" through the Senate, where it was approved, 65 to 1. Half a year later (June 11, 1948) he obtained Senate approval, 64 to 4, for the "Vandenburg Resolution" (Sen. Res. 239).

This directive to the President reaffirmed the hope of "international peace and security through the U.N." and urged "progressive development of regional and other collective arrangements for individual and collective self-defense . . . based on continuous and effective self-help and mutual aid," with the U.S. to be associated therewith "by constitutional process." It further proposed that America should "if necessary" seek "review" of the U.N. Charter and should meanwhile contribute "to the maintenance of peace by making clear its determination to exercise the right of individual or collective self-defense under Art. 51, should any armed attack occur affecting its national security." It also recommended "maximum efforts to obtain agreements to provide the United Nations with armed forces," plus "universal regulation and reduction of armaments under adequate and dependable guaranty against violation."

This solution of a problem of imperial power was less ingenious and majestic than that of Alexander of Macedon or Augustus Cæsar, but—for a time—was no less effective. By 1947–8 the North American republic, long dedicated to "isolation," "disarmament," and "peace," was already sufficiently alarmed by the words and deeds of its mortal enemies in the Scarlet Empire to seek safety in alliances, rearmament, and preparations for war. The semantic problem here posed was complicated by the obvious impotence of the United Nations (to whose perpetuation all good Americans were devoted as a symbol of global peace and unity) in the face of the feud between leviathan and behemoth, whose imaginary solidarity was the original bedrock of the U.N. Here, as always, men must cling to sacred words and rituals long after they have lost their meaning. Reversion to older words with unhappy connotations is confusing. The invention of new words capable of stirring men to feeling and action is so difficult an accomplishment as to require genius. American politics lost its last living genius on April 12, 1945.

The Vandenburg resolution was but a minor masterpiece of artistry. Yet it served. It equated "reform" of the U.N., and American control of the U.N., with the original ideal of the Charter, rearmament with disarmament, alliances with security, and, on the Pan-American model, coalitions to promote U.S. purposes with self-help, self-defense, mutual aid, and peace. The immortal mythology of "collective security" implicit in this verbiage we shall explore in a later chapter. The precipitate of the attitudes that assumed tangible, even if nebulous, form in the Vandenburg resolution was the North Atlantic Treaty signed in Washington April 4, 1949, by the Foreign Ministers of the United States, Canada, the United Kingdom, France, Italy, the Benelux States, Iceland, Denmark, Norway, and Portugal.

This Pact had significant precursors outside the area of Pan-American and United Nations affairs. In Fulton, Missouri, on March 5, 1946, Winston Churchill had urged an Anglo-American alliance to save "Christian civilization." On March 12, 1947, President Truman asked Congress for four hundred million dollars to support Greece and Turkey in the name of "helping free people to maintain free institutions and their national integrity against aggressive movements that seek to impose upon them totalitarian regimes." On June 5, 1947, Secretary of State Marshall publicly urged American economic aid to Europe, quite outside of the U.N., in the program that was to become known as the "Marshall Plan." Western suspicions of the East were increased, and the already warm Cold War was exacerbated, by Soviet refusal to participate or to permit Czechoslovakia or Poland to participate—all of this constituting one of the major blunders of Muscovite diplomacy and a triumph of petty pique and ideological dogmatism over rational calculations of self-interest. Following the February coup of the Communists in

Prague, Britain, France, and the Benelux States signed in Brussels on March 17, 1948, a fifty-year alliance treaty for economic collaboration and mutual defense under Article 51 of the Charter. On the same day President Truman endorsed the Brussels alliance, denounced the U.S.S.R., and recommended universal military training in America.

The signatories to the North Atlantic Pact reaffirmed faith in the United Nations and in "democracy, individual liberty, and the rule of law" and agreed (Art. 5) that "an armed attack against one or more of them in Europe or North America shall be considered an attack against them all; and consequently . . . each of them, in the exercise of the right of individual or collective self-defense recognized in Article 51 of the Charter of the U.N., will assist the Party or Parties so attacked by taking forthwith, individually and in concert with the other Parties, such action as it deems necessary, including the use of armed force, to restore and maintain the security of the North Atlantic area." A Council was provided for. "Armed attack" was defined to include (Art. 6) not only invasion of territory but assault on occupation forces, islands, ships, or aircraft—doubtless at some risk, although little thought was given to the possibility of hotheaded local commanders precipitating major international crises. Elaborate verbiage was employed to create the impression, and to convince the participants, that the enterprise was somehow a consummation of the original purposes of the United Nations. These obligations were ostensibly envisaged as an American guarantee of Western European security. When asked by Senator Hickenlooper, April 27, 1949, whether the United States was expected to send "substantial numbers of troops," Secretary Acheson replied: "The answer to that question, Senator, is a clear and absolute 'No.'" In less than two years the answer became "Yes," with the change indicating either lack of candor or lack of foresight on the part of the Secretary of State.[8]

[8] *The Chicago Tribune* commented editorially, May 1, 1949: "The bipartisan method is to assert that each step toward war is a step toward peace;

To trace through the successive steps by which this commencement led to the creation of an elaborate military and civilian bureaucracy of global scope to organize a defense of freedom against tyranny would be tedious and, for present purposes, pointless. By the spring of 1951 the ponderous machinery of NATO—partly in Paris where General Dwight D. Eisenhower initially presided over the "Supreme Headquarters of the Allied Powers in Europe" at the Hotel Astoria near the Arc de Triomphe, partly in Fontainbleau, partly in London, and partly in Washington—was being streamlined into nine committees (instead of fifteen) under a North Atlantic Council as "the sole ministerial body." Eisenhower was pleading for European unity. Washington was pushing the rearmament of Germany, negotiating accords for bases in Franco's Spain, subsidizing and arming Tito's Yugoslavia, and pressing for the accession of Greece and Turkey to the Pact—a consummation achieved by the time of the NATO conference in Lisbon in February 1952. By September 1, 1950, the United States had signed a mutual defense pact with the Philippines and was signing others with Australia and New Zealand to protect them from the common enemy—and from Japan, which Washington proposed to restore to independence and to protect and rearm as a new ally under the Treaty of Peace signed in San Francisco on September 8, 1951.

---

that each step is the last step that will be required; that the costs and the risks will be negligible. . . . The bipartisan boys believe that the same confidence men can work the same game on the same victims, world without end. They may be right." See also the editorial in the same paper, January 20, 1951: "Confidence Game." On the legal question of the compatibility of the Pact and the Charter, see Robert E. Elder's letter in *The New York Times* of January 1, 1950; my own comment thereon in the issue of January 8, 1950; F. B. Schick: "The North Atlantic Treaty and the Problem of Peace," *The Juridical Review* (Edinburgh: April 1950), pp. 26–70, and the various articles and editorial comments on this issue in *The American Journal of International Law*. This legal problem, although interesting, is academic in the light of the fact that the signatories of the Pact, in the face of Soviet intransigence and provocation, abandoned the concept of a concert of all the Great Powers, which was of the essence of the original U.N., in favor of the concept of an armed coalition for defense against Russia, with the U.N. thereby reduced either to a minor agency for the waging of war, cold or hot, or to nothing at all.

Other projects were pending for a vast Pacific coalition, a Near and Middle Eastern defense pact, and a universalization of the Grand Alliance to include all states save the enemy states and the stubborn "neutrals"—Sweden, Switzerland, India, Burma, and Indonesia—which refuse to align themselves with either half of One World against the other. The cause of American or Atlantic security was thus compounded with the cause of combating Red aggression all over the planet—and in some minds with the cause of slaying the Crimson Dragon in his native lair, though the latter enterprise evoked no enthusiasm outside of America. The common denominator was "defense" against a common foe. In its name, as so often happens, the defenders deemed it needful to extend their power toward the ends of the earth. In so doing they strove to act upon the premise, customary in the politics of power, that the loss of any position might entail the loss of all positions and that the wresting of any vantage point from the enemy might weaken his ability to hold any other.

The new "American Empire," stripped of its semantic embellishments, was thus an old-fashioned alliance against a pretender to global hegemony. Its only unique features lay in its inflation to worldwide proportions; in the skepticism of some of its lesser participants regarding its efficacy and purport; in the high degree of secret bitterness and concealed misunderstanding among its members; and in the general conviction that the wealthiest and most powerful State in the coalition must subsidize, arm, and protect all the rest, meanwhile insisting upon the "sovereign equality" of each and the need of sacrifice by all. The question of whether this program is to be regarded as a rational response to a challenge or as a phenomenon of aberration is a legitimate question that will be tentatively explored in the section that follows. Assuming it for the moment to be a rational response, what can fairly be said as to its structure and prospects in the terms we have here adopted for evaluating the works of the builders of Universal States?

The Myth that unites the collaborators is substantially the

same as that in whose name the late Cæsars of the Triplice sought to conquer the world: anti-Communism. Its content is clear in its negative aspects. Its adherents wish to avoid being liquidated and having their countrymen subjected to Red despotism. Some of them also hope to be able, eventually, to drive back the Marxist-Mongol barbarians to their homeland and there, if necessary and possible, to destroy them. The affirmative content of the Myth is more nebulous. It is not the "American Way of Life," for this set of beliefs, values, and practices (however defined), far from being accepted by America's allies, is a frequent source of contempt, envy, hatred, and despair. It is not "capitalism" (however defined), for the voters of Britain have rejected "capitalism," as have many of the governments of Western Europe, South America, and the rimlands of Eastern Asia. It is not "freedom" and "democracy" in the Anglo-American sense, since these ideals are all but unknown in Portugal, Spain, Yugoslavia, and the Arab lands, have long since ceased to have any substance among Germans and Japanese, and are clearly meaningless among the dark masses of Asia and Africa. It is not abhorrence of "aggression" as such, for the members of the coalition have displayed calm complacency toward any and all aggressions, including their own, so long as the aggressors were not Communists of the Muscovite sect. It is not "equality" among men and the "dignity" of Man, for these aspirations are commonly honored more in the breach than in the observance among the white men of the Grant Alliance who deal with men of darker skins in North America, the Caribbean, Africa, Oceania, and Asia.

Further analysis will support the hypothesis that the Myth of the *Pax Americana* has no positive content. Its negativism rallies to its support all who feel threatened by Communism or by other movements challenging the established order: liberals, conservatives, and reactionaries; democrats, clericalists, and feudalists; capitalists, colonialists, and potentially everyone who enjoys freedom and anyone who enjoys privilege and power and assumes, not unreasonably, that he can secure American aid if only he can show that he is menaced by "Communism." This diffuse quality of the Myth is not, in the short run, a weakness. In a time of worldwide social unrest, amid vague stirrings and passionate demands for "reform," the Myth can rally to its service all who feel jeopardized or outraged by the abominations of those who seek change. Only in the Americas, the Iberian Peninsula, Italy, Darkest Africa, and portions of the Orient, to be sure, can pleas for social justice easily be discredited and relegated to limbo by equating them with "red plots." Yet the device has its uses everywhere for those whose interests are best expressed in the aphorism: "Come weal, come woe; my status is quo." Such people are few in numbers but are frequently the possessors of wealth and influence. They can be united by the Myth. In their union is strength—albeit diluted by their own dissensions and by misguided efforts in some quarters to "liberalize" the Myth.

Authority in this system of power is, principally, the authority of dollars, flowing from the vast cornucopia of American industry and agriculture. James Harrington averred that "bread-givers are always law-givers." An old saw says: Who pays the piper may call the tune. How long, and under what circumstances, those who are bought will stay bought is another question. The military invincibility of America, particularly since the Korean War, is not as impressive to its pensioners as most Americans wish it to be. America's victories are products of geographical safety and the assembly-line rather than of martial ardor and strategic genius. The legends of the phalanx, the legion, the Mongol horsemen, the Janissaries, the Prussian Guards, the British dreadnoughts, and the Russian artillery and tanks have no convincing American equivalent save the atomic bomb—no longer a monopoly since 1949 and in any event ill-calculated to afford reassurance to those asked to rely upon it for protection.

Reputation for prudent statesmanship, often another source of authority, almost vanished altogether in December of 1950, when Prime Minister Attlee felt obliged to hurry to Washington to dissuade President Truman from his suspected intention of dropping atomic bombs on China. Nor did the subsequent dismissal of MacArthur, though welcomed by all of America's allies, save Chiang Kai-shek, revive America's reputation for farsighted diplomacy. America rules its world by dispensing dollars and goods to those willing to be seduced or unable to do without American largesse. Such empires, in the past, have been fragile and ephemeral. This one may conceivably endure longer if the miracle of American productivity continues—and if its surplus output can be distributed abroad in ways that promote continuing unity of interests and purposes.

The Adaptability of the American imperium is in one sense nil and in another sense infinite. To the degree to which Americans, with little experience in ruling an empire, expect all foreigners to learn English, worship wealth, and embrace Coca-Cola, cocktails, and modern plumbing, their talents for building enduring relationships of trust and understanding are negligible. To the degree to which they gladly accept into the camp of their allies all applicants, so long as they are anti-Muscovite, they are far more adept and flexible than their foes. The Kremlin tolerates no one who deviates from Stalinist orthodoxy. America generously offers the "glad hand," always full of dollars, to anyone and everyone who is anti-Stalinist: Fascists, Communists, and democrats; monarchists, republicans, and aristocrats; rich men, poor men, beggar-men, and thieves. This open-minded, tolerant, and democratic camaraderie in a common cause makes for a genuine universalism, mitigated only by the disposition of American policy-makers to act sometimes upon the assumption that those who accept any American favors should adopt all American policies. Under the pressure of necessity, Americans learned much between 1940 and 1950 of the arts of compromise and accommodation to alien ways. The final verdict on their learning is yet to be rendered. It is likely to depend upon other factors in the equation.

The Elite in the American world-State is, in global terms,

a strange congeries of anomalies: Latin-American dictators, British Socialists, Japanese industrialists, Arab chieftains, French Radicals, German carteleers, Italian clericalists, Yugoslav Communists, Spanish Falangists, and so on. But these are all allies, auxiliaries, or mercenaries. What manner of native leadership has America evolved for the accomplishment of its appointed task? It may be asserted, not unreasonably, that the rulership of America and of America's world has become the business, primarily, of businessmen, bankers, and bureaucrats (recruited partly from the ranks of industrialists and partly from the middle-class intelligentsia), supplemented in ever-increasing measure by career men in the arts of war. The agency of influence abroad is not, as with the enemy, a Party, a brotherhood of converts, or an amorphous mass of "fellow travelers," but the diplomatic, military, or economic "mission." American missions consist of well-paid officials who often live with their families in privileged quarters, drive their own cars, buy cigarettes at eight cents a pack and whisky at $1.50 a fifth in their PX's, and have little contact with the circumambient populace, which lives on a far lower level of material comfort and pays five or ten times as much for the same necessities of life. Such privileges are necessary, as they were in the Roman, Mongol, and Ottoman empires, to induce citizens who would prefer to live at home to assume posts in the provinces. They do not elicit affection among the provincials. But they often evoke admiration, respect, and obedience, which are more significant in the arts of power.

Is the new "American Empire" a success? Is it likely to endure, to fall apart, or to evolve into a government of all mankind? The future answers to these currently unanswerable questions would seem to depend less upon symbols, prestige, flexibility, and leaderhip than upon the ultimate purposes for which America's formidable power is to be used. A truly Universal State is here theoretically possible. Hans Morgenthau wisely comments: "The combination of the modern technologies of transportation, communication, and warfare, marshaled by the government of one super-power against the rest of the world, has for the first time in history made the conquest of the world possible. And what is more important still, it has made it possible for such a government, once it has conquered the world, to keep it conquered."[9] Yet Henry Adams in 1909 despaired of the "one-sided flabbiness of America, the want of self-respect, of education, of purpose; the intellectual feebleness and the material greed."[1] Brooks Adams half a century ago was no more hopeful. And in 1900 the Democratic platform declared, prematurely: "We assert that no nation can long endure half republic and half empire, and we warn the American people that imperialism abroad will lead quickly and inevitably to despotism at home."

The long experience of ages past gives appreciable weight to such doleful prognoses. Yet if we may assume for immediate purposes that America will continue to be ruled by reasonable men and not by madmen, then the issue might be said to depend upon which of three possible courses America is to pursue in dealing with all the vast problems of the great globe. One imaginable course is a reversion to "isolationism" in the face of successive frustrations abroad, accompanied by withdrawal from alien commitments and disinterest in the fate of mankind outside the American hemisphere. Such a solution would not be immediately disastrous. It might indeed be less so than some alternatives currently fashionable. But it would mean in the end—since no Power remains in Europe, Asia, or Africa to resist the Marxist behemoth of the Heartland—that the barbarians would infiltrate and flow into the vacuum thus left, with ultimate results for America unpredictable but undoubtedly hazardous.

Another and more probable course is the final unleashing by America, impatient of endless irritation and sacrifice, of a Holy War or Crusade to destroy the barbarian empire in a frenzy of heroic Messianism and establish by conquest an

[9] *In Defense of the National Interest* (Alfred A. Knopf; 1951), p. 59.

[1] Quoted in H. Stuart Hughes: *An Essay for Our Times* (Alfred A. Knopf; 1950), p. 162.

American world government. There is no present reason to believe that any such enterprise could succeed in its purpose. There are good grounds for supposing that its end result would be the destruction of European civilization, the fearful devastation of most of Eurasia, the reduction of the survivors to anarchy, and the demise of America into a war-wrecked police-state ruled by tyrant-demagogues, presiding above bloody altars and piles of rubble over a contest in arms admitting of no victory, no end, and no peace ever again in the lives of men. "A third struggle," wrote Winston Churchill in 1943, "will destroy all that is left of the culture, wealth, and civilization of mankind and reduce us to the level almost of wild beasts."

A third course—dull, unexciting, prosaic, but possibly more conducive to life—would be one of following the example of the Cæsars of ancient Rome, whose policy was neither one of withdrawal from the provinces in the face of outer threats, nor one of attempting to conquer, convert, or exterminate the barbarians, but quite simply one of defending the frontiers—by methods that proved effective in keeping the peace within the Empire for many centuries, and did not in the process wreck the civilization thus defended. Such a course, in military terms, required occasional extension of the frontiers to obviate dangers and occasional evacuation of outlying marches (e.g., Armenia, Mesopotamia, and southern Scotland by Hadrian, and Dacia by his successors) whose defense was too costly. It further required a nice adaptation of the needs of border warfare to the requirements of civilized living within the frontier. The Romans of old had aptitude for such a task. Whether the Americans of today can develop similar aptitudes remains to be seen. No other course seems likely to afford any reasonable promise of survival on any terms that civilized people would regard as tolerable. The question can best be left in the words of David L. Cohn:

> Technically competent, we are politically incompetent. "The object of war," says General MacArthur, "is victory." So it is—militarily. Its object, it seems to me, is peace. We have

won two wars in this generation and, twice losing the peace, now face a third world war. This is a measure, not only of our technical competence on the one hand and our political incompetence on the other, but also of our aptness for the short-term job and our ineptness for the long-term task; an endeavor at which Russia excels out of the reservoirs of her patience. . . .

Short-sighted, emotional, impatient, physically energetic but mentally lazy, possessors of a spectrum containing only the colors of black and white, devoted to "education" but wary of ideas and suspicious of "professors" in public life, corroded by our belief in the Easy Way and given to the pathetic illusion that complex problems will yield to a sovereign remedy, we swing, a capricious colossus, in a wide arc from pessimism to optimism, thereby bewildering our friends and enemies. . . .

Are we temperamentally fitted to pursue a policy of arming at home, arming our friends, aiding them economically, and fending off the Russians for years through the indeterminate future; the policy upon which we are embarked? This is a long-term policy and its successful application implies great patience on our part, willingness to stand to arms for years, the ability to deal skillfully with allies of many kinds and many minds, to pay a high price in men away from home, casualties, treasures. All this without any guarantee of how the policy will turn out. It is a common boast of ours that we can take it. But can we stand it? Is endurance coiled in our bowels? Would we not risk a world war with millions of casualties and the wreckage of our civilization rather than pay the high, if lesser, price of what may be loosely termed "containment" of our enemy; a price requiring us to restrain impetuosity on the leash of will? . . . Time alone will tell whether we can work the transformation.[2]

---

5. THE VOICE OF TERROR

Whenever in our time a war breaks out, there also breaks out, and especially among the most noble members of the people, a secret desire: they throw themselves with delight against the

[2] David L. Cohn: "The American Temperament," *The Atlantic Monthly* (September 1951), pp. 64–5.

new danger of death, because in the sacrifice for the fatherland they believe they have found at last the permission they have been seeking. The permission to evade their human purpose. War is for them a short-cut to suicide. It enables them to commit suicide with a good conscience.

—FRIEDRICH W. NIETZSCHE.

MANY ASPECTS of politics and opinion in the United States during the early years of the Cold War were puzzling to Europeans—and to some Americans. What meaning was to be given to thought-control, legislative inquisitions, and mass hysteria over "subversives"? Or to the nervous breakdown and suicide of a Secretary of Defense? Or to the elaborate confessions and accusations of ex-Communists, hailed as heroes by the press? Or to revelations that high officials and respected citizens had long been seditious conspirators or foreign spies? Or to widespread corruption in the public service? Such phenomena moved a few reflective observers to raise the question of whether the American reaction to the Russian challenge in the middle years of this century was a rational response to a problem or a possible evidence of mass insanity.

In favor of the more hopeful judgment is the circumstance that here, as in many past instances, an aspirant for global hegemony was countered and checked by his rivals and prospective victims through the familiar device of the organization and armament of a Grand Alliance by the most potent Power among them. The response was possibly obsolete, perhaps disastrous, and vitiated by new and more insistent versions of the ancient pretense that preparations for war were essential to preserve peace. Yet no one could imagine any politically practicable alternative. Henry A. Wallace's attempt to do so in the Progressive Party of 1948 (following his dismissal from the Cabinet in 1946 at the demand of James F. Byrnes) made him a prisoner of the Communists, a political failure, and finally a lonely outcast from all camps. President Truman's proposal to send Chief Justice Vinson to Moscow in October of the same year was promptly "vetoed" by Robert A. Lovett and George C. Marshall. The pattern of policy which emerged was, on the face of it, the sane reply of responsible men to intolerable provocation and incalculable peril. It appeared to be based on a correct perception of at least some aspects of reality. In its evident intent it was designed to create conventionally suitable means; i.e., alliances and arms, to attain a conventionally necessary end; i.e., the checkmating of a super-Power apparently bent on global dominion.

Whether the course embarked upon was operationally effective in results was a more difficult question. Up to 1952 the Russians had not unleashed their hosts against Western Europe or the Middle East, despite their obvious ability at any time to overrun both areas in a matter of weeks. This circumstance could be attributed to the "success" of the American policy of "deterring" them, first by way of threats of using the atomic bomb, and later by way of arming the menaced regions. On the other hand the same circumstance might be deemed an evidence of failure by those who may have hoped in dealing with the Russians to repeat the success of the Roosevelt Administration in dealing with the Japanese in 1941—when the prime question, as Henry L. Stimson put it, was "how we should maneuver them into the position of firing the first shot without allowing too much danger to ourselves." But if research and reflection should suggest, contrary to the oft-reiterated view of Winston Churchill, Leslie Groves, and others, that the Kremlin was not at all "deterred" or provoked by the atomic bomb, nor yet by European rearmament, but simply preferred to refrain (like the Mongols) from overrunning Western Europe by virtue of disinterest in such a course and apprehension over its possible effects on popular attitudes at home, then the problem of the pragmatic efficacy of the American program would become insoluble.

In support of the dismal hypothesis that the American course is primarily a phenomenon of psychopathology, the evidence that might be cited is too abundant for comfort.

This case has been presented in perhaps its starkest form by Dr. Alexander B. Mebane in the Summer 1950 issue of *American Perspective*, a worthy journal whose subsequent demise is possibly attributable to the reluctance of most Americans of our time to relish any perspective on their affairs. Since the issue is literally one of life or death, an extended quotation may be forgiven. Dr. Mebane begins by noting what is self-evident, but plainly unacceptable to most of his fellow citizens—namely, that an arms race in atomic weapons not only cannot achieve "defense" or "security," but is a perfect formula, particularly for America, for ever-increasing vulnerability and ultimate national extinction. He goes on:

The response of the United States to this situation is not a sane one. American foreign policy, in 1950, has departed so far from reality that it can be adequately described only in psychiatric terms. The type of psychosis involved, "delusional insanity," is that which results from inability of the personality to accept an existing situation of fact. Behavior is oriented with respect to a subjective world which differs from the unacceptable objective world. This results in actions which are out of adjustment to the real world.

Since what constitutes the "real" or "objective" world cannot in all cases be identified with certainty, it may be said that a certain degree of delusional insanity is universal and unavoidable. Clinicians concern themselves, however, only with cases in which the patient's subjective world is greatly out of harmony with the evidence of his senses. It is a case of this degree that is found in Washington today.

There are two lines along which delusional insanity can develop. (1) Toward "schizoid" conditions in which the personality shuts itself off from the world. The process is first noticeable in failure of appropriate emotional response, a "blunting of affect," and continues with progressive inattention to the environment. (2) Toward "paranoid" conditions in which the personality maintains touch with the world of actuality by "reinterpreting" it through an ever-more-comprehensive system of delusions ministering to the paranoid's self-esteem. The process begins with delusions of persecution and soon proceeds to delusions of grandeur (megalomania); the characteristic attitude is one of intense contempt and hatred for the rest of the world. The paranoid therefore becomes increasingly dangerous to others.

Dr. Mebane notes that "peace through strength" has always in the past meant war. The prevailing assumption that it is now the best means toward peace rests, he argues, upon the paranoid postulate of unmitigated Communist diabolism and the schizoid rationalization of Communist reasonableness which will *ex-hypothesi* cause American power to "deter" Communist aggression by making its risks too costly. The two assumptions are incompatible, since the enemy cannot at the same time be both a homicidal maniac and a human calculating machine. Dr. Mebane continues:

> But although the Paranoid Postulate implies the inevitability of atomic war, it supplies its own solution to this difficulty, for paranoia, whose keynote is *self-justification*, furnishes an outlook on life that is complete and self-sufficient. In the paranoid ethical system, the duty of fighting the enemy is an absolute one: to weigh the consequences would be dishonorable and cowardly. For the enemy, being implacable, will conquer the world unless we conquer him. And, since he is diabolical in nature, conquest of the world by the enemy is the very worst thing that could possibly happen to the human race. Therefore, if fighting the enemy means atomic war; if it means the destruction of most of the cities of the world; if it means the transformation of thousands of square miles into radioactive deserts; if it means man-made plagues; if it means the extinction of democratic government everywhere; if it means permanent radioactive pollution of the very oceans and of the air itself; *if it means the death of all living things*—all of these are *lesser evils.* In the paranoid ethics, what Russia might do to us if we failed to threaten her militarily must be considered to be *worse than the annihilation of the whole world.* This is the fundamental article of the paranoid faith—and it is a faith. It is a fanaticism.

On a lower level of abstraction, we may note that American policy-makers in the late 1940's and early 1950's, while possibly sane, were not necessarily wise. They had, for example, involved themselves in a series of enterprises designed to promote "freedom," strengthen "democracy," and enhance American power vis-à-vis Communist totalitarianism. Each was wholly plausible. But many of these steps seemed mathematically calculated to produce precisely the results sought to be avoided and to avoid exactly the results sought to be produced, as if high politics were an adventure in a nightmare or in the strange land described by Lewis Carroll in *Through the Looking-Glass*. The point is well put by Nathaniel Peffer:

> If one tries to survey the world today in a long perspective, there appears to be in progress a gigantic struggle, literally a struggle of giants, for planetary mastery. There is Russia, doing everything humanly possible to throw the world into the arms of America. There is America, doing everything humanly possible to throw the world into the arms of Russia. It is no doubt too early to predict the outcome, but the hypothesis may be ventured that since America, being inept in foreign politics for lack of experience—and only for that reason—seldom succeds in foreign politics, it will not succeed in this instance either, and that the world will be spared the embraces of Stalin, Molotov, *et al.* Yet that may be taking unwarranted comfort. It must be conceded that America is striving manfully to achieve its purpose. In subventioning Chiang Kai-shek and the ruling gang of his Chinese government, it strikes a mightier blow for the Russian suzerainty in Asia than ever has been struck by the Communists from Lenin and Trotsky to Stalin, Molotov and Zhdanov. In subventioning the equivalents in eastern Europe . . . it strikes a similar blow in that part of the world. Everywhere in the world we appear to be giving aid and comfort to those who, whatever their words may be when talking to Americans—how they have learned the lexicon of democracy!—desire only to return to the status of the past, meaning the preservation of their own privileges. We may not do so deliberately. We may not even do so consciously. Often we may do so in the immeasurable ignorance and innocence of European issues, thoughts, feelings, premises, attitudes.

which unfortunately, though naturally, characterize Americans. We may do so, too, only because we are being true to ourselves and it is unjust to ask of us that we be otherwise.[3]

So striking is the paradox here alluded to that some are disposed, in a curiously inverted sort of way, to attribute its architecture to the work of secret "Communist agents" in high places. Whatever its sources, the paradox is a reality. Only a few representative instances can here be touched upon.

The "great debate" over American strategy revolved in 1947–9 over the issue of whether in the event of war the Air Force through "strategic" atomic bombing could defeat and destroy Russia in a brief Blitzkrieg or the Army and Navy were to be regarded as also having a decisive part in the business. The anticipated war was universally assumed to be "total"—i.e., having no limits or purposes short of the annihilation of the enemy. No one remembered that Russia has never been defeated in a "total" war since the coming of the Mongols. The pleas of Herbert Hoover and a few other like-minded spirits for a reduction of American commitments to proportions commensurate with American power were without effect, since all the pleaders were obliged to equate Communism with total depravity—and a dedicated people waging holy war on sin cannot honorably tolerate any limitations on the scope of their crusade. In 1950-1 the issue shifted in *l'affaire* MacArthur to the question of whether America should "defend" Europe or wage "total" war on China, also unconquered by any invaders since the Mongols. The decision, temporarily at least, was to defend Europe. This task in turn was envisaged as a problem of matching or balancing, or at least checkmating, Russian land-power on the Continent.

This resolve, viewed in a context of rational calculations of the potentials of power involved, may well be deemed by future historians (if any remain) to have been from the out-

[3] Nathaniel Peffer, "Democracy Losing By Default," *The Political Science Quarterly* (September 1948), p. 334.

set wholly fatuous, as most informed Europeans at the time conceded in private but were unable to assert in public lest Americans be offended. Russia and its satellites had more than ten times as many divisions available for war in Europe as all Western European States, plus America, had in hand or in prospect. This disparity was viewed in Washington with the utmost alarm, on the assumption that the Russians would almost certainly do in the future what they had never in fact done in the past—i.e., conquer Western Europe—unless confronted locally with armed might capable of halting their expected onrush and driving them back to the steppes. The alternative prospect, on the model of 1940–4, of "liberating" a Continent already occupied by the enemy was apparently regarded as feasible in the Pentagon but was unthinkable to Europeans. The unbalance could be remedied (according to the Truman-Marshall-Acheson-Eisenhower dispensation) by building up fifty divisions in Western Europe by 1953 and one hundred by 1955 (though nothing was less probable), with the support of Spain and a rearmed Italy and Germany. General Eisenhower himself, however, told the Senators in March 1951 that twelve U.S. divisions in Europe as part of such a force (instead of the six proposed) could, in the event of war, hold the peninsula of Brittany against any conceivable Russian attack—a prognosis scarcely calculated to reassure even the Bretons.

The program of rearming Europe presented two difficulties, both apparently insoluble as these words were written. As for the German contribution, all the major cities of the Reich in 1951–2 were still wastelands of ruin and rubble, a visible fact that it seemed indelicate for military planners to mention. Even if German rearmament could be achieved in any effective fashion, the rearmed Reich, conforming to the immutable precepts of power politics and national interest, could be presumed to pursue German purposes, not American purposes—with no assurance that the two would coincide. American interests called for enlisting Germany in a coalition against Russia. German interests, obviously, could best be served by playing Russia and America against one another. In this familiar and always useful game the Russians, who currently held all the high cards, had centuries of experience, and Americans none whatever.

If, alternately and by some miracle, a revived *Wehrmacht*, whether in or out of a "European army," could be securely counted upon to fight Russia, the resulting equation would still be wholly inadequate to the task proposed. The enemy could match, still in a ratio of three or four to one if necessary, and for an indefinite future, any mobilization of military power in Western Europe which Washington, London, Paris, Madrid, Rome, and Bonn might be able to agree upon and attain. Hitler hurled against Russia 170 divisions in 1941 and 240 divisions in 1942. He was defeated and unable in 1943–5, with over 300 divisions in the East, to hold any line whatever against the foe. The Russia of 1953 is a still more formidable military Power, in terms of its own economy, apart from the satellite forces at its disposal in the event of any contest initiated by the West.[4]

The American enterprise, moreover—and this was the second difficulty—called for such sacrifices by the impoverished peoples of Western Europe as to jeopardize to the point of disintegration their heroic efforts to restore and maintain, with American aid, some semblance of prewar living standards. What Washington asked them to do their leaders agreed, reluctantly, to do since they remained dependent for solvency upon American subventions. But all knew that the

[4] Several distinguished scientists—including President James B. Conant of Harvard (see his "The Defense of Europe in the Atomic Age," Chicago Council on Foreign Relations, May 17, 1951) and President Vannevar Bush of the Carnegie Institution of Washington (speaking by radio March 4, 1951, under the auspices of the "Committee on the Present Danger")—argued that the end of the American monopoly of the atomic bomb required the building up of large land-forces in Western Europe to "deter" Communist aggression. On the specific issue here discussed, see "The Military Crisis of Western Europe," with quotations from British and French military authorities, by the late Max Werner, prepared for the Foundation for World Government, April 10, 1950. Max Werner concludes his searching analysis: "Western Europe cannot be defended by war; Western Europe can be defended only by a constructive peace policy."

enterprise was feckless. If the Russians did not attack, for reasons best known to themselves, the endeavor was unnecessary. If they did attack, the most that could be done would be too little and too late.[5] The Italian and French "neutralists," and the Germans whose slogan was "*ohne mich!*" had numerous counterparts in Britain.

In resigning as Minister of Labor on April 22, 1951, Aneurin Bevan (followed in his resignation by Harold Wilson, President of the Board of Trade) declared that the British rearmament program was "fantastically wrong" and "already dead," since American hoarding of raw materials and the American inflation rendered its goals unattainable. The scale and speed of the proposed rearming of the West were such "that the foundations of political liberty and parliamentary democracy will not be able to sustain the shock." He demanded that social welfare be given priority over rearmament as the only rational defense against the Communist menace. He insisted that Britain declare its independence of America's "ruinous" policy, not allow itself to be "dragged too far behind the wheels of American diplomacy," and not to "follow behind American capitalism, unable to restrain itself at all."[6]

[5] British Defense Minister Emmanuel Shinwell (Reuters dispatch of July 27, 1951) and Woodrow Wyatt, Under-Secretary for War (AP dispatch, July 15, 1951), in pleading for British rearmament, contended that Russia had 215 divisions under arms, plus 70 satellite divisions. The accuracy of such figures was questionable. What was not questionable was the capacity of the Scarlet Empire to match Western rearmament in a fashion that would maintain the disparity of 1946–50 whatever the West might do. This disparity, in the public utterances of Anglo-American officialdom, meant that Western Europe was "defenseless" before the Soviet colossus, although no military aggression in fact took place. This state of affairs appeared likely to continue indefinitely. The conclusion drawn, however, was not that the enterprise of matching Soviet military power on the Continent should be abandoned as pointless, but that such efforts should be doubled and trebled regardless of their appalling cost and self-evident futility. On the unwisdom of the entire American strategy here involved, see Walter Lippmann: "Breakup of the Two-Power World," *Harper's Magazine* (April 1950).

[6] For a defense of the Labor government's policy, issued prior to Bevan's resignation, see *Socialist Foreign Policy*, by R. H. S. Crossman, M.P. and Honorable Kenneth Younger, M.P. (London: Fabian International Bureau; Fabian Tract No. 287). For an exposition of the Bevan position, see the pamphlet in July 1951: "One Way Only: A Socialist Analysis of the Present

Such sentiments had a wider following in the British Isles and on the Continent than parliamentary votes and election results suggested. Many Europeans already knew that the militarization of America was jeopardizing their living standards and that the remilitarization of Europe which Americans were demanding would spell penury, regardless of whether its result was peace or war, to the advantage of no one save the Communists.

The Asiatic parallel of the American policy here under consideration need only be suggested. In 1950–2 the United States officially committed itself, despite the dismissal of MacArthur, to maintaining the French in Indochina, the British in Malaya, Chiang Kai-shek in Formosa, Syngman Rhee in Korea, and a reactionary regime in Japan. No other course was available to American policy-makers, since their imaginations could conceive of none. The alternative in each instance seemed in consequence to be a threatened triumph of Communism. The practical results in every case was the perpetuation of a political regime, a social order, and an economy that, cut off from Asiatic markets, must either disintegrate in the end or require American subsidies indefinitely. The proposed rearmament of Japan, odious to all the rest of Asia, rendered the problem all the more acute, despite the rituals in San Francisco on September 8, 1951, carried through in the face of Soviet threats—the ceremonial signing of a peace treaty with Tokio, coupled with a Japanese-American alliance.

The purely economic problem posed by this pattern of strategy was not *per se* insoluble. American security—and, as a means thereto, the subsidization of the whole global anti-Soviet "empire"—was assumed to require the building of prosperity and the amassing of power throughout Western Europe, the Near and Middle East, and Southeastern and Eastern Asia. Even so ambitious a goal as this was not neces-

---

World Crisis." The quotations in the text are from Bevan's address in the House of Commons, April 23, 1951. See also Bevan's book, *In Place of Fear*, (Simon and Schuster; 1952).

sarily beyond accomplishment—if all the resources and enormous productivity of America were devoted singlemindedly to the endeavor, at the sharp sacrifice of American living standards and the expenditure of vast treasure, much sweat, many tears, and some blood. Most of America's men of wealth and power did indeed exhort their fellow citizens to glad acceptance of precisely such a burden, arguing that the issue was one of freedom more precious than life itself to be defended against tyranny worse than death.

But the Americans of the midcentury, for all their genius in reducing complex issues to a simple "either-or," had come to relish so hugely the highest living standard in the world, and had begun to savor so delightfully the tempting, delicious, and deceptive fruits of total militarism, that they could make no such deliberate choice. Their decision instead—arrived at by the curious processes of a democracy in which the expectations of Big Business, Big Labor, and Big Agriculture were wholly sacred and the demands of Big Brass were almost sacrosanct—was to finance and arm all the peoples of Western Europe and Eastern Asia, at substantial profit to the American provisioners and armorers, and at the same time to maintain and improve American living standards through the pleasant but dubious device of inflation, and seek simultaneously to make America itself the most formidable military Power of all time on land, sea, and in the air.

Since American resources were finite, not infinite, this decision could scarcely be regarded as sane. In the words of Clarence B. Randall, President of Inland Steel Company: "The Administration wants to fight one half of the world, feed the other half, and at the same time maintain business as usual at home. It can't be done." The American response to the limited and local war in Korea was an annual defense-budget of sixty-one billion dollars (not including the cost of the war), which it was proposed to expand indefinitely in years to come. The figure proposed, amounting to over four hundred dollars for every man, woman, and child in the United States, exceeded by five billion dollars the entire federal budget for 1951. It constituted not only the largest "peacetime" military budget in history but was more than double the total appropriations of the United States in waging and winning World War I. No one, in Congress or out of it, dared question its size lest he be suspected of lack of patriotism, indifference toward national prosperity, or insufficient enthusiasm for combating the Red Devils.

The full results of the American decision of 1951 were happily not yet apparent a year later. But the inexorable consequences, already evident and certain to be aggravated in the years ahead, were: uncontrollable domestic inflation; an insidious and ever-expanding corruption in public life;[7] a steady dilution of civil rights to the point of general fear of

[7] The vast and amorphous story of corruption in America cannot here be told. But see frank and frequent editorials in *The Chicago Tribune* throughout the period under consideration and, in the old muck-raking tradition, *High Treason*, by Albert E. Kahn (Lear; 1950). See also Robert S. Lynd: "Our 'Racket' Society," *The Nation* (August 25, 1951), and columnist Ray Tucker's article (September 7, 1951), noting that the proposed investigation of the "China Lobby" had been killed because Secretary of the Treasury John W. Snyder and Attorney General J. Howard McGrath had "apparently convinced" President Truman that "the revelations would be politically dangerous" because those receiving fees from foreign governments to obtain favors in Washington would be found to include Acheson's law firm, Covington, Burling, Rublee, O'Brian and Shorb (representing at various times Pakistan, Colombia, Denmark, Iran, Peru, Sweden, and Poland), and law firms headed by former Attorney-General Homer S. Cummings (Spain, the Dominican Republic, Newfoundland), Clark Clifford (Indonesia), Oscar S. Cox (Italy, France, Belgium, Austria, Costa Rica), Robert R. Nathan (Israel, France), William J. Donovan (Siam), Donald Richberg and Seth Richardson (Chile and Panama), Paul V. McNutt (Korea), Manley O. Hudson (Egypt and Guatemala), and so on ad infinitum. Such arrangements were in no sense "corrupt," but were entirely lawful and legitimate, as were the arrangements whereby (according to the *Chicago Tribune* editorial of September 3, 1949, "A Nice Piece of Business," which, so far as I am aware, was never contradicted or made the subject of a libel suit) Anderson, Clayton & Co., the principal business of William Clayton, former Under-Secretary of State who helped push the Marshall Plan through Congress, secured up to midsummer of 1949 $100,000,000 of Marshall Plan orders, with Mr. Clayton personally profiting at the rate of $700,000 a year. Such arrangements between business and government were entirely "normal" and legitimate in the America of the Truman era. According to the National Industrial Conference Board (*The New York Times*, September 24, 1951), General Motors Corporation had obtained, since July 1950, $3,500,000,000 worth of war orders, or 14.7 per cent of the total, the Ford Motor Co. $1,000,000,000, or 4.2 per cent, and so on.

dissent from orthodoxy;[8] the supremacy of the military in the formulation of American policies at home and abroad; and the degeneration of American democracy to a point at which its leaders seemed rather more than likely to be finally confronted with the desperate choice of either launching a global war of annihilation which could never be won or terminated,[9] or inviting a postinflationary economic debacle of major proportions. Since the latter alternative was politically inconceivable, the former seemed the more probable, carrying with it the prospect of a garrison State, a wholly militarized economy, a repudiation of American traditions of freedom, and the rise of an indigenous Cæsarism, gloomily forecast by Oswald Spengler a generation ago—along with the reduction of much of Eurasia to anarchy and barbarism wholly beyond the power of a barbarized America to remedy or end.

The self-hypnosis of the American Commonwealth in the face of the Red Menace was most aptly illustrated in the circumstance that no public discussion of the actual alternatives open to the United States in world politics was any longer

[8] See below, pp. 287f.

[9] Walter Lippmann, in announcing the abandonment of his column "for some months to come" in order to write a book, *The Image of Man,* wrote three columns, "Total War and Co-Existence," (*The New York Herald Tribune,* June 18, 19, and 21, 1951) in which he expressed the following opinions:

> My own view is that in a total war between the Soviet orbit and the Atlantic Community the Soviet Government would be destroyed, the Soviet Empire would be demolished, Western Europe would sink into anarchy, and North America, victorious but weary, impoverished, and isolated, would find it hard to preserve the remnants of its freedom, harder still to bring back to life again the stricken civilization of the Western World.
>
> Put in other words, I believe that the United States would win the military victory against the Soviet Empire. The war, however, would be so devastating and so prolonged that in all of the Eurasian Continent there would be left no governments of sufficient power and authority to make peace and to restore order and to reconstruct the ruined world. . . .
>
> Insofar as the war was a total war and its aim was victory, the catastrophe would be well-nigh universal. Instead of its being the war to end war, which we fondly hoped for in 1917, it would be the war that could not be ended. This is the fundamental characteristic of the total wars of this century—that they have become increasingly more irreparably destructive and more hopelessly indecisive. . . .

possible in the 1950's. All advocacy of "peace" was equated with "Communism." All concern with the national interest was deemed unpatriotic.

The controversy over MacArthur in 1951 was not a debate as to how peace might best be restored and preserved and still less a disputation over how American interests might best be served in a dangerous world. The issue was quite simply one of whether America should fight China then or Russia later. General Bradley told the Senators that MacArthur's proposals, in the opinion of the Joint Chiefs of Staff, "would involve us in the wrong war, at the wrong place, at the wrong time, and with the wrong enemy." The nature of the right war, at the right place, at the right time and with the right enemy was made abundantly clear by other Administration spokesmen who opposed MacArthur's course solely on the ground that the Soviet Union might intervene before the United States was ready to fight Russia. "We must act with great prudence," declared President Truman on January 13, 1951, "pending the build-up of our national strength." We must weigh risks and avoid extension of hostilities "before we are ready," asserted Senator MacMahon, "until we get into a position to meet them." General Marshall: "We are not in a position now to take measures . . ." In short, America should fight China at the risk of Russian intervention only when America should be ready to fight Russia—which happy eventuality was, by implication, to be achieved by 1953 or 1954.[1]

In this context no diplomacy was possible save for the purpose of winning allies, weakening enemies, and preparing for Armageddon. The Secretary of State might still, on occasion, use words of wisdom and moderation.[2] But the

[1] See *Military Situation in Far East,* Hearing Before the Committee on Armed Services and the Committee on Foreign Relations, U.S. Senate, 82nd Congress, First Session (Washington, D.C.: U.S. Government Printing Office; 1951, 4 vols.) Cf. "The Meaning of MacArthur" in *Monthly Review* (Editors: Paul M. Sweezy and Leo Huberman), June 1951, pp. 33–49.

[2] See, for example, Dean Acheson: "What Is the Present? What of the Future?" in *The New York Times Magazine* (August 5, 1951). Cf. also *Our Foreign Policy,* Department of State Publication 3972 (September 1950).

screams of McCarthy, the temper of Congress, and the prevailing frenetic mood of people and press made it quite impossible for the President or State Department to seek any settlement of issues with Russia or China on any basis other than the "unconditional surrender" of the enemy. Any course of compromise was at once banned as "appeasement." Since no diplomacy is possible without bargaining, and no bargaining is conceivable without compromise, the greatest Power on earth here found itself stripped, by its own hallucinations, of its capacity to conduct foreign affairs on any basis other than what Philip E. Jessup once called "the erroneous notion that progress toward international peace can be made only by confronting power with greater power." [3] The power America amassed seemed likely never to serve any purpose other than wanton and senseless destruction, for Americans were unable to agree on any goals other than the negativism and nihilism of anti-Communism. That such a doctrine is likely to be ruinous to any Great Power was pointed out by William Graham Sumner in 1903 in words appropriate to the 1950's:

On Secretary Acheson's alleged incapacity for candor, and genius for evasion and equivocation, see Arthur Krock in *The New York Times* (July 20, 1951), and *The Chicago Tribune* editorial: "The Big Lies" (January 13, 1951).

[3] Philip C. Jessup in *The New York Times Magazine* (October 23, 1949). See also Ernest T. Weir (Chairman, National Steel Corporation, Pittsburgh): "Statement on Our Foreign Situation" (January 5, 1951); Henry Steele Commager: "An Inquiry into 'Appeasement,'" *The New York Times Magazine* (February 11, 1951); my own "Peace without Appeasement" (Chicago Council on Foreign Relations; 1951); and Hans J. Morgenthau, *Politics Among Nations* (Alfred A. Knopf; 1948) and *In Defense of the National Interest* (Alfred A. Knopf; 1951). The various addresses, pamphlets, and books by James P. Warburg, many of them issued by the Current Affairs Press, also represented a vigorous and brilliant effort to inject rationality into American foreign policy. George F. Kennan, original promulgator in 1947 of the "containment" policy, was seeking four years later to quiet the rising clamor for "preventive war." See his articles: "Is War with Russia Inevitable?" *The Readers' Digest* (March 1950), and "Let Peace Not Die of Neglect" *The New York Times Magazine* (February 25, 1951). Such efforts to suggest that problems of power must be settled by bargaining if they are not to be settled by war had little visible effect on American attitudes and policies during the period here dealt with, and often exposed their authors to slander and character-assassination.

If you want war, nourish a doctrine. Doctrines are the most frightful tyrants to which men ever are subject, because doctrines get inside of a man's own reason and betray him against himself. Civilized men have done their fiercest fighting for doctrines. . . . What are they all? Nothing but rhetoric and phantasms. Doctrines are always vague; it would ruin a doctrine to define it, because then it could be analyzed, tested, criticized, and verified; but nothing ought to be tolerated which cannot be so tested. Somebody asks you with astonishment and horror whether you do not believe in the Monroe Doctrine. You do not know whether you do or not, because you do not know what it is; but you do not dare to say that you do not, because you understand that it is one of the things which every good American is bound to believe in. Now when any doctrine arrives at that degree of authority, the name of it is a club which any demagogue may swing over you at any time and apropos of anything. . . . A policy in a state we can understand. . . . A doctrine is an abstract principle; it is necessarily absolute in its scope and abstruse in its terms; it is a metaphysical assertion. It is never true, because it is absolute, and the affairs of men are all conditioned and relative. . . .

Think what an abomination in statecraft an abstract doctrine must be. Any politician or editor can, at any moment, put a new extension on it. The people acquiesce in the doctrine and applaud it because they hear the politicians repeat it, and the politicians and editors repeat it because they think it is popular. So it grows. . . . It may mean anything or nothing, at any moment, and no one knows how it will be. You accede to it now, within the vague limits of what you suppose it to be; therefore you will have to accede to it tomorrow when the same name is made to cover something which you never have heard or thought of. If you allow a political catchword to go on and grow, you will awaken someday to find it standing over you, the arbiter of your destiny, against which you are powerless, as men are powerless against delusions. . . .

Your doctrine becomes an entity, a being, a lesser kind of divinity, entitled to reverence and possessed of prestige, so that it allows of no discussion or deliberation. The President of the United States talks about it and he tells us solemnly that it is true and sacred, whatever it is. . . . He says that, on account of the doctrine, whatever it may be, we must have a big navy. In this, at least, he is plainly in the right; if we have the doctrine, we shall need a big navy. . . .

[And] if you prepare a big army and navy and are all ready for war, it will be easy to go to war; the military and naval men will have a lot of new machines and they will be eager to see what they can do with them. There is no such thing nowadays as a state of readiness for war. It is a chimera, and the nations which pursue it are falling into an abyss of wasted energy and wealth. . . . It is a fallacy. It is evident that to pursue such a notion with any idea of realizing it would absorb all the resources and activity of the state; this the great European states are now proving by experiment. A wiser rule would be to make up your mind soberly what you want, peace or war, and then to get ready for what you want; for what we prepare for is what we shall get.[4]

So fantastic and potentially hideous were the most probable final consequences of the American response to the Communist challenge in the 1950's that allies and enemies were alike baffled as to how to cope with it. Among the few Americans still capable of independent thought and still bold enough to express their views, some suspected that the whole business was somehow a gigantic hoax. Thus the *Chicago Tribune*, with superficial plausibility, could say (August 2, 1951):

One thing about this Fair Deal crowd is that it is expert at getting rid of anything the taxpayer can earn. That is the one thing it can do. The country is going over a fiscal Niagara in a barrel and it would require extreme hardihood to say that the staves won't give when the bump comes. . . .

It is the job of Congress to introduce sense into these military proposals. The only way that that can be done is to introduce sense into the foreign policy that governs them. . . . Mr. Truman talks about strengthening the country to justify his incomprehensible figures. In fact, he proposes to weaken it irreparably. The prospect of gambling with the nation's solvency does not displease him, for his methods are calculated to

[4] William Graham Sumner: *War and Other Essays* (New Haven, Conn.: Yale University Press; 1911).

force the country into a socialist receivership if anything at all is to be salvaged. That way lies greater glory and profit for political spoilsmen, of which he is the leading example.

And thus Lawrence Dennis, one of the few perceptive and critical minds in a time given over to hysterical orthodoxy or discreet silence on the part of most intellectuals, wrote in his weekly analysis, *The Appeal to Reason* (August 4, 1951):

> What, in the way of public policy, is illogical, irrational and senseless, as well as immoral, must prove operationally unworkable. Crooked policies and crooked thinking about them must produce more and more crooks at all levels. Why shouldn't pressure groups be unscrupulous and unethical in trying to get all they can for their principals when they know that the nation's foreign policy which now determines about everything is shot through with bad faith and fraud? The very word "defense" is now as big a fraud as the honor system was at West Point. "Defense" has become nothing more or less than a monumental lie and a colossal racket to keep the political ins in and to keep up a war boom. The racket is generally considered too big and too well sold to be opposed. So, it is thought, the only smart thing to do about it is to exploit it as best one can for one's own and one's group interest. Both Truman and Stalin are winning the cold war or the defense racket here. Our defense is not defense. It is provocation. It is calculated to start a war we can't win and to keep up until total war begins an inflationary-military crisis that Communism can't possibly lose in the long run and that Truman is not likely to lose in the short run. From the point of view of American national interest, it is mad; from the point of view of Truman's political self-interest, it is masterly.

And thus Herbert Pell, erstwhile Congressman, Minister to Portugal, New York State Chairman of the Democratic Party, and member of the U.N. Commission for investigation of war crimes, in the *New York Times*, January 14, 1951:

> Peace is the only possible base for our civilization. It was built on peace, and without peace it will die. War will ineluct-

ibly end the customs and the outlook and the way of life, the ideals and the national purposes which we inherited from our fathers to be held as a sacred trust for our children. . . . Twice in our time we have seen that total war (and there really is no other kind possible) decides nothing, settles nothing, answers nothing and leads to nothing. Winner and loser, both are vanquished. . . . Today, does any sane person believe that a conflict with Russia will mean anything but mutual destruction and ruin? . . . It is manifest that a war with Russia will end in a collapse of common exhaustion. The representative of a shattered Russia will meet the emissaries of a worn and exhausted United States and devise a means by which both can survive without continuing mutual slaughter and destruction. Is there any person in the world who imagines any other result possible? . . .

Yet here, there and everywhere you hear the politicians shouting against compromise. . . . They have the effrontery to attack as cowards all who disagree with anything they shout. The whole thing is contemptible. . . . How much courage does anyone think it would take for me, 66 years old, living on an ample income quietly in the country, to clamor for war, to demand the sacrifice of a million men forty years younger than I and then end my heroic address with a bitter note of regret that my years or my grapevines prevented me from joining the brave boys whom I envy? Such words do not come from the mouths of heroes or of patriots but from the lips of self-seeking politicians hoping to ride into office on a wave of excitement that will conceal their own shortcomings. I have been in politics for forty years . . . and I know. Most of the political shouters think they are backing a winning horse —that's all. Twenty-five years ago thousands of American politicians attacked the Catholics to get the Klan vote. Today they follow McCarthy. Twenty years ago they said as they drank their bootleg liquor, "There's one more election in Prohibition." Today safe behind desks they think that war and hatred will keep their snouts in the public trough in 1952. It's as simple as that.

I am for peace. I am on the side of the angels of God who sang "Peace on Earth, Good Will to Men." They were not popular with those who filled the Inn and crowded Mary into the stables, but they were right all the same. Why not negotiate now, while the young men are still alive?

With all due respect to such views, it is more reasonable to assume that the American mood of the 1950's, and the public policies in which it found expression, were less the result of any "conspiracy" than the product of an elemental and widespread irrationality, born of deep psychic insecurities. These forces, which have destroyed many past civilizations, are not explicable in terms of any simple dishonesty, insincerity, or villainy any more than are the barbarian invasions, the Jehad of Islam, the Crusades, the wars of religion, or the Communist program of world revolution. The fact remains that all such operations set in motion forces and pressures that tend to become uncontrollable, irreversible, and irresistible—often eventuating in irreparable disaster. Though he manifestly had no plan for ameliorating a situation he viewed with justifiable alarm, General Douglas MacArthur uttered a truism when he spoke of "frantic endeavors" to arouse "a frenzy of fear throughout the land," promoting "a drift toward totalitarian role," "thought control," and other "stepping stones to dictatorial power." [5]

In the contemporary American case, it is arguable that the men of the Kremlin must themselves have been mad, or at least victims of horrible miscalculation, to have contributed to the emergence of any such Frankenstein monster as did, in fact, spring up from the fear and rage of Americans. But the American madness was *sui generis*. An old folk-proverb asserts that God takes care of little children, damned fools, and the United States. In His infinite mercy, He may yet save His American children from their self-appointed mission of destroying the world in the name of rescuing it from sin. But in the absence of divine intervention, only the most optimistic of observers and participants could suppose that the American course in the 1950's could end in anything other than tragic disaster. A few representative quotations from

[5] Address of General Douglas MacArthur in Cleveland, September 6, 1951.

the utterances of respected public figures must here suffice as evidence in support of this doleful hypothesis:

George H. Earle, former governor of Pennsylvania, April 26, 1946 and October 10, 1947:

> Soviet Russia is a menace far greater than the Nazis. The U.S. must prepare in self-defense to wipe out every town, city and village in Russia. . . . One nice little atomic bomb dropped on the Kremlin and the Russian people of 165,000,000 would fly to pieces with centrifugal force.

J. Edgar Hoover to the House Committee on Un-American Activities, March 26, 1947:

> Their objective is to overthrow the American Way of Life. . . . I would have no fears, if Americans realized the menace of Red Fascism. I do fear for the liberal and progressive who has been duped. . . . Communism is not a political party; it is an evil and malignant way of life—a disease that spreads like an epidemic, and quarantine is necessary to keep it from infecting the nation.

Charles A. Eaton, a former Minister of the Gospel, Chairman of the House Committee on Foreign Affairs, in the *American Magazine*, August, 1947:

> Americans are such good people that they are slow to recognize wickedness. . . . Compromise with Russia seems impossible. . . . They have no morals and no religion. . . . Russians are Slavs, which means captives or slaves. . . . But we still have the atomic bomb. . . . Once kicked out of decent society, Russia must either seek to regain good standing or be disciplined by the military action of the union of decent nations.

Governor Thomas E. Dewey, of New York: "The Red Czar Moves to Conquer Us," *Collier's*, February 10, 1951:

> At last the dreams of the Russian czars are coming true. . . . Stalin emerged as the greatest mass murderer of all history. . . . Does anyone think the Red Czar is going to stop now? . . . What the Russian time-table is no one knows. . . . Our very existence demands that we abandon every thought that we could remain alive in a Communist world. I say this not to show that all is lost. I say it be-

> cause we are in the most frightful crisis of all history; because we are divided in our councils, and because we are taking grossly inadequate steps for our own defense. . . . We can outproduce, outthink, out-organize and out-fight the Red slavemaster. We can beat him down to earth if we will only stop dawdling and get going.

Life magazine, January 22, 1951:

> No man can say just how the pure wickedness of Soviet Communism will ultimately be banished from the earth, as some day it will be banished. But what no man has a right to say is that we can live peaceably and happily *with* this prodigious evil. Meanwhile what must be said is that the Soviet empire, far from retreating, will continue to expand unless it is opposed with all our strength and all our mind and all our will. That includes the steady, calm and constant acceptance of the risk of all-out war.
>
> The President said last week that his chosen road—the road to a contrived peace with the present rulers of the present Communist system—is "the only realistic road to peace." It is not a realistic road to peace. It is not a realistic road to anything. It is the road our enemy wants us to take. It is the road to our defeat. It is the way to suicide. [The *Chicago Tribune* of April 2, 1951, commented editorially: "*Life* is misnamed. It ought to be called Death."]

Major General Robert W. Grow, U.S. Military Attaché in Moscow, July 1950—January 1952, whose diary was purloined in Frankfurt and published (March 6, 1952) by British Communist Richard Squires in East Germany:

> Communism must be destroyed! . . . War! As soon as possible! Now! It seems to me that the time is ripe for a blow this year (1951). We must start by hitting below the belt. This war cannot be conducted by Marquis of Queensbury [*sic*] rules. We must employ every subversive device to undermine the confidence and loyalty of Soviet subjects for their regime. . . . Anything, truth or falsehood, to poison the thoughts of the population!. . . . We must understand that this war is total and is fought with all weapons. . . . What should we do to fill out the vacuum after the Soviet regime is destroyed? . . .

We are now in a position to venture a tentative judgment, subject to correction by future events, on the question of whether Russia or America in the middle years of the twentieth century would appear to possess the requisite qualifications to undertake the task of achieving world government and a *Pax Orbis* by the sword. If the analyses attempted in the preceding pages can be deemed to have even a modicum of validity, the answer cannot be in doubt. Neither of the super-Powers of our time measures up to the exigencies of the enterprise. The circumstance that each of them, in the eyes of sophisticated West Europeans, consists of "barbarians" is irrelevant. Many World-States of the past have been established by barbarians. What is relevant to the issue is that Russia is dominated by intolerant inquisitors and unscrupulous fanatics, and America by unthinking sybarites and irresponsible neurotics.

These are not the qualities, whatever frenzied energies they may momentarily mobilize, which make possible the establishment of enduring world government through the military might of a conquering Power. Such qualities were conspicuously absent in the attitudes and conduct of the Pharaohs of Egypt, the captains of Alexander, the Consuls of Rome, the Caliphs of Islam, and the Khans of Tartary. In the current instance, moreover, no world government by the sword is conceivable save through the defeat and destruction of one Power by the other. This enterprise fascinates the morbid imaginations of many Americans and is an article of faith (albeit not necessarily of action) in the Scarlet Empire. In truth, the enterprise is wholly impossible of accomplishment by either side. Any effort to achieve it threatens the reduction of the survivors to despotism and savagery amid botched and bungled adventures in chaos, wherein the demented remnants of a decimated humankind can finally do no more than try to keep alive amid universal anarchy. These considerations, in an age of unreason, do not in the least preclude the possibility that Moscow or Washington or both will undertake the Great Crusade. They merely mean that whoever first seeks by the sword to unify the world of the twentieth century will perish by the sword and that the "victor" will find the task of restoring peace and order wholly beyond his powers. They mean, further, that all possibility of the political unification of mankind will disappear in the process and that the Great Society will sink into total disorder until centuries hence—if we may assume that some organized groups of human beings survive the holocaust—some primitive peoples, somewhere and somehow, resume the tasks of civilization.

We are left with the conclusion at this point in our inquiry that global peace by conquest cannot be achieved in the circumstances of the times in which we have the misfortune to live. Whether any alternative possibilities are available will be considered in the chapters that follow.

CHAPTER FIVE

PEACE BY TREASON

1. THE TRAITORS

> We must build gibbets on every mountain-peak and every high hill, all along the sky-line conspicuous gibbets, and if any person begins to say we have to save England or rescue France or avenge the Jews—take him up and hang him, he is pimping for war. If he says democracy, remember they pimped for war and they will again—take him up and hang him. Or if he says we must save Civilization: they said it: take them up and hang them. If they say, My Country, right or wrong—they are pimping for war, take them up and hang them. Higher than Haman. Hell, we'll have a fine orchard when the sun ripes the plums.
>
> —ROBINSON JEFFERS.[1]

KONRAD HEIDEN subtitled his first biography of Hitler, published in Zurich in 1936, "*Das Zeitalter der Verantwortungslosigkeit*," or "The Epoch of Irresponsibility." In it he sought to show how many of those who became victims of the Nazi terror had themselves raised the monster to power under the delusion that they were thereby buying protection from worse things. In his later work—difficult, definitive, and exciting—on the early career of the Nazi Cæsar, published in Eng-

[1] From *The Double Axe and Other Poems*, by Robinson Jeffers (Random House; 1948), pp. 17–18, reprinted by permission of the publishers. The passage is from *The Double Axe*, wherein Hoult Gore, slain in World War II, is restored to life by bitterness, hatred, and a will to revenge, and returns to denounce the warmakers and finally to murder all his family.

lish (Boston: Houghton, Mifflin; 1944) under its original title of *Der Fuehrer*, Heiden in his opening chapter quoted excerpts from a famous document purporting to set forth the strategic precepts of world-revolutionary conspiracy:

> We shall talk with the people on the streets and squares and teach them to take the view of political questions which at the moment we require. . . . We shall create unrest, struggle, and hate in the whole of Europe and thence in other continents. We shall at all times be in a position to call forth new disturbances at will, or to restore the old order. Unremittingly we shall poison the relations between the peoples and states of all countries. By envy and hatred, by struggle and warfare, even by spreading hunger, destitution, and plagues, we shall bring all peoples to such a pass that their only escape will lie in total submission to our domination.
>
> We shall stultify, seduce, ruin the youth. We shall not stick at bribery, treachery, treason, as long as they serve the realization of our plan. . . . In our arsenal we carry a boundless ambition, burning avidity, a ruthless thirst for revenge, relentless hatred. From us emanates the spectre of fear, all-embracing terror.
>
> We are the chosen, we are the true men. Our minds give off the true power of the spirit; the intelligence of the rest is instinctive and animal. They can see, but they cannot foresee; their inventions are purely corporeal. Does it not follow clearly that Nature herself has predestined us to dominate the whole world? . . .
>
> We shall paint the misdeeds of foreign governments in the most garish colors and create such an ill-feeling toward them that the peoples would a thousand times rather bear a slavery which guarantees them peace and order than enjoy their much-touted freedom. The peoples will tolerate any certitude we may impose on them, if only to avoid a return to the horrors of wars and insurrections. Our principles and methods will take on their full force when we present them in sharp contrast to the putrid old social order. Outwardly, however, in our "official" utterances, we shall adopt an opposite procedure and always do our best to appear honorable and cooperative. A stateman's words do not have to agree with his acts. If we pursue these princi-

ples, the governments and peoples which we have thus prepared will take our IOU's for cash. One day they will accept us as the benefactors and saviors of the human race. If any state dares to resist us, if its neighbors make common cause with it against us, we shall unleash a world war. By all these methods we shall so wear down the nations that they will be forced to offer us world domination.

Words similar to these have been written by, about, and against various groups of actual or alleged seditionists through the ages: early Christians, Albigensian heretics, Hussites, witches and warlocks, Gypsies, Protestants, Jesuits, Masons, Jacobins, Liberals, Fascists, Communists, Catholics. These particular words happen to have been written initially by a French lawyer, Maurice Joly, as part of a satire against Napoleon III, published in Brussels in 1864 under the title of *A Dialogue in Hell Between Machiavelli and Montesquieu.* This pamphlet was all but forgotten until 1905; when two leaders of the *Okhrana* or Tsarist Secret Police, Generals Oryevsky and Ratchkovsky, with the aid of a religious writer named Sergei Nilus, rewrote and reissued the pamphlet, giving it the form of the alleged secret minutes of the founding Congress of the Zionist movement, held in Basel in 1897. The new title of this forgery was *The Protocols of the Elders of Zion.* Hitler's co-worker, Alfred Rosenberg, first obtained a copy of it in Moscow in 1917. It has since been extensively used by anti-Semites as "proof" of the "Jewish World Conspiracy."

Those who believe in "world conspiracies" must be presumed, in the absence of convincing evidence to the contrary, to be victims of a contagious paranoia, shared with fellow believers. They feel themselves menaced with destruction —as in truth they are. The seeds of their doom are within themselves, deeply buried in unconscious intrapsychic conflicts. Since they are unaware of this secret, and could not admit it even if made aware, they must needs conjure up and locate the Devil, often with elaborate documentation, in the external world. They then find release in fighting the Devil and in exterminating his apostles. But almost invariably—and here we are in the presence of a masterpiece of madness—they are driven to go on to imitate the Devil, to "fight fire with fire," and to spin their own conspiracy as a means of saving the world from those who would destroy it. At this point others who do not wish to be "saved," or prefer salvation by some other prescription, become alarmed and more often than not conclude that fancy and fact are indistinguishable and that the plottings of those crusading against the Devil's Disciples can be frustrated only by adroit counterplots.

These familiar manifestations of human folly might seem to some irrelevant to the problem of world government. No universal empire has even been built in any such fashion. The procedures of propaganda and conversion and the devices of acquiring power which we have come to call, from ancient Hellenic and contemporary Spanish usage respectively, "Trojan horsemen" and "fifth columns," have often proved useful as adjuncts to conquering armies. But there is no case on record of any World-State being established solely, or even primarily, through the acts of conspirators bent upon subverting the status quo. Yet this fancy has long fascinated the imaginations of men, never more so than in our own time. And since it has deeply permeated the thoughts and deeds of the apostles of the *Pax Sovietica* and, more recently, of the *Pax Americana*—and has counterparts among the proponents of many other schemes of global dominion—some brief commentary on the phenomenon in its contemporary form is germane to the larger purposes of our inquiry.

The Communist world conspiracy has already been so elaborately and enthusiastically documented in America that no additional evidence need here be adduced,[2] even though

[2] See, amid the voluminous literature on the Communist world conspiracy, the numerous confessions and revelations of ex-Communists—e.g., Benjamin Gitlow, Louis Budenz, Elizabeth Bentley, Whittaker Chambers, *et al.* See also Everett M. Dirkson: *Communism in Action*, 79th Congress, Second Session, House Document 754 (Washington, D.C.: 1946); Martin Ebon: *World Communism Today* (McGraw-Hill; 1948); Richard Hirsch: *The Soviet Spies* (Duell, Sloan & Pearce; 1947); Alistair Cooke: *A Generation on Trial—U.S.A. vs. Alger Hiss* (Alfred A. Knopf; 1950); Ralph de Toledano and Victor Lasky: *Seeds of Treason—The True Story of the Hiss-Chambers*

failure to denounce Communist diabolism is currently equated with sympathy for its purposes and hence as evidence of treasonable intent. The risk will here be taken. A consideration of the origins, course, context, and consequences of aberrated and dangerous behavior-patterns is more useful in coping with them than the amassing of voluminous proof of their existence and the performance of rituals of exorcism, damnation, and purgation.

In his more cosmic moments, Marx conceived of his "class war" as being the result of impersonal economic and political forces, leading to "inevitable" consequences having no causal connection with the vices or virtues of any of the participants. But in his efforts to win converts, he took full account of the ways of men and depicted the Marxist Armageddon as a conflict between Good and Evil. Mankind was thus regarded as enslaved by a world conspiracy of "capitalists," and destined to be saved by a conspiracy of revolutionary "proletarians"—i.e., bourgeois intellectuals and agitators leading workers to a conquest of power, after which (as always) the leaders would rule the ruled for their own good and lead them to the Elysian Fields. Those to be saved must therefore exert themselves mightily in order to make certain that what was "inevitable" would indeed come to pass. There were here obvious elements of a "world conspiracy" (against the "world conspiracy" of "capitalism") long before 1917. But it happened that the Marxists who were first enabled to seize power in a great nation by virtue of the corruption and demoralization of war were Russians—i.e., heirs of the Petrine-Muscovite-Mongol-Byzantine tradition and, besides, actual conspirators who had spent their lives in an effort to overthrow an Autocracy by force and violence.

This circumstance colored with an indelible dye of conspiratorial self-adulation all Marxists the world over who

---

Tragedy (Funk & Wagnalls; 1950); Alexander Foote: *Handbook for Spies* (Doubleday; 1949); Robert E. Stripling: *The Red Plot Against America* (Drexel Hill, Pennsylvania: Bell; 1949); and Nathaniel Weyl: *Treason—The Story of Disloyalty and Betrayal in American History* (Washington, D.C.: Public Affairs Press, 1950).

came to worship at the shrine of Red Muscovy. Other Marxists, to be sure, condemned the self-anointed Messiahs as usurpers and impostors and demanded their crucifixion. But these, however loyal to their conception of the true faith, play a minor and often humiliating role in the global politics of our world. The comrades of the Muscovite persuasion are conspirators, plotting in dark and devious ways the overthrow of "capitalism"—all the while assuring themselves that they are serving the Brotherhood of Man. *In partibus infidelium*, their allegiance is to a foreign Power. Their purpose is revolution. Before June 22, 1941, and since August 14, 1945, they are therefore guilty of treason at least in the broadest and most vulgar sense of the epithet: men and women who love another country more than their own, who serve the other at the expense of their own, and who so hate and fear the ways and values of their homelands that they would risk their freedom and their lives (and those of all their countrymen) in order to refashion all things on the model of their Soviet Fatherland.

The opportunities available to these comrades in the lands outside the Scarlet Empire vary vastly from country to country, as do prevailing attitudes toward them and the personality types accordingly recruited into their ranks. The perennial spy-hunting and Red-chasing that preoccupy Americans have created a general impression that all Communists are Soviet intelligence-agents and that Soviet readiness to conquer the world, or at the very least Soviet acquisition of the atomic bomb, are attributable to the work of Communist rodents in the democracies. The impression is false. Moscow may wish to conquer the world, but is wholly unequal to the enterprise. Russian physicists, engineers, and industrialists were probably capable of achieving atomic fission without the aid of "secrets" filched by spies abroad.

The men of Moscow, moreover (unlike their counterparts in Washington), are far too shrewd, save in a few exceptional instances, to employ as spies or even as political broadcasters and other types of propagandists persons who are obvious rebels and renegades from the enemy camp. Such confessed Soviet espionage agents as Dr. Allan May Nunn and Dr. Klaus Fuchs were neither Communists nor open to the slightest suspicion of being Communists. Such cases as those of Alger Hiss, Judith Coplon, David Greenglass, Ethel and Julius Rosenberg *et al.*, while in no way invalidating the generalizations we are here concerned with, are more dubious, despite judicial convictions—though this is no place to discuss the doubts. It may be safely assumed that every Communist would like to be a Soviet spy if his Muscovite liege-lords were stupid enough to use him as such. Since in general they are not, his role is of a different order.

In France and Italy, where the support of one quarter of the electorate makes the comrades members of formidable and admirably organized mass parties, they have at their disposal most of the prerogatives of a "State within a State." Faithful converts can and do become parliamentarians, publishers, journalists, editors, trade-union officials, block captains, teachers, summer-camp leaders, theater-managers, and even merchants and bankers. Young men and women, inspired by the Vision and prepared to seek freedom through blind obedience and complete subjection, see careers opening out before them, embellished by the satisfaction of being held in awe and fear, if not in respect, by their pagan fellow-citizens. In Britain, where Communists are a negligible but tolerated minority, their function is that of eccentrics and cranks and their activities afford gratification only to those who enjoy such roles. In the United States, where their numbers are insignificant and their social purpose is to play the part of outcasts, their appeal obviously is only to those possessed of the stuff of which martyrs and masochists are made. Their common attributes are well put by Max Lerner (in *Actions and Passions*, Simon and Schuster, 1949, p. 55):

> I have always felt, and still feel, that the American Communist leaders are a pitiable group of second-rate men with no roots in American life, with no sense of the American mind, with no self-respect as free men, with no largeness and gener-

osity of view, turning and twisting in the gyre of their fettered dogmas, hating each other and hated by each other, nourished only by the vision of themselves as militants and revolutionaries and by their contempt for "liberals," fascinated by the Russian image and tied, in the end, to whatever their Russian heroes think good for both countries and the world.

Western politicians frightened of the Communist world conspiracy (or pretending to be frightened as a political device to win public approbation) have credited the Kremlin with devilish ingenuity in organizing a global network of agents and have credited the agents with diabolical cleverness in serving the purposes of the U.S.S.R. Both credits are undeserved. The Muscovite masters have never since the 1920's assumed that the comrades abroad could ever seize power unless, as in the late 1940's, they were either placed in power by Soviet armies (Eastern Europe) or were enabled (as in China) to conquer power by arms in a situation where a "bourgeois" regime left an utter vacuum by virtue of its own complete corruption and disintegration.

The role of the comrades in foreign parts is to serve, as best they can, the interests of Soviet foreign policy. Their best is seldom good and is often appallingly bad. The comrades in their own homelands are by definition traitors—never prudent and adaptable traitors but rather servile prisoners of their own orthodoxy and of the will of their Kremlin deities. The latter, in turn, have displayed over three decades a truly extraordinary capacity for muddling and blundering in the use of these tools, coupled with total lack of respect for their integrity or autonomy and, therefore, with repeated instances of deception, betrayal, and unscrupulous sacrifice of foreign brethren on the altars of expediency. The wonder is not that the comrades under these conditions have done so well as world conspirators. They have done miserably. The wonder is that they have held together at all.

The Western counterreaction to these feckless endeavors has been slow in developing and promises to be even more futile. The problem here is the same: how to cultivate traitors, foster treason, and instigate sedition and revolution in the enemy camp. The circumstances of the problem are wholly different and the imaginations of the organizers even more naïve, if possible, than those of their enemy "opposite numbers." The initial efforts of 1918–19 are all but forgotten, along with the lessons this failure might have taught. The quality of this fantastic episode of subversion and frustration is suggested by the conspiracy of Sidney Reilly, a British spy, with Boris Savinkov, Social Revolutionary terrorist (introduced to Winston Churchill by Reilly) to organize a counterrevolution in Russia in the summer of 1918. The attempt was drowned in blood, but only after the assassination of Volodarsky, German Ambassador Mirbach, and Uritsky, and the attempted assassination of Lenin by Fanya Kaplan, who obtained her gun from Savinkov.[3] Sedition and murder having failed to accomplish their purpose (as is usually the case), the champions of freedom against tyranny resorted to invasion, blockade, and subsidized civil war and were (as usual) defeated. Modern men for the most part are patriots. As such, they can be counted upon, whatever their resentments at their national rulers, to rally to their support when foreigners intervene and to fight to the death against all alien efforts to overthrow their governments either by internal treason or external assault.

This elementary proposition of contemporary political science has come to be understood, dimly and reluctantly, by the rulers of the Scarlet Empire. That it is currently not understood at all by democratic crusaders for the liberation of the victims of Red despotism is further evidence of the incapacity of the Western "Grand Alliance" to discharge ef-

[3] The details, with documentation, of the life and death of Sidney Reilly and of related conspiracies during the first years of Soviet regime can be found in *The Great Conspiracy,* by Michael Sayers and Albert E. Kahn (Boston: Little, Brown; 1946). This book, which I commended at the time of its publication, is now a kind of museum piece, since it is devoted to showing that the Soviet State from the outset was less an aggressor than a victim of aggression. In the perspective of 1952, this thesis is plainly preposterous. In any case, regardless of interpretation and evaluation, the facts set forth in this curious volume are, so far as my own knowledge goes, correct.

fectively the responsibilities of global rulership. World governments require Myths. But the myth-makers are required to act in terms of realities, not delusions. Imaginative exercises in "reconstructing" Russia so as to make it conform to Western expectations have long since become a favorite hobby of American publicists. Thus Herman Finer:

> The Soviet regime in Russia is the only system of government which seriously and inherently threatens a breach in a long reign of peace. The Soviet problem must be solved, for the Russian peoples' benefit as well as for that of the rest of mankind. But it must be solved only for a good and noble purpose; for peace, for justice, and for democracy. . . . A preponderant power, raised by conscience and poised in charity, must be held available throughout the years till democracy replaces despotism in Russia. If the Soviet rulers were overthrown would a widespread and long occupation be necessary thereafter? By no means. The people could govern themselves after temporary hardships. The incipient world organization would inherit a task of merciful assistance. But Russia belongs to the Russian people: assured of their democratic rights, and assisted in brotherhood to institute them, their lives and culture would be no menace to any other people.[4]

Thus George Kennan:

> What sort of Russia would we like to see before us, as our partner in the world community? . . . We may look, in the first place, for a Russian government which, in contrast to the one we know today, would be tolerant, communicative and forthright in its relations with other states and peoples. It would not take the ideological position that its own purposes cannot finally prosper unless all systems of government not under its control are subverted and eventually destroyed. . . . Secondly, while recognizing that the internal system of government is in all essential respects Russia's own business and may well depart drastically from our own, we are entitled to expect that the exercise of governmental authority will stop short of that fairly plain line beyond which lies totalitarianism. . . . The third thing we may hope from a new Russia is that it

[4] Herman Finer: *America's Destiny* (Macmillan; 1947), pp. 359 and 366.

will refrain from pinning an oppressive yoke on other peoples who have the instinct and the capacity for national self-assertion. In mentioning this matter, we are entering upon a delicate subject. . . .

These, then, are the things for which an American well-wisher may hope from the Russia of the future: that she lift forever the Iron Curtain, that she recognize certain limitations to the internal authority of government, and that she abandon, as ruinous and unworthy, the ancient game of imperialist expansion and oppression.[5]

Thus Paul G. Hoffman:

I am confident that the downfall of the present regime is inherent in its very structure. That confidence has been fortified by many astute observers, notably John Foster Dulles, General Douglas MacArthur, and George Kennan, along with a number of foreign ministers whose names I cannot disclose. The exact manner in which the Kremlin's tyranny will be broken is, of course, a matter of conjecture. So is the time. But the tensions that make a breakup likely are concrete and readily discerned. . . . All Soviet peoples live in virtual enslavement. . . . I am pinning particular hope for the downfall of the Kremlin on the will of peoples to rule themselves. . . . The best thing that could happen would be a revolution inside the USSR that would turn it toward democracy and thus provide a solid basis for enduring peace.[6]

[5] George F. Kennan: "America and the Russian Future," *Foreign Affairs* (April 1951), reprinted as Appendix II of *American Diplomacy, 1900–1950*, (University of Chicago Press; 1951). This article by the most intelligent and influential proponent of the policy of "containment" contains much wisdom, coupled with a cheerful discussion of how America ought, and ought not, to try to remake Russia after World War III, and a tacit assumption that while Russians who seek to remake America are immoral monsters, Americans who seek to remake Russia are angels of God. Mr. Kennan further postulates that America, obviously, possesses the power and capacity to remold the Russian community to our hearts' desire—a proposition that might deserve to be judged as evidence of insanity except for the fact that innumerable Americans, apparently otherwise sane, appear to share it.

[6] Paul G. Hoffman: *Peace Can Be Won* (Doubleday; 1951), pp. 171–3, 176, 177. It should be noted that these sentiments, written by a great public figure in 1951, are almost identical with those expressed by most other Western public figures in 1917–20. See Meno Lovenstein: *American Opinion of Soviet Russia* (Washington, D.C.: American Council on Public Affairs; 1941).

And thus Harold E. Stassen in *Man Was Meant to Be Free* (Garden City, N.Y.: Doubleday; 1951):

> The Iron Curtain has become a murderous network of barbed wire and machine-guns around an enormous prison of nations. . . . I look forward to the collapse of the Communist dictatorships and their ruthless, Godless systems. Beyond this, I believe will come the liberation and upward climb of mankind toward those better conditions that a free and democratic world *can* provide. . . . What I do urge is a great offensive for the cause of the freedom of mankind in the clash of ideas, of social orders—of economic systems and spiritual values.

Whether these consummations devoutly to be wished are to be achieved by example, gentle persuasion, tough propaganda, or atomic bombs and conquering armies is not usually made clear in the public utterances of those who advocate these blessings. What is clearly a part of the hypothesis is that America will perish unless Americans can somehow contrive to produce revolution in the Marxist imperium—a fantasy borrowed from the Muscovite Marxists and here reversed against them.

A catalogue of all the various and sundry earnest endeavors in this direction would be boring. The sequence is simple, and the consequence can be illumined by a few examples. On August 18, 1945, Secretary of State Byrnes demanded democracy in Bulgaria. Two days later Ernest Bevin insisted that "we must prevent the substitution of one form of totalitarianism for another." Long and involved Western efforts ensued to "democratize" Eastern Europe and the Balkans (a trick no one has ever turned thus far)—with Moscow rightly equating such efforts with an attempt to undermine Russian control of the Eastern marches, and Washington rightly equating Moscow's resistance with contumacious insolence and defiance of Western wishes. By January of 1948 Bevin was saying: "The issue is not simply the organization of Poland or any other country, but the control of Eastern Europe by Soviet Russia." Churchill agreed: "Who can ever believe that there will be permanent peace in Europe or in the world while the frontiers of Asia rest upon the Elbe?" Washington concurred *fortissimo.*[7] Since diplomacy and threats failed to alter the facts of life (and indeed made them worse), many Westerners concluded that war or revolution or both were requisite to achieve the desired diminution or overthrow of the Muscovite Power.

A bewildering multiplicity of organizations—often headed by apostate Communists or by *émigrés*, exiles, and refugees, and sponsored by Americans in the *Social Register*—had come into being by midcentury for the avowed purpose of effecting the emancipation of the enslaved populations living in misery under the Red Flag. The ultimate purpose of the "European Movement" (see p. 460f. below), declared Winston Churchhill, was "the deliverance" of Eastern Europe from "the grip of a tyranny more permanently devastating than that of Hitler." The Iron Curtain Refugee Campaign, endorsed by more than thirty state governors and headed by General Carl Spaatz (Chairman), Sumner Welles, and Admiral Richard E. Byrd, strove to expose Communist crimes against humanity and to sponsor Frontier Reception Centers and resettlement projects for fugitives from the Red Terror. The National Committee for a Free Europe, among its other enterprises, established a "Free Europe University in Exile" near Strasbourg and financed Radio Free Europe, whose programs were designed to conduct psychological warfare more vigorously than the official Voice of America, with the object of instigating revolution and promoting what *Life* magazine called "the necessary disintegration of the Soviet Communist system." General Lucius D. Clay in May 1951 praised the Munich broadcasts for having "the open and avowed aim to dethrone the Communist governments."

[7] See Vernon Van Dyke: "American Support of Free Institutions in Eastern Europe," Yale Institute of International Studies (removed in 1951 to Princeton), Memorandum No. 28 (August 10, 1948); Loy W. Henderson: "American Political and Strategic Interests in the Middle East and Southeastern Europe," *Department of State Bulletin* (November 23, 1947); and Constantine A. Fotitch: "The Liberation of Eastern Europe," *American Perspective* (June 1949).

The American Committee for the Liberation of the Peoples of Russia, Inc., was established in August 1951 under the Presidency of Eugene Lyons, with its committee including Professor William Yandell Elliott of Harvard, Isaac Don Levine, William Henry Chamberlin, and William L. White. Its announced goal was to unite all *émigré* groups in "a common front for a common dedication: the overthrow of the Soviet regime." Admiral Alan Kirk, former Ambassador of the U.S.A. to the U.S.S.R., became its president early in 1952. It proposed to co-operate with the "Council for the Liberation of the Peoples of Russia," formed at a conference in Stuttgart, with headquarters in Munich. The "Crusade for Freedom" of which General Clay was National Chairman and Harold E. Stassen chairman of the membership drive, secured sixteen million signers in 1950 and launched a campaign for twenty-five million adherents in September 1951, with meetings at Rockefeller Plaza and the Waldorf Astoria addressed by Vice President Alben W. Barkley and Cardinal Spellman. President Truman sent greetings and called the endeavor "an inspiring and effective attack against Red tyranny." The widespread popularity of proposals for instigating revolution in Russia was reflected in the book market, the cinema, and the radio.[8]

The liberation of Asia was no less dear to American hearts.

[8] James Burnham's *The Coming Defeat of Communism* (John Day; 1950) discusses "Political Subversive Warfare," along with military strategy. A popular thriller of 1951 was entitled *I Killed Stalin*, by Sterling Noel (Farrar, Strauss & Young; 1951). On America's Town Meeting of the Air, May 8, 1951, Mrs. Ada Siegel, Maurice Hindus, and John Scott discussed: "Is Revolution Possible inside Russia without War?" A striking illustration of the climate of American opinion was the apparent absence of any sense of impropriety on the part of the Admiral, the State Department, Congress, and most of the press when, on February 10, 1952, Admiral Alan G. Kirk, for two and a half years U.S. Ambassador to the U.S.S.R., assumed the chairmanship of the American Committee for the Liberation of the Peoples of Russia, Inc., explaining: "If the Stalinist regime is our enemy, the peoples enslaved by him in the Soviet Union are our friends. . . . It is my firm belief that they are overwhelmingly opposed to the Kremlin regime, hate its aggressive policies, and yearn for freedom from the Bolshevik yoke. . . . [The Committee will provide material and moral aid] to enable the fugitives from Stalin's tyranny now living in our midst to undertake practical anti-Soviet activities."

Before the China Institute in New York on May 18, 1951, Assistant Secretary of State Dean Rusk declared:

> The independence of China is gravely threatened. . . . The peace and security of China are being sacrificed to the ambitions of the Communist conspiracy. . . . We can tell our friends in China that the United States will not acquiesce in the degradation which is being forced upon them. . . . The Peiping Regime may be a colonial Russian government—a Slavic Manchukuo on a larger scale. It is not the Government of China. . . . It is not Chinese. It is not entitled to speak for China. . . . We recognize the National Government of the Republic of China [Chiang Kai-shek on Formosa]. . . . It more authentically represents the views of the great body of the people of China. . . . That Government will continue to receive important aid and assistance from the United States. . . . If the Chinese people decide for freedom, they shall find friends among all the peoples of the earth who have known and loved freedom.

Dean Acheson privately reprimanded Dean Rusk for using language so undiplomatic, but announced that the address represented no change of American policy. On April 14, 1951, the Voice of America, relayed from London to Eastern Europe, quoted a Washington correspondent to the effect that "British and American agents have maintained contact with Resistance forces in South China," that "aid has been flowing to such forces for many months," and that other agents had recently blown up a Peking power plant. In the face of British outcries of incredulity and anger, Downing Street, through Kenneth Younger, hastened to assert: "Needless to say, there is no truth in the allegations as far as the United Kingdom is concerned." In September Justice William O. Douglas aroused a storm of American press condemnation and threats of impeachment by declaring on his return from a journey to Asia that America should sponsor "land reform," cease to rely on "guns and dollars rather than ideas," and recognize the Peking regime as the only way of separating China from Russia. On September 13, 1951, no less than fifty-six senators signed a statement (circulated by

Senator William F. Knowland of California, with none of those asked desiring or daring to withhold approval) solemnly opposing "the recognition of Communist China or its admission to the U.N.," and averring that any recognition by Japan or any negotiation of a bilateral treaty between Japan and Red China would be "averse to the best interests of the people of both Japan and the United States."

Private American groups committed to the overthrow of the new government of China were too many to mention. They ranged from those who supposed that nonrecognition would produce collapse by a kind of black magic to those who envisaged the task in terms of bombardment, invasion, and occupation. One of the more active and more humanitarian in its objectives was the American Bureau for Medical Aid to China, of which Dr. Magnus I. Gregersen was president, with the directors comprising Lieutenant General Albert C. Wedemeyer; Mrs. Wendell Willkie; Hollis Powers Gale, investment banker; and Alfred Kohlberg, industrialist and chief sponsor of the China Lobby. In March 1951, Dr. Gregersen went to Formosa on an ECA mission. In its plea for funds, the ABMAC asserted: "In 1951 the struggle between the forces of darkness and the forces of light—between Communism and freedom—has irrevocably begun. Medical help is one weapon short of war available to us. . . ." [9]

The Congress of the United States, manifesting anew its habitual conviction that ideas are best fought with guns, finally brought itself to the point of appropriating funds to finance treason, sabotage, rebellion, guerrilla warfare, and perhaps *émigré* invasions of enemy countries. On September 19, 1951, Senate and House conferees, deliberating on the Mutual Security Bill, agreed to authorize expenditures of one hundred million dollars "for any selected persons who are residing in or escapees from the Soviet Union, Czechoslovakia, Hungary, Rumania, Bulgaria, Albania, Lithuania, Latvia and Estonia, or the Communist-dominated or occupied areas of Germany and Austria, and any other countries

[9] The ABMAC *Bulletin* (July-September, 1951).

absorbed by the Soviet Union to form such persons into elements of the military forces supporting the North Atlantic Treaty Organization or for other purposes."

All these activities zealously pursued on both sides of the line of battle for the peace of the world served a useful and perhaps necessary social function, as we shall see, though it was not quite what the sponsors supposed it to be. Before we consider its strange nature, it will be useful to glance briefly at other instances of attempted subversion—of a rather different character from those previously considered.

2. THE DEDICATED BRETHREN

> Peace can never be achieved by conferences or be decided by people who not only jabber, but who themselves go to war. This question was decided 1900 years ago in the teaching of Christ as this teaching was understood by Him and not as it has been perverted by the churches. All conferences can be summed up in a single dictum: All people are sons of God and brothers, and therefore they ought to love and not kill each other. Forgive my sharpness, but all these conferences invoke in me a strong feeling of disgust over the hypocrisy that is so obvious in them. . . . It is necessary to point out that the present state of affairs, especially the Hague Conference, has shown that nothing is to be expected from the higher powers, and that the resolution of this horribly destructive situation, if at all possible, will depend solely on the efforts of private individuals.
>
> —LEO TOLSTOY, 1900.[1]

COMMUNISTS in the lands of the so-called "Free World" are dedicated to the achievement of world peace through world unity. Anti-Communists within the Marxist World-State are also dedicated to world peace through world unity. The former seek to overthrow non-Communist governments, replace

[1] Quoted by Ernest C. Simmons: *Leo Tolstoy* (Boston: Little, Brown; 1946), pp. 576–7.

them with Communistic dictatorships, and unite all the earth under the hegemony of Marxist Muscovy. The latter seek to overthrow Communist governments; replace them with monarchies, aristocracies, or democracies; and unite all the earth under the ægis of Anti-Communism, Americanism, Atlanticism, Liberalism, Capitalism, Feudalism, Buchmanism, or some other of the many variants of the search for "freedom" through the liquidation of Red Despotism. Neither endeavor, even if globally successful, could conceivably eventuate in world peace through world unity. But both endeavors in their respective spheres are indistinguishable from treason—in the Scarlet Empire because counterrevolutoin and support of "American Imperialism" are plainly treasonable to the oligarchs of the status quo, and in the more or less democratic societies because revolution and support of "Soviet Imperialism" are no less obviously equivalent to "levying war against them or adhering to their enemies, giving them aid and comfort."

The case is less clear, in the New Atlantis at any rate, with respect to a great variety of other cults, sects, and movements unconnected with the "enemy" and yet bent upon peace through devices deemed dangerous to constituted authority and anathema to prevailing opinion. Such distinctions are clearly nonexistent in the new empire of Kubla Khan, since its rulers (unlike their Mongol precursors) tolerate no deviations from orthodoxy and regard all individual eccentricities of political attitudes as equivalent to "Fascism," "Trotskyism," "Titoism," and subversive service to "Wall Street." Even in the West, the imperatives of sovereignty—tolerant toward dissidents in the piping times of peace and plenty prevailing a century ago—move men under the harsher and more hazardous conditions of today to view all dissenters with suspicion. However unjustified such suspicions in any given case may be, and however unreasonable it would be here to identify non-Communist peace-seekers with "treason," it is none the less true by virtue of the very nature of the institution of the State that all who, for reasons of conscience, refuse to obey the orders of those who act in its name (including orders to kill and be killed) or decline to render obeisance to its symbols (e.g., Jehovah's Witnesses, who in their abhorrence of "idolatry" refuse to salute the flag) expose themselves, under the circumstances of our time of troubles, to general condemnation and sometimes to prosecution.

No adequate survey of pacifisms and "peace" movements can here be undertaken, nor is any such effort called for. These activities, thus far, are largely marginal and tangential to the mainstream of human conduct looking toward, or making for, world government. Neither need we puzzle ourselves with the intriguing problem of classifying such endeavors in terms of sources of inspiration, nature of activities, and content of programs. It will be sufficient to notice some typical ways in which many seekers after peace have sought, usually with no awareness of any lack of patriotism on their own part, to persuade their fellows to resist or defy the bellivolent commands of government; or to transcend national loyalties by building transnational or global loyalties through private efforts; or to checkmate and modify public attitudes and policies through pressure and propaganda.

In its genesis, the modern "peace movement" in the West had its roots in the religious and humanitarian conviction, best exemplified by the Quakers, that violence is immoral and un-Christian. It was in 1805 that David Low Dodge, a New York businessman who championed nonresistance to evil, published his pamphlet, "The Mediator's Kingdom Not of This World," arguing that all warfare is a negation of Christianity. On August 14, 1815, on the basis of his second pamphlet, "War Inconsistent with the Religion of Jesus Christ," he founded the first Peace Society. Later in the same year Dr. Noah Worcester of Massachusetts and two Friends (Quakers) in Ohio, without knowing of Dodge or of one another, founded two other Peace Societies. Quite independently, William Allen in London established in 1816, with its supporters initially limited to Friends, the Society for the Promotion of Permanent and Universal Peace—claiming to be the oldest of the Peace Societies, since the three American groups combined into the American Peace Society only in 1828, under the leadership of a New Hampshire sea captain, William Ladd. Until his death in 1841, Ladd was the chief American inspiration of the movement, and a successful advocate of collaboration between the American and British branches. The British brethren consistently opposed even defensive war on the ground that any forcible resistance to evil was unethical and irreligious. Regarding the politics of peace, they were more vague. The American brethren early championed "arbitration" and a "Congress of Nations," endorsed by the Massachusetts legislature in 1837.

Counterparts appeared on the Continent. Tracts and sermons poured out. Essay contests were numerous. Efforts at coordination among national group led to the first international Peace Congress in London in 1843. Ladd's successor, Elihu Burritt, a Connecticut blacksmith, took the initiative in summoning a second Congress in Brussels in 1848. About a thousand delegates, most of them British, assembled in an enthusiastic third Congress in Paris in 1849, under the presidency of Victor Hugo. A fourth followed in London in 1851 during the Great Exhibition. This initial exuberance waned with the advent of the Crimean War, which caused British and French nonresisters to be regarded as unpatriotic, and with the increasing devotion of their American colleagues to the cause of Abolitionism—which was to mean not peace but war.

During the half century that ended at Sarajevo the peace movement became worldwide and devoted its energies to the promotion of arbitration and disarmament. But the pristine simplicity of the early impetus was by now confused with the myriad notions of everybody concerned with "peace," from millionaires to anarchists. A dynamite manufacturer, Alfred Nobel, and an armor-plate maker, Andrew Carnegie, established prizes and endowments. The subversive notion of boycotting government as a means to peace and freedom evolved from David Thoreau's concept of civil disobedience through Tolstoi's Christian anarchism to Mohandas Gandhi's philosophy and technique of nonviolent resistance to authority. European Marxists dreamed of a "general strike" against war, as urged by J. Keir Hardie and Edouard Vaillant, to be proclaimed and organized by the Second International. The German Social Democrats were dubious. Jean Jaures's "compromise" formula implied revolution as a means of halting war. He was assassinated on the eve of Armageddon. Only the Russian Marxists followed such precepts. The Second International disintegrated under the impact of the patriotism of its national sections. The Peace Congress planned by the International Peace Bureau at Berne to meet in Stockholm in the late summer of 1914 never assembled.

A century of devoted labors for peace thus culminated in the singleminded devotion of most of mankind to the tasks of slaughter and destruction at the behest of the tribal gods. Two subsequent decades of even more ardent endeavors for peace were followed in 1939 by a far more complete and devastating dedication of men to murder and suicide in the name of *raison d'état*. A decade later all the world was furiously preparing for a third global contest in arms, which promised to be "final" and "decisive" only in the sense that the survivors seemed likely to revert to savagery regardless of the identity or ideals of the alleged "victors." Such blood-stained calendars and black horoscopes suggest one of two conclusions: either the "peace-seekers" were operating in a kind of moral and intellectual vacuum in which they were wholly unable to move the hearts and minds of men; or mankind, irremediably bent upon self-destruction, was incapable of responding to pleas for reason and for love. The record offers impressive evidence in support of both conclusions. But we must limit our analysis at this point to a few comments on the recent *leitmotifs* in this tragic symphony of frustration.

In World War I the various sections of the British peace-movement, co-ordinated since 1908 in the National Peace Council, found a voice in the "Union of Democratic Control," founded in October 1914 by E. D. Morel, Ramsay Mac-

Donald, Norman Angell, C. P. Trevelyan, and Arthur Ponsonby. (Morel was imprisoned in 1917 for violating the Defense-of-the-Realm Act.) Fenner Brockway collected signatures of war-resisters and helped to organize a "No Conscription Fellowship," which evolved in 1921 into the "No More War Movement" and a "War Resisters' International." Thousands of young people later signed the so-called "Oxford Oath," by which they pledged themselves never to bear arms for king or country. In America the Peace Society shifted in 1917 from opposition to war to advocacy of "war to end war," as did the Carnegie Endowment and the new "League to Enforce Peace," which helped pave the way for the League of Nations.[2]

The reader will here be spared the confused and futile history of the peace movement during the long armistice between World Wars I and II. A few tendencies are worthy of brief comment. The seditious pacifist-anarchist notion that war can be stopped if only enough people will refuse to fight, at the risk of jail, found little echo in the days of our years. It derives from Gandhi, Tolstoi, Thoreau—and more remotely, by some interpretations of the Gospel, from Jesus of Nazareth. In our time only handfuls of Quakers, other "conscientious objectors," and absolute pacifists have possessed the courage to act upon it and to invite contempt and punishment from their fellow citizens. There are still devoted souls who subscribe in varying degree to this ideal. At No. 3 Blackstock Road, London, is published *Peace News: The International Pacifist Weekly*. Early in 1951 it publicized the slogan of the Friends Peace Committee: "We think it wrong in the sight of God that men, of any age, should be forced to train to kill those with whom they should be friends." John S. Hoyland, Chairman of the National Council of the British Crusade for World Government, published eloquent pamphlets in 1950 under such titles as "Gandhi and World

[2] Useful guides, with bibliographies, to these movements are to be found in A. C. F. Beales: *The History of Peace* (Dial; 1931) and Merle E. Curti: *Peace or War—The American Struggle, 1636–1936* (Norton; 1936).

Government," "Federate or Perish," and "World Government and the Kingdom of God."

The National Peace Council, headed by Lord Boyd Orr, with the Rev. Henry Carter as chairman, continued without loss of public respect to work for peace (sans any extreme pacifist position), and to co-ordinate and report upon the activities of the multitudinous British peace-organizations.[3] The emergency "Peace with China Council" (144 Southampton Row), with Kingsley Martin as chairman and with a distinguished list of sponsors, organized local groups and filled large halls all over England in 1950–1 in a popular effort, devoid of any doctrinaire pacifism, to prevent the United States from plunging the U.N. and the Atlantic Alliance into all-out war with China.

Seekers after peace in the America of the 1950's had a harder row to hoe. The "Central Committee for Conscientious Objectors," with Ray Newton as chairman and endorsed by Clarence E. Pickett, Harry Emerson Fosdick, Pitirim A. Sorokin, and Albert Einstein, sought to defend religious pacifists from prosecution. The American Friends Service Committee strove valiantly to find bases of accommodation between the super-Powers.[4] Quakers were habitually regarded in America as amiable and harmless eccentrics. But their spiritual devotion to peace (shared by no other Christian denomination to anything like the same degree) aroused suspicions of treason in certain quarters in the mad America of the midcentury. The same was true of the "War Resisters' League" and of the "Fellowship of Reconciliation," founded in 1914, with A. J. Muste as national secretary at the time of writing. Comparable criticism was directed against such

[3] *The Peace Year Book,* 1951 Festival Edition, of the National Peace Council (London) provides, in a hundred-page pamphlet with a bibliography and other guides, an unusually complete list of British and foreign peace-organizations.

[4] See "American-Russian Relations: Some Constructive Considerations," A Report by a Working Party (Philadelphia: American Friends Service Committee; 1949), and the subsequent book: *United States and the Soviet Union: Some Quaker Proposals for Peace* (New Haven, Connecticut: Yale University Press; 1949).

atomic scientists (e.g., Cuthbert Daniel and Arthur Squires) who advocated unilateral disarmament as the only way to safety in a world in which competitive rearmament meant, so they believed, universal destruction.[5]

Among the more exciting ideas among the peace-seekers of our age of anxiety is the revolutionary conception that individuals can somehow transcend the parochialism of national sovereignty by proclaiming themselves "world citizens" and thus preparing the way on a mass scale for world government. In 1938 a "World Citizenship Movement" was launched in the United Kingdom. Its monthly periodical, *Humanity: The Journal of World Government and World Citizenship*, was published by United World Publications in Glasgow. Its chairman in 1951 was James Avery Joyce and its deputy chairman Hugh J. Schonfield. Among its sponsors were Vera Brittain, George E. Catlin, Lancelot Hogben, L. P. Jacks, Lord Boyd Orr, and (among Americans) Robert MacIver and Lewis Mumford. It offered tracts, lectures, and courses in World Citizenship. Similar activities on a smaller scale have long been carried on by the "World Citizens' Association" of Chicago. More recently, at Oberlin, Ohio, an American "World Citizenship Movement" has emerged, founded by Thomas Tchou, with Russell W. Davenport as first president (succeeded by John H. Holtvoight in 1951) and blessed by the National Education Association.

The most dramatic endeavors in this direction have taken place in France. Here Robert Sarrazac, in a kind of one-man campaign of "mundialization," induced scores of municipal councils in 1949–50 to declare their community part of the world community—an example followed by numerous local governments in Germany, the Low Countries, Scandinavia, and Britain. And here Garry Davis, bomber pilot and son of a band leader, renounced his American citizenship in 1948 in favor of "world citizenship" and, in mid-April of

[5] See pages 50–5 of Alexander D. Mebane's brochure, *Whither Must I Fly?* (1949), and the files of *The Christian Century* and the *Bulletin of the Atomic Scientists.*

1949, launched his "World Citizens' Pact" which summoned all to declare themselves citizens of the world and asserted that "all humanity is in a state of lawful defense against sovereign states, ideologies, and propagandas tending to justify recourse to war." His simplicity and flair for dramatic gestures, coupled with the obvious anguish of a mankind desperately seeking a way to salvation, led almost half a million people to sign his Pact. He returned to America on March 30, 1950, and in October applied for a restoration of his American citizenship. The "International Register of Citizens of the World" (4 rue Saint-Christophe, Brussels) continued to enlist adherents to the ideal of One World. Most among them are good patriots, conceiving of the duties of patriotism in global rather than national terms. A few, particularly in England, dream of a private "Commonwealth of World Citizens," all pledged never to fight one another in war and eventually capable, they hope, of negotiating with governments for the maintenance of peace.[6]

Such aspirations skirt the margins of treason, since it is of the essence of our cultural heritage in the system of States of which we are all a part that only those authorized to speak in the name of government are entitled to define citizenship and to prescribe the rights and duties of citizens. For private persons or groups to undertake such tasks smacks of subversion, particularly when their avowed purposes assert or imply that those who are to be true to the ideals promulgated may, and indeed should, disobey law and defy authority whenever public decisions demand action contrary to conscience. The

[6] The exhilarating campaign of M. Robert Sarrazac to "Mundialize" European local governments has nowhere been written up in any factual form, so far as I can discover. I was unfortunately unable to arrange an interview with him in Paris during my visit in 1951. The Foundation for World Government, which supported his efforts, has a dossier of stimulating essays from his pen but no systematic account of his endeavors—which are reminiscent of Robert Lee Humber, who, in the America of the 1940's, personally persuaded a score of state legislatures to endorse his resolution for world federal government. Thanks to the courtesy of Mary Lloyd, I have in my files a copy of *Le Midi Mondialiste, Numero Special*, Mars 1951, and some mimeographed material issued by various *Conseiles de Mondialisation*, illustrative of the methods and purposes of the movement.

Western theory and practice of popular sovereignty—i.e., the State is the People, or is answerable to the People, or derives its authority from the People—scarcely alters the case.

In the epoch of the modern tribal divinities, the vast majority of people in every land expect every citizen to do his patriotic duty by way of rendering exclusive allegiance to the Fatherland, bearing arms in its name, and killing and being killed on its behalf. The Western concept of minority rights, however, often affords some measure of protection to deviationists and eccentrics who scorn the normal duties of citizenship in their search for the *Civitas Dei*. The protection is strictly contingent upon negative abstention from warlike endeavors. Positive participation on the enemy's side is invariably treason. None of the movements thus far mentioned is seriously under such suspicion, for all are resolutely anti-Communist and each is banned as treasonable within the Scarlet Empire, where the rights of political and ideological minorities are nonexistent.

The situation is wholly different with respect to what is unquestionably the most multitudinous and vociferous of all "peace movements" of the midcentury: the so-called "Partisans of Peace." Here we are in the presence of a skillfully organized mass movement of Communist origin, with branches in all the major anti-Communist countries that still tolerate dissent. The organizers seek to serve the purposes of Soviet foreign policy through propagandistic activities designed to label Muscovite Marxists as champions of "peace" and supporters of American foreign policy as "warmongers." This circumstance, in the eyes of the discriminating observer, does not make all the participants mere agents or dupes of Moscow. The Kremlin may fairly be presumed to desire "peace" in global terms, since its interests would be best served thereby, with war deemed advantageous—and therefore permissible and moral—only when it is limited and localized. Many non-Communist "Partisans" sincerely, though perhaps mistakenly, believe that the Soviet Union wishes peace and that America is bent upon war, and thus assume, honestly and naïvely, that the cause of peace is best served by opposing American policies and supporting Soviet policies.

A "Congress of Intellectuals for Peace" was held in Wroclaw, Poland, on August 25, 1948. The introductory address by Alexander Fadeyev of the U.S.S.R. was an insulting assault upon Western culture and American civilization. Julian Huxley departed with the impression that the delegates were preaching war, not peace. In late March of 1949, under the auspices of the National Council of Arts, Sciences, and Professions, and without connection with the Wroclaw gathering (save that a few persons attended both), a "Cultural and Scientific Congress for World Peace" met at the Waldorf-Astoria Hotel in New York, amid picketing, misrepresentation, and controversy—though most participants supposed they were contributing to public enlightenment regarding the preconditions of avoiding war.[7] In Paris in April 1949 a "World Committee for Peace" emerged out of a distinctly pro-Communist Congress, where the term, "Partisans of Peace," was coined and Pablo Picasso's dove became the symbol of the movement. Another and even more pro-Communist "World Congress of Partisans of Peace," meeting in Stockholm in March 1950, formulated the "Stockholm Appeal," which, without condemning aggression or the use of other weapons of slaughter, demanded "unconditional prohibition of the atomic weapon as a weapon of aggression and mass annihilation of peoples," "strict international control," and the branding as a "war criminal" of any government "which first employs the atomic weapon against any country."

[7] See *Speaking of Peace* (Daniel S. Gillmor, editor), *A Report of the Cultural and Scientific Conference for World Peace*, National Council of the Arts, Sciences, and Professions, New York, 1949. My own exchange of views with Alexander Fadeyev is here reported verbatim. *The New York Herald Tribune* and *The New York Times* also reported the Conference in substantially accurate fashion. The account of it in *Time,* April 4, 1949, bore no relationship to the facts, but the publisher and editors refused to print any comment or correction, thereby conforming to the usual standards of integrity and veracity characteristic of the Luce publications in all such matters.

The Stockholm Appeal became the basis for a worldwide campaign to enlist signatures. On June 19, 1950, it was unanimously adopted by the Supreme Soviet of the U.S.S.R. According to Communist claims, it was subsequently signed by 115 million Soviet citizens, 204 million Chinese, 50 millions in the Soviet satellites, 20 millions in Germany, 16 millions in Italy, 15 millions in France, 2.5 millions in the U.S.A., and so on, up to an alleged global total of 500 millions—"a serious force," declared Marshal Bulganin, "and a dread warning to warmongers." The objectives of the campaign on the part of its initial organizers and sponsors were to capitalize upon universal desires for peace and universal distrust of America, to enlist sympathy for the Soviet Union, and to build a new type of "Popular Front" wherein Communists and non-Communists could again collaborate for shared purposes without the latter feeling used or abused or in danger of digestion by the former. The purposes of the non-Communist participants were, quite simply, to disseminate progapanda for peace without regard to the implications of their position or affiliations.

The "Partisans of Peace" evolved into a "World Peace Council," of which Professor Frederic Joliot-Curie became president. Even in hostile America, many seekers after peace were inveigled into supporting the cause through a "Peace Information Center" in New York, headed by Dr. W. E. B. DuBois, an "American Peace Ballot," an "American Peace Crusade," a "People's Congress and Exposition for Peace" in Chicago in late June 1951, and other ingenious devices. On February 25, 1951, the World Peace Council, meeting in Berlin, issued a new Appeal, demanding "the conclusion of a pact of peace among the Five Great Powers: the U.S.A., the Soviet Union, the Chinese People's Republic, Great Britain, and France. We would consider a refusal to meet and conclude such a pact, by the Government of any of the Great Powers whichever it might be, as evidence of aggressive design on the part of the Government in question." Again adroit semantic simplicity concealed stark realities.

Again millions of signatures were gathered. Such a pact, however drawn, would effect no change whatever in Soviet policies. An America arming furiously for war in the name of peace, fighting Red China in Korea, resolved on non-recognition of Peking, and committed in dealing with Moscow to "total diplomacy"—i.e., no diplomacy—could only reject such a proposal, and thereby convict itself by the proposal's own terms of "aggressive designs."

Such cleverness could not be ignored. On July 12, 1950, Dean Acheson denounced the Stockholm Appeal as "a propaganda trick in the spurious 'peace offensive' of the Soviet Union," a Communist plot, "an utterly cynical begging of the question," and a piece of "bitter hypocrisy" as shown by the fact that half the population of North Korea had signed the document prior to the launching of a war of aggression and conquest against South Korea. Warren Austin, in rejecting as "delivered to the wrong address" Joliot-Curie's proposal to send a delegation to the U.N. to explain the views of the World Peace Council, urged him to send the delegates to Moscow and Peking to convert the Red Sinners to the ways of rectitude and to loyal adherence to the U.N. Charter. Ernest A. Gross wrote Dr. DuBois: "We are not prepared to be used by the W.P.C. in its program of aiding and abetting aggression. . . ."[8]

In this wise, in the demented world of the 1950's, propaganda for "peace" became the major weapon of political warfare in the arsenal of the Muscovite Marxists, whose potentates outlawed "warmongering" by statute. In America adherence to the Great Crusade to defend peace and freedom against aggression and tyranny became the prime test of pa-

[8] See Donald H. McLachlan: "The Partisans of Peace," *International Affairs* (London: January 1951); "Peacegram," issued by the Peace Information Center of New York on behalf of the Stockholm Appeal; *The American Peace Crusader; The Bulletin of the World Peace Council;* Leon Dennen: "The Soviet Peace Myth," published by the National Committee for a Free Europe (1951); Press Releases of the U.S. Mission to the U.N., Nos. 1203 (May 25, 1951) and 1221 (June 20, 1951), and *Time's* horror picture and horror story of Communist perversity and mendacity in campaigning for peace, issue of September 17, 1951.

triotism, while all who sought peace by any methods other than war were open to suspicion of being enemy agents and traitors. Which side scored more points in this battle of words is a quite pointless issue. There are no victors in a contest in which sanity is the first casualty. When sanity is lost, peace of mind and peace on earth are alike doomed.

3. THE SCAPEGOATS

On the Day of Atonement, which was the tenth day of the seventh month, the Jewish high-priest laid both his hands on the head of a live goat, confessed over it all the iniquities of the Children of Israel, and, having thereby transferred the sins of the people to the beast, sent it away into the wilderness. The scapegoat upon whom the sins of the people are periodically laid, may also be a human being. At Onitsha, on the Niger, two human beings used to be annually sacrificed to take away the sins of the land. The victims were purchased by public subscription. All persons who, during the past year, had fallen into gross sins, such as incendiarism, theft, adultery, witchcraft, and so forth, were expected to contribute 28 *ngugas*, or a little over £2. The money thus collected was taken into the interior of the country and expended in the purchase of two sickly persons "to be offered as a sacrifice for all these abominable crimes—one for the land and one for the river." A man from a neighboring town was hired to put them to death. On the 27th of February 1858 the Rev. J. C. Taylor witnessed the sacrifice of one of these victims. The sufferer was a woman, about nineteen or twenty years of age. They dragged her alive along the ground, face downwards, from the king's house to the river, a distance of two miles, the crowds who accompanied her crying, "Wickedness! Wickedness!" The intention was "to take away the iniquities of the land. The body was dragged along in a merciless manner, as if the weight of all their wickedness was thus carried away." Similar customs are said to be still secretly practiced every year by many tribes in the delta of the Niger.

—JAMES G. FRAZER: *The Golden Bough*.[9]

[9] Sir James G. Frazer: *The Golden Bough* (Macmillan; 1940, one-volume abridgment), pp. 569–70.

DEATH has been the customary penalty for treason in all the times and climes of Man. In primitive cultures and barbarous epochs the exaction of the penalty has often been mingled in the public mind with notions once strange to us: the use of torture to obtain confessions or to insure that death should be preceded by suitable suffering; the equivalence of treason to heresy, blasphemy, and sacrilege on the premise that the rulers and dogmas of the State were sacred; and the ancient idea of human sacrifice to the gods, with the victim propitiating divinity by taking unto himself all the sins of the community and, by his death, absolving all from guilt. In our new age of barbarism, all these practices are again familiar. The conceptions underlying them are mingled and apotheosized in the Christian account of the secular circumstances and cosmic meaning of the death of Jesus of Nazareth—whose followers have ever since regarded as their holiest symbol an instrument of execution by torture whereby a divinely innocent prisoner was put to death for treason and heresy and, in dying, purified and saved all men.

That dissenters from orthodoxy and "enemies" of State or Church should die in agony was long taken for granted in Western culture. Joan of Arc was sainted by the Pope in A.D. 1920. Half a millennium earlier she had been sentenced by the Pope's agents to be burned to death as a witch, guilty of "high treason against God." On March 23, 1430—fourteen months before her own incineration—she wrote to the Hussite heretics of Bohemia:

> Do you think that you will escape punishment? Don't you know that God does not hinder your criminal undertakings . . . so that he can prepare for you punishment and sufferings the greater the more you rage? . . . To say the truth if I were not occupied with the wars against the English, verily I would already have gone long ago to find you. But in truth, should I not hear that you have mended your ways, I will perhaps leave the English and proceed against you, so that I shall, if unable by other means, starve out by the sword your stupid and stub-

born superstition and take away either your heresy or your life.[1]

In the Reformation, Martin Luther, outraged at the response of the serfs to his teachings, advised the princes: "Kill! Cut their throats! Burn, slay, crush the murderous and rapacious peasants!" The Emperor Charles V subsequently advised the Inquisition to follow his own example in dealing with heretics in the Netherlands "where all who remained obstinate in their errors were burned alive, and those who were admitted to penitence were beheaded." The battle-cry of the Scotch Presbyterians in the English Civil War was "Jesus and no quarter!"

The Inquisition, only lately regarded as a hideous relic of superstition, is again the central institution of our own age, as Dostoevsky foresaw in his immortal story of the Grand Inquisitor in *The Brothers Karamazov.* Under the leadership of its most memorable administrator, Father Thomas Torquemada (1420–98), the Spanish Dominicans or "Dogs of the Lord" burned thousands of heretics, led a "crusade" against the Moors, and expropriated and expelled a million Jewish families from Spain—to the ruin of the realm. In these trials of traitors, any witness who refused to testify against accomplices, friends, and relatives was himself deemed guilty of heresy. Confessions were commonly obtained by torture, including at times the torture of witnesses and of such lawyers as dared to defend the accused. In its later phases the Spanish Inquisition burned books as well as people and prosecuted scholars for "speeches suspected of heresy."

Lest Protestants take false pride in superior virtue in such matters, it is well to recall that in the Protestant as well as in the Catholic lands of the Atlantic community—over a period of several centuries, with authentic instances as late as the 1890's—tens of thousands of women were burned or otherwise tortured to death as "witches," usually under accusation

[1] Anatole France: *Vie de Jeanne d'Arc* (Paris: Calman-Lévy; 1908), Vol. II, p. 127, quoted by Hans Kohn: *The Idea of Nationalism* (Macmillan; 1945), p. 607.

of having had sexual relations with the Devil or of having brought misfortune on their neighbors through the practice of black magic. In 1692 in Salem, Massachusetts, a score of people, men and women alike, were hanged for witchcraft on the accusation of neurotic children. Of these things William Graham Sumner wrote in 1909: "If bad times should come again upon the civilized world . . . it must be expected that the old demonism would burst forth again and would reproduce the old phenomenon." [2] And Marion L. Starkey could write somberly in 1949 that "the urge to hunt 'witches' . . . has been revived on a colossal scale by replacing the medieval idea of malefic witchcraft by pseudo-scientific concepts like 'Race,' 'nationality' and by substituting for theological dissention a whole complex of warring ideologies." [3]

The chief effect, thus far, of the competitive efforts of each of the super-Powers of our epoch to foster treason in the other's camp has been to afford an abundant supply of "witches" to be ceremoniously prosecuted, tried, and sentenced. Other effects are problematical. Moscow may or may not have obtained significant atomic "secrets" from Western traitors. Washington has obtained little from "Iron Curtain" fugitives save "intelligence data"—which few are intelligent enough to evaluate correctly—and many thousands of destitute refugees, interspersed with spies, whom nobody knows how to dispose of. But both sides have indubitably obtained scapegoats whose widely publicized trials, incarcerations, or liquidations have brought comfort and joy to the populace and substantially strengthened the status quo in each camp.

A review of the record would be insufferably tedious. One of its curiosities is that the victims selected for inquisition in the Scarlet Empire—*e.g.*, Nicolai Petkov, Ferenc Nagy, Cardinal Mindszenty, Lazlo Rajk, Robert Vogeler, William

[2] William Graham Sumner: "Witchcraft," in *War and Other Essays* (New Haven, Connecticut: Yale University Press; 1911), p. 126.

[3] Marion L. Starkey: *The Devil in Massachusetts* (Alfred A. Knopf; 1949), p. ix.

Oatis, *et al.*—were invariably innocent victims of malice, induced to confess by torture, while their counterparts brought to justice in the American imperium were almost invariably found guilty of the gravest crimes by impartial judges and juries of their peers. So striking was this demonstration of the moral superiority of democracy over barbarism that Cardinal Spellman on February 6, 1949, in New York's St. Patrick's Cathedral, in a sermon entitled "Rebellion to Tyrants Is Obedience to God," called for a crusade against the Communist "crucifixion of humanity" and against the "followers of Beelzebub" and "the world's most fiendish, ghoulish men of slaughter."[4]

The most exhilarating manifestations of this political and social catharsis in the enemy camp were to be found in Red China in the years following the Communist assumption of power. According to officially broadcast accounts, the slogan of the Great Purge was: "Kindness to counterrevolutionaries means brutality to the people." In 1950–1 at Nanking three thousand people rallied to lodge denunciations. Among the victims, who were at once arrested, was a teacher of blind and dumb children. At Wuhan, ten thousand people followed suit. At Tsinan, arrested traitors were denounced by six thousand people demanding death, with the court obliging. In Chungking a girl demanded the execution of her mother for sabotaging the students' patriotic movement. Great crowds everywhere applauded the shooting of the condemned. In Shanghai in June 1951, newspapers reported public rejoicing at the mass execution of 284 traitors. Many culprits were accused of "arousing public wrath"—which

[4] The bare facts of these prosecutions, with references to sources, will be found in the articles on Bulgaria, Rumania, Hungary, Czechoslovakia, Poland, and the U.S.S.R. in *The New International Year Book* (Funk & Wagnalls), for the years 1945 to 1952. See also Bela Fabian: *Cardinal Mindszenty: The Story of a Modern Martyr* (Scribners; 1949); John Gunther: *Behind the Curtain* (Harpers; 1949); and *Breakdown: The Story of Michael Shipkov in the Hands of the* [Bulgarian] *Secret Police* (National Committee for a Free Europe; 1950).

could be placated only by the public liquidation of the accused.[5]

Western techniques for dealing with treason were less lethal, more refined, more humane, and more hypocritical, as befits an Anglo-American tradition that is wholly different from the Muscovite-Mongol tradition. The results were equally effective in silencing dissent and eliciting public approbation for an auto-da-fé. The American Republic in the 1950's was in precisely as much danger, clear and present, of being overturned by Communists as the Great Pyramid of Cheops is in danger of collapsing under an attack of mosquitoes. The Red Hunt was explicable in terms of two circumstances: American Communists were, if not agents of Moscow, at least loyal to Moscow far more than to Washington, while Washington was waging holy (albeit "cold") war against Moscow; and American Communists were convenient scapegoats for the sins of all, since almost no other Americans would dream of defending them, whatever their fate, and almost all other Americans were of one mind in regarding them as demons. So variegated and imaginative was the range of response to the challenge of the Red Devils that no systematic account of these phenomena can here be undertaken. A few representative instances must suffice to suggest the tenor of a totality.

The clue to the whole, so far as America was concerned, was the protean doctrine of "guilt by association"—or by innuendo, coincidence, or happenstance—originally developed in the late 1930's by the House Committee on Un-American Activities under the skillful leadership of Martin Dies. The doctrine found Executive expression in President Truman's "loyalty order" of March 1947, for the purging from the public service of "security risks," and Legislative approval in the McCarran (Internal Security) Act of 1950, described

[5] For representative accounts see *The Manchester Guardian* (April 27, 1951); *The New York Times* (June 21, 1951); and the report from Hong Kong in *The Atlantic Monthly* (October 1951).

by the American Civil Liberties Union as "the greatest threat to general civil liberties since the Alien and Sedition Acts of 1798." [6] Under its terms the State Department in early May, 1951, forbade Maurice Chevalier (among many other less famous figures) to enter the United States on the ground that he had signed the Stockholm Appeal and would therefore, presumably, be likely to corrupt American youth.[7] On February 9, 1951, Dr. W. E. B. DuBois, octogenarian Negro leader and erstwhile director of the "Peace Information Center" in New York (dissolved October 12, 1950) was indicted by the Justice Department for failing to register as a "foreign agent." (He was later found "not guilty.") In Madison, Wisconsin, on the Fourth of July of the same year, according to John Hunter, a reporter for the Madison *Capital Times*, 111 out of 112 persons approached refused to sign a "petition" composed entirely of excerpts from the Declaration of Independence and the Bill of Rights. The incident was satirized in *Pravda*, August 2, 1951, in an article entitled "Day of Lost Illusions."

Items: In Frankfort, July 3, 1951, the Eighth International Conference of Social Democratic Parties establishes a new "Socialist International," dedicated to endorsing American policy in Korea, fostering rearmament against the Red Menace, and fighting Communism tooth and nail. . . . Dr. Hewlett Johnson, Dean of Canterbury, criticizes Attlee in February 1951, for repudiating Stalin's bid for peace. In May he is barred from the U.S.A. and pelted with eggs and tomatoes in Canada. In July (after the Dean has gone to Russia to accept a "Stalin Peace Prize" and medal) Waldron Smithers, M.P., urges in the House of Commons that he be

[6] See *Security and Freedom: The Great Challenge*, American Civil Liberties Union, 30th Annual Report (June 1951); Edward E. Palmer (editor): *The Communist Problem in America—A Book of Readings* (Crowell; 1951); and Bert Andrews: *Washington Witch-Hunt* (Random House; 1948).

[7] Among influential American journals only *The Denver Post* saw fit to condemn this decision as absurd. Its editorial was reprinted in the Paris *Herald Tribune* of May 4, 1951 (see also the comment of Herbert Kupferberg in the same paper, May 2, 1951) and in *Paris-Presse-Intransigeant* of May 7, 1951.

tried for treason and publicly hanged (few Britons concurred). . . . On May 21, 1951, the U.S. Supreme Court, 8 to 1, holds that the California Un-American Committee is immune from suit for defamation of character. Justice William O. Douglas, dissenting: "May they sit as a board of censors over industry, prepare their blacklists of citizens, and issue pronouncements as devastating as any bill of attainder?" Yes. . . .

On June 4, 1951, the U.S. Supreme Court, in *Dennis et al. vs. U.S.*, upholds 6 to 2 the constitutionality of the Smith Act of 1940, under which a group of Minneapolis Trotskyites were first indicted and condemned (to the great joy of all Muscovite Communists) and under which Judge Harold R. Medina in October 1949, after a nine months' jury trial in New York, sentenced eleven leaders of the American Communist Party to jail terms of three to five years and fines of ten thousand dollars for "conspiracy to teach and advocate the overthrow of the Government by force and violence." Other arrests and trials follow. The American "schism in the soul" forbids open outlawry of the Communist Party but cheerfully sanctions the arrest and incarceration of Communists, the imposition of excessive bail, and the imprisonment of defending lawyers and contributors to bail funds for "contempt of court."

Justice Douglas, dissenting:

What petitioners did was to organize people to teach and themselves teach the Marxist-Leninist doctrine. . . . The opinion of the Court does not outlaw these texts nor condemn them to the fire, as the Communists do literature offensive to their creed. . . . The Act, as construed, requires the element of intent—that those who teach the creed believe in it. The crime then depends not on what is taught but on who the teacher is. That is to make freedom of speech turn not on *what is said*, but on the *intent* with which it is said. Once we start down that road we enter territory dangerous to the liberties of every citizen.

Justice Black, dissenting:

These petitioners were not charged with an attempt to overthrow the Government. They were not charged with non-verbal acts of any kind designed to overthrow the Government. They were not even charged with saying anything or writing anything designed to overthrow the Government. The charge was that they agreed to assemble and to talk and publish certain ideas at a later date. The indictment is that they conspired to organize the Communist Party and to use speech or newspapers and other publications in the future to teach and advocate the forcible overthrow of the Government. No matter how it is worded, this is a virulent form of prior censorship of speech and press, which I believe the First Amendment forbids. I would hold Par. 3 of the Smith Act authorizing this prior restraint unconstitutional on its face and as applied.

But let us assume, contrary to all constitutional ideas of fair criminal procedure, that petitioners although not indicted for the crime of actual advocacy, may be punished for it. Even on this radical assumption, the only way to affirm these convictions, as the dissent of Mr. Justice Douglas shows, is to qualify drastically or wholly repudiate the established "clear and present danger" rule. This the Court does in a way which greatly restricts the protections afforded by the First Amendment. The opinions for affirmance show that the chief reason for jettisoning the rule is the expressed fear that advocacy of Communist doctrine endangers the safety of the Republic. Undoubtedly, a governmental policy of unfettered communication of ideas does entail dangers. To the Founders of the Nation, however, the benefits derived from free expression were worth the risk. They embodied this philosophy in the First Amendment's command that Congress "shall make no law abridging . . . the freedom of speech, or of the press. . . ." I have always believed that the First Amendment is the keystone of our Government, that the freedoms it guarantees provide the best insurance against destruction of all freedom. . . .

Public opinion being what it now is, few will protest the conviction of the Communist petitioners. There is hope, however, that in calmer times, when present pressures, passions and fears subside, this or some later Court will restore the First

Amendment liberties to the high preferred place where they belong in a free society.

Senator Joseph R. McCarthy of Wisconsin, June 14, 1951, charges in the Senate that Dean Acheson and George C. Marshall are parties to a "conspiracy" to weaken the U.S.A. in order to facilitate its conquest by the U.S.S.R. . . . On March 2, 1951, the U.S. Post Office, acting on an order issued by the Department of Commerce, refuses to continue mailing the *Bulletin of the Atomic Scientists* to subscribers behind the "Iron Curtain." . . . In the May-June 1951 issue of the Soviet journal, *History Teaching in Schools*, N. M. Goldberg and V. A. Orlov argue that Soviet students must be taught American history to demonstrate "imperialism as the highest and last stage of capitalism" and to show that the U.S.A. "now heads the anti-democratic camp of international reaction, of instigators of new wars. . . . It is important to show its special aggressiveness and predatory tendencies." . . . Martin Dies (as reported in the *Chicago Tribune*, July 5, 1951) in staging a "political comeback" in Texas by accusing Roosevelt and Truman of coddling Communists and raising Russia to the position of a "world menace." . . .

These developments, taken together, meant that Marxist Muscovy and its allies and satellites were dealing with dissenters very much as they had always been dealt with throughout most of Eurasia. What was lost in the process was not the reality of freedom, since these communities had never enjoyed anything of the kind save in tattered shreds and evanescent patches. What was lost was merely the Marxist vision or promise of a new freedom which had never in fact been fulfilled. What America was losing in its fear of subversion was of a different order. A long legacy of personal liberty, constituting the major distinction between democracy and totalitarianism, appeared in process of being sacrificed in the name of defending democracy against totalitarianism.

This result did not flow from the mere incarceration of

Communists. Indeed an open and honest outlawry of the Party, or even a ceremonial shooting at sunrise or boiling in oil of all admitted Communists, with leaders impaled on stakes or nailed to crosses, would have been less destructive of the American tradition. It was rather the method of supression through the formula of "conspiracy to teach and advocate" and the atmosphere engendered through "guilt by association," "subversive lists," loyalty oaths, and the slow poison of universal suspicion, that wrought the damage. A powerful contributing factor was the heroization by Congress, press, and public of all ex-Communists—Elizabeth Bentley, Louis Budenz, Whittaker Chambers, *et al.*—who manifested the intensity of their repentance (and secured lucrative lecture engagements, teaching posts, and publishing contracts) by sweepingly accusing all and sundry unpopular figures of having been Communists. The end point of these processes was already clearly visible by midcentury.

In the Schneiderman Case of 1943, with Wendell Willkie representing the defendant, the Supreme Court had held that naturalization could not lawfully be revoked on the plea that membership in the Communist Party was *per se* evidence of disloyalty. Justice Frank Murphy: "We should not hold that petitioner is not attached to the Constitution by reason of his possible belief in the creation of some form of World Union of Soviet Republics unless we are willing so to hold with regard to those who believe in Pan-Americanism, the League of Nations, Union Now, or some other form of international collaboration or collective security which may grow out of the present holocaust. A distinction here would be an invidious one based on the fact that we might agree with or tolerate the latter but dislike or disagree with the former." After the Dennis decision of 1951, some were quick to point out, as one journal put it, that "if the right to preach and advocate has been withdrawn from Communists, then, by the court's own terms in the Schneiderman decision, the proponents of Atlantic Union and of the United Nations have no better right to preach and advocate these causes. . . . The court says that Communism is an illegal conspiracy. Does that not also make Atlantic Union and U.N. illegal movements? By Justice Murphy's logic we can discern no other meaning and effects."[8]

That such groups would be prosecuted was wholly improbable. The fact remained that the First Amendment to the Constitution had been emasculated by the Congress and Supreme Court of the United States. No one could henceforth feel free, regardless of his motives, to speak, to assemble, and to organize for any unpopular purpose with any assurance that his right so to do was adequately protected.

The drift and muddle of things, under the whiplash of fear, was clear enough long before the Court gave judicial sanction to legislative violation of the Bill of Rights. Robert M. Hutchins put the matter cogently, albeit vainly, at the 237th convocation of the University of Chicago in June of 1949:

> We hear on every side that the American way of life is in danger. I think it is. I also think that many of those who talk the loudest about the dangers to the American way of life have no idea what it is. And, consequently, no idea what the dangers are that it is in. You would suppose to listen to these people that the American way of life consisted in unanimous tribal self-adoration. Down with criticism, down with protests, down with unpopular opinions, down with independent thoughts.
>
> Yet the history and tradition of our country make it perfectly plain that the essence of the American way of life is its hospitality to criticism, protest, unpopular opinion, and independent thought. The great American virtue was courage. We ought to be afraid of some things. We ought to be afraid of being stupid and unjust. We are told that we must be afraid of Russia. Yet we are busily engaged in adopting the most stupid and unjust of the ideas prevalent in Russia, and are doing so in the name of Americanism. The worst Russian ideas are the police state, the abolition of freedom of speech and the right of opposition, and the notion that the individual exists for the state. These ideas are the basis of the cleavage between East and West. Yet every day, in this country, men and women are being de-

[8] *The Chicago Daily Tribune*, "Birds of a Feather" (August 7, 1951).

prived of their livelihood or at least of their reputations by unsubstantiated charges. These charges are then treated as facts in further charges against their relatives or associates.

We do not throw people into jail [i.e., in 1949] because they are alleged to differ with the official dogma. We throw them out of work. The heart of Americanism is independent thought. The cloak-and-stiletto work that is now going on will not merely mean that many persons will suffer for acts that they did not commit, or for acts that were legal when committed, or for no acts at all. Far worse is the end result which will be that critics, even of the mildest sort, will be frightened into silence. Stupidity and injustice will go unchallenged because no one will dare to speak out against them. The way to fight ideas is to show that you have better ideas. No idea is any good unless it is good in a crisis. You demonstrate the failure of your ideas if, when the crisis comes, you abandon them or lose faith in them or get confused about them to the point of forgetting what they are. The American idea is freedom.[9]

The sacrifice of freedom in America, and the liquidation of the hope of freedom in the Scarlet Empire, would have been a small price to pay for security and peace. But neither good was purchasable at such a price. Hypothetically, any human community can discharge its accumulated aggressions and alleviate its tensions by putting its sins on scapegoats, reducing its dissenters to the status of pariahs and moral lepers, and indulging in the ritualistic persecution of those branded as outcasts and outlaws. External conduct, in theory, should then be more pacific than it might otherwise be, if fears and hates had no internal targets. In practice, no

[9] See also Henry Steele Commager: "Who Is Loyal to America?" in *Harper's Magazine* (September 1947); Jerome Davis: *Character Assassination* (Philosophical Library; 1950); Owen Lattimore: *Ordeal by Slander* (Boston: Little, Brown; 1950); David Lilienthal: *This I Do Believe* (Harper; 1949); George Marion: *The Communist Trial* (Fairplay Publishers; 1949); and O. John Rogge: *Our Vanishing Civil Liberties* (Gaer; 1949). The extent to which the libertarian tradition in America suffered further erosion in 1950 and thereafter, under the spell of what William O. Douglas called "the black silence of fear," is set forth in Henry Steele Commager and others: *Civil Liberties under Attack* (Philadelphia: U. of Pa. Press; 1952); Merle Miller: *The Judges and the Judged* (Doubleday; 1952); and "How Free Is Free?"—a special issue of *The Nation*, June 28, 1952.

civilized community seems ever to have turned the trick.

On the contrary, intolerance begets fanaticism and often initiates a process of brutalization in which all "civilized" conceptions of human relations progressively deteriorate. By the 1950's this process was well under way in both halves of One World. Amid the manifold uncertainties of the final outcome, it was at least certain that those deemed traitors would not only fail in the enterprise of subverting tyranny and establishing freedom, unity, and peace on new foundations, but would themselves be sacrificed on the altars of bloodthirsty totemic deities.

CHAPTER SIX

PEACE BY PLANNING

1. THE FUNCTIONALISTS

Government without the foundation of any active functioning society would be either a mere policeman or a tyrant. Among the Lincoln papers recently made public there was a note, written some ninety years ago, which put the whole idea in Lincoln's own plain way: "The legitimate object of government is to do for a community of people whatever they need to have done but cannot do at all or cannot do so well for themselves in their separate and individual capacities. In all that the people can individually do as well for themselves the government ought not to interfere." In the world at large economic and social activities could be linked and dealt with jointly on a wider scale without intruding upon local politics or being held up by different ideologies. Unity in diversity is the genius of modern society, and the only promising foundation for an international system. The greater the number of nations concerned the greater and more intractable is the element of diversity. We are not likely to get peace by trying to argue nations into giving up what divides them, but only by striving practically to strengthen what unites them. It is not merely a question of preventing strife and conflict. The modern state can no longer be merely a police state, nor can any international system be merely that. Peace must be seen as an active, working peace through practical and continuous association in every day affairs. Historically speaking, the international problem of our time is not how to keep the nations peacefully apart, but how to bring them actively together.

—DAVID MITRANY.[1]

OUR INQUIRY, thus far, has been negative in its conclusions regarding the possibility of establishing effective world government in our time through conquest or subversion or some combination of both. If the conclusion be thought unduly pessimistic, the lethal opiates of ignorant optimism are readily available for those who feel need of them. The fact of the matter would seem to be that the Great Society of our era, while desperately in need of world government if it is to survive, is so constituted that most formulas advanced for arriving at the goal are unacceptable to the peoples who compose it. These peoples have been conditioned by past experience to reject, by and large, all proposals for radical new departures in the management or mismanagement of their common affairs. Nevertheless, a number of other approaches to the problem deserve places on our agenda.

One among them, more talked and written about in Britain and on the Continent than in America, may be labeled "functionalism," in contrast to "federalism," "collective security," "imperialism," "revolution," or what you will—though it should not be assumed that this approach is wholly incompatible with its alternatives. It proceeds from the conservative and wholly reasonable assumptions on the part of its proponents that no radical rearrangement of international relations in our Great Society is politically feasible; that the Great Society is nevertheless in process of progressive unification; that the prime vehicles of unity are private and public agencies devoted across national frontiers to serving specific common wants and needs of men and women—economic, administrative, technical, professional, intellectual, æsthetic,

[1] Quoted from the pamphlet, "World Unity and the Nations," by David Mitrany and Maxwell Garnett (*Towards World Government*, No. 3, The National Peace Council, 144 Southampton Row, London, W.C. 1, undated but apparently 1950).

avocational, and so forth; and that the political unification of the world can best be promoted by supporting and encouraging the greatest possible proliferation of such activities.

This hypothesis has in our time received its most articulate formulation in England.[2] Empiricism is a prime component of the British tradition. Its adherents are skeptical in equal measure of French rationalism, German metaphysics, Russian Messianism, and American propensities to insist that everybody must either conform to some preconceived ethical ideal (usually undefined beyond the level of slogans) or else suffer the wages of sin. David Mitrany has long contended that human efforts to work together are usually unsuccessful or transitory when based upon prior agreement as to general principles and specific procedures, but are highly successful when prompted by common wants and shared purposes co-operatively fulfilled through the trial and error of experience, with machinery devised *ad hoc* to meet problems as they arise. He argues further that international administrative agencies survive general wars in which international political institutions are demolished, and that national sovereignty is seldom attenuated by frontal attack but is often diluted through the collaboration of administrators and experts working together to promote transnational goals. "Sovereignty cannot in fact be transferred effectively through a formula, only through a function"—with the resulting multiplication of functional agencies eventuating in practice if not in theory in "federation by installments."[3]

Lord Boyd Orr—first director-general of the U.N. Food and Agriculture Organization, winner of the Nobel Peace Prize in 1949, and sometime president of the National Peace Council and of the World Movement for World Federal Gov-

[2] See, for example, James Avery Joyce (editor): *World Organization—Federal or Functional* (London: Watts; 1945); David Mitrany: *A Working Peace System—An Argument for the Functional Development of International Organization* (London: National Peace Council; 1946); and the additional references and excellent summary in Alan de Rusett: *Strengthening the Framework of Peace* (London: Royal Institute of International Affairs; 1950), pp. 44–66.

[3] David Mitrany: ibid., pp. 9 and 51.

ernment—regards "functionalism" and "federalism" as complementary, rather than antithetical, approaches. The functional agencies of the League of Nations survived its political demise. The specialized agencies of the United Nations are its greatest contribution to peace. But they can approach the goal, it is argued, only if supplemented with the political apparatus of a world federation based upon consent. Lord Boyd Orr's proposals of 1946 for a World Food Board, with effective authority to cope with the nutritional needs of mankind, is illustrative of his viewpoint.[4] The project, approved by the FAO, was rejected by Washington and London and ignored by Moscow.

Mr. Aake Ording was the initial sponsor and director of UNICEF (United Nations International Children's Emergency Fund) of which Dr. Ludwik Rajchman became director until 1951. Through an adroit co-ordination of the activities of private or nongovernmental international organizations, governments, and U.N. agencies, all spurred by simple humanitarian sentiments, UNICEF in the late 1940's contributed mightily to the salvation of the health, and often the very lives, of millions of children, babies, and expectant mothers throughout the world. Aake Ording was asked by the Carnegie Endowment for International Peace and the "International Committee of the Non-Governmental Organizations having Consultative Status with the Economic and Social Council of the U.N." (heaven help the name, but this is what it was called and what, in fact, it was!) to prepare a memorandum on the relationship between unofficial international organizations and the United Nations.[5]

Mr. Ording herein argued that the bewildering variety of existing private international organizations demonstrate Man's propensity to unite across frontiers in pursuit of good; that men everywhere are reaching out to unite humanity in

[4] See Lord Boyd Orr: *Food—The Foundation of World Unity* (London: National Peace Council; 1948).

[5] See Aake Ording's Report: "The Non-Governmental Organizations: Some Proposals for Immediate and Long-Term Consideration," May 31, 1949.

the pursuit of such objectives; and that hitherto-passive Western proletarians and colonial natives are hereby, for the first time, finding the means to act together on a world scale to define and serve their common needs. But national governments and the U.N. are alike too remote from the lives of men to give expression to these needs and to act upon them. The task therefore falls to nongovernmental associations, and upon these as a foundation must be built the temple of a new world order. Men and women will continue to meet across frontiers as members of their vocations and professions. Their "functional" organizations will deal with their common problems. Only in this way, argues Ording, can world government ever become a living reality. National governments should, therefore, consult constantly with such groups. Public international organizations should give them not only consultative status, but authority to make decisions and to take action in their respective spheres. The organizations themselves must give mankind a vision of unity in a Great Society dedicated to economic abundance and social well-being for all its members. Ultimately a World Congress of nongovernmental organizations must supplement, as a functional parliament, a world convention of peoples in the quest for world government through the planned promotion of human welfare.

This new "political pluralism," extended to the international community, postulates that men can never find peace by studying the "causes of war" and seeking to frighten themselves with the horrors of combat, but can approach the goal only through constructive, co-operative efforts to promote common objectives. A hundred or so "public international unions" now exist for such purposes. Almost a thousand "private" international organizations carry on activities on a more or less global scale directed toward aims that are, at least roughly, suggested by their names: the International Chamber of Commerce, the International Astronomical Union, the League of Red Cross Societies, the Institute of International Law, the World Alliance for International

Friendship through the Churches, the International Association for Labor Legislation, the Boy Scouts, the Girl Scouts, and so on. Meanwhile, Aake Ording became (as of 1951–2) secretary-general of the "Union of International Associations" (nongovernmental) which has its headquarters in the *Palais d'Egmont* in Brussels, publishes a monthly *Bulletin* and a *Yearbook of International Organizations*, and serves as a clearing house, service agency, and information center.[6]

These heartening and even exciting developments in Man's struggle for a new *Pax Orbis* are vitiated by the circumstance that nobody gets excited about them and that the mass of mankind, with rare exceptions, knows nothing of their existence even when benefiting in invisible ways from the activities here suggested. But an evaluation, however tentative, of the promise of the functional approach requires some consideration, however brief, of those attributes of the contemporary Great Society which have given rise to the hopes here expressed.

2. MERCHANTS AND MARKETS

> In business, as in other spheres of human activity, the grand old virtues are nice to listen to, uncomfortable to practice. Competition involves risk, enterprise requires effort, initiative forces the human animal to get up from his favorite position, which is resting on his hind quarters. Why fight about a market when you can divide it? Adam Smith, who knew his businessmen, observed in a famous passage that they rarely got together without launching a conspiracy. The conspiracy was to stop cutting each other's throats—and cut the consumer's instead. The dignified name for this is a cartel.
>
> —I. F. STONE in *PM*, August 18, 1943.

[6] See the publications of the UIA in Brussels; Lyman C. White: "Peace by Pieces—The Role of Non-Governmental Organizations," in *The Annals of the American Academy* (July 1949), pp. 87–97, and his book, *International Non-Governmental Organizations* (New Brunswick, New Jersey: Rutgers University Press; 1951) for details of these activities and hypotheses.

The "Liberals" of the nineteenth century, as exemplified by Richard Cobden (1804–65) and John Bright (1811–89), believed that worldwide free trade would promote world unity and world peace. Let governments cease to fetter private business across frontiers and all the planet would become a prosperous market for the exchange of goods and services, with Adam Smith's "invisible hand" insuring that each, in pursuing his own gain, would promote the well-being of all. A global economy, based upon competitive free enterprise among businessmen and an attitude of *laissez faire* on the part of politicians, would lead, it was assumed, to a global polity—or, better yet, would make any such development unnecessary, since the "natural order" (as the Physiocrats termed it) would insure harmony and peace. "The spirit of commerce," Immanuel Kant had written in his *Perpetual Peace*, "is incompatible with war." "Free trade," said Cobden, "would have the tendency to unite mankind in the bonds of peace."[7]

In a world given over to business, contended the successors of the "Manchester School," all mankind would ultimately be bound together in shared abundance by unbreakable ties of economic interdependence. Cobden and Bright were both ardent apostles of peace, arbitration, nonintervention, and disarmament. As recently as 1910 Norman Angell argued in *The Great Illusion* that these bonds of commerce had developed to a point at which another major war would impoverish and bankrupt victors and vanquished alike with no nation gaining any fruits of victory. Therefore, since men are rational beings . . . ?

No such simple faith is available to the "liberals" of the later twentieth century, who have seen all such hopes turned to ashes in the fires of neomercantilism, economic nationalism, and military imperialism. Victorian individualism is forever dead. "The mental and social framework postulated by a *laissez-faire* economy," comments Werner Levi wisely,

[7] Richard Cobden: *Speeches on Questions of Public Policy* (edited by John Bright and James E. Thorold Rogers), London, 1870, Vol. II, p. 421.

"does not exist internationally."[8] Yet here, as always, verbal formulæ that once evoked affirmative emotional responses persist in men's minds long after they have ceased to have any relevance to realities. The United States—for generations past and still today the exemplar *par excellence* of tariff "protectionism" and other restraints upon trade—championed "free trade" (in theory) under Woodrow Wilson, and more recently sought (in principle), under the Hull-Roosevelt dispensation, to induce all the world to return to a "Manchester School" conception of international economic relations. The Atlantic Charter of 1941 asserted, cautiously, that America and Britain would "endeavor, with due respect for their existing obligations, to further the enjoyment by all states, great or small, victor or vanquished, of access, on equal terms, to the trade and to the raw materials of the world which are needed for their economic prosperity."

The U.N. Charter reiterated this ideal, as did innumerable spokesmen in the U.N. Economic and Social Council and other intergovernmental agencies dedicated to reducing national barriers to trade. Washington initiated the sessions in 1945 in London, New York, and Geneva (where numerous reciprocal trade agreements were signed in November 1947), which culminated at Havana (March 24, 1948), at the U.N. Conference on Trade and Employment, in the signature of the Charter of an International Trade Organization, by which "free trade" was to be promoted. The qualifications, exceptions, and "escape clauses" in the document suggested that the goal was an obsolete aspiration rather than a living reality.

The measure of futility and self-deception implicit in such rituals is to be found in the fact that the official American champions of "free trade" have not only continued to practice the most extreme "protectionism" through a variety of devices in restraint of trade, but have bested all their rivals in mak-

[8] Werner Levi: *Fundamental of World Organization* (Minneapolis, Minnesota: University of Minnesota Press; 1950), p. 88. Dr. Levi's long chapter on "The Organization of Economics" merits careful reading.

ing international commerce less a source of wealth and welfare than a weapon of politics and strategy. By midcentury the United States had reduced its own trade with the new "enemy" to the vanishing-point, had brought heavy pressure to do likewise on its European allies (none of whom could afford to dispense with East-West exchanges of goods), and had banned imports of cheese and butter from its European allies (so that American producers could charge more in the American market) to the ruination and despair of many European exporters. The cream of the jest was exemplified at Geneva on September 27, 1951, when Willard L. Thorp for the U.S.A. persuaded the other parties to the General Agreement on Tariffs and Trade (sponsored by the U.S.A. and designed to prevent commercial discrimination) to approve American commercial discrimination against Czechoslovakia—motivated solely by strategic and political considerations, and these, as usual in American foreign policy, having no demonstrable relationship to the attainment of any rationally defined objective.

This and many other comparable instances are a *reductio ad absurdum* of the notion that freedom of trade is to be had, or would promote peace and unity if it were to be had, in a world community whose national segments are irrevocably dedicated to the passionate pursuit of power politics and war. When, as Spengler prophesied, "politics conquers economics," the commercial interdependence of nations not only ceases to be a basis of unity, founded upon common interests, but is itself attenuated, to the common impoverishment of all, by politically dictated embargoes, quotas, and boycotts designed either to penalize or weaken the "enemy" or to swell the bank accounts of domestic producers at the expense of domestic consumers. In such a context private or intergovernmental "planning" to reduce obstacles to commerce offers small hope of restoring or creating a truly global economy, with efficient geographical division of labor, and a world market within which goods and services are freely exchanged on the basis of prices competitively determined by supply and demand.

With the slow demise of competitive free enterprise or *laissez-faire* capitalism, and the progressive breakdown and disappearance of the "automatic" mechanisms of the free market for the most efficient utilization of productive resources, the Great Society has long since entered upon an era of "economic planning"—i.e., the conscious and purposeful allocation of capital, labor, land, and materials through more or less centralized decision-making by lawgivers, managers, and bureaucrats, private or public. But there is no planning as yet (save with regard to a few commodities, such as wheat, and a few services, such as mail delivery) on anything resembling a global scale. Most plans for lesser areas, moreover, have objectives that are either tangential or antithetical to the promotion of peace and the increase of the wealth and comfort of mankind. Communist planning aims at industrialization in preparation for "inevitable" attack and for the building of a fully socialized, and ultimately communized, economy of abundance. Fascist planning aimed at war and conquest as the only means toward full production and full employment in sick societies where peace spelled depression, disintegration, and civil strife. American (and North Atlantic) planning aims at disposing of surpluses, enriching producers, and preparing for Armageddon.

Amid plans and plans, there is no plan to achieve peace and plenty for all the men and women who comprise the Great Society. All are hypnotized by stereotypes causing them to regard any such goal as a bloodless abstraction and leading them to suppose that their purposes can best be served by pursuing with singleminded devotion the particular "interests" of local tribes, sects, and cults—falsely equated with humanity and the will of God.

This is not the place to expound the mythology, ecschatology, nonsense, and wisdom of "planning," nor to consider the question of whether "planning" means the end of "freedom" (*à la* Hayek, Mises, Henry Hazlett, and the *Chicago Tribune*) or signifies the dawn of "liberty" (*à la* Lenin, Clement Attlee, Mao Tse-tung, the first New Dealers, and the Technocrats). These questions, as commonly posed, are literally meaningless, since none of the verbal abstractions employed has ever been defined in terms that have concrete meaning in peoples' lives—save (alas!) occasionally among the oligarchs of the Scarlet Empire. It is enough to note a sequence in the evolution of a symbol, and of the practices of power-holders in yielding to group pressures in the name of the symbol.

The "planning" of the Mercantilists, two and three centuries ago, was a business of government regulating business to the end of enhancing the power and prosperity of the nation-State. When the "bourgeois revolution" in the Netherlands, England, America, France, and elsewhere later cast down the monarchies and aristocracies committed to these habits, its beneficiaries initially demanded public policies that would leave entrepreneurs free to pursue profits in whatever ways they found most profitable. Very soon, however, the same entrepreneurs perceived that profits would be handsomely enlarged by a return to public "planning" in the form of tariffs, subsidies, tax exemptions, governmental promotion of exports, and governmental protection of private investments abroad—with politicians, diplomats, and strategists, for diverse motives, eagerly concurring in the new dispensation.

This condition of affairs contributed powerfully to reducing the Great Society to the miseries of Great Wars and Great Depressions, followed by more Great Wars. Since these bestial progeny of the coupling of neomercantilism with power politics were universally deemed to be unwanted bastards, men bestirred themselves to sterilize the parents and subject the offspring to euthanasia. These laudable endeavors took the form, particularly in America, of a new type of public "planning"—e.g., the Reciprocal Trade Agreement Program of 1934—planned to put an end to planning in the interest of restoring competitive free trade. This effort having failed to attain its goal, all the rulers of all the major and minor Western nations dedicated themselves with new enthusiasm to new forms of regulation of business by government (to the advantage of both and the ultimate impoverishment of everybody else) through income taxes, currency depreciation, exchange controls, export quotas, import embargoes, wage-fixing, agricultural subsidies, price-fixing, public spending, and, finally, colossal rearmament. Motives were mixed. Some sought full employment and economic stability through the devices favored by the late Sir John Maynard Keynes. Others sought private profits through public favors. Still others (e.g., the British Laborites), strove for Utopia. But the ultimate common denominator of the new "planning" was preparation for war in defense of peace.

Given this record, only an ignoramus could suppose that "economic planning," national and international, as practiced in the 1950's, offered reasonable hope of contributing in the long run to the wealth, health, and happiness of the human species. Its immediate consequences were prosperity, corruption, and a frenzied scramble for public handouts. Its ultimate consequences promised to be not the more abundant life but total death, with the dynamics of the process so advanced and so inexorable that no man and no groups of men could any longer act effectively to halt the drift and muddle toward disaster or even question the purposes or probable consequences implicit in the deeds of its architects.[9]

Meanwhile under the relentless impact of Western science, technology, and economics the Great Society—with no one in particular planning or even foreseeing its structure and direction—has assumed a shape that bodes ill for its durability or

[9] Recent literature, popular and erudite, relevant to these matters is too voluminous for listing here. I have found useful data and suggestive ideas in Werner Levi: ibid.; Eugene Staley: *World Economy in Transition* (Council on Foreign Relations; 1939); Lewis Browne: *Something Went Wrong* (Macmillan; 1942); Nicholas Doman: *The Coming Age of World Control* (Harper; 1942); and the pertinent portions of L. Larry Leonard's excellent text, *International Organization* (McGraw-Hill; 1951).

its ultimate integration into a viable world order. Glib generalizations about "economic interdependence" and a "world economy" conceal rather than reveal the life experiences of our time which matter most to the majority of men and women and thereby influence the future through their collective hopes and deeds. Western European civilization, on both shores of the Atlantic, has in the course of the past few centuries profoundly disturbed and altered the life-ways of all the peoples of Eurasia, Africa, and the Americas, thanks to a temporary and ephemeral Western superiority in industrial and commercial techniques and in military and administrative science. The result has not been the emergence of a truly world economy. It has rather been the fantastic enrichment and enlargement of the Atlantic communities at the expense of brown men, yellow men, and black men, with none of the pigmented brethren sharing in the process save the Japanese, before their downfall. In these operations the colored peoples have suffered defeat, exploitation, and humiliation—and enjoyed higher birth-rates, lower death-rates, currently better living standards, and prospectively greater poverty than they ever knew before white men intruded into their affairs.

The fact remains that most of mankind is still desperately poor, living lives of ignorance, squalor, disease, and indignity. Such has doubtless been the fate of most of mankind in all past ages. The contemporary difference consists in this: that more and more of *les miserables* in the non-Atlantic world have been exposed to, and influenced by, Western European and American conceptions of economic abundance and human decency and have thus come to believe, rightly or wrongly, that somehow or other they can attain similar blessings for themselves—through colonial rebellion, national "independence," expropriation of investments, "democracy," "socialism," "capitalism," "Communism," or other Western gadgets and clichés. Such hopes may well prove fatuous. Human testicles and ovaries produce people in such abundance, wherever famine and plague are even slightly alleviated, that the resulting multitudes may be forever condemned to poverty. But men act out their hopes. Most of mankind has now been led to hope, sometimes by the example of the American "way of life" and sometimes by that of the U.S.S.R. and, more recently, of Red China, that industrialization and "planning" offer promise of literacy, health services, schools, factories, "culture," and a better life.

That this aspiration, whether or not obtainable, is at least potentially a global revolutionary ferment, is suggested by the current distribution of income among the members of the human race. Statistics are often suspect and deceptive. In this instance they would appear to bear some relationship to reality. According to the estimates of U.N. experts (*National and Per Capital Income: 1949*, Statistical Office of the U.N., October 1950) average per-capita annual income in U.S. dollars in 1949 was distributed as follows:

U.S.A., $1,453; Canada, $870; New Zealand, $856; Switzerland, $849; Sweden, $780; United Kingdom, $773; Denmark, $689; Australia, $679; Norway, $587; Belgium, $582; Luxembourg, $553; Netherlands, $502; France, $482; Iceland, $476; Ireland, $420. These communities comprise the "wealthy" people of our world.

The well-to-do include: Israel, $389; Czechoslovakia, $371; Finland, $348; Argentina, $346; Uruguay, $331; Venezuela, $322; Western Germany, $320; U.S.S.R., $308; Poland, $300. The poor are far more numerous: Cuba, $296; South Africa, $264; Hungary, $269; Portugal, $250 (Spain unreported but probably much less); Italy, $235; Austria, $216; Chile, $188; Panama, $183; Yugoslavia, $146; Colombia, $132; Greece, $128; Costa Rica, Lebanon and Turkey, $125; Mexico, $121; Brazil, $112; Egypt, Japan, Peru, and Syria, $100.

The desperately poor, living on the barest margin of existence (less than $100 per capita), comprise unhappily almost half of mankind: El Salvador, $92; Nicaragua, $89; Iraq and Iran, $85; Paraguay, $84; Honduras, $83; Guatemala, $77; Dominican Republic, $75; Ceylon, $67; India,

$57; Bolivia, $55; Pakistan, $51; Afghanistan, $50; Philippines, $44; Ecuador, Haiti, Saudi Arabia, and Yemen, $40; Liberia and Ethiopia, $38; Burma and Thailand, $36; Korea, $35; China, $27; and Indonesia, $25.

These figures, probably inaccurate in detail but substantially correct in their comparative value, will repay careful study. In the North Atlantic communities sensitive observers have, of late, become aware of the appalling poverty of the less-privileged peoples and have been casting about—under the impetus of fear or guilt or charity or brotherhood—for ways and means of bringing the world's poor to a level of life less glaringly penurious in contrast to Western opulence. Some aspects of this endeavor will be touched upon in the following section. What has not aroused serious attention, at least since 1776 when Adam Smith published his *Wealth of Nations,* is the question of why a few hundred million people in North America and Northwestern Europe have, in the past few centuries, become ten to twenty times wealthier than a majority of mankind. This circumstance, when it is apprehended at all, is commonly but erroneously assumed to be eternal and is vulgarly attributed to providence, destiny, the American way of life, race, blood, religion, cleverness, or some other irrelevant "cause."

While the dimensions and complexities of the problem forbid its exploration here, a few hypotheses are in order—the more so as they call attention to certain facets of the chronic "world crisis" of our time which cannot safely be ignored in any effort to describe the Great Society or to calculate the prospects of the emergence of a global polity. The riches of the West are attributable, in the simplest sense, to science and technology. What these boons to mankind (lately regarded more and more widely as a curse and a nemesis in the light of Man's abuse of them) might have achieved, or may yet achieve, in the way of the unification of the world, were they at the disposal of men like gods, is a problem of idle speculation or of creative imagination. They have in fact been used by extremely human beings for the tangible and practical goals of profit and power. In practice, therefore, their use has led to the global hegemony of the Western Powers, the fabulous enrichment of the Atlantic communities, and the genesis of a confused and multiform "world revolution" throughout Eastern Eurasia, the Orient, the Middle East, Africa, and Latin America, where vast masses of humanity have been stirred from ancient lethargy and moved to new resentments and new hopes by the impact upon them of white men with machines.

Western wealth is a product of the application of the new science and technology to the exploitation of the "frontier" —i.e., the material and human resources of the "backward" or "undeveloped" areas of the earth. America grew rich in the course of the "winning of the West." Europe grew rich through the exploitation (in all meanings of the word) of African and Asiatic colonies and of overseas markets for goods and capital. Most colonies, to be sure, have not "paid" in the sense of enriching all the population of the metropolis, though British India, the Belgian Congo, and Dutch Indonesia were notable exceptions. But the Western peoples long enjoyed the advantages of superior skills, special privileges for the selling of goods and investment of capital, and favorable "terms of trade" whereby dear manufactures could be exchanged for cheap foodstuffs and raw materials from the "colonial" economies of the world.

These relationships between Atlantic merchants and remote markets among the darker peoples are now, for all practical purposes, at an end. The how and why of this process lie beyond our immediate horizon. During the first half of the twentieth century Europeans wasted their substance in recurrent total wars. By midcentury Americans were bent upon wasting their wealth in militarism in preparation for future war. The "Schism in the Soul" of Western culture led men to suppose that these self-destructive activities were a necessary price to pay for the protection of "freedom" against "tyranny." The men of the year A.D. 2000 may well take a somewhat different view. They may see in these patterns of behavior not only the causes of the decline of Europe and the stagnation of America, despite its colossal productivity in the service of Mars, but the sources (along with earlier adventures in colonialism) of that "awakening" of Asia and Africa which was to bring to a close the happy status enjoyed by the Atlantic peoples between 1550 and 1950. They will perceive that these processes first made Western Europe, once it became incapable of supporting itself any longer through privileged trade relations with the poorer two thirds of the world, the pensioner of the United States—and then confronted America with a dilemma by the terms of which its rulers seemed obliged either to subsidize the rest of the Atlantic community or else to dispose of its surpluses through more global wars in which no meaningful victory could ever be won.

Further imaginings regarding things to come would here be fruitless. It suffices to note that the revolt of Asia against the white man's rule spells *finis* to those attributes of the "world economy" which were the preconditions of Europe's (and, less directly, America's) phenomenal prosperity in the nineteenth and early twentieth centuries.[1] This condition of affairs might fairly be regarded as more likely to produce global anarchy than world unity, save in the minds of those unaware of this condition of affairs. Meanwhile, the processes preceding the economic decline of the West created, for a time, the appearance of a Great Society and a World Economy. Within this context, sundry adventures in the "functional" unification of mankind were undertaken, with variable though interesting results.

[1] I am not aware of any published systematic analysis of the processes of world politics here touched upon. Some suggestions are offered, however, by Walter Prescott Webb in "Ended: 400-Year Boom—Reflections on the Age of the Frontier," in *Harper's Magazine* (October 1950), and in Edgar Ansel Mowrer's article, "What Asia Wants," in the same issue of the same journal.

3. THE BUREAUCRATS

Not until we evaluate the personality of man in the light of his whole environment can we escape the consequences of seeing life in false perspective. Today men seem politically hypnotized. Yet much of that which is necessary and good for us goes on irrespective of our political strivings—the sunshine, the rain, the blossoming of the flowers, the ripening of the harvests, the passing of the seasons. The hills stand still, friendships remain precious, men and women fall in love, children play and dream, and the stars look down on human life. It has been said that we cannot argue ourselves out of a dilemma, and given many of the values that are commonly held today, there may be no way out of the international dilemma. We can, however, raise ourselves above the dilemma by considering problems from a new level of comprehension, imagination, objectivity, and insight. A deeper appreciation of the totality of life may permit us to have the mental ability and restraint necessary to control the vast forces unleashed by science, which today have revealed the bankruptcy of international political institutions as they are and the insufficiency of man's purpose to channelize them. Dominating all the international problems of today may be the problem whether or not man can control the great things which he has invented, whether or not he has the morality to use what he has created or must succumb to his creations.

—LINDEN A. MANDER.[2]

A GREAT SOCIETY may exist and flourish without quite being what it seems to its builders to be. It may be fragmented into stubborn sovereignties and riven by rivalry for power among them. It may move not toward but away from the bright and open fields of a global economy, a world market, and universal freedom of movement of people and goods and ideas. Yet it may still be a community of sorts wherein men come to-

[2] Linden A. Mander: *Foundations of Modern World Society* (Stanford University Press; 1947, revised edition), p. 912. This judicious and eloquent volume, having been written as a textbook, has not in my opinion received nearly the attention it deserves.

gether effectively across frontiers to serve particular common interests. From this fact stems the functionalist's hope of "peace by pieces" through the building, by slow accretions, of ever-greater interdependence among the earth-dwellers. An assessment of the hope requires some familiarity with the international organizations, public and private, that have sprung up to fulfill men's shared needs and wants.

Their number has become baffling. The third issue of *The Year Book of International Organizations* (Geneva: 1950) is a volume of 900 pages. State Department Publication No. 3655, February 1950, requires 335 pages to describe briefly the major public International Organizations in which the United States participates—grouped as "general" (3), agricultural and fisheries (4), commodity (7), economic and financial (6), educational, scientific, and cultural (8), occupation and peacemaking (9), political and legal (3), regional (2), social and health (12), transport and communication (11). The monthly *Bulletin of the Union of International Associations* regularly lists new private organizations established since the most recent enumeration—for example, in the issue of February 1951: the International Association of Gerontological Societies, the Union of International Technical Associations, the European Union of the Cinema, the International Congress for the Liberty of Culture, the International Association of Universities, the International Society of Musical Libraries, the Federated Union of Hygienists of Latin Tongues, the International Council for Building Documentation, the European Committee for Cooperation of Machine-Tool Industries, and so forth.

Happily, compilations and descriptions of the almost-innumerable organizations now functioning in scores of fields of common interest are readily available elsewhere and need not be offered here.[3] Nongovernmental associations of like-minded men and women, united for shared purposes

[3] Aside from the works mentioned, including Mander, see the excellent accounts, supplemented with admirable bibliographies, in L. Larry Leonard: *International Organization* (McGraw-Hill; 1951).

across political boundaries, are at least as old in Western civilization as the Roman Church. Public administrative agencies set up by agreements among governments are a more recent device, virtually unknown before the establishment in 1815 at the Congress of Vienna of the international Rhine Commission. So successful was this enterprise in regulating traffic for the benefit of all that it became the prototype of the European Danube Commission, founded in 1856, and for numerous other bodies to administer international waterways in a fashion preserving in form the "sovereignty" of the riparian States and achieving in fact the promotion of navigation and commerce with a minimum of national interference. The International Telegraphic Union was also established in 1856. On the initiative of American, German, French, Swiss, and other postal administrators, the Universal Postal Union came into being at Berne in 1874. Scores of other "public international unions" have since emerged, each in response to a widely acknowledged public need and each designed to co-ordinate, systematize, and regulate the activities of public administrators. Their work, if confined within national frontiers in a system of jealous sovereignties, was of minimal public service or, sometimes, of none. But their work served well the needs of all men and women in the Great Society when the national pieces of the jig-saw puzzle were fitted together into a transnational pattern on the simple principles of compromise and accommodation verbalized in the phrase "all for one and one for all"—or, still more simply, in the Golden Rule.

We are here in the presence of a political invention of impressive ingenuity and utility. Its place in the larger web of politics in Western culture will be considered below. What is at once heartening and discouraging in this connection is the disposition of humankind to try to transfer formulas that have proved effective in dealing with some kinds of problems to other kinds of problems where their applicability and efficacy are occasionally striking, often limited, and frequently futile and altogether irrelevant.

Much of the elaborate machinery of the League of Nations and the United Nations reflects a conscientious effort to apply the "administrative" or "bureaucratic" approach toward international problems (and nothing invidious is here implied by "bureaucratic") to a variety of human needs that, in the nature of the case, can never be well served by purely national action. It has long since become a cliché to say that the League, albeit a "political" failure, was a shining success in coping with humanitarian, social, economic, and other allegedly "nonpolitical" problems. It is similarly asserted by many that the U.N., while of dubious value as a vehicle for promoting peace among rival super-Powers, has brought multitudinous blessings, and even some semblance of unity, to a disunited and weary humanity through the administrative activities of its "specialized agencies."[4] The validity of these judgments may be taken for granted, though a critical evaluation in detail would require concrete examination of truth and consequences in scores of specific instances. A few, considered briefly, will serve to illumine the issue here posed and to document a tentative conclusion regarding the "functionalist" hypothesis as a whole.

To take first two extreme instances of a negative character, more illustrative of the well-meaning follies of lawyers than of the humane fantasies of bureaucrats, the U.N. "Genocide Convention" and the "Declaration of Human Rights" (approved by the General Assembly, December 10, 1948, and subsequently "implemented" by a so-called Covenant of Human Rights) suggest the futility of seeking to accomplish by "law" what people are unwilling to do in fact. As for the former instrument, comment is scarcely needed. To make mass murder an "international crime" in a world whose governments and peoples are devoting themselves with passionate conviction to preparations for mass murder (in the name of "peace," "liberty," "survival," or "crusades for freedom") is equivalent—with less humorous and more ghastly impli-

[4] See, as one example, J. Alvarez del Vayo: "Voice of Humanity," in *The Nation* (June 23, 1951).

cations—to prohibiting the sale of alcoholic beverages in a community incurably addicted to drinking alcoholic beverages. Noble proclamations of "universal" human rights in a world in which such rights are nonexistent among most of its peoples and are rapidly yielding to the imperatives of military Cæsarism among the remainder is not to contribute to the dignity of the human spirit but to give testimony to the feebleness of the human mind. "Everyone," says the U.N. Declaration, "has the right to life, liberty, and security of person. . . . No one shall be held in slavery or servitude. . . . No one shall be subjected to torture or to cruel, inhuman or degrading treatment or punishment. . . . All are equal before the law. . . . No one shall be subjected to arbitrary arrest, detention or exile. . . . All shall be presumed innocent until proved guilty . . . no attacks upon honor or reputation . . . freedom of thought, opinion and expression . . . peaceful assembly and association" and so on . . .

These "rights" are among the fairest aspirations of mankind. They do not exist, and have never existed, in Eastern Europe and in all of Asia and Africa. They are currently in process of attenuation in the United States by the President, Congress, and the Supreme Court, with the evident approbation of press and public. Their survival in the British Isles and Western Europe may prove temporary. A Great Society dedicated to orthodoxy, intolerance, and crusades cannot be persuaded to respect rights through the schizoid utterances, however eloquent, of the same people who are bent upon destroying them. Rights are meaningless when power-holders respect the rights only of those who obey them and agree with them. This is the situation in Marxist Eurasia and is rapidly becoming the situation in America. Under these circumstances no "declarations" or "covenants" can have the force of law or halt the drift toward despotism.[5]

[5] The California Court of Appeals in 1950 held unconstitutional a state law regulating alien land-tenure on the ground that it was in conflict with Article 55 of the U.N. Charter—which, as a ratified treaty, is part of the "supreme law of the land," whereby all signatories agreed to promote "universal respect for, and observance of, human rights and fundamental free-

Such proclamations have value as symbols when they mirror the aspirations of new nations, classes, or creeds rising to ascendancy in the name of liberty. When addressed to weary peoples sinking into anomie in the name of war for peace, they are not only futile but are a disservice to sanity to the degree to which they cause people, summoned by destiny to rethink the shape of the future, to take comfort in stereotypes already irrelevant to the present.

An enterprise in international lawmaking of a different and somewhat more hopeful character is represented by the International Labor Organization. Its actual achievements and prospects reduces to the level of wishful thinking the title of its recent chatty and charming volume, *Lasting Peace the I.L.O. Way* (Geneva; *ILO*; 1951), and the implication of its director-general, David A. Morse, in his Foreword that here is to be found "the basis for universal and lasting peace." What is here to be found is a commendable and partly successful effort to achieve uniformity in the labor legislation and social security laws of the nation-States, and to make such measures as conducive as possible to the health, wealth, and happiness of those who work for wages. The machinery, originally set forth in Part XIII of the Treaty of Versailles in 1919, comprises the International Labor Conference, made up of two government delegates, one employer delegate, and one labor delegate from each member State; the Governing Body, elected by the Conference and consisting of governmental, employer, and labor representatives in the proportions of 16-8-8; and the International Labor Office, charged with research, documentation, publications, and

---

doms for all without distinction as to race, sex, language, or religion." This effort to make an international convention the legal basis for the definition of constitutional powers of local government and constitutional rights of individuals might be deemed by some a heartening advance toward the federal principle of world organization. The decision, however, provoked indignant outcries among defenders of national sovereignty. See *The Chicago Tribune* editorial of August 1, 1951, "Ambition Unrestrained," commenting acidly on Oscar Schachter's article on this problem in the *Vanderbilt Law Review* and accusing him, by favoring the California decision, of having "forfeited the right to be considered an American."

publicity—all of which functions have of late been admirably handled. The end products of the deliberations of these bodies comprise draft Conventions (ninety-eight in number by April 1951), submitted to the participating States for formal ratification, and Recommendations (eighty-eight thus far) regarding national labor legislation.

Many workers in many lands have unquestionably benefited from these endeavors. The durability of the ILO is itself the best evidence of its capacity to serve human wants without running afoul of national sovereignty. For twenty years it functioned as part of the apparatus of the League of Nations. With the death of the League in World War II, it moved to Montreal—and later back to Geneva as an integral, yet separate, part of the machinery of the U.N.

Despite hopes and pretenses to the contrary, such an institution cannot and does not promote peace among nations. No wars have ever been fought over differences in labor laws. Wars are fought over questions of power, and to these the relationship of the status of wage-earners is at most tangential. Mankind is served by the ILO on a different level. Its Conventions deal with such matters as hours of labor, women in industry, minimum age of employment, hazardous occupations, workmen's compensation for accidents, sickness and old-age insurance, safety regulations, vacations, collective bargaining, and the like.

All has been accomplished in these spheres that anyone could expect to be accomplished in the world of separate sovereignties. Labor legislation is a national, and sometimes a local, function. The ILO cannot make law, but can only recommend laws and submit draft accords for ratification as a basis of national law. Russia is not a member (save from 1934 to 1939) nor is Red China, though Albania, Bulgaria, Czechoslovakia, Finland, Hungary, and Poland are among the sixty-two member States. The limits of the efficacy of the ILO are indicated by the fact that none of its ninety-eight Conventions, drafted during a third of a century, has been ratified by all the members, nor has any single member ratified as many as two thirds of these agreements. Bulgaria has ratified 62, France 52, the United Kingdom 49, New Zealand, Chile and Czechoslovakia 35, The Netherlands, Argentina, and Poland 34, Mexico and Sweden 33, and so on, down to the States that have ratified half a dozen or fewer (Afghanistan, Ceylon, Dominican Republic, Egypt, Ethiopia, Guatemala, Iceland, Liberia, Syria, and Thailand) and those which have (1951) ratified none at all: Bolivia, Costa Rica, Ecuador, El Salvador, Haiti, Indonesia, Iran, Israel, Lebanon, Panama, Philippines, Vietnam. The United States has ratified only six ILO Conventions. Between ratification and effective enforcement through national legislation the gap is often still great.

Another and even more puzzling adventure in international collaboration and bureaucracy is represented by UNESCO—the United Nations Educational, Scientific and Cultural Organization. Its Constitution boldly declares that "since wars begin in the minds of men, it is in the minds of men that the defenses of peace must be constructed, that ignorance of each other's ways and lives has been a common cause, throughout the history of mankind, of that suspicion and mistrust between the peoples of the world through which their differences have all too often broken into war; that the great and terrible war which has now ended was made possible by the denial of democratic principles . . . and that peace must be founded upon the intellectual and moral solidarity of mankind." For reasons set forth elsewhere in these pages, each of these statements (save the last Kantian precept), though almost universally regarded as a truism, is in fact a falsehood or an irrelevancy. Since all human conduct begins in the "minds" of men, the initial statement says nothing meaningful about war or about minds. Nor is war ever a product of ignorance, in the sense here implied, nor of autocracy, any more than peace is a product of knowledge or of democracy.

We are here confronted with another variant of the psychological phenomenon displayed in the publicity of the ILO.

In a world dedicated to war and desperately hungry for peace, every endeavor deemed good by significant numbers of men is equated in the minds (or at least in the press releases) of its proponents with "peace" or, sometimes, with victory in "war for peace." UNESCO, with its General Conference, Executive Board, and Secretariat, exists to foster the enrichment and diffusion of knowledge across frontiers through the collaboration of educators, scientists, writers, and artists. The purpose is admirable and approved in principle by all save the self-appointed custodians of tribal bigotry. Even Communists (i.e., devils) approve, though the U.S.S.R. will have none of UNESCO. But the purpose and the ingenious planning devoted to its furtherance have no immediate or even remote relationship to the problem of peace, for peace requires global government, and government requires Myth, Authority, Adaptation, and an Elite, all of which have as much to do with the otherwise useful activities of UNESCO as the flowers that bloom in the spring.

The self-imposed dilemma in which this organization has thus involved itself has, after much travail, found a "solution" of a kind. UNESCO's numerous worthy projects of research and publication have contributed to knowledge but not to peace—unless one chooses to fall into the semantic trap of supposing that knowledge is virtue or that truth is freedom, and that freedom plus virtue equals peace. UNESCO, to be sure, has published a survey of *Tensions Affecting International Understanding* (by Otto Klineberg, Social Science Research Council, 1950) and *Contemporary Political Science: A Survey of Methods, Research, and Teaching* (UNESCO, 1951) and was instrumental in the establishment of an International Political Science Association in 1949.[6] It has given no support, however, to such constructive but "controversial" endeavors as Henri Brugman's "College of Europe" in Brussels and Alexandre Marc's "World Federal-

[6] See Unesco/SS/MPS/Conf. 1/7, October 10, 1949, Paris, containing a Summary Report of the Conference of Political Scientists at UNESCO House, a list of participants, and the Constitution of the new International Political Science Association.

ist University" in Paris.[7] Director General Dr. Jaime Torres Bodet concluded the sixth General Conference of UNESCO by declaring in Paris (July 11, 1951) that the 150 resolutions approved had "solidified" the common aim "to consolidate international peace based on respect for human rights." He welcomed the admission of Western Germany, Japan, Vietnam, Laos, and Cambodia to membership; the proposals to combat illiteracy and promote adult education; the plans to draw up a universal copyright-convention and to prepare a scientific and cultural history of mankind; the appeal for an increase in newsprint production; the allocation of ninety thousand dollars for the education of Arab refugee children from Palestine; and so forth. *Osservatore Romano* expressed regret that UNESCO had neglected religion as a means toward peace through education. . . .

Since peace is not a product of education, but only of the effective organization of central power in the community within which peace is sought—and since propaganda, perquisites, and even persecution, but not "understanding" *per se*, are possible devices for the organization of power, UNESCO's confusion of ends and means is complete. Former Deputy-Director (1947–50) Walter H. C. Laves has argued that UNESCO should positively "promote peace," rather than concern itself vaguely with "international understanding," by fostering universal "knowledge of certain elementary facts," such as "(a) war anywhere endangers everyone; (b) nations depend upon each other for economic welfare; (c) people are different; (d) human rights are essential to peace; (e) the U.N. is indispensable today."[8] This formulation suggests the nature of the resolution of UNESCO's dilemma. Of Dr. Laves's "elementary facts," the second and third are self-evident, the fifth is meaningless in the absence of a definition of "indispensability" to whom and for what, while the

[7] See *Message de Paix*, November 1950, No. 9, published in Namur (Belgium), and *World Government News* (New York: December 1950), pp. 11–12.

[8] Walter H. C. Laves: "UNESCO and the Achievement of Peace," *The Political Quarterly* (London: April–June, 1951), pp. 163–74.

first and fourth are false. In a system of sovereignties lacking common government, war endangers only those who engage in it or choose to feel endangered by it. "Human rights," moreover, have often been slogans in the name of which men have fought one another. But the roots of war lie in the politics of power and, more deeply, in the unregenerate and unredeemed nature of Man, and have no more to do with "rights" than with "democracy" or "the white man's burden" or "trade follows the flag" or "King and Country," "Throne and Altar," "Rescue of the Holy Sepulcher," or the "Glory of Allah."

UNESCO's dilemma, perhaps inevitably, has been resolved by an acceptance of the premises of "collective security," the validity of which will be considered in the following chapter. In August of 1950 the Executive Board unanimously endorsed U.N. resistance to aggression in Korea, and undertook to promote "a full understanding of the principles of the U.N. action for peace and security." This decision, as Percy W. Bidwell puts it, settled the long dispute as to whether UNESCO "was to be purely cultural (i.e., non-political) or whether it was to take sides in the cold war. Now it has chosen political action." [9] In July 1951 the General Conference pledged full co-operation in U.N. efforts to maintain peace by war. Here we behold a "functional" organization whose actual function was from the outset confused in the minds of men with "peace"—and whose ultimate fate, in a world where everybody wages war in the name of peace, has therefore been complete "politicalization" and conversion into a weapon of warfare wielded in support of

[9] Foreword to Frederick S. Dunn: *War and the Minds of Men* (Harper, for the Council on Foreign Relations; 1950). This suggestive little volume illumines the dilemma of UNESCO and resolves it simply: UNESCO must adapt itself to the global struggle for power by supporting "Freedom" against "Tyranny," as the two terms are currently defined in the Atlantic community. See also Charles S. Ascher: "The Development of UNESCO's Program," and Reinhold Niebuhr: "The Theory and Practice of UNESCO," both in *International Organization* (February 1950); Byron Dexter: "Yardstick for UNESCO," *Foreign Affairs* (October 1949); and Senator William Benton: "How Far Can Unesco Reach?" address to the U.S. National Commission (April 13, 1950).

one group of belligerents against another. This denouement is doubtless a consummation devoutly to be welcomed by all who suppose that peace and freedom are best promoted by mobilizing good nations to fight bad nations. It suggests, however, that "functionalism" as an approach to peace through world government is subject to appreciable limitations, at least in such a world as the one in which we happen to live.

The situation is no different with respect to most functional organizations, established or proposed, in the realm of economic collaboration among states. Throughout the Scarlet Empire all such organizations, it goes without saying, are directed toward enhancing the economic and military power and serving the political purposes of the Communist oligarchy. In Atlantica, their conterparts have more and more come to play a comparable role. As of 1951–2 the U.N. Economic Commission for Europe, under the leadership of Gunnar Myrdal, was still functioning feebly as a link between East and West. The vast and sprawling bureaucracy of the OEEC or Organization for European Economic Cooperation came into being, on the other hand, as an auxiliary of the "Marshall Plan" and has as its task the promotion of economic viability, stability, and progress in the Western European marches of the American Empire in the face of the Muscovite menace.[1]

The Schuman Plan, though not yet in effect at the time of writing, is worthy of note as an effort not merely to achieve economic integration in a given area with respect to specific industries, but to outflank and thereby "solve" a political problem through the creation of an international bureaucracy for the co-ordination, control, and planning of business activities. On May 9, 1950, French Foreign Minister Robert Schuman invited all European States to join in drafting a treaty to merge their coal and steel industries into a single market.

[1] See, among O.E.E.C. publications, *L'Organisation Européenne de Cooperation Économique: Historique et Structure* (Paris: Mai 1951); *European Economic Cooperation: A Survey* (May 1951); and *Annual Reports on European Recovery Program* (Paris: O.E.E.C.; 1949 f.).

Western Germany, Italy, and the Benelux States accepted.

A series of projected supranational institutions with limited but essentially sovereign powers over coal and steel finally emerged from protracted discussion: a High Authority to be elected for a six-year term by the participating governments, with its members not representing, or responsible to, national administrations but answerable to a Common Assembly, composed of delegates of the signatory States in proportions to be agreed upon. The High Authority would have power to tax the production of the coal and steel industries, to issue binding directives, to levy fines on violators, to lend and borrow funds, and to make studies and recommendations. Its budget would be fixed by the Assembly, which could compel its members to resign by a two-thirds vote of censure. A special Council of Ministers would co-ordinate the work of the High Authority with national economic policies and would fix tariff rates on coal and steel imported from outside the areas covered by the Plan. A new Court of Justice would settle disputes and could nullify acts of the High Authority, Assembly, and Council of Ministers taken in excess of their powers. A Consultative Committee would act as an advisory liaison agency between the High Authority on the one hand and producers, labor, and consumers on the other.

Within the region of the Plan, the equivalent of a customs union would be achieved with respect to steel and coal—i.e., tariffs and other restrictions on the movement of these commodities among the members would be lifted and uniform rates would be applied by all to nonmember States. Accords among producers to restrict competition by fixing prices, allocating markets, or discouraging technological progress would be outlawed, though the High Authority might, if it chose, authorize agreements for joint selling, specialization, and mergers. Within the "single market," exceptional transition-arrangements were contemplated for the high-cost Belgian coal industry and the uneconomical Italian steel industry. But in principle the iron ore of Lorraine, the coal of the Saar, Belgium, and Westphalia, and all the blast furnaces and rolling-mills scattered through the valleys of the Ruhr, the Rhine, the Moselle, and the Po would be enabled to function on a Continental scale, as do their counterparts in America and Russia. A fifty-year treaty, elaborately devised to achieve these purposes, was initialed at the Quai d'Orsay on March 19, 1951, and formally signed on April 18 by cabinet ministers of the six participating States.[2]

No "functional" project of recent vintage engendered such high hopes, conflicting interest, manifold doubts, and unforeseen complications. The Schuman Plan was variously hailed or assailed as a method, or *the* method, of making war between France and Germany henceforth impossible; as a new version of the European Steel Cartel of 1926; as the precursor of European federation; as a prospective boon or curse to coal miners and steel workers; as a guarantee of competition or a threat of monopoly; as a victory of "free enterprise" or a triumph of "planning," "bureaucracy," or "socialism." Its actual author appears to have been Jean Monnet. Its first impetus came not from the Quai d'Orsay but from the Office of the "Monnet Plan" around the corner in the rue de Martignac. Aside from the French coal mines, which are nationalized, the Western European coal and steel industries are privately owned. Their owners displayed no ardor for integration, control, and direction at the hands of bureaucrats. French and German conservatives were enthusiastic (on the basis of differing expectations) while French Socialists were lukewarm and German Socialists were bitterly opposed. Conservatives and Laborites in England were alike skeptical and of one mind in rejecting British participation. American diplomats were fulsome in their praise, American businessmen doubtful. . . .

Only future decisions can reveal what is to come of the

[2] The treaty is in process of ratification at the time of writing. Among the already voluminous literature, see Department of State Publication 4176, *An Analysis of the Schuman Plan*, reprinted from the *Bulletin* of April 2, 1951; *The Times* (London: April 23, 24, 1951); *Le Monde* (Paris: April 20, 1951); William Diebold, Jr.: "Imponderables of the Schuman Plan," *Foreign Affairs* (October 1950); and Clarence B. Randall (president of Inland Steel): "European Steel: Monopoly in the Making," *The Atlantic Monthly* (October 1951).

Plan. Its motivation was primarily political—i.e., to integrate Western Germany as an equal member into a West European community, but under international supervision adequate to thwart *revanche* and to prevent or at least control German rearmament. Its method was economic-bureaucratic, with no one certain before the event whether the machinery would expand or restrict production, increase or reduce wages and other costs, raise or lower prices to consumers, and strengthen or weaken private capital. The end of "peace" here striven for would be well served if the political objective could be attained—and, what is more doubtful, if that objective could be shown to constitute a step toward "peace." The means proposed might or might not promote the end already defined. They might conceivably serve the same purpose in some different fashion, or prove to be of no use whatever. As of 1952 the Plan appeared no less likely than other enterprises in international bureaucracy to serve certain human needs, and no more likely to insure peace.

As a final instance among our samples of the type of approach to world order here under discussion, let us consider the much discussed program usually designated as "Point Four." In his Inaugural Address of January 20, 1949, President Truman asserted that "in the coming years, our program for peace and freedom will emphasize four major courses of action"—(1) unfaltering support to the United Nations; (2) continuation of our programs for world economic recovery; (3) strengthening of freedom-loving nations against the dangers of aggression, and:

> Fourth, we must embark upon a bold new program for making the benefits of our scientific advances and industrial progress available for the improvement and growth of under-developed areas. More than half the people of the world are living in conditions approaching misery. Their food is inadequate. They are victims of disease. Their economic life is primitive and stagnant. Their poverty is a handicap and a threat both to them and to more prosperous areas. For the first time in history, humanity possesses the knowledge and the skill to relieve the suffering of

these people. . . . I believe that we should make available to peace-loving peoples the benefits of our store of technical knowledge in order to help them realize their aspirations for a better life. And, in cooperation with other nations, we should foster capital investment in areas needing development. Our aim should be to help the free peoples of the world, through their own efforts, to produce more food, more clothing, more materials for housing, and more mechanical power to lighten their burdens. . . . This should be a cooperative enterprise in which all nations work together through the United Nations and its specialized agencies wherever practicable. It must be a world-wide effort for the achievement of peace, plenty, and freedom. . . . Guarantees to the investor must be balanced by guarantees in the interest of the people whose resources and whose labor go into these developments. The old imperialism—exploitation for foreign profit—has no place in our plans. What we envisage is a program of development based on the concepts of democratic fair-dealing.

The widespread and often fervent interest aroused by this and similar proposals to raise living standards among the impoverished masses comprising more than half of mankind has its sources in various foci of attention—and on various levels of awareness of the facts of life in the twentieth century. The battle hymn of Communism proclaims, speciously but boldly: "Arise, ye prisoners of starvation! Arise, ye wretched of the earth! For justice thunders condemnation, a better world's in birth. No more tradition's chain shall bind you. Arise, ye slaves! No more in thrall. The world shall rise on new foundations. You have been naught: you shall be all. . . ." If, as is commonly supposed, the wretched and the starving are the easiest and most eager converts to the banner of the Scarlet Empire, then the West's most effective weapon against the foe is, *ex hypothesi*, the wherewithal and "know-how" to alleviate starvation and wretchedness.

Some have embraced this cause as a means of winning the Cold War, others in the hope of ending it. Such a program is urged by some on simple grounds of humanitarianism and

Christian duty, and by others on the basis of the contention that if America does not dispose of its vast outpouring of capital and goods in some such constructive fashion, its riches will choke the assembly lines or will be consumed in the waste of war to the ruin and impoverishment of all. Still others see in such a program the germ of uniting all mankind in a common creative task and the nucleus of the world government of days to come.

Stringfellow Barr's trenchant and lucid pamphlet, "*Let's Join the Human Race*" (University of Chicago Press; 1950), is the most eloquent plea thus far published for a "Point Four" approach to the needs of men and the unity of the world. He urges the establishment of a "World Development Authority" as an international public corporation, to raise funds by public sales of bonds, to invest the proceeds in the development of "backward" areas, and to promote the political unification of mankind by meeting the universal needs of all peoples. He concludes:

> But let's be frank with ourselves. We have of late been forming habits of fear, not hope. We may go on as we have gone: arming, taxing ourselves, crying that the godless are at our gates. If we do, I think that all mankind will be heavily punished, the guiltless with the guilty. Part of our punishment will be that, refusing to see the world's oneness or our common destiny, we shall suffer each in his separate nation. A further collapse in the world economy would bring famine to India but not to us. It would bring us unemployment instead, and on a vast scale—poverty in the midst of plenty. We would have sent our sons all over the globe to put down revolution, and we would probably be rewarded in the long run by revolution at home. I have not urged this as the reason for acting, because I do not believe that the best reason for health is to escape the painful symptoms of disease. The best reason for health is this: a healthy man is a complete and proper man.
>
> But if we insist in treating symptoms, I think that mankind—and particularly that little portion of it called American—is in for very rough weather. Maybe a third World War may be needed to teach us. If so, when it is over, we may still arise and

act. The tools to work with may by then have been very nearly destroyed and the work may by that time be much harder to do. But there is a chance that we may have more wisdom, too. And wisdom, armed with simple tools, might succeed where rich folly had failed.

Scott Buchanan's earlier memorandum, "*World Government and World Development*" (Foundation for World Government, May 1, 1950), points in a similar direction, as do the contributions of Harlow Shapley, James P. Warburg, Benjamin A. Javits, and many others.[3] On February 2, 1950, Senator Brien McMahon of Connecticut proposed that the United States should offer to Russia and the world, on condition of Soviet acceptance of an effective system for international control of atomic energy, a disarmament and development program under which America, with other States following suit proportionately, should reduce its arms expenditures from fifteen billion to five billion dollars a year, and invest the remaining ten billions annually for five years in the economic progress of the world community. Half a year later Walter Reuther, President of the CIO, called for the expenditure through the U.N. of thirteen billion dollars a year for the next hundred years "to wipe out human misery and

[3] See, among the growing literature on this theme, "World Security through International Resources Development," by Hermann Herrey and Harlow Shapley (privately printed by the authors; 1949); James P. Warburg: "Point Four" and "Turning Point Toward Peace?" (The Current Affairs Press; 1949 and 1950); Benjamin A. Javits: *Peace by Investment* (Funk & Wagnalls in association with United Nations World; 1950); J. B. Condliffe and H. H. Hutcheson: "Point Four and the World Economy," Foreign Policy Association, Headline Series, No. 79 (January–February, 1950); Peter G. and Dorothea S. Franck: "Implementation of Technical Assistance," International Conciliation Pamphlets, No. 468 (February 1951), Carnegie Endowment for International Peace; and the invaluable monographs prepared by the Public Affairs Institute of Washington, D.C.: Dewey Anderson and Stephen Raushenbush: "A Policy and a Program for Success"; James Rorty: "Engineers of World Plenty"; Harold R. Isaacs: "Two Thirds of the World"; Morris Llewellyn Cooke and others: "Ground Work for Action"; Stephen Raushenbush: "People, Food, Machines"; Wallace J. Campbell and Richard Y. Giles: "Helping People Help Themselves"; Seymour E. Harris: "Foreign Aid and Our Economy"; and Morris E. Rosenthal: "Where Is the Money Coming From?" See also J. Keith Killby: "Reuther and Colombo Plans," *Federal News* (London: April 1951).

desperation, to win the sympathy and support of hundreds of millions of people and strip the Kremlin of its power to exploit them and sacrifice them in battles of aggression."

The steps already taken along the path thus charted, while short and halting, are yet too many to admit of any résumé of the itinerary. The American Congress, seldom given to boldness in matters other than military, voted appropriations that were almost microscopic in comparison with funds approved for arms. The U.N. launched a technical-assistance program. At the Colombo (Ceylon) Conference of Foreign Ministers of the British Commonwealth in January, 1950, Mr. Spender of Australia proposed, and secured approval of, a program for devoting almost £2,000,000,000 over a six-year period to the development of agriculture, industry, transport, and health and educational services in South and Southeastern Asia. On November 10, 1950, Gordon Gray (aided by Edward S. Mason as his deputy and a staff of nine, including Kermit Gordon) Submitted a *Report to the President on Foreign Economic Policies* (Washington, D.C.: Government Printing Office; 1950) in which a third of the pages dealt with "undeveloped areas and economic development programs."

President Truman's "International Development Advisory Board," of which Nelson Rockefeller was chairman, made public on March 11, 1951, a report entitled "Partners in Progress," based on the premise that free peoples were faced with "two main threats. One is military aggression and subversion. The other is hunger, poverty, disease, and illiteracy." The Board made proposals designed to increase American private investment abroad from one billion to two billion dollars annually by way of "tax incentives," new treaties, an insurance program, an "International Finance Corporation" as an affiliate of the International Bank for Reconstruction and Development, and the creation of an office of "Assistant Overseas Economic Adviser" to "encourage the maximum and most effective use of private enterprise." President Truman expressed appreciation: "The Point Four concept, properly carried out, is essential to the successful defense of the free world. . . ."

Leroy D. Steinbower, U.S. Representative on the U.N. Economic Employment, and Development Commission, commenting on May 17, 1951, on the report entitled "Measures for the Economic Development of Under-Developed Countries," asserted that "in the current fiscal year, the United States is spending over a quarter of a billion dollars on programs of technical and economic assistance to the under-developed areas"—aside from Export Import Bank loans of $566,000,000 in 1950, International Bank loans of $284,000,000, and private direct investments of American capital abroad of $1,100,000,000.

Lest such figures should be regarded as evidence that the U.S. and the U.N. were already embarked in midcentury on a comprehensive global program of raising the productivity and living standards of the world's poor relations, it is well to recall that no such program had emerged, save in shreds and patches, and that the U.S. in 1952 was scheduled to devote over fifty billion dollars to preparations for war in the name of peace. "The proportion of resources that have to be devoted to defense," declared Mr. Steinbower in the commentary quoted above, "are very substantial and have to have the highest priority." Since resources are not infinite, a Great Society whose symbols and values and conflicts for power are such that priority must always be given to armaments cannot devote very much to the welfare of the most miserable part of mankind—the more so as many of *les miserables* in China, Indochina, Burma, Malaya, and elsewhere had already decided perversely that Communism had more to offer than Capitalism as a way to the good life. The prime objective of Western policy, plainly, was not to raise living standards in Communist-controlled areas but to endeavor to increase misery to the point where apathy, rebellion, or collapse would ensue.

The central difficulty, however, was of a different order. What was called for, if the "bold new program" was to have any appreciable effect, was the type of boldness urged by Stringfellow Barr, James P. Warburg, Henry A. Wallace, Walter Reuther, Senator McMahon, and others who perceived that nothing significant could be achieved without some type of World Development Authority, possessed of vast funds for investment, and wholeheartedly supported by the governments and peoples of the wealthy Atlantic communities. Even such an agency might well flounder and fail unless its direction were dedicated to two revolutionary goals: channeling capital away from the traditional enterprises devoted to private profit and national power into projects of development having no connection with the armament industries and unlikely to pay dividends for many years; and fostering such changes in the social and economic structure of "backward" areas as would make investments productive without "exploitation" of native workers, bribery of native landlords and bureaucrats, and alien infringements on local sovereignty. Quite apart from the arms race, which made the whole issue academic, these conditions seemed unlikely to be met by the rulers of America (the only important source of investment capital), for the American elite in the 1950's was dedicated to promoting private profit at public expense and to supporting with money and arms the feudal gentry and corrupt officialdom of virtually all the "colonial" communities of the world. Two comments by conservative economists are sufficient to suggest the obstacles in the way of the necessary reorientation.

What is the President proposing? He is proposing that in order to induce American private investors to risk their funds abroad, *we are to allow these private investors to keep the profits of their investment, but to force the American taxpayers to assume the losses.* Such a proposition needs merely to be stated plainly to show that it would be preposterous and intolerable. The private investors and investment bankers who applaud this proposition are short-sighted beyond belief. It could only lead to the control and eventual nationalization of all foreign investments.

Such an arrangement, moreover, would not remove or in the least reduce the risks of foreign investment. It would merely *transfer* those risks from the investor to the taxpayer. The taxpayers would pay for the investor's losses abroad out of the proceeds of their own businesses at home. This proposal, like most proposals of the so-called Welfare State, rests on the fundamental assumption that nearly every domestic and foreign problem can be solved simply by seizing still more from the American taxpayers and handing it over to someone else.—HENRY HAZLITT.[4]

The mere listing of the steps that would have to be undertaken to assure an expansion of output and income in an under-developed country reveals the utter implausibility of the view that they could be carried out by the existing governments of most under-developed countries. The crucial fact rendering the realization of a development program illusory is the political and social structure of the governments in power. The alliance of property-owning classes controlling the destinies of most under-developed countries cannot be expected to design and to execute a set of measures running counter to each and all of their short-run vested interests. If to appease the restive public, blue-prints of progressive measures, such as agrarian reform, equitable tax legislation, etc., are officially announced, their enforcement is willfully sabotaged. The government representing a political compromise between landed and business interests cannot suppress the wasteful management of landed states and the conspicuous consumption on the part of the aristocracy, cannot suppress monopolistic abuses, profiteering, capital flights, and extravagant living on the part of the businessmen. It cannot curtail or abandon its lavish appropriations for a military and police establishment providing attractive careers for the scions of wealthy families and a profitable outlet for armaments produced by their parents—quite apart from the fact that this establishment serves as the main protection against popular revolt. Set up to guard and to abet the existing property rights and privileges, such government cannot become the architect of a policy calculated to destroy the privileges standing in the way of economic progress and to place the property and the incomes derived

[4] Henry Hazlitt: *Illusions of Point Four* (Irving-on-Hudson, New York: Foundation for Economic Education; 1950), pp. 31–2.

therefrom at the service of society as a whole.—PAUL A. BERAN.[5]

These obstacles to the raising of living standards, among the world's poor are not, under all imaginable conditions, insuperable. They are merely of such character and magnitude that they can scarcely be overcome within the social, political, and ideological context of American foreign policy and the Atlantic alliance in their midcentury patterns. Communism as a method of destroying feudalism, partitioning and then collectivizing landed estates, and promoting industrialization through the planned investment of socialized capital—all by means of political dictatorship and ruthless regimentation—has demonstrated, at least in Transcaucasia and Central Asia, what is possible in the way of elevating illiterate, exploited, apathetic, and disease-ridden peoples into flourishing communities possessed of schools, libraries, hospitals, factories, and theaters.

But the "Point Four" program is envisaged by most of its proponents as an alternative to social revolution, not a means toward it—and as an antithesis, rather than an imitation, of Communism. Posed in these terms, the problem may reasonably be deemed insoluble *per se*, and quite irrelevant to the issue of war and peace—unless it should somehow, in ways not now foreseeable, furnish a means whereby American assembly lines, swiftly geared to the tasks of anticipated war, could find outlets for their vast production in markets less lethal than those of Mars. Meanwhile, most of the miserable masses of mankind in the slums of Asia and Africa seemed likely to be left to their own devices or to alien example, inspiration, or leadership in their yearning for a more abundant life.

[5] Papers and Proceedings of the 63rd Annual Meeting of the American Economic Association, reprinted in *Monthly Review* (August 1951), pp. 131–2.

4. WORKS WITHOUT FAITH

"He's admitted into certain rooms, but they're only a part of the whole, for there are barriers behind which there are more rooms. Not that he's actually forbidden to pass the barriers, but he can't very well push past them once he has met his chiefs and been dismissed by them. Besides, everybody is watched there, at least so we believe. And even if he did push on further what good would it be to him, if he had no official duties to carry out and were a mere intruder? And you mustn't imagine that these barriers are a definite dividing-line; Barnabas is always impressing that on me. There are barriers even at the entrance to the rooms where he's admitted, so you see there are barriers he can pass, and they're just the same as the ones he's never yet passed, which looks as if one oughtn't to suppose that behind the ultimate barriers the bureaux are any different from those Barnabas has already seen. Only that's what we do suppose in moments of depression. And the doubt doesn't stop there, we can't keep it within bounds. Barnabas sees officials, Barnabas is given messages. But who are those officials, and what are the messages? . . ."

—FRANZ KAFKA: *The Castle* (New York: Alfred A. Knopf; 1947), p. 226.

THE MINIATURE "case studies" of selected functional organizations offered in the preceding pages could be multiplied and expanded many times without altering significantly the conclusion they suggest. That conclusion comes to this: "Functionalism" as a highway toward unity and peace in the sundered and fragmented community of the earthlings is a road well traveled and well worth traveling—not because any such blessed destination lies at journey's end but because many pleasant way-stations are scattered along the route, each worth visiting for its own sake. The travelers are a team, however, moving in a vehicle so curiously contrived that no motion is possible, and no station is ever attained, unless all are of one mind in wishing to arrive and are agreed as to the itinerary and the tempo of the trip. Should any among them deny the desirability of reaching a given point or insist upon using the facilities there available against others—or should all fall out among themselves as to the what and how and why of a particular segment of the passage—then the carriage halts abruptly and the voyagers never come to the hoped-for wayside inn or restaurant.

But no matter how many stopping-places are reached and relished, the alleged destination—the unification in amity and the governance in peace of all mankind—lies always beyond the horizon as a tempting and maddening mirage. For this road leads to no such haven. Even if it did, our travelers, albeit often willing enough to move together toward nearer goals, are quite unwilling to sacrifice their identities and their private purposes in the ways required to arrive at the far-off, divine event.

Put differently, we are here concerned with a process of "depoliticalization"—if so barbarous a term be permissible in the absence of any other descriptive of the phenomenon. Functional international organizations of the more successful sort arise and flourish and fulfill their functions because they deal with matters that governments and peoples have agreed, passively or expressly, to take out of the realm of politics. Administration begins where politics stops. Consensus and agreement on a common purpose by all or most of the nation-States make it possible for managers and experts to deal systematically and scientifically with questions of practical means toward an end that all accept. The possibility is contingent upon such acceptance—which signifies, in turn, that politicians and patriots cease to be interested in the objective, save for their desire to enjoy a specific public service with a minimum of delay and friction and a maximum of economy and efficiency. Shared wants and needs admit of being dealt with as administrative problems when they are removed from the misty spheres of problems of power and of the passionate loves, hates, and fears of men, and come to be envisaged in a context of rational adaptation and invention in the service of the interests of all.

So impressive (to the few who have paid attention) is this process of reducing "political" quarrels to "administrative" problems, and so multitudinous have become the areas of human activity in which it has operated, that enthusiasts have hopefully assumed that the process must ultimately embrace—or, at any rate, ought to embrace—all human interests and thus replace power politics with a planetary bureaucracy unselfishly serving the welfare of mankind. That the process, in its successive proliferations, is capable of contributing toward the realization of so noble a goal no one can reasonably deny, though quantitative measurement of this factor in the total complex equation is plainly beyond our powers. What is overlooked or neglected in the elaboration of these hopes is that men, as presently constituted, continue to cling to their public fears, hates, and loves, and to find other purposes to "politicalize" and shout about in the struggles for power among the great and sovereign leviathans and behemoths.

The test of the competence of a good administrative agency is very much like the test of the competence of a good heart, a good radio-tube, a good kidney, or a good motor-car engine. If it functions so well that its owner is unaware of its existence, its efficiency is admirable. As soon as its beneficiary becomes conscious of, and begins worrying about, its functions, then something is surely awry with the mechanism. The old proposition which holds that government best which governs least may be debatable. But there can be no debate over the proposition that the administrative agency is best which performs its tasks so anonymously, silently, and smoothly that all its customers support its endeavors and share in its services with a minimum of awareness of its very existence. Despite advertising campaigns put on by propagandists and public-relations advisers, the criterion of success in international, as in national and local, administration is public unconsciousness of the work of the administrator. H. G. Wells, in one of his rare "blind spots," once put the point very well, without realizing the import of what he was writing:

> The typical *ad hoc* organization is the Postal Union, which David Lubin, that brilliant neglected thinker, would have had extended until it controlled shipping and equalized freights throughout the world. He based his ideas upon his practical experience of the mail-order business, from which he derived his very considerable fortune. From that problem of freight adjustment he passed to the idea of a controlled survey of world production week by week and month by month, so that a shortage here or a glut there could be foreseen and remedied in time. He realized the idea in the form of the International Institute of Agriculture at Rome, which in its hey-day made treaties like an independent sovereign power for the supply of returns from nearly every government upon earth. The war of 1914 and Lubin's death in 1919 checked the development of this admirable and most inspiring experiment in *ad hoc* internationalism. Its history is surely something that should be made part of the compulsory education of every statesman and publicist. Yet never in my life have I met a professional politician who knew anything whatever or wanted to know anything about it. It didn't get votes; it seemed difficult to tax it; what was the good of it?[6]

The good of it was great precisely because people took it for granted. The symbols and practices of politics which arouse public attention are those which crystallize conflicting patterns of behavior and divergent definitions of value. When such cleavages are obscured or forgotten in pursuit of a common aim, no one is any longer interested save the experts concerned with its realization.

There is nothing in human experience or in the nature of the political animal to render credible the supposition that this process can somehow be extended to embrace all the public interests of mankind. Men live not by bread alone but by belief and faith and loyalty shared with their fellows, along

[6] H. G. Wells: *The New World Order* (Alfred A. Knopf; 1940), pp. 118–19.

with common fears and hatreds. These needs have thus far been met largely through passionate allegiances to the symbols of tribes, nations, or empires jostling one another in uneasy rivalry. What has always been need not always be. But no amount of "functionalism" seems likely, by itself, to alter the age-old pattern—save in a possibly dangerous direction.

It is at least arguable that when sovereignties bargained and fought over concrete stakes—e.g., markets, waterways, natural resources, and the like—their conflicts were limited to attainable goals. To the degree to which such interests become "depoliticalized" and transferred to the rational realm of international administration, frictions among sovereignties tend to become focused on such moral intangibles as "freedom" or "truth" or "justice." With respect to these, no honorable compromises are possible through diplomacy, and no meaningful victory can be won in war, short of the extermination of the alleged disciples of injustice, falsehood, and despotism. A quarrel of kings over weights and measures or control of a river or postal charges can be settled and ended one way or another. A feud among rival and sovereign demagogues over the meaning of "liberty" admits of no adjustment or termination. The "functionalists" would be indignant at the imputation that their admirable work has thus contributed to the frequency and ferocity of holy wars or Crusades. Without insisting that this is the case, we must none the less take cognizance of the relationships here suggested.

The futility of the functional approach when applied to problems of *Realpolitik* is vividly illustrated by the case of uranium and plutonium—and with a brief glance at this disturbing story of frustration, we may well leave the whole matter. With the advent of nuclear fission and the use of its hideous power to obliterate Hiroshima and Nagasaki, many men of wisdom, including Albert Einstein and Robert M. Hutchins, contended that the unleashed atom could be harnessed to the service of mankind, instead of becoming the probable means of Man's self-destruction, only through the creation, by global international agreement, of some type of world government with planetary powers of legislation and administration in the field of atomic energy. The resolution adopted by the U.N. General Assembly on January 24, 1946, envisaged a more modest goal. A U.N. Atomic Energy Commission should prepare proposals for international exchange of scientific information "for peaceful ends," "control of atomic energy to the extent necessary to insure its use only for peaceful purposes," "the elimination of national armaments of atomic weapons and of all other major weapons adaptable to mass destruction," and "effective safeguards by way of inspection and other means to protect complying states against the hazards of violations and evasions."

The Commission did not meet until June. On March 16, 1946, the Lilienthal-Acheson proposals ("*A Report on the International Control of Atomic Energy*," Department of State document 2498) were released in Washington. They contemplated, on the model of TVA, a U.N. Atomic Development Authority as an international public corporation to own and operate all the world's uranium and thorium mines, as well as all laboratories and plants using fissionable material in dangerous form, and to conduct all atomic research, inspection, licensing, and leasing, to the ends of preventing manufacture of atomic bombs and of making atomic energy and its by-products available for the works of peace. Whether this "functionalist" proposal would have proved acceptable had the U.S.A. stood by it, and had Soviet policy in Iran that spring not provoked the beginning of the Cold War, we shall never know. Common interest in avoiding the suicide of the human race, it might have been supposed, would have been sufficient to foster global agreement to take the whole issue out of the arena of power politics and make it a problem of administration. In reality neither the Truman Administration nor the Stalin regime, each seeking strategic advantages, was prepared to do anything of the kind—with results now known to everyone.

The gist of the matter can be put briefly.[7] Bernard Baruch on June 16, 1946, combined the Lilienthal-Acheson proposals with insistence on "condign punishment" of violators through an end of the Security Council "veto" in atomic matters. David Lilienthal and Chester I. Barnard had vainly warned Baruch in May that the injection of the "veto" issue was "meaningless" and could lead only to a "blind alley." He insisted that the U.S.A. would discontinue the production and stock piling of atomic bombs only at some indefinite future date, when satisfied that the successive stages of international control were operating effectively to prevent any other nation from producing nuclear weapons—and only on condition that the control plan be enforced by the threat of war, "legalized" in advance by revision of the U.N. Charter. Two days later Gromyko, on behalf of Moscow, proposed a treaty to forbid the production and use of atomic weapons and to provide for the destruction of all stockpiles within three months, with a U.N. committee to recommend measures of inspection and control.

From these initial positions Washington and Moscow never deviated in any material detail. The subsequent discussions were therefore not "negotiations," since negotiations require bargaining and compromise. The "functionalist" approach failed because both super-Powers were bent upon playing politics with the atom. The U.S.A. put forward proposals certain to be rejected by the U.S.S.R.—which in turn put forward proposals certain to be rejected by the U.S.A. Washington sought to prolong its monopoly of atomic bombs

[7] For a fuller account see L. Larry Leonard: *International Organization* (McGraw-Hill; 1951), pp. 276–95, and the present writer's *International Politics* (McGraw-Hill; 1948, 4th edition), pp. 918–37, and "Atomic Diplomacy: Deadlock and Prospects" (Chicago Council on Foreign Relations; 1950), where an attempt was made to offer a "constructive" and "practicable" proposal. Amid the mushrooming literature on these questions, the most incisive criticism of U.S. policy is offered by Patrick Blackett: *Fear, War, and the Bomb* (McGraw-Hill; 1949). Frederick Osborn, "The U.S.S.R. and the Atom," *International Organization* (August 1951), restates the official and familiar view that the Baruch proposals were a masterpiece of wisdom and altruism and that the U.S.S.R. refused to accept them because of obstructionism, wickedness, and total depravity.

by championing a scheme whereby no other nation could acquire any. Moscow sought to win time to break the American monopoly—an accomplishment announced by President Truman on September 23, 1949. The race for the H-Bomb followed. The war to come promised to resemble the famous duel that Abraham Lincoln never fought. He was challenged and given his choice of weapons. He proposed shotguns at five paces. The challenger dropped the idea. Whether Americans and Russians would be equally prudent seemed questionable.

The test of diplomatic success in the looking-glass world of the Atomic Age is not agreement but prevention of agreement, plus ability to put the blame on the other side. The new objective all sublime, moreover, is not to "depoliticalize" problems in the interest of a functional-administrative solution, but rather to politicalize all existing functional organizations and make global administration, even in inconsequential matters, all but impossible. Under such conditions, "functionalism" has no future.

Little need be said of the sequel to our tale. The advent of the Soviet bomb rendered obsolete the Baruch Plan, along with America's global strategy for resisting the Communist barbarians. But this fact evoked no modifications of policy —in which respect it resembled Cineas' famous discourse, which, wrote Plutarch, "gave Pyrrhus pain but produced no change in his plans." In a frenzied quest for complete security, which is never attainable in the world of men, the super-Powers arrived at complete insecurity along what Patrick Blackett has called "the road to anxiety neurosis and the madhouse."

CHAPTER SEVEN

PEACE BY WAR

1. THE AGELESS FABLE

Credo quia absurdum. —ORIGEN.

IN THE YEAR 1306, a wealthy French lawyer named Pierre Dubois wrote a treatise entitled *De Recuperatione Terræ Sanctæ*. The author was a contemporary of Dante—who hoped that a *Pax Orbis* might somehow be restored by the Holy Roman Emperor. Dubois knew better. He addressed his work to Philip the Fair and dedicated it to Edward I. In it he proposed that the princes of Europe should unite to rescue the Holy Land from the Infidels. To promote unity and further the purposes of the original Crusaders, Dubois urged the establishment of a Council of Europe and a Court. The Pope was to be President of the former, with appellate jurisdiction over the latter. Lawbreakers and peacebreakers would be excommunicated and suffer war against them by all the other members of the Council. Nothing came of this proposal. But it had the merit, at least, of recognizing that separate sovereignties cannot easily be united unless they are dedicated to a common purpose to be pursued against a common foe.

A century and a half later the amazing Hussite heretic, George Podebrad—who spent his life fighting the Pope and was the only Bohemian and the only non-Catholic ever to be King of Bohemia—proposed (1464) holy war against the Turks as a means of uniting Europe's princes, all of whom should conclude pacts of perpetual friendship and renounce war among themselves. The coalition he envisaged would function through an Assembly of diplomats, a Court to settle disputes, and a Syndic to receive financial contributions. The Assembly would have authority to fix quotas of military forces and to wage war. Despite Papal hostility, Podebrad managed to conclude pacts with Hungary and France, but was otherwise frustrated in his endeavor.

Later writers, grappling with the same problem, arrived at the simple and now long familiar notion that peace among sovereignties can best be preserved by having all sovereigns solemnly compact to wage war against any sovereign who might take the sword. Since in theory none could resist all others leagued against him, each would be deterred from aggression and peace would be forevermore secure. The fact that this formula, known in our time as "collective security," is based on false premises and has never worked in practice—and, as we shall see, cannot conceivably work in the very nature of our system of States—has not prevented successive generations of philosophers, politicians, and peace-seekers from embracing it with an ardor exceeded only by their naïveté.

The tale of this fable is much too long to be retold in detail.[1] A few of the more famous "classics" devoted to its elaboration will suggest the course of this unending search for the horn of the unicorn. In 1623 an obscure French monk, Emeric Crucé, published *Le Nouveau Cynée* (*The New Cineas*) as an indictment of war and a plan for perpetual

[1] The literature of "peace," envisaged in these terms, is as staggering in volume as it is operationally useless in content. Helpful compilations are to be found in Edith Wynner and Georgia Lloyd: *Searchlight on Peace Plans—Choose Your Road to World Government* (Dutton; 1949, revised edition); Sylvester J. Hemleben: *Plans for World Peace through Six Centuries* (University of Chicago Press; 1943); and Sir John A. R. Marriott: *Commonwealth or Anarchy? A Survey of Projects of Peace from the 16th to the 20th Century* (Columbia University Press; 1939).

peace. Wars are fought, said he, for honor, for profit, for reparation of wrong, and for the exercise of the troops. But all is waste and vanity since there is "more dishonor to fear than glory to hope for in war." The essence of his remedy is this: "Choose a city, where all sovereigns should have perpetually their ambassadors, in order that the differences that might arise should be settled by the judgment of the whole assembly. . . . If anyone rebelled against the decree of so notable a company, he would receive the disgrace of all the other Princes, who would find the ways to bring him to reason." The chairmanship of the assembly would rotate among the Great Powers, all of whom would agree to wage war against any defiant prince.

So passionate is Man's desire for peace in a world in which men love war, and so addicted are people to preferring easy wishes to hard realities, that Crucé's wholly fatuous conception has not only undergone no significant change in three centuries—though the best minds of the race have devoted themselves to the problem—but is actually far more widely accepted as wisdom in the 1950's than in the 1620's. Much ado about nothing is monotonous if unleavened by wit and whimsy. These qualities are conspicuously lacking in the solemn and moralistic disquisitions of the advocates of peace by war. A few voices will be enough to suggest the dull uniformity of the formula here considered, although the owners of the voices, curiously, were on the whole people not dull but often bright and sometimes sparkling. A false idea, if superficially plausible and infused with hope, can reduce even the finest minds to inanity.

Crucé's contemporary, the Duc de Sully, Hugenot financial adviser to Henry of Navarre, set forth in his memoirs a scheme for peace which he described, with little basis in fact, as the "Grand Design of Henry IV." The program was intended to humble the House of Hapsburg. It was frustrated, according to Sully, by the death of Queen Elizabeth in 1603 and by the assassination of Henry in 1610. Europe should be permanently divided into fifteen States, in each of which uniformity of religion was to be achieved. All would unite in a General Council of sixty-six members, in which France, England, Spain, Austria, Sweden, Denmark, Lombardy, Italy, Poland, and Venice would each have four commissioners, chosen for three-year terms. The Council, supplemented by six regional councils, would discuss all problems and pacify all quarrels among the nations. All members would contribute quotas to a European Army of 200,000 foot, 50,000 horse, 200 cannon, and 120 vessels of war—which force would be employed to carry out the decisions of the Council and to punish any sovereign who defied its will. Messrs. Tardieu and Herriot, Premiers of France, made similar proposals to the League of Nations General Disarmament Conference of 1932. The idea of a European Army was revived two decades later under the inspiration of the Council of Europe, René Pleven, Winston Churchill, Truman, Acheson, and Eisenhower. Unlike old soldiers, some superstitions and delusions neither die nor fade away.

Quaker William Penn published his *Essay Toward the Present and Future Peace of Europe* in 1693. He proposed a General Diet, Estates, or Parliament of all princes to meet periodically to settle disputes. "If any of the sovereignties that constitute the imperial States shall refuse to submit their claims or pretensions to them, or to abide and perform the judgment thereof, and seek their remedy by arms, or delay their compliance beyond the time prefixed in their resolutions, all the other sovereignties, united as one strength, shall compel the submission and performance of the sentence, with damages to the suffering party, and charges to the sovereignties that obliged their submission." Since all war, held Penn, is waged to keep, to recover, or to conquer territory, the Imperial Diet can keep the peace by adjusting territorial disputes. Voting strength in the Parliament should be based upon national wealth: 12 units for the Holy Roman Empire, 10 each for France and Spain, 8 for Italy, 6 for England, 3 for Portugal, 10 each for Turkey and Muscovy, and so on. Peace would thus be preserved, friendship among princes would be fostered, they would be enabled to marry for love instead of reasons of state, and "the reputation of Christianity will in some degree be recovered in the sight of Infidels."

At the time of the Conference of Utrecht the erudite Abbé St. Pierre published *A Lasting Peace Through the Federation of Europe* (1713), which he sent to the French Minister, Fleury. The statesman commented: "You have forgotten an essential article, that of dispatching missionaries to touch the hearts of Princes and to persuade them to enter into your views." The Abbé proposed an alliance of all States which should guarantee the territory of all its members, suppress revolutions, and maintain monarchs on their thrones. The allies would oppose by arms any Power that should refuse to give effect to its judgments or make treaties contrary to them. Utrecht was to be designated as the City of Peace. Each State would maintain agents there who would constitute an assembly, authorized to keep the peace and, by a majority vote, to enact all laws necessary and proper to achieve the objective.

Forty-three years later Jean-Jacques Rousseau—scallywag philosopher of Geneva, libertine, social theorist, and madman—wrote his famous commentary (under the same title) on the Abbe's work, though it was not published until 1761. Here Jean-Jacques proposed a league of nations, misnamed a "federation," wherein the members would form a perpetual and irrevocable alliance and create a Diet or Congress, with a rotating presidency and fixed quotas of financial contributions and armed forces, which should settle all disputes, guarantee the territorial integrity and existing form of government of all members, and wage war against any member defying its conclusions. Rousseau was too wise to assume that his plan was likely to be accepted:

> This is not, of course, to say that the sovereigns will adopt this project . . . but only that they would adopt it if they took counsel of their true interest. . . . All that I do assume in them is understanding enough to see their own interest, and courage enough to act for their own happiness. If in spite of all

this, the project remains unrealized, that is not because it is Utopian; it is because men are crazy, and because to be sane in a world of madmen is in itself a kind of madness.

This form of madness is chronic. The brilliant apostle of "utilitarianism," Jeremy Bentham, published his *Principles of International Law* on the eve of the French Revolution. Here he argued, long before such arguments were popular, that war never "pays"—forgetting that the joys men derive from mutual murder and suicide are not to be measured in monetary terms. He urged disarmament, free trade, the abolition of secret diplomacy, and the emancipation of colonies as the keys to peace. A common court of judicature, he opined, would contribute to the same end. A common tribunal would aid in the process and should be empowered to place any recalcitrant state under the "ban of Europe." The objective, he believed, could also be served by common concentration on the building of an Atlantic-Pacific canal across Nicaragua in a new State of "Junctiana."

The celibate philosopher of Königsberg (now Kalinengrad) Immanuel Kant, published his *Zum Ewigen Frieden* (*Toward Eternal Peace*) in 1795. In customary Kantian fashion, he here argued that people are "rational" and "just," and that governments, if properly constituted, would also be rational and just—and, being so, would combine to promote rationality and justice. Reason makes peace a duty. Wars of extermination "would allow eternal peace only upon the graveyard of the whole human race. Such a war, therefore, as well as the use of the means which might be employed in it, is wholly forbidden." States ought to give up their "wild and lawless freedom, to accept public and enforceable laws, and thus to form a constantly growing World-State of nations." Since they are unwilling to do so, hope for peace must rest in a loose union, devoted to commerce and to "republican" constitutionalism. If all governments represent their peoples, war will be unlikely. Kant's "Articles of Perpetual Peace" postulated the independence of all States, nonintervention, disarmament, world citizenship, and (more vaguely) collective armed action by a League of Nations against any state that should defy "the decision of the common will according to law." Some elements of what we have come to call federalism are implicit in the Kantian formula, but its prime implication, obscured in metaphysics, is that peace can be kept by arrangements for the waging of war by States upon States.

Since 1800 this idea has been expounded by such a multitude of peace-seekers that a mere listing of their hortatory efforts would fill many pages. A few samples will indicate the tenor of the whole, with each writer horrified by the madness, murder, and waste of war and striving somehow to propose a better way of adjusting international conflicts. William Jay, son of John Jay, in his *War and Peace* (1842) observed: "We make daily great improvements in Natural, there is one I wish to see in Moral, Philosophy: the Discovery of a Plan, that would induce & oblige Nations to settle their Disputes without first Cutting one another's Throats." His purpose was to show that "war is a demon whose malignant influence is felt at all times and in all places" and that "every war, without exception, involves guilt and must be offensive to the Deity." Moreover, "every war is professedly defensive, while scarcely any is so in fact. It will be difficult to specify a single instance in which a war might not have been averted by honest and sincere negotiation, or by a sacrifice far less costly to either party than the prosecution of hostilities." Nations should therefore outlaw war by treaty and submit all disputes to arbitration. Jay is vague as to what should be done with defiant sovereignties. But most of his contemporaries had no doubt as to the answer: military coercion.

Elihu Burritt, the "learned blacksmith," set forth his plan for a Congress of Nations at three conferences of peace-seekers in Brussels (1848), Paris (1849), and Frankfurt (1850). In the triumph of freedom and democracy he saw the harbinger of the unity of mankind. A constituent assembly of peoples, composed of elected delegates, one for each million souls in Christendom, should codify international law, establish a "high court of nations," and discuss other forms of co-operation. As a pacifist and as an American supremely confident that all problems can be solved by "passing a law," Burritt ignored the question of enforcement. The Hague conferences of 1899 and 1907, also ignoring this crucial issue, achieved substantially what Burritt had urged—with results highly useful but scarcely calculated to demonstrate that sovereignties would renounce war if only they were provided with machinery for arbitrating or adjudicating their controversies.

Benjamin Franklin Trueblood, a Quaker, saw the need of arrangements beyond these devices and yet not geared to enforcement through armed violence. In *The Federation of the World* (1899), he expressed a higher hope: "A great international state, coextensive with the surface of the globe, with some sort of government directing the general interests of the race and compatible with local self-government, is the necessary and inevitable outgrowth of the nature of man and of society, under the action of the divinely ordained social processes, and that regeneration and reconstruction of humanity which Christianity is bringing about." General acceptance of arbitration, coupled with a moral improvement of mankind would, he hoped, lead to world federalism, with no need of the coercion of States by States.

But such voices were lonely. In the nineteenth and twentieth centuries the prevailing views of Western mankind—and ultimately the policies of governments—toward the nature of the problem of peace have been focused on the hypothesis (usually regarded as a self-evident fact) that war can be abolished through an alliance or organization of all sovereigns to punish by force of arms any sovereign violating peace. A final instance, albeit an influential one, must here suffice to prove the point.

At a conference in Independence Hall in Philadelphia, in mid-June of the year of blood 1915, there was established the League to Enforce Peace, with ex-President William

Howard Taft and Senator Henry Cabot Lodge, Sr., among its prominent supporters. Its program embodied four proposals: (1) the establishment of an International Judicial Tribunal to adjudicate legal disputes; (2) creation of a Council of Conciliation, with an Executive Committee, to deal with political differences; (3) periodical gatherings to codify and modify international law; and (4) arrangements for compelling States to refrain from war, to submit quarrels to pacific settlement, and to accept the decisions arrived at—ranging from moral suasion and social ostracism to collective diplomatic ruptures, economic boycotts, and military coercion.

At a second conference in Washington in 1916 Senator Lodge endorsed "entangling alliances" as a means of enforcing peace and Woodrow Wilson cautiously approved the plan of the League, enunciating high moral principles and expressing his conviction that the American people were willing to "become a partner in any feasible association of nations formed in order to realize these objects." On January 22, 1917, in an address to the Senate on "A World League for Peace," Wilson went farther:

> In every discussion of the peace that must end this war it is taken for granted that that peace must be followed by some definite concert of power, which will make it virtually impossible that any such catastrophe should ever overwhelm us again. . . . It is inconceivable that the people of the United States should play no part in that great enterprise. . . . These are American principles, American policies. We can stand for no others. And they are also the principles and policies of forward-looking men and women everywhere, of every modern nation, of every enlightened community. They are the principles of mankind and must prevail.

This conception bore strange fruit in the League of Nations Covenant of 1919. With the complex structure and tangled international law of the Geneva experiment, "made in America" and repudiated by America, we are not here concerned. What is relevant to our inquiry is the League method of keeping the peace. Its elements of investigation, conciliation, mediation, arbitration, and adjudication are as old as Athens, Babylon, and Egypt, and have never, in any past or present system of States, achieved a *Pax Orbis* or even any temporary facsimile thereof, for reasons implicit in the very nature of political relationships among separate sovereignties. The new element in the Geneva scheme was "collective security" through "international sanctions."

Novelty resided not in the idea, which as we have seen was centuries old, but in its translation into an institution, brought into being through solemn international commitments. Even the practice had adumbrations in older times. The Treaty of Westphalia, signed in Münster in 1648, obliged all parties (Art. 123) "to defend and protect all and every article of the peace against anyone . . . and if it happens any point shall be violated, the offended shall before all things exhort the offender not to come to any hostility, submitting the cause to a friendly composition, or the ordinary proceedings of justice." By Art. 124: "Nevertheless, if for the space of three years the difference cannot be terminated by any of those means, all and every one of those concerned in this transaction shall be obliged to join the injured party, and assist him with counsel and force to repel the injury, being first advertised by the injured that gentle means and justice prevailed nothing." Similarly the Treaties of Chaumont and of the Quadruple Alliance of 1814–15 contemplated the collective use of force against aggression or revolution. Under their terms the Concert of the Powers authorized Austria and France, respectively, to resort to armed intervention to suppress liberal rebellions in Italy and Spain in 1821–3.

The League scheme of "sanctions" was none the less an innovation in terms of the high hopes placed upon it, the vast literature evoked by it, and the completeness of its ultimate failure and repudiation. On the false analogy of the policeman and the malefactor in civil societies, the framers of the Covenant sought to give practical effect to the conception once expressed by the Royal Institute of International Affairs:

"Sanctions are measures taken in support of law. It is of the essence of law that its sanctions are applied with and by the general authority, not by any individual. With the substitution of the word 'state' for the word 'individual,' this is true in principle, and ought to be true in fact, of the sanctions of international as well as of national law." [2] On the basis of this premise, the drafters of the Covenant framed its Article 16 as follows:

> 1. Should any Member of the League resort to war in disregard of its covenants under Articles 12, 13, or 15, it shall *ipso facto* be deemed to have committed an act of war against all other Members of the League, which hereby undertake immediately to subject it to the severance of all trade or financial relations, the prohibition of all intercourse between their nationals, and the nationals of the covenant-breaking State, and the prevention of all financial, commercial or personal intercourse between the nationals of the covenant-breaking State and the nationals of any other State, whether a Member of the League or not.
>
> 2. It shall be the duty of the Council in such case to recommend to the several Governments concerned what effective military, naval or air force the members of the League shall severally contribute to the armed forces to be used to protect the covenants of the League.
>
> 3. The Members of the League agree, further, that they will mutually support one another in the financial and economic measures which are taken under this Article, in order to minimize the loss and inconvenience resulting from the above measures, and that they will mutually support one another in resisting any special measures aimed at one of their number by the covenant-breaking State, and that they will take the necessary steps to afford passage through their territory to the forces of

[2] The Royal Institute of International Affairs: *International Sanctions* (London: Oxford University Press; 1938), p. 4. This excellent study reviews in some detail the theory and practice of League sanctions, with particular reference to 1935–6. See also David Mitrany: *The Problem of International Sanctions* (London: Oxford University Press; 1925); Sir John Fischer Williams: "Sanctions under the Covenant," *British Yearbook of International Law* (1935); and William E. Rappard: *The Quest for Peace* (Cambridge, Massachusetts: Harvard University Press; 1940).

any of the members of the League which are cooperating to protect the covenants of the League.

4. Any Member of the League which has violated any Covenant of the League may be declared to be no longer a Member of the League by a vote of the Council concurred in by the Representatives of all the other members of the League represented thereon.

The suppositions originally entertained by the authors of these words are clear enough. Said Woodrow Wilson in 1919: "Suppose somebody does not abide by these engagements, then what happens? An absolute isolation, a boycott!" M. Augustin Hamon spoke of "an isolation that is complete, absolute, a revival of medieval excommunication." In its Resolution 14, of October 1921, the League Assembly interpreted Article 16 to mean that moral and economic measures of "increasing stringency" should be taken against peace-breaking States before recourse was had to any military measures. War for peace should be resorted to only if the "criminal" declined to yield to the "will of the community" in the face of diplomatic reproof, nonrecognition of the fruits of aggression, embargoes, and boycotts. But the advocates of "collective security," then as now, have never been in doubt but that the final and most effective method of promoting peace is war—however paradoxical the proposition might appear to a man from Mars. The point is well put in the Royal Institute Study already quoted:

> Neither an angry man nor an angry nation will listen to argument. A nation whose passions have been inflamed, whether by the policy of another government or by the propaganda of its own, may not be deterred from attacking another State by the certain prospect of the severest economic measures of which the world disposes. To deal with this contingency, the world has only one resource—to employ overwhelming force to bring to an end the private use of force by an individual State. Indeed, some have argued that this measure is the only real sanction against a breach of the rule of law, that it is useless to seek for less onerous substitutes, since they are pre-ordained to futility.[3]

[3] Op. cit., p. 114.

The best test of truth, said Justice Holmes, is "the power of the thought to get itself accepted in the competition of the market." By this test the theory of "collective security" is unquestionably valid, for it has been honored with all but universal acceptance in the Great Society of the twentieth century. But the pragmatist will test the truth of hypotheses not by their popularity alone—since men are ever prone to confuse hopes and wishes with reality—but by their utility and their operational consequences when put to the test of practice. "Collective security" has twice been so tested in our time, on a world scale. The observable results of these experiments merit careful attention.

---

2. TRAGEDY AT GENEVA

> For God's sake help us. Get something done that will really harm the Italian armies and not merely the Italian people. . . . Rally your husbands, brothers, sons, and force them to use their massed strength to compel the parliaments and rulers to take action. Do I ask you purely selfishly to do this? No. We are only a small race; but I am seventeen and its leading daughter, and I know, as you know, that if Mankind lets armies and gas destroy my country and people, Civilization will be destroyed too. We have a common cause, you and I. Why therefore do not all do something to drive off this common danger to Humanity, this agony, this death by bombs, shells, and gas, before it again establishes itself as it is doing here now, soon to spread fatally to your homes and your menfolk too? Italian aggression and gas have set Humanity a test. If you fail to help us now, we all shall die.
>
> —PRINCESS TSAHAI'S APPEAL TO THE WOMEN OF THE WEST, April 27, 1936.

THE GENEVA EXPERIMENT in peace by war has been described in many volumes, along with its poignant failure—with an aftermath more ghastly than anything that could conceivably have happened had this quixotic enterprise never been attempted. Since I have elsewhere written of the same at length,[4] a bare résumé of this sorry tale will here do to suggest the anatomy of folly and the physiology of futility. This is the sordid drama—destined to be re-enacted on another stage fifteen years later—of a Great Society incapable of facing realities and bent upon converting falsehood into truth by ritualistic incantation having no relationship to the facts of life or to the actual purposes of the players. "Where there is no vision the people perish."

Benito Mussolini, pseudo-Cæsar, decided in the year 1933 to conquer Ethiopia—for "reasons" not germane to our immediate inquiry. The issue, said the Duce to General Emilio de Bono, must be resolved "not later than 1936." Preparations were made during 1934. Despite provocation in the armed clash of December 5, 1934, at Wal-Wal in the Ogaden Desert, followed by Italian demands for apologies and reparations, De Bono reported that the Negus (Ras Tafari Makonnen, crowned in 1930 as Haile Selassie, King of Kings, Chosen of God, Conquering Lion of the Tribe of Judah, and alleged descendant of King Solomon and the Queen of Sheba) would not attack. "In case the Negus should have no intention of attacking us," rejoined Mussolini, "we ourselves must take the initiative."

The problem posed by this decision was simplicity itself

[4] See Arnold J. Toynbee: *Survey of International Affairs*, 1935, Vol. II (London: Oxford University Press; 1936); L. Larry Leonard, op. cit. pp. 135–54; and my own *Europe on the Eve: The Crises of Diplomacy, 1933–1939* (Alfred A. Knopf; 1939). The voluminous post-World-War-II diaries, memoirs, and published documents have added personal and political details but have not altered the "plot" or "moral" of these events. At Chatham House in April 1951, Professor Toynbee concurred in this judgment. In what follows I have therefore refrained from burdening the reader with post-war documentation and contemporary "revelations" of little consequence. Documentary references for the facts and quotations in this section will be found in the three works cited above. In my own earlier volume I expressed belief in the theoretical possibility of "collective security." In the light of subsequent events and reflections, I now regard this belief as mistaken. "Collective security" in all imaginable contexts is unworkable for reasons amply set forth in the text of the present chapter. See also F. P. Walters: *A History of the League of Nations* (London: Oxford University Press; 1952, 2 vols.).

—in the eyes of those whose stereotyped image of world order is a picture of a society of virtuous sovereignties sworn to uphold "the rule of law" and to "enforce peace" by the collective coercion of criminal sovereignties. Italy was bound by nine treaties (seven signed and ratified by the Fascist regime)—from the Anglo-French-Italian pact of December 13, 1906, to the Argentine Anti-War Treaty of October 10, 1933—to safeguard the integrity and independence of Ethiopia and to submit all disputes to conciliation, arbitration, or adjudication. Both Italy and Ethiopia were members of the League, as were Britain, France, and the Soviet Union. All Members had agreed (Art. 10 of the Covenant) "to respect and preserve as against external aggression the territorial integrity and existing political independence of all Members of the League" and had assumed the obligations of "collective security" set forth in Art. 16. Nothing could be clearer than the duty of Italy to keep the peace, the duty of all other League Members to wage war on Italy in the event of Italian aggression against Ethiopia, and the certainty in this event that the aggressor, if not deterred beforehand from crime by this awful prospect, would be caught red-handed and would be halted and punished—much as a common criminal is arrested by the sheriff, hailed before the judge, tried before a jury of his peers, solemnly sentenced, and cast into jail.

That such clarity and simplicity in conception should, in execution, turn into complexity, obfuscation, and the co-operation of the "police" and the "criminal" to take the life of his victim was (and still is) a source of endless mystification to the convinced disciples of collective security and international sanctions. The apparent enigma exists only because the facts of the society of nations bear no relationship to the fancies projected upon it by the advocates of this intriguing formula. Statesmen use moral and legal abstractions to influence public attitudes—since no public is able to admit that international politics is a competition for power. But States act out of interest. To confuse one's interests with the verbiage of ethics and law is to act blindly, rashly, and fatuously. To see one's interests plainly, to serve them boldly, and to clothe the result in the language of legalism and moralism is to act adroitly and effectively. The lofty expectations of the naïve may even appear, in the latter situation, to be fulfilled. Yet such hopes are certain to be shatteringly disappointed when moral and legal obligations have been so defined that action or inaction dictated inexorably by interest are manifestly inconsistent with the "duties" previously assumed, and thus require violation and repudiation as the lesser of two evils.

The uses, abuses, or disuses of the power at the disposal of policy-makers in London and Paris were here decisive. Moscow, under the guidance of the genial Maxim Litvinov, was fully committed to "collective security," but was neither able nor willing to take action alone against Rome. Washington was not only not a Member of the League but was committed to a so-called "neutrality" policy under which sales of arms were to be impartially banned to both belligerents with no distinction between the aggressor and his victim. This arrangement was highly beneficial to Italy and fatally injurious to Ethiopia. It was compared by John Bassett Moore to the "new chastity, which encouraged fornication in the hope that it might reach the stage of legalized prostitution." The efforts of Secretaries Hull and Ickes to discourage, through "moral suasion," American shipments to Italy of oil and other strategic materials not banned by law were without effect. Paralysis in Geneva and Fascist propaganda in America had appreciable influence in making the United States the unwitting economic ally of the lawbreaker. This curious result was not the fruit of the pursuit of any national interest whatever (indeed every actual American interest in the situation was wholly ignored or betrayed), but of an irrational chase after a will-o-the-wisp.[5]

[5] See John Norman: "Influence of Pro-Fascist Propaganda on American Neutrality, 1935–1936," in D. E. Lee and G. E. McReynolds (editors): *Essays in History and International Relations in Honor of George Hubbard Blakeslee* (Worcester, Massachusetts: Clark University; 1949).

The interests of Britain and France were defined by their policy-makers not at all in terms of abstract ideals, in or out of the Covenant, but in terms of sympathy for Fascism and the hope of enlisting Mussolini's support against Hitler. On the former theme Winston Churchill had said in Rome, as early as January 20, 1927, that he could not help "being charmed by Signor Mussolini's gentle and simple bearing and by his calm, detached poise. . . . I should have been whole-heartedly with you from the start to the finish in your triumphant struggle against the bestial appetites and passions of Leninism. . . . Your movement has rendered a service to the whole world. . . . Italy has provided the necessary antidote to the Russian poison. Hereafter no great nation will go unprovided with an ultimate means of protection against the cancerous growth of Bolshevism." And as late as 1951 Mr. Churchill in his memoirs of the war found only one fault with the greatness of Il Duce: he gambled unwisely, betrayed the wrong allies, and joined the losing camp. "Even when the issue of the war became certain, Mussolini would have been welcomed by the Allies. . . . He could have timed his moment to declare war on Hitler with art and care." [6]

Other British and French diplomats, bureaucrats, and plutocrats—as fearful of Communism as their American counterparts were to be a decade later—were even more ardent in their admiration for Hitler, Hirohito, and Mussolini. To thwart Fascist ambition, to discredit the Blackshirt regime by inflicting upon it a diplomatic defeat, or, still worse, to bring it to military disaster by using force to halt its agression—and thereby invite its downfall and possible Red revolution in Italy—were all unthinkable to Paris and London in 1935–6. Fascism was to be helped, not hindered. If the result

[6] At the time of writing, the portion of Churchill's memoirs dealing with the fall of Mussolini is being serialized, with the book to be published in 1952. Anglo-French upper-class admiration for Fascism in its Italian, German, Spanish, and Japanese forms as a factor influencing policy at Downing Street and the Quai d'Orsay in the 1930's is discussed, with documentation and quotations, in my *Europe on the Eve*, pp. 332–46. I find nothing in postwar publications and revelations which alters the essential validity of this evaluation.

was to be the conquest of Ethiopia, the collapse of the League, and the exposure of "collective security" as a farce and a fraud, these ills could better be born than the alternative.

The actual policies of the Western Powers, as distinct from their pretended policies, are scarcely open to retrospective criticism for being "immoral." Whatever serves national interest is "moral" in the jungle world of power politics. The policies in question were reprehensible only because they were operationally false and thereby produced consequences that were the antitheses of those expected, and damaged most grievously the interests they were intended to serve. Logic is important in law. Ethical standards are relevant to morality. But in the politics of rival sovereignties, nothing counts but results. In the present case, the results were calamitous.

Pierre Laval, renegade Socialist and crypto-Fascist, struck a complex diplomatic bargain with Mussolini in Rome on January 7, 1935. Its secret essence, elaborately denied by Laval at the time, was that France would acquiesce in the projected Italian subjugation of Ethiopia in return for the hope of Italian support in championing Austrian independence and opposing the rearmament and expansion of the Nazi Reich. Hitler repudiated the disarmament clauses of the Treaty of Versailles in mid-March, with the Western allies acquiescing and wooing Italian favor all the more fervently. All winter, spring, and summer Italian troops and arms poured through Suez to Eritrea and Somaliland in open preparation for the invasion. Sir John Simon, chief architect of Western acquiescence in the Japanese seizure of Manchuria from China in 1931–2, blandly assured Commons that these activities were not "aggressive in character."

All Ethiopian efforts to secure preventive or protective action through the League were skillfully evaded or thwarted by Downing Street and the Quai d'Orsay. Sir John Maffey's Interministerial Commission, in a report to the Foreign Office of June 18, 1935 (by coincidence the same day on which the new Foreign Secretary, Sir Samuel Hoare, exchanged letters with Ribbentrop whereby Britain gave approval to German naval rearmament), held that "no vital British interest exists in Ethiopia or its neighborhood sufficient to oblige His Majesty's Government to resist a conquest of Ethiopia by Italy," although certain Ethiopian border territories ought in this case to be annexed to the Sudan, Kenya, and British Somaliland. By September 3, when the arbitral tribunal ruled absurdly that neither Italy nor Ethiopia had been responsible for the clash at Wal-Wal, Ethiopia had appealed seven times for League action looking toward a pacific settlement and had seven times been put off. When Haile Selassie in July urged Washington to remind all parties of the Pact of Paris, President Roosevelt refused to act, and expressed confidence that there would be no resort to war—although the State Department had known for over a year of Mussolini's decision to conquer Ethiopia.

In short, the Western Powers in this first test case of "collective security" rejected utterly the Wilsonian contention that "any war anywhere is everybody's business" and decided that the projected Italian aggression was either "none of their business" or was a business they ought to promote in the hope of favors from the would-be conqueror. The difficulty in the way of the latter enterprise was not so much the law of the Covenant, which only the Ethiopians took seriously, but the mood of the British public, which had permitted itself to be persuaded that "collective security" could be made to work. In the "British National Peace Ballot," organized by the League of Nations Union, almost half the British electorate expressed its views—announced on June 27, 1935. By an overwhelming majority, the voters approved both economic and military sanctions against aggression. This, to say the least, was awkward for Stanley Baldwin, Neville Chamberlain, Anthony Eden, Sir John Simon, Sir Samuel Hoare, *et al.*, whose government was contemplating an autumn election. Baldwin hastened to assert that the League "remains the sheet-anchor of British policy." In late September, Hoare proclaimed at Geneva that his country stood "for steady and collective resistance [meaning 'assistance'] to all acts of unprovoked aggression." In the campaign preceding the polling of November 14, 1935 (in which the Baldwin Cabinet won 431 out of 615 seats), the most widely displayed Tory campaign poster was a picture of the Covenant with a fist planted upon it, over the caption: "Our word is our bond."

This spectacle and all that followed it must impress those who believe in the fable of "collective security" as a monstrous and indecent exhibition of prevarication, hypocrisy, and black villainy, perpetrated incredibly by the most respected and responsible statesmen of the democracies. To those who understand that "collective security" is a delusion, this episode is merely a tale of squirming, equivocation, and finally successful connivance in aggression on the part of politicians who were neither very imaginative nor particularly cognizant of the actual interest of their States.

During the spring and summer of 1935 London and Paris saw to it that Ethiopia could buy no arms. At a three-power conference in London in mid-August, Eden and Laval offered to Rome "economic concessions" and "territorial adjustments" in Ethiopia. Il Duce replied: "If you offered me all of Ethiopia on a silver platter, I would refuse it, for I have resolved to take it by force." Since force was bound to prove embarrassing to the Western statesmen, who faced a difficult problem, they hopefully tried the silver platter. In September the League Council and Assembly referred the problem to committees. Here in Geneva on September 10 Hoare and Laval agreed to rule out "military sanctions, naval blockade, the closure of the Suez Canal—in a word, ruling out everything that might lead to war" with Italy. Both men then solemnly proclaimed their fidelity to the League Covenant. The Council Commission of Five on September 18 proposed "territorial adjustments" and Italian economic exploitation of Ethiopia (called "international economic assistance"), but Mussolini was contemptuous. . . .

On the eve of war, Laval wanted to know whether Britain

was willing to apply Art. 16 in the event of aggression in Europe. Hoare circuitously said no. Hitler gave assurances that Germany would not join Italy nor attack France during the coming crisis, while Mussolini let it be known that Italy would not respond with war to economic and financial sanctions so long as they did not impede the conquest. A viable bargain was thus struck. On October 1 Il Duce, with great eloquence and fanfare and amid tremendous popular enthusiasm, ordered the invasion. On October 3 Addis Ababa informed the League Council that Ethiopia was being bombed by Italian planes and invaded by Italian troops. Haile Selassie rallied his primitive warriors: "It is better to die free than live as slaves."

The comedy at Geneva was played out to its end, with sundry amusing twists. On October 7 the Council adopted the report of its Committee of Six, holding that Italy had "resorted to war in disregard of its covenants," despite Baron Aloisi's protest that the invasion was "quite legitimate" and "even within the framework of the Covenant." The Assembly concurred on October 11 and established a committee "to consider and facilitate the coordination of measures" under Art. 16 (League procedure, like U.N. procedure, vindicates Clifford Odets's comment in *Rocket to the Moon:* "The Universe must be managed by a committee. No one man could make so many mistakes!") By October's end most League members had accepted proposals to embargo all arms, loans, credits, and sales of a few strategic materials to Italy; to ban some imports from Italy; and to give one another "mutual support" (whatever that might mean) in the application of economic and financial "sanctions" against the peace-breaker. All of this was play-acting, save for the small States, which hoped pathetically that "collective security" might somehow be made effective. Italy's war could have been stopped within a week by closing the Suez Canal and banning oil exports to Italy. Neither step was ever taken or even seriously considered —under the pretense that Mussolini would in that case have waged war against the Western Powers. As is now known, and was then known, he would have abandoned his enterprise in favor of a "defensive" posture. The simple fact of the matter is that Paris and London wanted Il Duce to succeed in his adventure. The mockery of "sanctions" promoted this purpose, because it enabled Mussolini to convert a potentially unpopular war of conquest into the plausible facsimile of a patriotic crusade against the "degenerate democracies" at Geneva.

The tergiversations of the democracies were too complex to review here. Laval perceived at November's end that the U.S.S.R. and the lesser Powers were favorable to "oil sanctions," which would have compelled Italy to halt the war. He therefore maneuvered adroitly to postpone League consideration of this issue. On December 8 he cooked up a "peace" scheme with Hoare whereby Haile Selassie should cede most of his country to Mussolini, make half of the remainder an Italian sphere of influence under League auspices, and convert all of it into an Italian "protectorate." The Ethiopian government was thus offered a choice between assassination and suicide. Mussolini was contemptuous, as usual, since he knew that contempt was safe. But the British Parliament and public were outraged when the news of the Hoare-Laval "deal" leaked out. Baldwin sacrificed Hoare on December 18, replacing him with Anthony Eden. Laval resigned for other reasons in late January. But Eden, Sarraut, and Flandin, and after them Blum and Delbos, pursued identical policies.

The finale was foreordained. Hitler, sensing the drift of things, repudiated the Treaty of Locarno and sent Nazi troops into the demilitarized Rhineland on March 7, 1936. There was no Western retaliation beyond verbiage. *Der Fuehrer*, after all, was merely preparing to attack Russia. The West, so its leaders hoped, might well play the role of *tertius gaudens*. Henceforth Paris excused its connivance in Mussolini's aggression on the pretext that all the Western Powers must stand together, while London excused its connivance in Hitler's aggression on the pretext that "collective security" must be vindicated vis-à-vis Italy. Discussion of oil sanctions had meanwhile been resumed in February. Il Duce bombastically threatened "war." Flandin asked for postponement. Eden appealed for "peace." The League Committee of Thirteen endlessly debated trivialities, in the face of Italian use of poison gas against the Ethiopians, and finally urged "negotiations." Paul Boncour asserted in late April that "conciliation must continue until it arrived at its goal." Salvador de Madariaga was puzzled: "We can only work for conciliation in the somewhat illogical and difficult form of a conciliation between an aggressor and his victims." On April 20 the Council addressed a "supreme appeal" to Rome—and adjourned.

Marshal Badoglio's armies, using tanks and planes, dropping incendiaries and mustard gas on defenseless villages, bombing hospitals and Red Cross camps, maiming and blinding thousands of peasants, marched to their triumph of "civilization" over "barbarism." Addis Ababa was taken by the invaders on May 5, 1936. Mussolini shouted victory and proclaimed the King of Italy "Emperor of Ethiopia." Haile Selassie fled to Jerusalem and then proceeded to London and Geneva. Churchill, Baldwin, Chamberlain, Eden all asked that "sanctions" be lifted in the name of "peace." Cabinet supporters cried out at the Labor Opposition: "Do you want war?" Leon Blum's "Popular Front" followed Tory guidance. On June 30 the Assembly opened the "debate" that was to be the requiem of the League of Nations. Haile Selassie spoke:

> I am here today to claim that justice which is due to my people and the assistance promised it eight months ago, when fifty nations asserted that aggression had been committed in violation of international treaties. None other than the Emperor can address the appeal of the Ethiopian people to those fifty nations. . . . I pray to Almighty God that He shall spare to the nations the terrible sufferings that have just been inflicted on my people. . . . The deadly rain that fell from the aircraft made all those whom it touched fly shrieking with pain. All those who

drank poisoned water or ate infected food also succumbed in dreadful suffering. In tens of thousands the victims of Italian mustard gas fell. It is in order to denounce to the civilized world the tortures inflicted on the Ethiopian people that I resolved to come to Geneva. . . . God and history will remember your judgment. . . . Is it the Covenant that needs reform? What undertakings can be of any value if the will to keep them is lacking? . . . What measures do you intend to take? Representatives of the world, I have come to Geneva to discharge in your midst the most painful of duties for the head of a state. What reply have I to take back to my people?

The reply was never in doubt. Litvinov denounced the betrayers of the Covenant. Blum bespoke peace. On July 4, 1936, by a vote of 44 to 1 (Ethiopia), with 4 abstentions, the Assembly approved Van Zeeland's resolution to end the "sanctions" imposed under Art. 16. Within two years most League members recognized Italian title to Ethiopia. Eleven members of the League withdrew, including Italy. Others disappeared: Ethiopia, Austria, Czechoslovakia, the Spanish Republic, Poland, Norway, The Netherlands, Belgium, France. . . . The last political act of the League Council was the expulsion of the Soviet Union from membership (December 14, 1939) for aggression against Finland. No such step had ever been taken or even considered against Japan, Italy, or Germany. Communist aggression was intolerable. Against Fascist aggression the League Powers did nothing until almost all was lost. The flames of World War II, already devouring Europe, were ignored at Geneva. The Council and Assembly never met again, save for the Assembly session of April 8, 1946, which voted that "with effect from this day . . . the League of Nations shall cease to exist." Death had occurred a decade earlier. The corpse was now interred.

For those who strive to find poetic justice in the incalculable consequences of international anarchy, comfort is to be derived from the circumstance that Haile Selassie ultimately returned to his kingdom in the wake of British armies; Mussolini and his mistress, Clara Petacci, were shot on April 27,

1945, and their bodies strung up by the feet in the Piazza Loretto in Milan; Laval fell before a firing squad on October 14, 1945; *et cetera.* But these are irrelevancies. World War II could have been averted, not by "collective security" and "sanctions," but by *Realpolitik*, alliances, and arms wielded in time by statesmen dedicated to the interests of their States and unconcerned with the uses of delusions, even for purposes of deception. There were no such statesmen in the "Free World." Millions therefore died in agony. Europe bled, burned, and decayed. The colossi of East and West partioned the ruins, established the "United Nations," and then quarreled over the wreckage. . . .

---

3. FAILURE AT LAKE SUCCESS

> The world is a stupendous machine, composed of innumerable parts, each of which being a free agent, has a volition and action of its own; and on this ground arises the difficulty of assuring success in any enterprise depending on the volition of numerous agents. We may set the machine in motion, and dispose every wheel to one certain end; but when it depends on the volition of any one wheel, and the correspondent action of every wheel, the result is uncertain.
>
> NICCOLÒ MACHIAVELLI: *On Fortune, Chance* . . .

HUMAN CAPACITY to learn from past experience often appears to be inversely proportionate to the number of humans involved in the experience. An individual, unless hopelessly aberrated, does not usually persist in trying to saw wood with a hammer or make a silken purse from a sow's ear once he perceives that such endeavors are unsuccessful and may entail injury and damage as well. Small communities frequently relinquish policies and enterprises that prove in practice ill suited to serving their needs. But when most or all of mankind has persuaded itself of the efficacy of a given formula for achieving an end that all, in principle, accept, then it is commonly the case that no amount of misery encountered in pursuit of the prescription suffices to lead men's minds to the conclusion that the formula is unworkable and merits abandonment. On the contrary, such mass frustration readily begets mass fanaticism in worshipping the source of failure with a fervor that waxes in proportion as the failure becomes more dismal, calamitous, and complete.

"Collective security" through "international sanctions" is a formula that most of the governments and peoples of the earth have come to regard in the twentieth century as the only possible means of preserving law and order in the society of sovereign States. That this formula is futile and indeed productive of more, rather than less, anarchy and violence has been experimentally demonstrated beyond reasonable doubt in the minds of reasonable men. But since men in the mass are unreasonable, they cling to the formula even more passionately in the 1950's than in the 1930's. They strive mightily to convince themselves that what is by nature unworkable can yet be made to work through sheer doggedness—or through the presumed efficacy of some clever trick or subtle symbol not hitherto "sold" with sufficient salesmanship, but, if well advertised, guaranteed to succeed through a mystic abracadabra. Each effort fails, precisely as failure has greeted Man's past efforts to learn geography by assuming that the earth is flat, to combat disease by burning witches, to fathom the cosmos through geocentric astronomy, or to promote religiosity by torturing heretics and fighting infidels. But each failure, as in all these other instances until recently, is but a spur to new efforts to validate falsehood, rationalize superstition, and claim magical cures through fetishes and incantations.

In fairness to human frailty and wisdom, it must be acknowledged that the original architects of the United Nations, as successor to the League of Nations, perceived for a brief time that the Geneva theory of "collective security" required substantial modification if "peace" was to be served thereby. This perception was less a result of insight or logic than of the imperatives of "sovereignty" on the part of the surviving Great Powers—and of the reluctance of statesmen to re-experience the political embarrassments bred by moral abstractions and sweeping commitments which no government concerned with national interest could possibly make the bases of policy. The diplomatic intricacies of this innovation are less important for our purposes than its essence. By the same token we are not here concerned with the bureaucratic and legalistic complexities of the U.N.—interesting and important as they may be—but only with the theory and practice of the United Nations as an instrumentality of peace by war.[7]

The Charter of San Francisco, based on the recommendations of the conferees at Dumbarton Oaks, as amended at Yalta and in subsequent diplomatic exchanges, was the work of 50 national delegations, comprising 282 delegates, 1,444 assistants, 1,058 members of the International Secretariat, 2,636 journalists and radiomen, 2,252 Army and Navy aides, 800 Boy Scouts, 400 Red Cross workers, 188 telephone and telegraph operators, among others. The average produc-

[7] Among the more useful and penetrating studies of the U.N. are: Eduardo Jiminez de Arechaga: *Voting and the Handling of Disputes in the Security Council* (Carnegie Endowment for International Peace; 1951); Norman Bentwich and Andrew Martin: *A Commentary on the Charter of the United Nations* (Macmillan; 1951); Eugene P. Chase: *The United Nations in Action* (McGraw-Hill; 1950); Clyde Eagleton: *International Government* (Ronald Press; 1948, revised edition); Herbert V. Evatt: *The Task of Nations* (Duell, Sloan & Pearce; 1949); J. Eugene Harley: *Documentary Textbook on the United Nations—Humanity's March Toward Peace* (Los Angeles, California: Center for International Understanding; 1950); Paul Hasluck: *Workshop of Security* (Melbourne, Cheshire: 1948); H. Field Haviland, Jr.: *The Political Role of the General Assembly* (Carnegie Endowment for International Peace; 1951); Julia Emily Johnsen (compiler): *United Nations or World Government* (H. W. Wilson; 1947); Hans Kelsen: *The Law of the United Nations* (Praeger; 1950); Hersch Lauterpacht: *International Law and Human Rights* (Praeger; 1950); John Maclaurin (pseud.): *The United Nations and Power Politics* (Harpers; 1951); Hans J. Morgenthau (editor): *Peace, Security and The United Nations* (Chicago University Press; 1946); Gilbert Murray: *From the League to U.N.* (London: Oxford University Press; 1949); Pitman B. Potter: *An Introduction to the Study of International Organization,* (Appleton-Century, Crofts; 1948, 5th edition); Louis B. Sohn: *World Law, Cases and Materials* (Foundation Press; 1950); Louis Wirth and others (edited by Quincy Wright): *The World Community* (University of Chicago Press; 1948).

tion of documents daily was 500,000 pages—with a high of 1,700,000 pages on the best day. Of the 111 Articles of the Charter, only those relevant to "collective security" need here be considered. The "Security Council," entrusted with "primary responsibility for the maintenance of international peace and security," consisted of five "permanent members" (U.S.A., U.S.S.R., U.K., France, and China) and six "non-permanent members" elected for two-year terms by a two-thirds vote of the Assembly. This body was charged with dealing with disputes or situations likely to endanger peace, and with making recommendations for a settlement. In the event of a breach of the peace (Arts. 39–54), the Council was empowered to ask member States to break off diplomatic and economic relations with the peace-breaking State and to have recourse to demonstrations, blockades, or military action carried on by national contingents under orders of the U.N. Military Staff Committee—subject to special agreements and (Art. 51) to "the inherent right of individual or collective self-defense if an armed attack occurs."

The fathers of the Charter originally perceived that international coercion of sovereignties could not possibly result in peace but only in universal war if, perchance, the sovereignty to be coerced should be a "Great Power." The Yalta formula, as subsequently interpreted at the Golden Gate, was incorporated in Art. 27:

1. Each member of the Security Council shall have one vote.

2. Decisions of the Security Council on procedural matters shall be made by an affirmative vote of seven members.

3. Decisions of the Security Council on all other matters shall be made by an affirmative vote of seven members including the concurring votes of the permanent members; provided that, in decisions under Chapter VI ["Pacific Settlement of Disputes"], and under Paragraph 3 of Article 52 [pacific settlement of local disputes through regional agencies], a party to a dispute shall abstain from voting.

The meaning of this verbiage was that any permanent member might "veto" any proposal for collective coercion or even for investigation or recommendation (which might initiate a "chain of events" leading to enforcement action) and might also veto a decision as to whether any given question was "substantive" or "procedural." It was self-evident that none of the Big Five would ever assent to its own coercion by the others and might, under the Charter, prevent any coercion of any State if it so chose. The contention of many critics that these arrangements were outrageous in placing the Great Powers "above the law" is the fruit of a misconception of the very nature of the global system of sovereignties. Any coercion of a Great Power, as the framers of the Charter plainly perceived, is a formula not for law, peace, and order but for global war.

This recognition of the realities of power, as we shall see, was to be short-lived in the abrupt evolution of the U.N. from a semblance of a world community to a weapon of American diplomacy against Soviet imperialism. The original formula, however, had at least the merit of facing facts. The crucial point at issue has been well put by one of the American architects of the Charter, Leo Pasvolsky:

> In the field of the maintenance of international peace and security, a choice had to be made between giving the new organization the authority to settle international disputes and to enforce its decisions, or empowering it only to promote and facilitate the settlement of international controversies and disputes by the nations themselves. Those who determined this country's position and the representatives of the other countries participating in the international negotiations, came to the conclusion that it was not possible to go beyond the second alternative. . . . It appeared clear at the time that the American people would not consent to a situation in which American armed forces could be used for joint international action without this country's consent. . . .
>
> It was obvious that the only way in which the United States could safeguard itself in this regard was to have a system under which no decision involving the actual or potential use of armed force could be made without its consent. It was equally

obvious that the only way in which this could be done in practice was for the same principle to apply to the other major nations. In other words, the system of voting would have to be such that any decisions of the kind I have just described would require the unanimous consent of the major nations. This is the so-called veto.

There were no illusions as to the limitations that such an arrangement would impose upon the effectiveness of the proposed organization, nor as to the possibility that the great privilege which the major nations thus claimed for themselves might be abused. It was clear that under such a system any one of the major nations would be in a position, not only to stop action against itself, but to stop any collective action. The underlying theory, however, was that if one of the major nations were to prove recalcitrant, or were to refuse to abide by the rules of international behavior that were being inscribed in the Charter, a situation would be created in which the recalcitrant nation might have to be coerced; and it was apparent that no major nation could be coerced except by the combined forces of the other major nations. This would be the equivalent of a world war, and a decision to embark upon such a war would necessarily have to be made by each of the other major nations for itself and not by any international organization.[8]

The San Francisco prescription postulated a "concert" of Great Powers as a means to peace rather than the naïve formula of peace through a war of all peace-loving States against any peace-breaking State. Nothing that has occurred since 1945 vitiates the wisdom of this view—which is less a modification in detail than a repudiation in principle of the classical theory of "collective security." What occurred in fact, however, led to a repudiation of the repudiation in the so-called "Free World" and to a reversion to the original unworkable hypothesis, with results implicit in all action based upon false premises or moralistic self-deception.

The advent of cold war between the American leviathan

[8] Leo Pasvolsky: "The United Nations in Action," *Edmund J. James Lectures on Government* (University of Illinois Press; 1951), pp. 79 f.

and the Muscovite behemoth unhappily coincided with the very first meetings (in London) of the U.N. General Assembly and Security Council in January 1946. The Kremlin, having fully availed itself of the opportunities presented by Western abdication and Nazi aggression to impose its power on Eastern Europe and the Balkans, seemed to Downing Street and the State Department about to do the same in Iran—since Moscow refused (at first) to withdraw its troops by the appointed date. Disputation over the Iranian issue set the tone of U.N. debates during the first year, and for all the years thereafter. Thanks to American wealth and general fear of Communism, U.S. spokesmen soon discovered that they could mobilize, with little effort, a majority of votes in the Council and Assembly against any position taken by Moscow. The temptation to use this advantage was too great to resist. In the late 1940's American delegates over and again, on all issues great and small, rallied majorities against the Kremlin, pressed questions to a vote, and then accused the Soviet delegates of "obstructionism" or opposing the "will of the majority."

The propagandistic "victories" thus won were gained at the price of destroying the initial premise of the United Nations. Moscow's delegates responded to each such challenge in the Security Council with a "veto"—i.e., a negative vote on a resolution commanding the support of a majority of the members, including the votes of the U.S.A., Britain, France, and China—with the latter State represented by the rump regime of Chiang Kai-shek long after his downfall. America would have used the veto as freely as the Soviet Union if the latter had ever been able to rally a "majority" against Washington. In fact, America had no need to do so, and pressed its own advantage to the full. In consequence almost half a hundred Soviet vetos had been cast in the Security Council by the end of 1951, with Washington rejoicing each time at this new proof of Soviet "intransigence." The real import of this development was well put by Walter Lippmann as early as 1947:

No good and nothing but harm can come of using the Security Council and the Assembly as an arena of the great dispute, or of acting as if we did not realize the inherent limitations of the Charter and thought that somehow we could by main force and awkwardness use the U.N.O. to overawe and compel the Russians. All that can come of that is to discredit the United Nations on issues it cannot settle and thus to foreclose the future of the U.N., which can begin only if and when these issues have been settled. Judging by the speeches in the Greek affair of the British and American delegates, Sir Alexander Cadogan and Mr. Herschel Johnson appear to be acting on instructions which treat the U.N. as expendable in our conflict with Russia. It is a great pity. Nothing is being accomplished to win the conflict, to assuage it, or to settle it. But the U.N., which should be preserved as the last best hope of mankind that the conflict can be settled and a peace achieved, is being chewed up. . . . It is implicit in the policy [of the Truman Administration] that the U.N. has no future as a universal society, and that either the U.N. will be cast aside like the League of Nations, or it will be transformed into an anti-Soviet coalition. In either event the U.N. will have been destroyed.[9]

This indeed is what took place, with extraordinary rapidity. By 1947–8 the U.N. had become, as regards its role in world politics, a minor branch of the Department of State and a façade for a coalition against "Soviet aggression." A case can be made out for the expediency of such procedures as weapons of *Realpolitik* if the premise be granted, as is here cheerfully done, that American national interests could best be served by organizing as many States as possible for the task of opposing, restricting, "containing," and, perhaps in the end, destroying the Soviet power. No plausible case can be made out, save by the semantic devices of hypocrisy, for the pretense that the result represented the vindication of "justice," "freedom," "righteousness," and the "rule of law" through the "enforcement of peace" via "collective security" against international "criminals." Alliances and coalitions of the virtuous against the wicked—i.e., of "our" side against

[9] Walter Lippman: *The Cold War* (Harper; 1947), pp. 58–9.

"their" side—are always useful and often necessary. To sell the public the sacrifices of blood and treasure which these national interests require, by reference to "international morality" and promises of the Millennium, is frequently expedient and often justified by the imperatives of national survival. But it is folly for the actors, and tragedy for all concerned, when responsible policy-makers persuade others, and ultimately themselves, that such devices of power politics are in fact equivalent to world government, or at least constitute a method of maintaining peace through a collective war of all against each.

By the shores of Lake Success in the 1940's and '50's, as by the shores of Lake Geneva in the 1930's, what was quaintly called "police action" against "aggression" was never attempted or even considered by the democratic Powers except when the "aggressors" were Communists. (Most U.N. meetings were held at Flushing Meadow in the reconditioned plant of the Sperry Gyroscope Company until May of 1951, when the U.N. moved to its new Manhattan skyscraper and the plant at Lake Success was reconditioned for war production.) The Korean War was the fourteenth controversy to come before the Security Council since its establishment. Of the preceding thirteen, the first was the complaint of Iran, supported by Britain and the U.S.A., over the continued presence of Soviet troops in its northern provinces, and the second and third were retaliatory Soviet complaints against Britain for waging war on Greek rebels and using Japanese troops to fight the Indonesian independence movement. Syria and Lebanon next complained (February 4, 1946) over the presence of British and French troops on their soil. In all these instances, the troops in question were ultimately withdrawn and the existence of "aggression" was debatable. The Indian-Pakistani hostilities over Kashmir, the Corfu Channel case, the "Spanish Question," the Egyptian complaint over British troops, Trieste, Czechoslovakia, and the Berlin blockade likewise involved no clear issues of lawless resort to force. But in three instances prior to Korea, U.N. members resorted to force in plain violation of the Charter, and other U.N. members applied no "sanctions" to the lawbreaker, in plain violation of the duties they had assumed in the Charter. The obligations in question are clear and unequivocal:

> Article 1. The purposes of the United Nations are: 1. To maintain international peace and security, and to that end: to take effective collective measures for the prevention and removal of threats to the peace, and for the suppression of acts of aggression or other breaches of the peace, and to bring about by peaceful means, and in conformity with the principle of justice and international law, adjustment or settlement of international disputes or situations which might lead to a breach of the peace. . . .
>
> Article 2. . . . 3. All members shall settle their international disputes by peaceful means in such a manner that international peace and security, and justice, are not endangered.
>
> 4. All members shall refrain in their international relations from the threat or use of force against the territorial integrity or political independence of any State, or in any other manner inconsistent with the purposes of the United Nations.

In July 1947, Australia and India summoned the Security Council to intervene in the war unleashed by The Netherlands against the Javanese natives fighting for the independence of Indonesia. When Dutch forces in December 1948 unleashed a *Blitzkrieg* and captured the Indonesian leaders, the U.S.A. charged The Netherlands with having violated the cease-fire agreement of August 1, 1947. The Security Council mediated, sent observers, and finally did nothing in view of procedural wrangles and reluctant Dutch acknowledgment of Indonesian independence on November 2, 1949. In mid-September 1948 India invaded the princely State of Hyderabad and abruptly extinguished its "independence." Amid jurisdictional confusion, the Security Council did nothing. In February 1948 the Council considered the two-month-old war unleashed by the Arab States against Israel. Both Council and Assembly long bandied about sundry resolutions calling for a cease-fire and a truce—which was finally negotiated, early in 1949, by Dr. Ralph Bunche, as U.N. mediator. Meanwhile, the governments of the Atlantic Powers had connived in the Arab aggression. When the Israelis, unaided, decisively defeated the invaders, most of the U.N. members accepted the facts of life, recognized Israel, and admitted the new State to membership (May 11, 1949).

Since none of the "aggressors" in these instances could be regarded as acting on behalf of the U.S.S.R. or international Communism, no coercive action was taken or even discussed. In the Indonesian case the Dutch aggressors, despite ephemeral successes, were beaten by the rebels and finally yielded up an old and rich colony to its inhabitants. In the case of Hyderabad the aggressors were at once triumphant, with no other government having the slightest concern in the matter. In the case of Israel the Arab aggressors were vanquished by their intended victim. In each case the threescore sovereignties gathered together in the U.N. each acted according to its interests, as its policy-makers understood them, and not at all in accordance with any principle requiring every State to wage war on any State resorting to force.

This age-old and immutable rule of politics, operative in all systems of sovereignties and rendering forever inoperable all schemes of "collective security," was in no sense negated but was on the contrary fully confirmed by the responses of national policy-makers, and of their spokesmen in U.N., to the challenge of the Korean War. We are here in the presence of the first instance (widely hailed as a "new era" in the "enforcement of peace") of the application in the name of an international organization of "military sanctions" against an aggressor. Since the record of this enterprise has been reported in millions of words in the public prints and is still fresh, at the time of writing, in the recollection of all readers, a bare outline of events will serve to suggest the essentials of the matter. By way of anticipating conclusions, they come to this:

National policy-makers playing the ancient game of power politics embarked on enterprises of aggrandizement which were based, on both sides, on erroneous calculations of the power at the disposal of the enemy, and thus came to grief. One side clothed its purposes in the verbiage of Oriental resistance to Occidental "imperialism," the other in the verbiage of an international "police action" against "criminals." Both sides suffered final defeat, thanks to an equipoise of fighting capacity in which neither could overcome the other. "Collective security" proved, as always, to be a mockery, useful only for purposes of deception and self-deception, with the outcome determined not by irrelevant abstractions but by the realities of the relative military might of the States immediately involved. But in the end, as always, politicians, pressmen, and publics persisted in ignoring realities and clinging to the irrelevancies in a desperate endeavor to convert nonsense into sense through semantic incantation.

In the bloodstained record of the "civilized" cultures of mankind, there is no novelty in recourse to military violence by men against men. The Korean War of 1950–2[1] was a limited and localized episode in butchery and devastation, comparable in these respects to hundreds of similar episodes in the politics of the Western State system and of its precursors. If these hostilities merit the space here given to them, the justification of such attention lies less in the techniques of violence displayed (the political and diplomatic background and the military history of the enterprise we shall leave to others) than in the circumstance that the conflict was from the outset a bewildering confusion of class warfare, ideological rivalry, "power politics," and "collective security."

[1] A bibliography of the Korean War would serve little purpose here. The background is summarized in Sydney D. Bailey: *The Korean Crisis* (London: National Peace Council; 1950) and in Robert T. Oliver: *Why War Came in Korea* (Fordham University Press; 1951). The serious student should of course consult the voluminous U. N. documents on the matter and the records of the Security Council and General Assembly, along with the *Bulletin of the Department of State* and the files of *The New York Times*. The most readily available source for the Communist version of events is *Korean Independence*, published weekly in Los Angeles in English and Korean by a Korean group committed to the North Korean regime.

Since men ambivalently love and hate warfare, the question of "war guilt" exercises their imaginations with respect to all major adventures in mass murder and destruction. The issue is usually posed in terms of who first attacked whom. Whole libraries are devoted to this question in connection with the outbreak of hostilities in Europe in 1914. As regards the initiation of violence between 1931 and 1941, the problem is simpler, since the "aggressors" were relatively frank. The question of "responsibility" in 1950 is also quite simple. The allegation of Pyongyang, Peking, and Moscow, echoed by Communists the world over, that the Korean hostilities were instigated by the United States and initiated by its South Korean "puppets" has not to date been substantiated by any credible evidence. The South Korean, U.S., and U.N. contention that the North Korean government deliberately organized and launched a massive invasion with the object of uniting Korea by force is supported by ample evidence and reasonable inference from the course of events, and will here be deemed correct.

The hypothesis that the invasion was ordered in Moscow was immediately seized upon and generally accepted by officialdom in Washington and at Lake Success. This view admits, at present, of no conclusive proof or disproof. That Muscovite influence in Pyongyang was sufficient to veto a recourse to force can scarcely be questioned. Moscow's failure to do so makes the Kremlin at least an accessory to aggression. Also self-evident is the fact that the North Korean army had been trained by Russian advisers and sufficiently well equipped with Soviet tanks, mobile artillery, planes, and small arms to conquer South Korea in the absence of outside intervention. (Washington had deliberately denied heavy weapons to the South Korean forces, in the certainty that had they been made available Syngman Rhee would have carried out his long-publicized project of invading and conquering North Korea.)

Millions of words of speculation have been published in the West in efforts to explain why Moscow here "unleashed war." The Kremlin, said some, took seriously the January 1950 utterances of Truman, Acheson, Louis Johnson, Omar Bradley, *et al.*, to the effect that American strategic interests in South Korea and Formosa were not sufficient to warrant military intervention and that these areas lay beyond the U.S. "security zone" in the Pacific. Moscow, so ran the argument, therefore expected no American action in defense of territories already "written off." Stalin's Politburo, argued others, fully anticipated the U.S. and U.N. response, the probable course of military events, and the inevitable Chinese intervention, and thus achieved, without risk or commitment, a Machiavellian masterpiece of trickery designed to discredit the U.N., to provoke the U.S. into taking the road to suicide through militarism and Fascism, and to involve and erode American military might in a series of hopeless wars on the rimlands of Asia, coupled with a major and unending conflict with China. On balance, it is unlikely that the rulers of the Scarlet Empire were either so naïve as the first hypothesis suggests or so clever (or insane) as the second postulates.

In all probability the men of Moscow played no active role in the business, beyond equipping the North Korean army. Kim Il-sung either acted on his own initiative or advised Moscow of his plan. In the former case (which is plausible in the light of the propagandistic delay and confusion displayed by Moscow, Peking, and Communist centers elsewhere immediately after the outbreak of hostilities), the Kremlin could either make the best of an unauthorized *fait accompli* perpetrated by an "ally" or sternly order the abandonment of the enterprise. Since it promised, at the outset, to be successful and, if so, to be highly advantageous to the U.S.S.R. in its global duel with the U.S.A., the decision was in favor of the former course. If, on the contrary, Pyongyang consulted Moscow in advance, we are obliged to conclude that the Kremlin's comment must have amounted to this: We neither authorize nor forbid this experiment in violence; if you swiftly conquer South Korea, good; but if you do not and are faced with American military intervention, do not expect us to dispatch troops to your rescue or even to supply you with the additional tanks, guns, planes, and technicians which will then be necessary to defend North Korea against counterinvasion; the adventure is risky; the risk is yours; we assume no obligations; we have doubts; we wish you well. . . . Which of these alternative suppositions comes closer to truth, no one in the West can yet say. In either case, the Muscovite role was less one of direct instigation than one of passive acquiescence.[2]

What is more pertinent to our inquiry is the way in which U.S. policy-makers, pursuing American national interests as they understood them, went to war at once against the invaders of South Korea, mobilized the U.N. as a supporting force, and then depicted their policy as a "police action" against "crime," allegedly constituting the first instance of successful "collective security" through "international military sanctions" against "aggression."

The actual results were of a different order. They entailed the crushing defeat of the armies of the United States by Communized Oriental "Gooks"; the belated recovery of American military initiative through a massive accumulation of sea power, air power, and firepower; the irresponsible use of the victory thus won to provoke Chinese intervention; and the experience of another humiliating military debacle, followed by a second recovery and a stalemate wherein both sides, while claiming victory, acknowledged defeat and strove for "peace" only because the war could obviously never be won and seemed otherwise unlikely ever to be ended.

In the first two years of conflict, all of Korea was laid waste with fire and sword; millions were reduced to savagery, beggary, or agonized death; over 110,000 American casualties were suffered and 20,000 Americans were slain by the foe (far more than the combined total of American casualties in

[2] For an excellent analysis of these imponderables, see Wilbur W. Hitchcock (a former member of the U. S. Military Government in Korea): "North Korea Jumps the Gun," *Current History* (March 1951), pp. 136–44.

the War of the Revolution, the War of 1812, the Mexican War, and the Spanish-American War); the U.N. was vitiated as a vehicle of peace; and "collective security" was so plainly discredited that all sane men and women would have recoiled from it in horror save that they were hypnotized by their fears and delusions.

The response of the rulers of America to the news of June 25, 1950, was conditioned by two closely related facets of past experience: four years of global cold war against "Soviet Imperialism"; and the loss of China to the "enemy" in 1949. The latter disaster admits of a simple explanation, derived from the palpable fact that most men are patriots and xenophobes. Communism triumphed in the Russian civil war of 1918–20 because the U.S. and its allies subsidized, armed, and supported the forces of anti-Communism embodied in the White Armies. Communism triumphed in the Chinese civil war of 1945–9 because the U.S. subsidized, armed, and supported the forces of anti-Communism embodied in the regime of Chiang Kai-shek. The self-evident conclusion, validated by all historical experience, that foreign intervention in a civil war fought by well-organized opposing factions on the territory of a major national community almost invariably results in the defeat of the faction accepting foreign aid has always been, and still remains, wholly beyond the vision of American policy-makers in the White House, State Department, Pentagon, and Congress. America devoted itself after 1949 to "explaining" the Communist conquest of China not at all in terms of its actual causes, but by reference to "Soviet plots," espionage, treason, subversion, "Communists" in the State Department, Roosevelt's "treachery" at Yalta, and all other irrelevancies under the sun.

Having "lost" the Chinese war, some Washington policy-makers, to be sure, were disposed to accept the universe, however distasteful, and to contemplate with reluctant equanimity (at the turn of the year 1949–50) the probability of a Communist conquest of Formosa and the necessity of ultimately recognizing the Peking regime for what it was: the government of China. But the psychopathology and skulduggery of many Senators and Congressmen rendered such a course inexpedient. The Truman Administration, having preached holy war against Communism for years with political and economic results highly advantageous to the possessors of political power and industrial securities, welcomed an opportunity to vindicate its anti-Communism and to capitalize further upon Congressional and public ardor for crusading against Red Sin. A rational definition of national interest (in the judgment of this writer) would have dictated unilateral American military intervention in Korea against Communist aggression, with no extension of the conflict to China and with no attempt to make the U.N. a tool of American purposes. The course adopted was one of combining defense of South Korea with an open challenge to Red China and the mobilization of the U.N. in support of American policy—with the sequel fatal alike to the U.N. and to the Korean enterprise as both were originally conceived.

News of war in Korea led to immediate Presidential authorization to General MacArthur to give material aid to the government of Syngman Rhee, and to a White House Conference on June 26, 1950. According to Louis Johnson, then Secretary of Defense, Dean Acheson urged immediate American intervention and commitment of U.S. sea and air forces against the invaders. The respresentatives of the armed services pointed out difficulties, but apparently took no definite position. Several Senators urged consultation with Congress, but Tom Connally was "crotchety and fussy" about this suggestion, which "died aborning." At noon of June 27 President Truman issued a public statement:

> In Korea the Government forces, which were armed to prevent border raids and to preserve internal security, were attacked by invading forces from North Korea. The Security Council of the United Nations called upon the invading troops to cease hostilities and to withdraw to the 38th parallel. This they have not done but, on the contrary, have pressed the attack. The Security Council called upon all members of the

United Nations to render every assistance in the execution of this resolution.

In these circumstances I have ordered United States air and sea forces to give the Korean Government troops cover and support.

The attack upon Korea makes it plain beyond all doubt that Communism has passed beyond the use of subversion to conquer independent nations and will now use armed invasion and war. It has defied the orders of the Security Council of the United Nations issued to preserve international peace and security. In these circumstances the occupation of Formosa by Communist forces would be a direct threat to the security of the Pacific area and to United States forces performing their lawful and necessary functions in that area.

Accordingly I have ordered the Seventh Fleet to prevent any attack on Formosa. As a corollary of this action I am calling upon the Chinese Government of Formosa to cease all air and sea operations against the mainland. The Seventh Fleet will see that this is done. The determination of the future status of Formosa must await the restoration of security in the Pacific, a peace settlement with Japan, or consideration by the United Nations. I have also directed that United States forces in the Philippines be strengthened and that military assistance to the Philippine Government be accelerated.

I have similarly directed acceleration in the furnishing of military assistance to the forces of France and the associated States in Indo-China and the dispatch of a military mission to provide close working relations with those forces.

I know that all members of the United Nations will consider carefully the consequences of this latest aggression in Korea in defiance of the Charter of the United Nations. A return to the rule of force in international affairs would have far-reaching effects. The United States will continue to uphold the rule of law. I have instructed Ambassador Austin, as the representative of the United States to the Security Council, to report these steps to the Council.

The program thus announced went far beyond armed resistance to aggression in Korea. It was one of identifying a purely American policy with the U.N., of asserting that "Communism" was now bent upon "war" in defiance of the U.N., and of unilateral military intervention against Red China in Formosa and against the Viet-Minh in Indo-China, with no consultation of any kind with America's allies or other members of the U.N.

Meanwhile, the Security Council (which the U.S.S.R. had been boycotting since January in protest against its refusal to replace Chiang Kai-shek's appointees with delegates from Peking) had been advised by the U.N. Commission in Korea that South Korea was the victim of "a calculated coordinated attack prepared and launched with secrecy," and of a "well-planned, concerted, and full-scale invasion." On June 25—after the American decision to intervene had already been reached—the U.S.A. called the Security Council together (with the U.S.S.R. unrepresented and with China represented by the agent of the Kuomintang despite recognition of Peking by Britain, India, and other U.N. members) and proposed a resolution that the other members accepted. It held "with grave concern" that "the armed attack upon the Republic of Korea by forces from North Korea . . . constitutes a breach of the peace"; called for "immediate cessation of hostilities" and North Korean withdrawal to the 38th parallel; and summoned all members "to render every assistance to the U.N. in the execution of this resolution and to refrain from giving assistance to the North Korean authorities."

When the invaders paid no heed, the Council on June 27 recommended that "members of the U.N. furnish such assistance to the Republic of Korea as may be necessary to repel the armed attack and restore international peace and security in the area." A third resolution of July 7 recommended that all such assistance be "made available to a unified command under the U.S.," requested "the U.S. to designate the commander of such forces," and authorized the unified command "at its discretion" to "use the U.N. flag in the course of operations against North Korean forces, concurrently with the flags of the various nations participating."

The United Nations thus committed itself, despite doubts

and reservations among many members, to an American war in Korea in the name of peace. Such action would, of course, have been "vetoed" by the Soviet spokesman had he been present. His absence is further evidence that the invasion was not planned in, or ordered by, Moscow. Gromyko on July 4 denounced the U.S.A. for unlawful intervention and "aggression" in Korea, and condemned Trygve Lie and the Security Council for "a gross violation of the Charter." An American appeal to Moscow (June 27) to "disavow responsibility for this unprovoked and unwarranted attack" and to "use its influence with the North Korean authorities to withdraw their invading forces immediately" evoked Soviet replies (June 29) accusing South Korea and its supporters of responsibility for aggression and declaring (July 6) that the U.S. naval blockade of the Korean coast was "a new act of aggression" for which the Soviet Union would hold Washington "responsible." Efforts by Attlee and Nehru during July to elicit Soviet "co-operation" for the restoration of peace in Korea were fruitless.

The American decision was influenced by the happenstances that U.S. troops were available near by (Japan) for intervention, that a U.N. Commission was already on the scene, and that the Soviet boycott of the Security Council prevented a "veto" against collective military action. The war for peace nevertheless went badly. General MacArthur assumed command. On June 30 President Truman ordered the use of U.S. ground forces in Korea, the bombing of targets north of the 38th parallel, and the naval blockade of enemy ports. Chiang Kai-shek's offer to send 33,000 Nationalist troops from Formosa to Korea was rebuffed. The invaders promptly occupied Seoul, advanced southward, defeated American and South Korean forces at Suwon and Chonan, drove relentlessly to the Kum River before Taejon, took the city on July 20, and by early August had penned their foes into a small area north of Pusan on the south coast, defended along the Naktong River. Only by the narrowest of margins did the most formidable Power in the world avoid having its forces driven into the sea from the remote peninsula chosen by the enemy as an arena of battle.

During August the efforts of the invaders to take Taegu and then march on Pusan were beaten back by stout American defense. In mid-September MacArthur executed a daring and successful counterblow: an amphibious landing at Inchon, followed by the liberation of Seoul, September 26–9. Co-ordinated offensives of U.S. forces, breaking out of the Taegu-Pusan perimeter, effected a junction with the liberators of Seoul, and forced the surviving invaders to flee for their lives back to the 38th parallel. On October 1 MacArthur summoned the North Koreans to surrender under penalty of total defeat and destruction. South Korean troops simultaneously crossed the parallel.

Swift as was this abrupt reversal of the always-uncertain fortunes of war, it was to be followed by even more astonishing twists of destiny, displaying in extreme and alarming form the apparent incapacity of American policy-makers to foresee the consequences of their own decisions. In this mad and tangled counterpoint of incompetent *Realpolitik*, political myopia, strategic blundering, and feckless gestures of "collective security," we may conveniently review first the course of war and diplomacy to their tragic end and then consider *seriatim* the acts of the bitter comedy played out at Lake Success.

On October 9, 1950, as MacArthur "for the last time" demanded that the enemy surrender, American forces crossed the 38th parallel. During the next fortnight Wonsan and Pyongyang were taken, while the government of Syngman Rhee, back in ruined Seoul, insisted that it be given authority over all of North Korea. By October 26, South Korean troops had reached the Yalu River and the Manchurian frontier. By November 20, U.S. troops also reached the Yalu in the northeast. On November 24, MacArthur launched his "final battle" to end the war by Christmas, with the intention of occupying all the south bank of the Yalu and destroying all enemy forces in North Korea. Within a week this offensive fell to pieces in a major military disaster.

As early as October 11, Peking had announced that it would "not stand by idly" if U.S. forces crossed the 38th parallel and sought to reach the Yalu. In succeeding weeks, Peking repeatedly declared that China's security was menaced by U.S. "aggression" in Korea and Formosa and by bombing raids into Manchuria, that it would intervene unless American forces halted at the parallel, and that its terms for peace were evacuation of foreign troops from Korea, withdrawal of the Seventh Fleet from Formosa, and Red China's admission to the U.N. All such warnings were ignored in Washington and by MacArthur's headquarters in Tokyo, despite advice from Indian and other sources that they were seriously meant. Chinese "volunteers" now began moving across the Yalu to aid the North Koreans. MacArthur indignantly declared on November 6 that "alien" forces had massed "a great concentration" in the "privileged sanctuary" of Manchuria and that the Chinese intervention was "one of the most offensive acts of international lawlessness of historic record." With the breakdown of his offensive, he asserted (November 27) that the Chinese had precipitated "an entirely new war," which must be dealt with "within the councils of the United Nations and the chancelleries of the world."

By December 5, Chinese and North Korean armies had retaken Pyongyang. U.S. forces in the northeast were partly trapped and captured and partly evacuated by sea at Hamhung, which was abandoned by Christmas eve. On December 25 Syngman Rhee's regime fled to Pusan from Seoul, which fell once more to the enemy on January 4, 1951, after being set afire by the now-defeated "liberators." On January 6, MacArthur's headquarters forbade newsmen to use the word "retreat." The invaders took Wonju on January 9 and Inchon on January 21, striving to outflank and encircle their antagonists in south-central Korea. General Matthew Ridgway's counteroffensive in February, labeled "Operation

Killer," turned the tide once more, though MacArthur announced that no decisive defeat of the Communist armies and no effective campaign north of the 38th parallel would be possible so long as the Chinese intervention gave the enemy numerical superiority. Ridgway opined (March 12) that an end of the war at the parallel would be "a tremendous victory."

Battered Seoul changed hands for the fourth time on March 14, 1951, when Allied forces re-entered its ruins once more. On March 24 MacArthur publicly offered to negotiate a truce with the enemy commanders, announced that he had again ordered his forces to cross the 38th parallel, and threatened China with the "risk of imminent military collapse" should the Western Powers decide to expand their military operations. By the end of March, U.S. forces were once more north of the parallel, taking Hwachon and the near-by dam in mid-April and losing them again a week later in the face of a massive enemy counterassault, which, however, was blunted and turned back early in May. Allied forces again crossed the parallel, were again driven back, and once more surged over the line in late May in operations that had now become as monotonous and meaningless as they were murderous. Killing continued all through the summer and fall of 1951, while truce negotiations at Kaesong and later at Panmunjom were initiated, interrupted, resumed, deadlocked, broken off, and strung out for months in a tedious misery of frustration, with neither side, as in the Wars of Religion, knowing how to win, interrupt, or end an armed conflict in which no victory was possible.

Meanwhile most Americans—seemingly eager to fight Russia, and infuriated by the incredible spectacle of their best troops being beaten by Koreans and Chinese—went mad. The signs of the madness were many, from military appropriations increased from fifteen billion to sixty billion dollars per year, to President Truman's hint of dropping atomic bombs on China—which obliged Prime Minister Clement

Attlee to fly to Washington and explain to the President (December 4–8, 1950) that Britain would have no part in such folly. The conference succeeded in preventing any such fateful step, but failed altogether to harmonize or reconcile differences of British and American policies toward China. London, while supporting the U.S. and U.N. war against aggression, sought peace with Peking. What Washington sought was a mystery to everybody, including everyone in Washington—until MacArthur temporarily clarified the issue, precipitated the culminating American madness of 1951, and then left the matter, amid demagoguery and confusion worse confounded, more mysterious than ever.

Heroes and geniuses are laws unto themselves. Yet they often guess wrongly in their estimates of what "the lesser breeds without the law" will tolerate. *L'affaire* MacArthur, albeit among the most bizarre episodes in the entire history of American public life, cannot here be discussed.[3] The General, *de facto* potentate of Japan since 1945, had long displayed symptoms of supposing that he was solely responsible for policy in the conduct of the Korean War—a supposition not *per se* unreasonable, since no one in Washington exhibited any symptoms of responsibility. His threats to China were frequent. On April 5, 1951, it became known that he had written to Congressman Joseph Martin that he believed Europe could be defended against Communism only in Asia, and that a "Second Front" should be opened on the Chinese mainland by Chiang Kai-shek's Formosan troops, aided by the U.S.A. His conviction that the Korean War

[3] See John Gunther: *The Riddle of MacArthur* (Harpers, 1951); the two million words of testimony in *Military Situation in the Far East:* Hearings Before the Committee on Armed Services and the Committee on Foreign Relations, U.S. Senate, 82nd Congress, 1st Session (Washington, D.C.: U.S. Government Printing Office; 1951); Richard H. Rovere and Arthur M. Schlesinger, Jr.: *The General and the President* (Farrar, Strauss & Young; 1951); Lawrence Dennis, *The Appeal to Reason,* issues of March 31, 1951, and subsequently; "Impeach Truman," a *Chicago Tribune* editorial of April 12, 1951; "After MacArthur" and "Fighting for a Draw," *The Economist* (London), April 14, and April 28, 1951; and "MacArthurism sans MacArthur" in *l'Observateur* (Paris), April 26, 1951.

could somehow be won by all-out bombing of Manchuira and unlimited war on China, at whatever risks of Soviet intervention, was long a matter of record.

On April 11, 1951, the President accused the General of insubordination and relieved him of all his commands, appointing General Ridgway as his successor and explaining that MacArthur's policies involved "very grave risks of starting a general war." The inimitable "isolationist," Senator Taft, at once joined MacArthur (and McCarthy) in urging war on China. The subsequent spectacle of ticker-tape parades, ham acting, Congressional hearings, witch-hunting, political idiocy, public hysteria, and utter confusion would best be forgotten by America and the world, were it not for the fact that the policies or lack of policies of the government of the United States made more of the same inevitable. Few sane citizens could quarrel with the substance of the General's subsequent public indictment of the Administration for irresponsibility, inconsistency, and general befuddlement in foreign policy. Still fewer could accept the General's own demagoguery (despite his refreshing mastery of the English language, in contrast to the ghost-writers of the President who dismissed him)—as illustrated, to take but a single ex-example, in his speech to the American Legion in Miami: "There is little doubt that the yielding of Formosa and the seating of Communist China in the U.N. were fully planned when I called upon the enemy commander in Korea on March 24 to meet me in the field to arrange armistice terms. . . . The opposition I expressed . . . unquestionably wrecked the secret plan to yield on these issues as the price of peace in Korea."

The level of "statesmanship" here displayed on all sides was not unrelated to the fact that in Korea during the months of tragedy thousands of young Americans were done to death, tens of thousands of Koreans and Chinese were slain, and millions were left homeless, hungry, and destitute in a military adventure based upon hideous miscalculations and directed toward unattainable goals. The immediate crime was that of the North Korean Communist leaders. The proximate crime was that of the deluded apostles of "collective security." The ultimate crime, as always, was that of a mankind enamored of sin in the name of virtue. The horrors of the Korean War—with its atrocities of terrorism, butchery through firing-squads, mass attacks, wholesale destruction of villages by napalm bombs, and indiscriminate massacre of Asiatic peasants by American aviators—had its contemporary parallel in Indo-China and Malaya and its age-old precedents in Man's inhumanity to Man. Mark Twain's embittered "War Prayer," irreverent but immortal in the eloquence of its truth, is still the most graphic commentary on the consequences of international anarchy:

> O Lord our God, help us to tear their soldiers to bloody shreds with our shells; help us to cover their smiling fields with the pale forms of their patriot dead; help us to drown the thunder of the guns with the cries of the wounded, writhing in pain; help us to lay waste their humble homes with a hurricane of fire; help us to wring the hearts of their unoffending widows with unavailing grief; help us to turn them out roofless with their little children to wander unbefriended through the wastes of their desolated land in rags and hunger and thirst, sport of the sun flames of summer and the icy winds of winter, broken in spirit, worn with travail, imploring Thee for the refuge of the grave and denied it—for our sakes, who adore Thee, Lord, blast their hopes, blight their lives, protract their bitter pilgrimage, make heavy their steps, water their way with their tears, stain the white snow with the blood of their wounded feet! We ask of One who is the spirit of love and who is the ever faithful refuge and friend of all that are sore beset, and seek His aid with humble and contrite hearts. Grant our prayer, O Lord, and Thine shall be the praise and honor and glory, now and ever. Amen.

To unravel the incredibly tangled fiction of "collective security" in the Korean War would require several lengthy volumes. Only the gross anatomy of confusion can here be sketched. The central and crucial fact may be indicated at the outset. The campaign was universally regarded in the West as an "international police action" against "aggression." Thirty-eight governments in the U.N. pledged support. Fifteen sent troops. But the entire operation was in fact an American enterprise. Nine tenths of the foreign forces were supplied by the U.S.A. Nine tenths of Allied casualties were suffered by Americans. Other contributions were mere tokens to placate Washington and give comfort to those who supposed that here for the first time all the world was waging a holy war for peace. By midwinter of 1950–1, 250,000 U.S. soldiers, sailors, airmen, and marines had been dispatched to Korea to aid or, more often, to replace a fluctuating but roughly equal number of South Korean troops. All other U.N. contingents totaled less than 26,000 men.[4] Most British troops in Asia were already engaged in fighting Communists in Malaya. Most French troops were similarly engaged in Indo-China. Each sovereignty, as always, was guided by its interests. Those with least power and least responsibility were the least inhibited in urging military adventures upon others—as when El Salvador on November 18, 1950, demanded that the U.N. General Assembly condemn the Chinese reoccupation of Tibet as an act of "unprovoked aggression."

In the vote in the Security Council on the Resolution of June 25, 1950 (proposed by Ernest A. Gross of the U.S.A.), Yugoslavia abstained, the U.S.S.R. was absent, and affirmative votes were cast by Britain, France, "China" (i.e., Formosa), Ecuador, Cuba, Egypt, India, Norway, and the U.S.A. In the vote of June 27, endorsing the Truman decision for military intervention and requesting all U.N. members to employ armed force against aggression in Korea, India and Egypt abstained while Yugoslavia voted in the negative. Although Nehru informed Trygve Lie on the 29th that his government accepted the recommendation, India refused to send any troops and persisted in efforts aimed at mediation and at the

[4] Up to the time of writing there had been no significant change in these proportions, despite U.S. efforts to secure greater support from its U.N. allies.

admission of Red China and the return of the U.S.S.R. to the Council. In the vote of July 7 India, Egypt, and Yugoslavia all abstained. Pyongyang, later joined by Peking and Moscow, held that these and all subsequent acts of the Council were illegal because of the nonparticipation of the Soviet Union, the exclusion of Communist China, and the Charter's requirement of unanimity of the permanent members for all substantive decisions. The U.S. and U.N. pretense that these acts were not "decisions" but only "recommendations" (like those of the League Council in the fall of 1935), and the argument that an abstention could not be construed as a negative vote, did not alter the fact that the original intent of the framers of the Charter was here ignored in pursuit of a purpose staunchly opposed by the governments of India, China, and Russia, whose peoples comprised half the human race.

Of the fifty nations to whom Lie appealed on July 14, 1950, to send combat troops to Korea, thirty-five declined or failed to reply. Thailand, Turkey, Greece, Australia, and a few others later gave affirmative answers. Meanwhile Jacob A. Malik returned to the Security Council and assumed its rotating presidency during the month of August. His efforts to have the Kuomintang representative expelled and delegates from Peking and Pyongyang admitted were all defeated by the American majority. Chou En-lai's accusation that the U.S.A. was guilty of aggression in Formosa led to a close vote on September 11 (Sir Gladwyn Jebb presiding) on a Soviet resolution to invite Communist China to appear before the Council to present its complaints of American aerial attacks on Manchurian territory. Britain, France, Norway, Yugoslavia, India, and the U.S.S.R. voted in the affirmative (one less than a legal majority), while Egypt and Ecuador abstained and the U.S.A., "China," and Cuba voted against. The forty-fourth Soviet veto, cast on September 6, killed a resolution condemning North Korea for continued defiance. The forty-fifth veto (September 12) killed a motion for a U.N. Commission to investigate Chinese charges of border violation by the U.S. Soviet resolutions demanding the withdrawal of foreign troops from Korea and condemning the U.S. for "barbarous" bombing of civilians were voted down.

The more likely it appeared toward the end of summer that the U.N. forces might be driven out of Korea altogether, the more numerous were the voices raised in favor of punishing Red Sin in kind by uniting all of Korea by force. Syngman Rhee insisted that the U.N. must impose "unconditional surrender" on the North and give his own regime sovereignty over all the land. Warren R. Austin told the Council as early as August 17 that once peace should be restored, the Republic of Korea, with U.N. aid, should have authority throughout Korea. In a Chicago address of September 8, Lie declared that a withdrawal of the invaders to the 38th parallel would be unacceptable, and that "the aim of the U.N. is and must be a united and independent Korea." The General Assembly, meeting on September 19, voted down an Indian resolution for the admission of Communist China and a Soviet resolution for the expulsion of Nationalist China. Indonesia was admitted as the sixtieth member on September 28. On the same day, with Sir Gladwyn holding the issue "procedural" and hence not subject to a veto, the Council voted 7 to 3 (U.S., Cuba, and "China" opposed) to invite Peking to send a representative on November 15 to present its case against U.S. "aggression" on Formosa. The "American majority" was no longer safe. . . .

On October 2 the U.S.S.R. proposed a Korean cease-fire, withdrawal of foreign troops, and national elections to be supervised by a U.N. Commission on which Moscow and Peking would be represented. American and British lawyers—here, as often, the bane of all rational diplomacy, since they envisage international relations in fairy-tale terms of "police," "judge," "jury," and "criminal"—indignantly rejected the proposal on the ground that North Korea must be penalized, not treated as an equal. Percy Spender (Australia) urged U.N. forces to cross the parallel. India warned that any such step would provoke Chinese intervention. All warnings to this effect from New Delhi and Peking were blithely ignored by

Truman and Acheson, Attlee and Bevin, Pleven and Schuman, Lie and MacArthur. To the U.N. (i.e., U.S.) Commander the U.N. governments had for all practical purposes abdicated all control over the course of events in the Far East, with calamitous results.

In the complex skein subsequently woven at Lake Success, one thread was spun out and raveled into ultimate shreds and dust by the American policy-makers, who were resolved to carry through with lawyerlike precision their determination to transform the U.N. into an instrument of war at the disposal of Washington. Under the Charter, no such role was possible in the Security Council so long as the U.S.S.R. was a member. Marshall had therefore sponsored the creation of the "Little Assembly" (Interim Committee on Peace and Security) in September 1947, in the hope that it might somehow be used to coerce Communist aggressors. Acheson now moved to use the General Assembly as a whole as the tool of this purpose, seeking through ingenious formulas to bypass the clear intent of the Charter and to furnish the Assembly, permanently and for use in all wars to come, the fortuitous advantages which the U.S. had by accident enjoyed for the conduct of hostilities in June and July of 1950. Under American pressure the Assembly on November 3, 1950, approved a lengthy resolution (52 to 5 with 2 abstentions) called "Uniting for Peace," but meaning, as usual in such matters, "Uniting for War." All members were asked to maintain armed forces to "promptly be made available for service as U.N. units." A fourteen-member "Collective Measures Committee," from which the Soviet bloc was excluded, was set up to plan the application of economic and military sanctions; a "Peace Observation Commission" was created to investigate situations endangering peace and security; and the Assembly itself, to meet on twenty-four hours' notice, undertook to supersede the Security Council by "making appropriate recommendations to members for collective measures, including in the case of a breach of the peace or act of aggression the use of armed force when necessary."

This new enterprise in peace by war suffered the fate of all its predecessors—and of all its successors to the end of time. Beneath the vast and foggy cloudbanks of verbal obfuscation, the terrestrial design for power in the autumn of 1950 was simple enough. Inspired by the success of the Inchon landing and the liberation of Seoul, the U.S. and U.N. committed themselves to the counterconquest of North Korea. Peking made it clear beyond all question that it would never permit MacArthur's troops to station themselves on the Manchurian frontier. This decision was not "dictated in Moscow" nor attributable to ideological sympathy of Chinese Communists for Korean Communists. It was a product of the most ancient and elementary considerations of *Realpolitik*. The U.S.A. had proclaimed itself the implacable enemy of the Peking government, banned it from the U.N., insulted and denounced it on every possible occasion, intervened in Formosa, resumed its policy of subsidizing Chiang Kai-shek, blockaded the Chinese coast, made sporadic aerial attacks on Manchuria, and otherwise made it plain beyond doubt that Washington's purpose was, if possible, to destroy the revolutionary regime and restore the Kuomintang.

On October 7, the General Assembly gave final approval for U.N. military action throughout Korea to unify the country. On October 12, the U.N. Interim Committee on Korea resolved that the U.N. Command should take over the administration of the North. Peking drew the necessary conclusions. When Chinese armies began pouring over the Yalu in late October, the U.N. was faced with the unpleasant issue of waging "war for peace" against a Great Power, immediately adjacent to the theater of battle, inhabited by one fifth of the human race, and in command of large, well-trained, and war-seasoned military forces. The Security Couneil hesitated.

On November 24, as MacArthur launched his "final offensive," which was to end in disaster, a Peking delegation arrived at Lake Success. The Council on November 8 had invited Peking to participate in discussion of MacArthur's charges of Chinese intervention in Korea. Chou En-lai refused, but accepted the earlier invitation to discuss "American aggression" in Formosa. Dr. T. F. Tsiang (agent of Chiang Kai-shek), supported by John Foster Dulles, proposed a U.N. inquiry into charges that Russia was threatening peace by supporting the Chinese Communists. But the proposal was withdrawn when it became clear that no two-thirds majority in the Assembly could be mobilized for such a step in view of European alarm at the direction of American policy. Wu Hsiu-chuan, agent of Peking, took his place at the Council on November 27. In reply to the accusations and threats of Warren Austin, he bitterly and elaborately denounced the U.S.A. and demanded that the Council admit Red China to the U.N. and "condemn, and take concrete steps to apply severe sanctions" against America for its "criminal act of armed aggression against the territory of Formosa, and armed intervention in Korea." On November 30 Malik vetoed Austin's resolution calling for withdrawal of Chinese troops from Korea.

The U.S. now took the issue to the Assembly, newly streamlined as an agency to condemn and punish international "criminals" by use of military force. But no force was available, apart from the forces already in Korea, reeling back in defeat—nor would any imaginable force have sufficed to "enforce peace" on China save through a major, interminable, and inconclusive world war. Washington pressed for branding Peking as an "aggressor." America's allies were horrified and paralyzed. A dozen Asian and Arab countries, under India's leadership, appealed to Peking and Pyongyang not to send their armies south of the 38th parallel, and proposed a cease-fire and subsequent negotiations on all Far Eastern problems. Britain and Yugoslavia supported the proposal. This and other similar efforts failed. Washington was intransigent. Peking at this stage of hostilities would assent to no armistice without admission to the U.N. and American withdrawal from Korea and Formosa. Wu Hsiu-chuan denounced the cease-fire plan as a "trap" and took his leave in mid-December. The U.S. now sought to pressure its European allies into condemning, blockading, and attacking China. Nehru warned of disaster.

After complex and futile attempts in various quarters to thwart American folly, the Assembly yielded as if hypnotized and on February 2, 1951, adopted a slightly diluted resolution (44 to 7 with 9 abstentions) finding that "the Central People's Government of the People's Republic of China, by giving direct aid and assistance to those who were already committing aggression in Korea and by engaging in hostilities against U.N. forces there, has itself engaged in aggression in Korea"; demanding Chinese withdrawal; calling upon all States to aid the U.N. in Korea and refrain from helping the aggressor; and requesting a subcommittee of the "Collective Measures Committee" to consider "as a matter of urgency . . . additional measures to be employed to meet this aggression," subject to possible action by a "Good Offices Committee" to arrange a cease-fire. The legalists now rejoiced that judge and jury had tried and sentenced the "criminal" and that nothing remained but to execute the sentence. In short, the U.S. had browbeaten the U.N. into agreeing to wage war on China and, obviously, on Russia as well should Moscow come to Peking's support under the alliance treaty of 1950.

How such a war would promote "peace" was clear to no one except MacArthur and some elements in Pentagon, the State Department, Congress, and the American press. In reality the American "victory" at Lake Success was meaningless. Apart from the Soviet bloc, India and Burma voted in the negative while Egypt, Indonesia, Pakistan, Saudi Arabia, Sweden, Syria, Yemen, Yugoslavia, and Afghanistan abstained. Virtually all of Asia and the Moslem world were thus opposed to the American program. Of the delegates supporting the U.S., almost all suspected anxiously that Washington policy-makers were bent upon total war against

China. They were themselves resolved, despite the resolution, to have no part in such madness.[5]

In February the Assembly rejected Soviet proposals to condemn the U.S. for aggression against China. The "sanctions committee" met and studiously did nothing, despite American insistence on speedy preparations for war. The Good Offices Committee (Louis Padilla Nervo, Nasrollah Entezam, and Sven Grafstrom) bestirred itself to find a peaceful exit from the impasse. U.S. spokesmen now began to hesitate and to explain that they were not as bellivolent as they sounded. The Asian and Arab States resumed their efforts for peace. The crusading Trygve Lie began to back water. London expressed firm opposition to any "sanctions" against China. Faced with an insoluble dilemma of his own making, the American President made MacArthur his scapegoat. On May 18, to be sure, the Assembly yielded anew to American importunities and voted an arms embargo against China and North Korea, 47 to 8, with Afghanistan, Burma, Egypt, India, Indonesia, Pakistan, Sweden, and Syria abstaining and the Soviet bloc taking no part on the ground that the whole proceeding was "illegal." Appeals from Washington for more U.N. troops for Korea produced none.

In the end the U.N. was reduced to such vacuity by the uses the U.S. had made of it that it could neither make peace nor wage war. The cease-fire negotiations of 1951–2, registering the defeat of both sides in a war no one could win, were initiated by Jacob Malik's broadcast of June 23, by American-Soviet consultations in Moscow, and by exchanges of messages between General Ridgway and the Communist commanders, leading to parleys at Kaesong and later at Panmunjom. Washington stopped talking about "liberating" and "unifying" all Korea and penalizing China for "aggression." Peking stopped talking about Formosa and entry into

[5] For details see the debates and documents of the General Assembly for this period; the *United Nations Bulletin* (February 15, 1951); Lillie Schulz: "Peace: Why It Was By-Passed," *The Nation* (February 17, 1951); and Richard H. Rovere: "Letter from Lake Success," *The New Yorker* (February 10, 1951).

the U.N. While the talks went on, men killed men on "Heartbreak Ridge" and in a hundred other arenas of mechanized murder. The "negotiations" (ostensibly in the name of the U.N. but in fact conducted exclusively by U.S. agents) assumed the eerie quality of an endless nightmare, as in a Kafka novel, because neither side could quite acknowledge the fact of defeat. Both continued to strive, interminably and hopelessly, for some illusion of victory through diplomatic haggling or further butchery aimed at, but never attaining, some strategic or propagandistic advantage over the enemy.

None of this mattered, save to those who suffered or died as a result. What mattered—though none would grant the point—was that "collective security" had again been exposed as a formula not for peace but for war, not for law but for savagery, not for order but for anarchy, not for victory but for futility and tragedy. That its advocates denied the reality of these self-evident facts and continued to worship folly before brazen idols and bloody altars can only be deemed further proof of Man's incurable addiction to delusions.

---

4. THE INVINCIBLE DELUSION

In one combination or another, these three superstates are permanently at war, and have been so for the past twenty-five years. War, however, is no longer the desperate, annihilating struggle that it was in the early decades of the twentieth century. It is a warfare of limited aims between combattants who are unable to destroy one another, have no material cause for fighting, and are not divided by any genuine ideological difference. This is not to say that either the conduct of war, or the prevailing attitude toward it, has become less bloodthirsty or more chivalrous. On the contrary, war hysteria is continuous and universal in all countries, and such acts as raping, looting, the slaughter of children, the reduction of whole populations to slavery, and reprisals against prisoners which extend even to boiling and burying alive, are looked upon as normal, and, when they are committed by one's own side and not by the enemy, meritorious. But in a physical sense war involves very small numbers of people, mostly highly trained specialists, and causes comparatively few casualties. The fighting, when there is any, takes place on the vague frontiers whose whereabouts the average man can only guess at, or round the Floating Fortresses which guard strategic spots on the sea lanes. In the centers of civilization war means no more than a continuous shortage of consumption goods, and the occasional crash of a rocket bomb which may cause a few scores of deaths. War has in fact changed its character. More exactly, the reasons for which war is waged have changed in their order of importance. Motives which were already present to some small extent in the great wars of the early twentieth century have now become dominant and are consciously recognized and acted upon. . . . It is always the same war. . . . The primary aim . . . is to use up the products of the machine without raising the general standard of living.

—GEORGE ORWELL: *1984* (New York: Harcourt, Brace; 1949).[6]

THE CONFUSION in the minds of men over "collective security" in the twentieth century has many sources, as numerous and protean as the very roots of the "schism in the soul" of Western mankind in its final "time of troubles." Yet it seems not unreasonable to suggest that the genesis of disorder lay in the coupling of two concepts of great antiquity into an unhappy and unholy union wherein neither could any longer be distinguished from the other. One concept was forever false and could never be made true under any imaginable circumstances. The other was unquestionably true and could never be made false unless and until the system of sovereignties prevailing currently throughout the world should be subverted

[6] Reprinted by permission of Harcourt, Brace & Co., New York, from the late George Orwell's exciting and horrifying fantasy of 1984, pp. 186–9. Orwell did not explicitly postulate that the belligerents in his nightmare world of days to come would fight in the name of "collective security," but in most other respects his brilliant portrayal of the probable shape of the second half of the twentieth century closely corresponds to trends easily visible as early as 1950–1, including the slogan "War Is Peace."

or abolished by a "world revolution" of a scope and magnitude hitherto unknown in the civilization of the West.

The false concept in this befuddled marriage of convenience is precisely the doctrine of "collective security" in its classical form—i.e., the notion that peace among competing sovereignties is possible through pledges and plans for a war of all against each. The hypothesis in practice is wholly fallacious, as we have seen. Such experiments produce many interesting consequences. But peace is never among them. Policy-makers in sovereign States act in accordance with what they conceive to be the interests of their State in each situation. The interests thus defined are invariably a product of more or less prudent calculation of risks and advantages. This generalization is not invalidated by the grotesque spectacle of tiny military units fighting to no purpose in Korea in 1951 at the behest of the governments of Colombia, Turkey, and Thailand—all of which hoped thereby to gain substantial benefits from Washington. To run great risks in the name of some abstract conception of "community interests," taken seriously by no sovereignty and regarded by all as the negation of "common sense," is a pattern of action no sovereignty ever indulges in.

If adequate motivation is always lacking for "collective security," in the very nature of every system of sovereignties, what is even more clearly lacking is that relationship of power which might conceivably make the coercion of one by all a feasible enterprise. Despite the fictions of international law and the anthropomorphic fantasies of popular patriotism, States are not individuals bearing toward one another the bonds of person to person in civil society and acting as members of an organized polity. If the seventy-odd "sovereignties" of the contemporary world were all roughly equal in size and power (and if they were impelled toward the pattern of conduct here postulated, as assuredly they would not be), then any combination of 69 to 1 or 68 to 2 or 67 to 3 or even 60 to 10 might hypothetically present such an overwhelming combination of the forces of virtue against vice that those tempted to viciousness would be deterred from crime, or promptly and cheaply penalized should they yield to temptation. In fact the "Powers" range in extent and fighting capacity from two "super-Powers" and several "Great Powers" through sundry "Middle Powers" to a myriad of minuscle "Powers" possessed of no power whatever.

The tiniest among them, being incapable of "aggression," are never in need of "coercion." The mightiest among them cannot be coerced by the others without a world war resulting. This self-evident circumstance—quite clear to the framers of the U.N. charter but almost forgotten by policy-makers in Washington and by their obedient servants at Lake Success in 1950–1—plainly means that the formula of "peace" through the coercion of sovereignties by sovereignties spells general war whenever the proposed victim of coercion is sufficiently formidable to offer effective resistance. London and Paris were pleased to pretend that this was the case with Fascist Italy in 1935. London and Paris knew that this was the case in 1950 in the face of MacArthur's folly in demanding war on China.

Three further considerations reduce to nonsense the presuppositions of Dubois and Podebrad, Rousseau and Kant, Wilson and Litvinov, Acheson and Lie. Sovereignties are not permanently divisible into categories of "peace-loving" and "aggressive." Every sovereignty in the world, however pacific now, has been "aggressive" and "expansionist" at some time in the past and will revert to sin at some future date. Every sovereignty now "aggressive" has exhibited some time in the past, and will exhibit some time in the future, a passionate solicitude for the status quo. It is, moreover, impossible in any operationally effective terms to indict a nation, particularly if it be large and well-armed. The attempt spells general war. Even if the leaders of the vanquished are "tried" and hanged by the victors, following wholesale bloodshed and destruction, as at Nuremberg and Tokyo after 1945, the result is not the triumph of the rule of law, but only the promotion of savagery.

Thus Joseph Addison in *The Spectator* (July 19, 1712): "I have more than once found fault with those general reflections which strike at Kingdoms or Commonwealths in the gross; a piece of cruelty which an ingenious writer of our own compared to that of Caligula, who wished the Roman people had all but one neck, that he might behead them at a blow." Edmund Burke similarly warned: "Nations do not behave as individuals, nor can they be treated as individuals are treated." "The 'policeman-burglar' analogy," says the Royal Institute of International Affairs, in a British masterpiece of understatement, "has been responsible for much loose thinking and slovenly argument." [7]

Finally, as a corollary proposition, it may be observed that "war for peace" involves as grave risks for the "sheriff" as for the "criminal," and is therefore in practice unacceptable to all governments and peoples which feel themselves in no immediate danger from any specific "aggression." Walter Lippmann in his column of January 15, 1951, put the point aptly:

The trouble with collective security is, if I may reprint something I wrote back in 1946, that "when the issue is less than the survival of the *great* nations, the method of collective security will not be used because it is just as terrifying to the policeman as it is to the lawbreakers. It punishes the law-enforcing states, at least until they have paid the awful price of victory, as much as the law-breaking states. Therefore it cannot be used as a method of ordinary and continuing enforcement, for example as a means of insuring the inspection of laboratories and plants working with fissionable material. There would be little surgery if the surgeon had to amputate his own arm when he was called upon to amputate the patient's leg. There would be little en-

[7] Royal Institute of International Affairs: *International Sanctions*, p. 6. For some additional and suggestive commentaries, see Charles Reith: *Police Principles and the Problem of War* (London: Oxford University Press; 1940); C. R. M. F. Crutwell: *A History of Peaceful Change in the Modern World* (London: Oxford University Press; 1937); and the October 1951 issue of *World Politics* (Center of International Studies, Princeton University Press), particularly the articles of Felix Gilbert: "The 'New Diplomacy' of the 18th Century"; Arnold Wolfers: "The Pole of Power and the Pole of Indifference," and Raymond I. Garthoff: "The Concept of the Balance of Power in Soviet Policy-Making."

forcement of law in our cities if in order to arrest burglars, murderers and violators of the traffic ordinances the police had to start a fight in which the courthouse, the jail, and their own homes were likely to be demolished. Men will not burn down the barn in order to roast a pig: the method of collective security is, I repeat, too crude, too expensive, and too unreliable for general and regular use. It proposes to achieve peace through law by calling upon great masses of innocent people to stand ready to exterminate great masses of innocent people. No world order can be founded upon such a principle; it cannot command the support of civilized men, least of all of democratic men who respect the individual and consider it the very essence of justice to distinguish between the guilty and the innocent, the responsible and the irresponsible."

This falsehood has in our time been wedded to an age-old truth, with the partners blended into one by the intimacy of their unfortunate fusion. The truth is as old as international politics: a Power feeling itself threatened by another more powerful should seek allies and cultivate coalitions to give the "aggressor" pause or, if need be, overcome him in ordeal by battle. The uses of alliances, well-contrived and directed toward attainable ends, are clear to all. The record of experience reveals conclusively that alliances do not promote peace, since their ultimate purpose, usually, is victory in war. But neither do they *per se* encourage war, since their efficacy in intimidating enemies and deterring or postponing recourse to arms has frequently been demonstrated. Their customary purpose in recent centuries has been to prevent—by diplomacy, by war, or by both—the aggrandizement of any one Power or combination of Powers to a point at which the independence of all the rest might be jeopardized. No one who accepts the values of national sovereignty can reasonably question the utility and necessity of such arrangements in the kind of international system in which we live. The repudiation of such devices is rational only for those who hope for the conquest of all sovereignties by one or who urge such a fusion of sovereignties as will put an end, through a co-operative world government, to the ancient game of rivalry for power among sovereignties.

In our era the delusion of "collective security" has been inextricably mingled with the realities of the "balance of power." A grand alliance defeated the German bid for global hegemony in 1918. A greater grand alliance frustrated the German-Italian-Japanese bid for world mastery in 1945. A still greater grand alliance, *ex hypothesi*, was called for in midcentury to thwart Communist ambitions to take over the planet, since the comrades were already masters of China, Russia, and all of eastern Europe. On the other side of the line of conflict, a comparable coalition appeared imperative since America controlled Japan, Western Germany, all West Europe, and the Mediterranean and was evidently bent upon "containing," encircling, outflanking, and, if possible, demolishing the Scarlet Empire.

Within the confines of this bipolar pattern of power, it was doubtless inevitable that one side or the other, taking cognizance of widespread illusions, should identify its purposes with the superstition of "collective security." Washington and Moscow alike had long worshipped this idol. Whichever was more successful in mobilizing the lesser sovereignties in the service of its purposes was bound to present these purposes, and to seek to further them, not in terms of "national interest," nor even in terms of the "balance of power," but in terms of the unity of all the virtuous sovereignties against the wicked. In this contest, Washington won hands down and thereby became the focal point—through the U.N., the Truman Doctrine, the Atlantic Alliance, and other devices—for a grandiose adventure in "collective security" as an attractive façade for a Grand Alliance "made in America" against the enemy coalition.

Here, as always, the objective of such combinations is not "peace" as such, but the prevention of the foe's further aggrandizement, lest he reach a point of power at which defense would become hopeless. In the pursuit of this end, peace is promoted if the enemy is sufficiently intimidated by the aggregation of power arrayed against him to refrain from an open test of force, or if both coalitions, like Triple Alliance and Triple Entente for a decade before 1914, are able to strike bargains and resolve crises without general recourse to the sword. War is fostered if the tactics of intimidation are unsuccessful or if the defenders of the status quo conclude that they have more to gain than to lose by precipitating a showdown or a preventive war against their antagonists. In August 1950, Secretary of the Navy Francis Matthews urged such action, contending that it would "win for us a proud and popular title—we would become the first aggressors for peace." Despite semantic confusions, what is in fact striven for in such matters is neither "war" nor "peace," which are merely different contexts in which the struggle for power is pursued, but rather the maintenance of the "balance" in order that each sovereignty may survive and none may overwhelm the rest.

That America's Great Coalition against Marxist Muscovy was weakened, not strengthened, by its identification with the hallucination of "collective security" was wholly unappreciated by the vast majority of Americans. Yet it is clear that under the goad of Communist aggrandizement and intransigence the U.S., with the connivance of its allies, perverted the U.N. from its original purpose and sought to transform it from a forum of diplomacy into an agency of psychological warfare and armed hostilities. The resulting alliance, all sicklied o'er with legalistic and moralistic abstractions and pretenses of universality, was less capable than most such combinations of acting prudently and responsibly, and was far less adapted than old-fashioned alliances to the necessary tasks of bargaining, localization of conflicts, and negotiation of limited accords.

Indeed, it was the essence of the Acheson dispensation, with its slogan of "total diplomacy" (meaning no diplomacy whatever), that the U.N. should repeatedly be used as a cloak for refusal to discuss questions that could only be settled by negotiations among Great Powers. Every issue referred to the

Council or Assembly, with their usually obedient American majorities and their full publicity for all clashes of views and interests, represented the loss or postponement of an opportunity to employ diplomacy for the accommodation of differences. The effort, moreover, to arm the U.N. as a world-wide coalition of peace-loving states for war in the name of peace against aggression, was foredoomed to futility from beginning to end. The "enemy" comprised two of the five Great Powers and ruled one third of the human race. His coercion through "sanctions" meant World War III. In the eyes of most Asiatics, furthermore, the "aggressor" in Chinese-American relations in 1950–1 was not China but America. Britain, France, and most of America's lesser allies in the U.N. had no enthusiasm for the enterprise and no intention of contributing toward it.

On all these grounds, the marriage of America's aberrated *Realpolitik* with the myth of "collective security" through the U.N. represented no service to peace, to America's interests and purposes, or to the future usefulness of the U.N. itself. At the time of writing the States of the Soviet bloc, preferring to employ the U.N. forum for propaganda purposes, had not yet withdrawn from the organization despite its conversion into an agency of Pentagon and the State Department. It was arguable, as of 1952, that the only remaining value of the U.N. in world politics lay in the shadowy circumstance that in its corridors America's allies were able to confer with one another with reasonable regularity for the purpose of devising means of obstructing and restraining the more exuberant of America's policy-makers. This value is not to be minimized. But it has obviously no relation to the proper and effective function of a Grand Alliance or to the global role intended for the U.N. by the framers of the Charter.

These circumstances did not prevent presumably responsible politicians and publicists from continuing to talk nonsense in their efforts to elicit public approbation for the policies they were bent upon pursuing. Some were engaging in deliberate deception. Others believed sincerely in the fallacies and irrelevancies they preached. To draw invidious distinctions between them in these terms would be uncharitable. A few sample utterances are nevertheless in order by way of suggesting the flavor of the whole.

Senator Paul H. Douglas of Illinois, July 5, 1950:

Once the United Nations called upon its members to lend military aid first to the United Nations and then to Korea itself in forcing the invaders back to the boundary line at the 38th parallel, any use of armed force by us was not an act of war, but instead merely the exercise of police power under international sanctions. For war is the anarchic use of force by one nation against another for the purpose of imposing its own will and in the absence of an international authorization. What we are really doing in Korea is to serve as a police force to carry out the decision of the United Nations that its member nations should help to repel the invasion of South Korea. We are, therefore, serving as agents of an international authority designed to protect the peace of the world and not as anarchic or self-appointed users of force. It is indeed probably in only such a manner that an international police force could as a practical matter be created. It would not be born in a vacuum. We can only hope that when the present emergency has been ended that the free nations will learn this lesson and will establish a permanent international police force which can be used in just such situations as that which has arisen.[8]

The American Association for the United Nations, Peoples Section *Bulletin*, April, 1951:

The principle of collective security is as sound today as when the United Nations took action to repel the aggression against the Republic of Korea on June 25th. The nations must profit by experience. The experience in Korea clearly demonstrates the necessity for improvement in collective security action. In the first place, troops must be designated in advance for call by the Security Council or the General Assembly; an adequate United Nations military staff must plan in advance for

[8] "The Constitutional and Legal Basis for the Action of President Truman in Using Our Armed Forces to Repel the Invasion of South Korea," Address to the Senate by Paul H. Douglas, July 5, 1950.

their coordination and command. . . . The United States should urge the United Nations immediately to implement the "Uniting for Peace" resolution adopted by the fifth General Assembly, which provides for the designation of forces to be available . . .

Ambassador Warren R. Austin, at the 42nd Annual Convention of Rotary International, Atlantic City, May 28, 1951:

> Thanks to the lessons of Korea, we have found the way to prevent the United Nations from ever again being caught unprepared in the face of aggression. From here on, an act of aggression should find the United Nations ready and able to organize quickly and efficiently the resources of its members, who have the will to obey the call of duty. The Uniting-for-Peace Resolution, approved last fall by 51 member states, has made it possible for the veto-free General Assembly to organize resistance to aggression whenever the Security Council fails to perform its primary duty by reason of the exercise of the veto. . . . I shall be able very soon to transmit to the United Nations, on behalf of the Government of the United States, a specific statement of the types and strength of the national armed forces which will be maintained by the United States of America, in accordance with our Constitutional processes, for service as United Nations units.

Ambassador Austin's promise had a sequel. The "Collective Measures Committee" on April 11, 1951, despatched its questionnaire to all U.N. members and asked replies as "a matter of urgency." The U.S. reply, presented by Ernest A. Gross to Trygve Lie, was not delivered until June 8. After listing U.S. forces engaged in Korea, it asserted that "the United States Government regards the maintenance of these forces" as "fulfillment at this time of the purposes of the recommendations of the General Assembly in the Uniting for Peace Resolution." Any actual "ear-marking" of forces to serve the U.N. was indefinitely deferred, to be kept "under constant review in the light of changing circumstances and in furtherance of the policy of the U.N. to build up an effective collective security system. Accept, Excellency, the renewed assurances of my highest consideration." Other replies were similarly dilatory, vague, and evasive. No sovereignty on earth had any actual intention of placing its troops at the disposal of the U.N. All understood full well that the campaign in Korea was a "U.N." operation in name only.

Lest it be supposed that such renewed validations of reality are capable of modifying the verbalizations of statesmen, a few further contemporary utterances may be noted.

John Foster Dulles in *Advance* (April 1951), organ of the Congregational Christian Churches:

> This year, for the first time in all time, a world organization moved with force to halt aggression. It seemed that the hope of ages had come true. Whatever may now be the disappointments, we can know that the sons of the United Nations who in Korea lay down their lives do so for the noblest cause for which men ever died in battle. . . . [Unfortunately, the result may be] a full scale foreign war. . . . When it comes to straight military strategy, the free world seems, momentarily, in a mood of some confusion and without any agreed deterrent program.

Secretary of State Acheson, June 1, 1951, to the Senate Armed Services and Foreign Relations Committees:

> The operation in Korea has been a success. Both the North Koreans and the Chinese Communists declared it to be their purpose to drive the United Nations forces out of Korea and impose Communist rule throughout the entire peninsula. They have been prevented from accomplishing their objective. It has been charged that the American and allied forces fighting in Korea are engaged in a pointless and inconclusive struggle. Nothing could be farther from the fact. They have been magnificent . . . [Yet] no one can predict when the fighting will stop and when the aggression will end.

Trygve Lie, June 25, 1951:

> One year ago—on June 25, 1950—the United Nations made a great decision. For the first time in history a world organization acted to meet armed aggression with collective force. Because of that action, and because of the courageous and self-

sacrificing fight waged by United Nations forces in Korea, the development of collective security against war anywhere in the world has been greatly advanced. The men who are fighting and dying under their national flags and the flag of the United Nations serve the noblest of all causes. They are fighting to prevent a third world war. . . . They have won a great victory for the United Nations and for peace. . . . For all who love peace, June 25 should be a day of tribute to the men who have fallen in this cause. It should be a day of rededication to the purpose of establishing firm collective security under the United Nations to prevent future armed aggression anywhere in the world.

Of other efforts to achieve peace by war, there was no end. As early as July 1949, Senators Elbert Thomas and Paul H. Douglas introduced a Resolution asking for "a supplementary agreement under Article 51 of the Charter," whereby U.N. members would agree, on the basis of a two-thirds vote of the Assembly, including any three of the five permanent members of the Council, to come to the military aid of any victim of attack. The State Department took a dim view of this proposal but, as we have seen, sought to achieve the same objective through the Assembly Resolution of November 3, 1950.[9]

The empty dream of an "international police force" to keep peace by waging war on warmakers—always meaningless in view of the actual distribution of power among sovereignties—remains no less popular among some types of peace-seekers

[9] On these and related proposals, see Hamilton Fish Armstrong: "Coalition for Peace," *Foreign Affairs,* October, 1948; Paul H. Douglas, "United to Enforce Peace," *Foreign Affairs* (October 1951); *Revision of the U.N. Charter,* Report of the Committee on Foreign Relations, 81st Congress, 2nd Session, Senate Report No. 2501 (September 1, 1950); "Congress and the United Nations," by Carl Marcy and Francis O. Wilcox, *Foreign Policy Reports,* Foreign Policy Association (May 15, 1951). For a broader perspective and a provocative analysis of the background of such issues see John Somerville: *The Philosophy of Peace* (Philosophy Books; 1950) and his supplement, "War and Peace in the Great Debate: Gen. Eisenhower's Premises and Gen. MacArthur's Conclusions" (Chicago: The National Committee for Peaceful Alternatives; 1951). Many searching and disturbing questions regarding these and other aspects of the Korean "police action" are raised in I. F. Stone's *The Hidden History of the Korean War* (New York: Monthly Review Press; 1952).

than it was centuries ago. The "Commission to Study the Organization of Peace" (policy-making agency of the American Association of the United Nations) proposed on July 16, 1951, that a U.N. supreme commander be designated to apply "collective measures" against aggressors under the direction of a "Permanent Collective Security Commission" and a "Temporary Political Coordination Committee."

Ely Culbertson, Chairman of the "Citizens Committee For U.N. Reform," has long urged his ingenious formula for a "Quota Force Plan" under which an international army—"a kind of Foreign Legion of fighters for peace"—would be recruited from nationals of the lesser States and would be so cleverly contrived as to be able to defend all victims of aggression, aided if need be by the armies of the Great Powers, and at the same time render aggression against any Great Power "*impossible*." The details of this proposal require no discussion here, since it is based on the usual false premises of "collective security," plus some others conjured up by Mr. Culbertson himself, who shows little talent for understanding the meaning of "federalism" or comprehending that world politics, unlike bridge, is not a game played according to fixed rules and won or lost on the basis of calculations of mathematical probability.[1]

[1] The Culbertson "Quota Force" program has at least the merit, rare enough in most proposals for peace by war, of recognizing the power factors in the international equation. It is nevertheless irrelevant, despite the wide and often enthusiastic attention it has aroused, because it assumes that "aggressors" can be deterred or at least defeated if only a sufficiently formidable and ingenious machinery of military coercion can be mobilized against them. All history and logic refute the assumption. See Ely Culbertson: *Total Peace* (Doubleday; 1943), the publications of the "Citizens Committee for U.N. Reform," 16A East 62nd Street, New York City; and Ely Culbertson, "Plan for a U.N. Police Force," *The New American Mercury* (December 1950). The "Culbertson Plan," like numerous other schemes for "peace," had become by midcentury a rallying-point for many whose basic premise was either the desirability or the inevitability of a Western war with Russia. The CCUNR as of 1951, however, included among the members of its National Council others of different views, such as George S. Counts, Max Eastman, Sidney Hook, Norman Thomas, *et al.* Mr. Culbertson, though born in Russia of an American father and Russian mother, has displayed no startling acumen as an analyst of Russian policies and purposes. In a letter to *The New York Times* (April 14, 1951) he cried havoc and opined that the Politburo "will renounce its historic design for a Communist World State and retreat behind

As a final example of this approach, the project of the late Lord Davies is noteworthy. He established a "Society for the Promotion of International Law and Order," and for years propounded through its stimulating journal, *The New Commonwealth* (Thorney House, Smith Square, London), the notion that peace could be maintained through a vaguely defined "International Equity Tribunal" and an "International Police Force" to beat down aggressors. The genial, yet mordant, comment of H.G. Wells says all that needs to be said of this scheme:

> My old friend and antagonist Lord David Davies, for instance, has recently succumbed to the infection [of peace by war]. He was concerned about the problem of a World Pax in the days when the League of Nations Society and other associated bodies were amalgamated in the League of Nations Union. He was struck then by an idea, an analogy, and the experience was unique for him. He asked why individuals went about in modern communities in nearly perfect security from assault and robbery, without any need to bear arms. His answer was the policeman. And from that he went on to the question of what was needed for states and nations to go their ways with the same blissful immunity from violence and plunder, and it seemed to him a complete and reasonable answer to say: "An international policeman." And there you were! He did not see, he is probably quite incapable of seeing, that a state is something quite different in its nature and behaviour from an individual human being. When he was asked to explain how that international policeman was to be created and sustained, he just went on saying "international policeman." He has been saying it for years. Sometimes it seems to be the League of Nations, sometimes the British Empire,

---

her rightful frontiers only under the compulsion of an ultimatum, and only if it estimates that the American superiority in atomic weapons is still so decisive that Russia would lose the war even if she could temporarily seize Eurasia. It follows that the chances are at least one in three that Soviet Russia will attack during 1951; and if she attacks, it will probably be during the summer months rather than the spring months, when Central Europe is a sea of mud. If Soviet Russia does not attack this summer, then the odds are five to one or better that the attack will be made next summer, when scores of atomic bombs will be added to her stock pile. Far from relaxing, we must redouble our efforts."

sometimes an international Air Force, that is to undertake this grave responsibility. The bench before which the policeman is to hale the offender and the position of the lock-up are not indicated. Finding our criticisms uncongenial, his Lordship went off with his great idea, like a penguin which has found an egg, to incubate it alone. I hope he will be spared to say "international policeman" for many years to come, but I do not believe he has ever perceived or ever will perceive that, brilliant as his one inspiration was, it still left vast areas of the problem in darkness.[2]

Apart from the inexorable record of events, the *reductio ad absurdum* of peace through "collective security" was attained—with of course no such thought in the minds of the editors and contributors—in *Collier's* magazine of October 27, 1951. Here, in 130 pages illustrated with many horrendous pictures and maps in color, twenty-two able writers and sundry artists—most of them presumably sane and responsible people—presented in one package the most effective piece of Communist propaganda ever written by anti-Communist Americans, the most naïve of all reaffirmations of American Messianism and Millenniarism, the most convincing exhibit of the political psychopathology of the U.S.A. at midcentury, and, somewhat incidentally and unintentionally, the most exquisite satire on "collective security" ever printed. Captions: "Russia's Defeat and Occupation, 1952–1960," and "Preview of the War We Do Not Want." Cover: A sturdy and handsome Marine, "MP—Occupation Forces," with grenade ready and bayonet poised, and U.S. and U.N. flags on his helmet, in front of a map in which Eastern Europe, the Ukraine, and the Baltic States are "occupied," Moscow is "Occupation HQ," and Leningrad is renamed "Petrograd." Contents: Well-written fiction, with Robert E. Sherwood, Edward R. Murrow, Hal Boyle, Hanson W. Baldwin, and Lowell Thomas leading off, followed by Arthur Koestler, Oksana Kasenkina, Marguerite Higgins, Stuart

[2] H. G. Wells: *The New World Order* (Alfred A. Knopf; 1940), pp. 78–9.

Chase, Walter Ruether, J.B. Priestley, Erwin Canham (editor of the *Christian Science Monitor*), Walter Winchell, Allan Nevins, Red Smith, Philip Wylie, John Savage, Kathryn Morgan-Ryan, Senator Margaret Chase Smith, Harry Schwarz, Howard Brodie, and Bill Mauldin.

World War III is here described from the happy perspective of A.D. 1960. It begins with a Stalinist attempt to assassinate Tito, followed by a satellite and then a Soviet invasion of Yugoslavia in May 1952. Truman comes to the defense of virtue against vice. The U.S. and most of the U.N. members declare war. Atomic bombing of Russia begins in highly humanitarian fashion, "avoiding completely population centers" and concentrating on "legitimate military targets only." Red Army invades Western Europe and launches terroristic atomic attacks on America. Invaders are halted and crushed on Christmas Day, 1952, by a barrage of atomic artillery shells, which the Russians (apparently) never thought of. Liberation of the Russian people from the frightful Communist tyranny becomes the goal of the war. U.S. suicide-parachutists destroy the Soviet A-bomb plant in the Urals. By 1955 hostilities cease, with complete Red defeat and occupation of enemy territory. The delighted survivors among the Russians avidly read translations of *Collier's*, *Time*, *Life*, *Reader's Digest*, *The Saturday Evening Post*, and even the "measured cadences" of Walter Lippmann and the "dramatic prose" of Walter Winchell. They replace the Moscow Ballet with *Guys and Dolls*.

Comes "Freedom—at long last." Women are emancipated. God is worshipped. "Free" trade unions are established. Education is restored by Allan Nevins. An enjoyable time is had by all at the Moscow Olympics. The liberated slaves take over, after a brief interval of famine and chaos following the collapse of the Soviet regime. Democracy is revived with the aid of Arthur Koestler. One party gives way to twenty-two, with the Monarchists leading. A brave new Russia is born out of the rubble through the beneficent aid of UNIHOPE, UNITOC, UNIPROD, and other U.N. agencies. By 1960 everybody loves everybody and the Millennium is at hand.[3]

This symptomatology of collective megalomania is here worthy of comment only because it suggests, quite accurately, the most probable short-run consequences of "collective security" in the atomic age. (The ultimate results, obviously, will not be the advent of Utopia, but the descent of all of Western culture into breakdown and barbarism.) The campaign, of course, is a U.N. "police action" waged in the "name of collective security." Since the power of the enemy is matched by his viciousness and stubbornness, the war for peace, as here graphically described, involves the wholesale destruction of London, other Western European cities, Detroit, New York, Hanford, Chicago, Washington, Philadelphia, Boston, Los Angeles, Norfolk, Bremerton, ("casualties greatly lessened by improved civil defense procedures"), Moscow, Kharkov, Kiev, and indeed most other Russian cities. Millions perish. But the gay survivors achieve heaven-on-earth, by miraculous processes and ethereal motivations that only the publishers and editors of *Collier's* (Edward Anthony, Louis Ruppel, Richard Chaplin, Gordon Manning, *et al.*) can reasonably be expected to explain. . . .

Peace in an ever-fluctuating system of rival sovereignties, unequal in fighting-capacity and dedicated to the pursuit of security and power through aggrandizement and defense, is possible for greater or lesser intervals of time only through the adroit practice of diplomacy by responsible statesmen seriously concerned with minimizing or postponing recourse to violence. "Permanent" peace is possible only through a permanent termination of the game of power among rival

[3] Among the numerous commentaries on this phantasmagoria, see D. F. Fleming: "Collier's Wins World War III," in *The Nation* (November 10, 1951), and subsequent observations and letters in later issues. This issue received widespread attention in the British, Continental, and Soviet press. Thomas J. Hamilton, in reporting in *The New York Times* of November 11, 1951, on the U. N. Assembly session in Paris, wrote: "The October 27 issue of *Collier's Magazine* . . . is providing Communist delegates with material for constant attacks on the alleged aggressive aims of the United States."

sovereignties. This goal has never been attained, and cannot in the nature of the case ever be attained, through the solemn dedication of all sovereignties to self-abnegation or the "outlawry of war" or "disarmament" or universal pledges to wage war against warmakers. This goal is attainable only through the subjugation of all sovereignties by one, with a World-State emerging out of victory—or through the voluntary merging of sovereignties in a global polity, with a World-State emerging out of agreement. The first solution has many times been achieved in past civilizations. It is unattainable in our own, for reasons set forth elsewhere in these pages. The second solution has never been attained. Yet it deserves to be regarded (unlike "collective security") as within the realm of the humanly possible. We shall therefore move on in our inquiry to an exploration of this hope.

CHAPTER EIGHT

PEACE BY CONTRACT

---

1. E PLURIBUS UNUM

I am for coercion of law—that coercion which acts only upon delinquent individuals. This Constitution does not attempt to coerce sovereign bodies, states, in their political capacity. No coercion is applicable to such bodies, but that of an armed force. If we should attempt to execute the laws of the Union by sending an armed force against a delinquent state, it would involve the good and bad, the innocent and the guilty, in the same calamity.

—OLIVER ELLSWORTH TO THE CONNECTICUT STATE CONVENTION IN DEFENSE OF THE PROPOSED CONSTITUTION OF 1787.

EDWARD AUGUSTUS FREEMAN (1823–92) was among the more prolific of England's nineteenth-century historians. He insisted on the oneness of human experience, on the necessity of using original sources, and on the enduring heritage of Rome as the key to the unity of European civilization. His fifteen-volume *History of the Norman Conquest*, though remarkably wrong on a number of matters in the light of later scholarship, is still a fascinating work. Among the more suggestive of his many books is his *History Of Federal Government From The Foundation Of The Achæan League To The Disruption Of The United States*, Volume I, *General*

Introduction: History of the Greek Federations (London and Cambridge: Macmillan; 1863).

This 700-page tome is largely given over to an account of the leagues of the Greek City-States from the Peloponnesian War to the Roman conquest. Freeman defined federal government as "any union of component members, where the degree of union between the members surpasses that of an alliance, however intimate, and where the degree of independence possessed by each member surpasses anything which can fairly come under the head of merely municipal freedom [p. 2]." He deemed "good" those federal arrangements wherein the central authority operated on individuals, and "bad" those in which it operated on the member states—though all twentieth-century political scientists would deny that the latter device was "federal" and would describe it as the essence of a "confederation" or *Staatenbund*, as distinct from a *Bundestaat* or true federation. Freeman envisaged federalism, rightly enough, as a kind of compromise between large and small states—or, as we should prefer to say, between a unitary nation or imperium and a dispersion of sovereign authority among a multiplicity of lesser polities. While denying (p. 92 f.) that the Civil War in America was evidence against the viability of federalism, he did not conceive of the formula as being widely applicable to the governance of mankind:

> A Federal Government does not secure peace and equal rights to its whole territory so perfectly as a modern Constitutional Kingdom. It does not develop the political life of every single citizen so perfectly as in the ancient city-commonwealths. But it secures a far higher amount of general peace than the system of independent cities; it gives its average citizens a higher political education than is within the reach of the average subjects of extensive monarchies. This form of government is a more delicate and artificial structure than either of the others; its perfect form is a late growth of a very high state of political culture. It is even more than other forms of government essentially the creation of circumstances, and it will even

less than other forms bear thoughtlessly transplanting to soils where circumstances have not prepared the ground for it [p. 89]. . . . A Federal Union must depend for its permanence not on the sentiment but on the reason of its citizens [p. 114].

Freeman begins his Preface (dated January 2, 1863) with the comment: "I trust that no one will think that the present work owes its origin to the excitement of the War of Secession in America. It is the first installment of a scheme formed long ago, and it represents the thought and reading of more than ten years." He promised a second volume on the Swiss and German leagues "to follow the present with all reasonable speed," though "I cannot fix any certain time for its appearance." Volume II never materialized, nor was the original volume ever revised or republished in a second edition.

In a world of men given to aggression as their normal response to frustration, it is unhappily true that no set of symbols for promoting solidarity, and no set of legalistic devices for reconciling liberty with authority, can offer any guarantee that men will achieve brotherhood in co-operative pursuit of the tasks of peace rather than butcher one another in heroic devotion to the duties of war. Yet the precepts of "federalism," evolved by trial and error in various widely separated areas, have lately impressed more and more reasonable observers as offering greater promise of "peace on earth, good will to men" than any other formula for order in communities of States.

The remoter origins of federalism cannot here be traced, nor is space available for accounts of functioning federal governments—Switzerland, Austria, Yugoslavia, The Netherlands, Canada, Australia, Mexico, Brazil, the U.S.S.R., the U.S.A., *et al.* A few definitions and distinctions, all of them part of the stock in trade of descriptive and comparative political science, are nevertheless in order. Even the best-informed citizens of federations are often confused as to the distinguishing characteristics of the system of power under which they live, and are therefore unable to evaluate the possible applicability of its principles to the problem of international order.[1]

All hierarchies of political authority in communities larger than a village involve some distribution or division of powers between central and local officials. In the most extensive polities of the past, this division has most commonly been made by the central authority itself—whether Pharaoh, Cæsar, or Tsar; Senate, Parliament, or National Assembly—with provinces, counties, townships, and municipalities possessed of only such lawmaking, executive, and judicial competence as may be allotted to them by the central power, the human incarnations of which are empowered by law to give, to change, or to take away authority from the lesser and local powers. Such was in principle the method of allocating public functions between the whole and parts in the Roman, Ottoman, and Mongol empires. And such is the national method in the United Kingdom, France, and Italy, and the

[1] In the voluminous literature of federalism, the following works are particularly helpful: Alfred Mitchell Bingham: *The United States of Europe* (Duell, Sloan & Pearce; 1940); Sanjib Chaudhuri: *A Constitution for the World Government* (Calcutta: The Author; 1949); David D. Davies: *A Federated Europe* (London: V. Gollancz; 1940); Alfred Cyril Ewing: *The Individual, The State and World Government* (Macmillan; 1947); Howard O. Eaton and others: *Federation, the Coming Structure of World Government* (Norman: University of Oklahoma Press; 1944); Gilbert Leon Guerard: *Europe, Free and United* (Stanford, California: Stanford University Press; 1945); Edouard Herriot: *The United States of Europe*, Translated by Reginald J. Dingle (Viking; 1930); Arthur N. Holcombe: *Our More Perfect Union* (Cambridge, Massachusetts: Harvard University Press; 1950); Robert Maynard Hutchins: *St. Thomas and the World State* (Milwaukee: Marquette University Press; 1949); William Ivor Jennings: *A Federation for Western Europe* (Macmillan; 1940); Julia Emily Johnsen (compiler): *Federal World Government* (H. W. Wilson; 1948); Sir John Arthur Ransome Marriott: *Federalism and the Problem of the Small State* (London: Allen & Unwin; 1943); Raleigh Colston Minor: *A Republic of Nations; A Study of the Organization of a Federal League of Nations* (London: Oxford University Press; 1918); Vernon Nash: *The World Must Be Governed* (Harper; 1949, 2nd edition); Oscar Newfang (translated from French by Pierre Gault): *World Federation* (Barnes & Noble; 1939); Oscar Newfang: *World Government* (Barnes & Noble; 1942); Walter Alison Phillips: *The Confederation of Europe; A Study of the European Alliance, 1813–1823, as an Experiment in the International Organization of Peace* (Longman, Green; 1920, 2nd edition); Emery Reves: *The Anatomy of Peace* (Harpers; 1945); K. C. Wheare: *Federal Government* (London: Oxford University Press; 1946).

local method within the several units (states, provinces, cantons, republics) of existing federal unions. This mode of achieving a geographical division of powers has traditionally come to be regarded as the essence of a so-called "unitary" government. What particular powers are wielded by central or local bodies, and how extensive or circumscribed they may be, are irrelevant to the problem here in hand, the heart of which is the question of what authority determines the distribution.

At the opposite pole from the "unitary" principle is the not-uncommon arrangement among separate and independent societies wherein each retains full authority over its own affairs but all agree—usually by treaty or by some covenant, charter, or even "constitution" indistinguishable from a treaty save in name—to vest certain powers in common agencies. Most alliances and coalitions are of this character. When the delegation of authority to common bodies is more or less permanent, and the authority transferred includes some power of decision-making beyond mere diplomatic consultation, the arrangement is often dignified by the name "league" or "confederation."

Here the member States determine the division of powers between the parts and the whole. Each participant ordinarily retains a right of abrogation of the treaty or secession from the league if dissatisfied with the results of the transfer of power, or with the interpretation put upon it by others, or with revisions of the arrangement agreed upon by co-signatories. Such were the ancient Greek confederacies, when they were not mere façades for the hegemony of a dominant Power. Such was the government of the United States under the Articles of Confederation (1781–9) and of the Confederate States of America (1861–5). In its contemporary shape the British Commonwealth also displays these attributes, although it is unique in representing a devolution of power from the initial supremacy of the Parliament at Westminster to the full independence of the overseas units. The League of Nations and the United Nations are further instances, albeit of a looser character, of confederations in this sense.

Intermediate between these extremes are the true federations or federal unions—the essence of which is a division of powers between central and local agencies by means of a written constitution that, in theory, reflects the consensus, or "general will," or "popular sovereignty" of all the communities thus united. The distribution of authority set forth in the document admits of no modification by either central or local organs acting alone. Both must participate in sanctioning change through an amending process whereby representatives of the whole and of the parts must assent to any enhancement or diminution of the previously accepted powers allocated to each. The authority to determine the distribution thus resides in neither the central nor the local entities, but in another and transcendant power assumed to be superior to both and to delegate a portion of its "sovereignty" to the government of the union and another portion to the governments of the constituent areas comprising the federation.

With the metaphysical nature of "sovereignty," and the scholastic question of whether it is or it not divisible, we need not here concern ourselves. If the term be taken to refer to that authority in a commonwealth which, in the last analysis, is above law and above government in the sense of being regarded as the ultimate source of both, then sovereignty in a unitary State resides either in the national government or some element thereof (*e.g.*, the ruler in absolute monarchies, the House of Commons in contemporary Britain) or, as in France and Italy, in the people of the nation expressing their view through a constitution whereby specific powers are conferred upon government and specific limitations are imposed upon their use. Sovereignty in a league or confederation, conversely, remains in the member States. In a federation it reposes in the people of the entire union and is manifested in the processes of drawing up and amending the state and federal constitutions whence the local and central governments derive their legal authority.

A further, and indeed fundamental, distinction between federations and confederations has to do with the way in which central decisions are locally enforced. In a league or confederacy the central agencies, having no power to legislate for individuals but only for the member States as corporate entities, must of necessity rely upon good faith on the part of the local authorities in the participating units, supplemented by exhortation or (where some semblance of "collective security" is part of the system) by the armed coercion of one by all or of the parts by the whole. In a federation, on the other hand, the government of the union has power to make law, within such limits as the federal constitution prescribes, with the resulting legislation enforceable on individuals throughout the union through the action of both federal and state agencies of law-enforcement and adjudication.

This distinction was rightly deemed crucial by those who first framed the Federal Constitution of the U.S.A. in 1787. George Mason of Virginia said that "punishment could not in the nature of things be executed on the states collectively, and therefore that such a Government was necessary as could directly operate on individuals, and would punish those only whose guilt required it." James Madison held that "the use of force against a state would look more like a declaration of war than an infliction of punishment, and would probably be considered by the party attacked as a dissolution of all previous compacts by which it might be bound. . . . Any Government for the states formed on the supposed practicality of using force against the unconstitutional proceedings of the states would prove . . . visionary and fallacious."

Edmund Randolph: "There are but two modes by which the end of General Government can be attained; the first is by coercion as proposed by Mr. Patterson's plan. Second, by real legislation, as proposed by the other plan. Coercion is impracticable, expensive, cruel to individuals. It tends also to habituate the instruments of it to shed blood and riot in the spoils of their fellow citizens, and consequently trains them up for the service of ambition. We must therefore resort to a national legislation over individuals." Hamilton was even more emphatic: "To coerce the states is one of the maddest projects that was ever devised. A failure of compliance will never be confined to a single state. . . . The thing is a dream, it is impossible. . . . What is the cure for this great evil? Nothing, but to enable the national laws to operate on individuals, in the same manner as those of the states do." [2]

Federalism implies two spheres of law, general and local, each enforceable not by the coercion of states by states but by action against lawbreaking individuals on the part of law-enforcement authorities. The relationship between the two spheres in every genuinely federal system presupposes that local officials are bound by federal law as well as by local law and that federal law, properly enacted within the constitutional scope of federal authority, prevails over local law when the two conflict. This is of necessity the case since the purpose of the whole arrangement is the replacement of the anarchy of separate sovereignties by the union of united sovereignties. The principle has never been better stated than in Art. 6 of the U.S. Constitution of 1787:

> . . . This Constitution, and the laws of the United States, which shall be made in pursuance thereof, and all treaties made, or which shall be made, under the authority of the United States, shall be the supreme law of the land; and the judges in every state shall be bound thereby, anything in the Constitution or laws of any state to the contrary not withstanding.
>
> The Senators and Representatives before mentioned, and the

[2] These quotations from the "Founding Fathers" will be found in Max Farrand (editor); *The Records of the Federal Convention of 1787* (New Haven, Connecticut: Yale University Press; 1923) Vol. I, pp. 34, 54, 164–5, 256, 284, 320, 339–40. Many of these arguments are eloquently reiterated in *The Federalist Papers*, especially Nos. 15–22. For a fuller commentary on these questions, see "The Dilemma of the Peace-Seekers," *The American Political Science Review* (February 1945), and "Toward the World State," *The Scientific Monthly* (July 1946).

members of the several state legislatures, and all executive and judicial officers both of the United States and of the several states, shall be bound by oath or affirmation to support this Constitution; but no religious test shall ever be required as a qualification to any office or public trust under the United States.

Federalism also presupposes dual citizenship. In a federal union every citizen is at the same time a citizen of the federation and of one of its component units (including such lesser local units as may grant citizenship), with all the rights and duties which each such status entails.

Other details vary from case to case. But several other common features of federal systems should be noted. Every federal government, unlike central agencies in an alliance, league, or confederation, is financially independent of its constituent parts, in that it does not rely upon local appropriations, subventions, or grants but possesses power to levy taxes on individuals and to raise its own revenues in other ways, independently of the disposition of the local units to support it or to withhold or delay support. Every federal government, moreover, possesses power to issue bonds, to borrow and lend, to appropriate and expend funds for the common defense and the general welfare, to regulate interstate and foreign commerce, to administer or regulate systems of communication, and to coin money. With few exceptions every political federation of states is also a postal union, a customs union, and a currency union.

Last but far from least, every federal government involves some scheme of representation in the federal legislature whereby, in most instances, a bicameral lawmaking body consists in one chamber of an equal number of representatives from each member state, regardless of population, and of a number of representatives in another chamber proportionate to the population of the local units. Federal legislation usually requires a majority vote in each chamber and approval by a nationally elected federal executive official. This was the heart of the "Great Compromise" between the large and small states in the Philadelphia Convention of 1787. The principle of the equality of states in an upper house and of the representation of populations in a lower house has shown itself to be viable, and indeed indispensable, for the effective formation and functioning of federal unions in virtually all instances in which the federalist hypothesis has been put to the test of practice.

---

2. THE PARLIAMENT OF MAN

> What a large amount of moral firmness, intelligent foresight, and supple adaptation this world authority will have to possess, more than ever necessary in critical moments when, in the face of malevolence, people of good will need to be supported by authority! After all our past and present trials, should we dare to say that the resources and methods of government and politics today are adequate? In truth, it is impossible to solve the problem of a world political organization without agreeing to leave the beaten track from time to time, without appealing to the experience of history, and to a sane social philosophy, or even to some kind of vision from creative imagination.
>
> There, Gentlemen, is a vast field of work, study, and action. You have understood this and looked it squarely in the face; you have the courage to spend yourselves for this cause. We congratulate you. We would express to you our wishes for your entire success and with all our heart we will pray to God to grant you His wisdom and help in the performance of your task.
>
> —POPE PIUS XII TO WMWFG, April 6, 1951.

IN THE FIRST YEAR of the second half of the twentieth century an idle pedestrian in the capital of France, exploring the charms of ancient streets, might conceivably have wandered in search of curiosities down the rues du Havre and Amsterdam from the Gare Saint-Lazare in the direction of the Place de la Concorde. Proceeding in as straight a line southward as the thoroughfares of Paris permit, he would presently have come to the rue Vignon, running along the eastern edge of the VIIIe Arrondissement, midway between the Havre-Caumartin Metro Station and the Greek-temple Church of the Madeleine.

This long and narrow street is dull, neither old nor new, neither rich nor poor. It is lined with small shops and third-class apartments and office buildings. If our pedestrian, crossing west to east diagonally from the excellent little restaurant of *la Fermé des Matthurins* to No. 18, across from a tiny dress-shop (*Pour Madame et Bébé*), had peered into a small, untidy courtyard, he would have seen a number of signs beside a cavelike stairway. Among them were small placards informing him that on the upper floors were to be found the offices of WMWFG—the "World Movement for World Federal Government," of the "*Conseil Mondial pour L'Assemblée Constituante des Peuples*," and of the "*Mouvement pour la Fédération des Peuples—Association Adhérente au Mouvement Universel pour Une Confédération Mondiale—Toute l'Europe unie dans un Monde uni!*"

Further exploration would have revealed small and dingy offices, crowded with old desks, primitive filing-cabinets, Mimeographing machines, and tables of literature. The inmates? A French stenographer or two; a few able and devoted women—American, British, or French—donating their labor to a cause; and occasionally a slightly shabby gentleman and scholar, French or foreign, obviously indigent and yet devoting some hours each week (stolen from a busy, harried, and unlucrative life) to the same cause in the face of feeble funds, few supporters, and the vast and oppressive apathy of the world. The WMWFG moved its offices in 1951 to The Netherlands (369 Keizersgracht, Amsterdam) for reasons of economy. . . .

Across the Channel in London our pedestrian—if still interested in such puzzling phenomena—could find their counterparts in concentrated form on Buckingham Street, extending from the Strand to the Thames Embankment gardens, roughly halfway between the Aldwych semicircle and Charing Cross Station. At the corner he passes a gaping hole where once a building stood before the Blitz. Proceeding down the slope of the left sidewalk along a narrow way lined with shops, new flats, and old lofts, he comes upon an antique six-storied structure at No. 20 filled with cramped and cheap offices, housing the headquarters of "Federal Union, Ltd.," the "Crusade for World Government," "World Citizens," and several other affiliated or similarly inspired organizations. Here again, in a somber semi-Dickensian atmosphere of hideous poverty and indomitable good cheer, are the few stenographers, the women volunteers, the Mimeograph machines, the crops of pamphlets, and the directors—wondering at times, in spite of themselves, whether their toil and sacrifice can move a largely indifferent mankind.

Other offices are to be found amid the ruins of Frankfurt, in Rome, and elsewhere on the Continent—though none with comparable purposes is tolerated behind the "Curtain" or anywhere within the Scarlet Empire. Such offices in New York, Washington, and Chicago are more opulent, as befits the mood and means of the American leviathan. But even here the spirit at midcentury is strikingly similar: the fervor of conversion to a creative idea, the frustration of functioning with funds and personnel never adequate to the tasks in hand, the discouragement of public apathy, and the inspiration of trying to save the world from its own folly.

When where and by whom the idea was first propounded that federalism offers a possible ideological and institutional basis for replacing anarchy by order in the entire human community is a problem best left to the historians of ideas, social doctrines and political inventions. Some early adumbrations of this notion, albeit seen through a glass darkly, were touched upon at the outset of the preceding chapter. Despite Victor Hugo, William Ladd, Alfred Lord Tennyson, and the work of some of the nineteenth-century "peace societies," organized efforts on behalf of international federation on a planetary scale are largely a development of the twentieth century, and more particularly of the years immediately preceding and following World War II.

These endeavors, from the late 1930's to the middle 1950's, suggest a bewildering kaleidoscope of iridescent patterns, ever changing, coalescing, dividing, and overlapping in a confused mosaic of organizations, factions, and sects. The interested reader can readily secure reams of literature from each and all. To seek to unravel all the tangled controversies and feuds over ends and means among and within the various groups (all with their rebels, heretics, schismatics, and secessionists) would serve no purpose save to demonstrate anew that men and women who are agreed upon purposes are still addicted to quarreling over methods, and to show what has already been shown: that the fashioning of world government is not a simple but a fearfully complex task. Our more modest enterprise is to suggest, by sampling, a few *leitmotifs* in the symphony or cacophony of movements striving for world federation.

It is still a moot point to what group belongs the honor of first having championed federalism as a basis for world order, during the years we are here considering, and of having sought to win friends and influence people on behalf of the cause. Among contenders for the prize is assuredly the "Campaign for World Government," established in Chicago in 1937 by the Lloyd family of Winnetka as an educational and liaison agency for sundry peace-seekers and church organizations. Its leading lights have at various times included Edith Wynner, Georgia Lloyd, her sister Mary, and her brother, William Bross Lloyd, Jr.

In the autumn of 1938 three Britishers, Derek Rawnsley, Charles Kimber, and Patrick Ransome took the first steps toward founding "Federal Union, Ltd.," in London. In the following spring a panel of advisers was named: Lionel Curtis, Lord Lothian, Wickham Steed, and Barbara Wootton—even as "Federal Union, Inc.," emerged in the U.S.A. in the wake of the publication of *Union Now.* While the American group was dedicated to a federation of democracies in the face of threatened totalitarian aggression, the British movement held more emphatically that such a "nuclear" union should and must lead toward a universal world federal government. W.B. Curry's *The Case for Federal Union* (Penguin Books; 1941) played in Britain a role somewhat comparable to that played in America by *Union Now* and *Union Now with Britain* (New York: Harpers; 1938 and 1941).[3]

The simple and eloquent author of these volumes, Clarence K. Streit, arrived at his vision of world federation while reporting League of Nations news from Geneva for the *New York Times*. Father of Federal Union, Inc.; ardent advocate of Anglo-American federation after the fall of France; founder of *Freedom and Union*, established in 1946 as the journal of his movement; and grandfather of Federal Union's progeny, the Atlantic Union Committee (born in March 1949)—Streit became the prime inspiration and the modest Messiah of the American movement for a federation of democracies.

While no single figure in the British movement has attained the stature of Streit, much of the burden of recruiting, organizing, pamphleteering, and speaking has been ably carried by J. Keith Killby, Secretary of Federal Union, Ltd., since 1946. Once a "free-lance pacifist," he spent several years in New Zealand and Australia and joined Federal Union while a member of the British Army. He served King and Country at Knightsbridge and El Alamein and in Sardinia and Italy. He has been a member, and often a leader, of such organizations as the National Peace Council, the Crusade for World Government, the WMWFG, the European Union of Federalists, and the United Nations Association.[4] British federalists envisage their ends and means in generous and catholic terms. Federal Union, Ltd., is the British branch of WMWFG. As of 1951–2, under the presidency of the Rt.

[3] Curry quotes freely from, and acknowledges full indebtedness to, Streit's *Union Now*. It was my privilege to write a short introduction to the American edition of the Curry book (1942). The factual data in this and the ensuing section are drawn from a voluminous file of leaflets, pamphlets, speeches, notes on personal interviews and public meetings, and other fugitive material assembled at home and abroad in 1950–2. The references that follow are limited to books, articles, and pamphlets still available from the publishers or in the larger libraries of the Atlantic community.

[4] See *Federal News* (organ of Federal Union Ltd.), January 1951.

Hon. Lord Beveridge, K.C.B., it simultaneously championed European Federation, Atlantic Federation, and World Federation and favored, as roads toward the goal, amendment of the U.N. Charter, a World Constituent Assembly, political action to elect federalists to Parliament, the strengthening of functional agencies, and the promotion of regional unions.[5] Most Americans would regard such open-mindedness as immoral. All Russians would regard it as impossible.

The federalist ferment in America in midcentury bubbled and boiled in many minds, in many places, and in many forms. Robert Lee Humber, an American long a businessman in Paris, returned to his homeland in the wake of the Nazi conquest of France and induced the legislature of North Carolina (March 13, 1941) to adopt his "Declaration of the Federation of the World." In subsequent years he traveled from capital to capital as a kind of one-man lobby, and persuaded more than a score of state legislatures to do likewise, although some later reversed themselves amid the confusions of ever-hotter Cold War. In mid-March of 1946 the Rollins College Conference at Winter Park, Florida, endorsed "a constitutional federal government" of the world as "the only way by which we can assure our survival and preserve our liberties." Said Justice William O. Douglas to the atomic scientists, political leaders, and publicists there assembled: "Our goal should be a world government representing the peoples of the world, functioning under an international bill of rights through a legislature, judiciary, and executive." In its final appeal the Conference called for the transformation of the U.N. Assembly into a global federal parliament.

In the same month Harold C. Urey told the American Association for the Advancement of Science, meeting in St.

[5] See "Policy Statement 1951" of Federal Union Ltd., 20 Buckingham Street, London. For an admirable survey of these and related movements, both British and American, including Lionel Curtis's "Minimalist" proposals, see Chapter iv (pp. 67–113) of Alan de Rusett's *Strengthening of the Framework of Peace* (London: Royal Institute of International Affairs; 1950). A helpful sketch of the major groups is provided in Alfred Lilienthal: *Which Way to World Government?*, Foreign Policy Association Headline Series No. 83 (September–October, 1950).

Louis, that without world government applied science in the atomic age "may lead to a complete destruction of our civilization." Six months later, in Chicago, the Annual Conference on Science, Philosophy, and Religion was assured by Thomas K. Finletter that "only world government applying law can do away with international war," and by Waldemar Gurian that world government was impossible because Russia would never accept it. In November 1946, the electorate of Massachusetts voted 9 to 1 in favor of converting the U.N. into a world federal government, while General Carlos P. Romulo and "World Federalists, U.S.A., Inc." made public appeals for such a step.

As pristine enthusiasm was followed by sober concern about concrete proposals and political action, fusions and fissions became the order of the day. As early as October 1945, at the Dublin, New Hampshire, conference of federalists, the ranks divided into a majority favoring global federation and a minority (Clarence K. Streit, A. J. G. Priest, Owen J. Roberts, Michael Williams, and Stringfellow Barr, through the latter subsequently joined United World Federalists) favoring a nuclear union of the Atlantic democracies. In February 1947, at Asheville, North Carolina, representatives of World Federalists, Americans United for World Government, Student Federalists, World Republic, World Citizens of Georgia, and the Massachusetts Committee for World Federation merged into "United World Federalists," which came to include many secessionists from Federal Union who rejected the Streit formula in favor of the universalist ideal. In the autumn Henry Usborne, brilliant and handsome Labor M.P., eloquently addressed many meetings throughout America on behalf of global federation.

The project of electing delegates to a Peoples' World Convention, envisaged as a useful device of mass education, was discussed at a conference at Pocono Pines, Pennsylvania, in late June 1948, on the invitation of Albert Einstein, Grenville Clark, Hubert Humphrey, Leo Szilard, Carl Van Doren, and Stringfellow Barr (Henry Usborne also attending), with financial support from Anita McCormick Blaine of Chicago. Interested and inspired by these discussions, she shortly made an offer of a million dollars to further the cause of world government. Mrs. Blaine and Scott Buchanan, another trustee of the fund, were both members of the Progressive Party and friends of Henry A. Wallace. In consequence of frictions and suspicions engendered by what Stringfellow Barr called anti-Communist "hysteria" and "guilt by contagion," the Pocono enterprise came to nothing. The Continuing Committee of the Pocono Conference dissolved. Mrs. Blaine's grant became the basis of the Foundation for World Government, which donated $50,000 to the (British) Crusade for World Government, nothing to Fyke Farmer's domestic "crusade," (see below) and various amounts to other groups —and then decided to finance research rather than organizations, with special emphasis on problems of the economic development of backward areas.[6]

These frictions and confusions, which have their parallels among federalists in Western Europe and elsewhere, may easily suggest to skeptics or cynics that all the movements we are here considering are much ado about nothing. It is quite possible that nothing may come of these efforts save high hopes, much verbiage, and final failure. Such a result, however, should rejoice the hearts only of those who despair of men's capacity to achieve reason and order in their common affairs. All of the new federalists, without exception, are aiming at a world revolution to be achieved not by conquest or subversion but by persuasion and agreement. As in all revolutions, whether fulfilled or abortive, those who are inspired by the Vision are bound, precisely because of the intensity of their conviction, to quarrel among themselves about the right road to heaven. When, as in our time, the incentive to action is less the flowery fragrance of the Elysian Fields than

[6] For details, see Stringfellow Barr's "Final Report on the Pocono Conference" (privately printed; 1948). Among Dr. Barr's other notable contributions to the Federalist cause are his *The Pilgrimage of Western Man* (Harcourt, Brace; 1949) and *Let's Join the Human Race* (University of Chicago Press; 1950).

the hot breath of hell upon the necks of the seekers for salvation, the searchers for safety are even more likely to bicker to no purpose, since fear is ever an evil counselor. Yet the desirability or attainability of the destination is not to be judged by the degree of quibbling among the devotees.

It may be useful to set forth in summary form the positions, emerging from chaos, of the major groupings dedicated to the ideal of global federation—and then of those, in the section following, committed in principle, or by considerations of expediency, to partial or regional union.

PAX ORBIS?—United World Federalists, with almost fifty thousand members in 1949, was not only the largest single group in WMWFG, but exceeded the combined membership of all other organizations in the Movement. Under the presidency of Cord Meyer, Jr. (author of *Peace or Anarchy*, Boston: Little, Brown; 1947), and, since 1948, of Alan Cranston, UWF has championed the transformation of the U.N. into a global federal government with specified and narrowly limited powers to keep the peace. Partial federation is envisaged as a second best choice in the event of Soviet refusal to participate, and then only in terms of a geographically limited union open to all nations willing, sooner or later, to join. UWF has worked actively to commit Congress and state legislatures to this position through resolutions and constitutional amendments—all of which efforts have doubtless "educated" lawmakers and citizens, but produced few concrete results to date.[7]

The temper and direction of UWF, at the time of writing, can be suggested by its officers, among whom (1951–2) were, aside from those already named, Cass Canfield, Grenville Clark, Norman Cousins, William O. Douglas, Mrs. J.

[7] "World Government" resolutions in the Congress of the U.S.A. have been too numerous to review here. See "Proposals for World Government before Congress" by Percy E. Corbett, Yale Institute of International Studies, Memorandum No. 34 (March 25, 1950); Alfred M. Lilienthal: ibid.; and the several Congressional hearings of 1949–50 on the various proposals advanced, none of which, to date, has been endorsed in committee or acted upon by Congress as a whole.

Borden Harriman, W. T. Holliday, Robert E. Sherwood, Raymond Swing, and Vernon Nash.

We believe that peace is not merely the absence of war, but the presence of justice, of law, of order—in short, of government, and the institutions of government; that world peace can be created and maintained only under a world federal government, universal and strong enough to prevent armed conflict between nations, and having direct jurisdiction over the individual in those matters within its authority.

Therefore, while endorsing the efforts of the U.N. to bring about a world community favorable to peace, we will work to create a world federal government with authority to enact, interpret and enforce world law adequate to assure peace:

1. by urging use of the amendment processes of the U.N. to transform it into such a world federal government;
2. by participating in unofficial conferences, whether of private individuals, parliamentary or other groups seeking to produce draft constitutions for consideration and possible adoption by the U.N. or by national governments in accordance with their respective constitutional processes; and
3. by pursuing any other reasonable and lawful means to achieve world federation.

House Concurrent Resolution 64, sponsored at the time of its maximum Congressional support by 105 Representatives and 22 Senators, asserted:

That it is the sense of the Congress that it should be a fundamental objective of the foreign policy of the U.S. to support and strengthen the U.N. and to seek its development into a world federation open to all nations with defined and limited powers adequate to preserve peace and prevent aggression through the enactment, interpretation, and enforcement of world law.[8]

Vox Populi?—The PWC ("Peoples' World Convention") achieved a "Steering Committee" in September 1948 (elected

[8] For further details consult the voluminous literature issued by United World Federalists, Inc., 7 East 12th Street, New York City, particularly *The Federalist*, a monthly journal initiated in April 1951 in place of the U.W.F. edition of *World Government News*, 15 Moore Street, New York City.

at the Luxembourg Congress of WMWFG), under the chairmanship of Henry Usborne. The objective was to convene at Geneva in December 1950 a gathering of elected representatives, one per million of population, to formulate, ultimately, a World Constitution to be submitted to the U.N. and to national governments for ratification. The "Mondialization" movement in Western Europe, and Garry Davis's "International Registry of World Citizens," are ideologically akin to PWC. After much travail a "convention" of sorts did in fact meet in Geneva at the end of December 1950—of which more anon.

The dedicated souls responsible for PWC early convinced themselves, though not very many other people, that world government is unattainable without popular education and public pressure upon politicians for action. These preconditions they sought to promote by the device already indicated. In 1946 Mary and Georgia Lloyd, Edith Wynner, Harris Wofford, and a few other Americans evolved the idea of a "Peoples' Convention." A similar approach was propounded at the same time by the "*Front Humain des Citoyens du Monde*," in which J. Allemand Martin, P. Montuclard, and Robert Sarrazac were chief figures, and by a group of British M.P.'s meeting under the leadership of Henry Usborne and eventually establishing the "Crusade for World Government." This group, endorsed by almost a hundred British parliamentarians, distributed cards pledging the signers (some sixteen thousand in England by 1951) to vote in the projected unofficial election of delegates, if and when held. In March 1950 John Fitzgerald, Secretary of the Proportional Representation Society, became Chairman of the National Executive of the "Crusade," which became a membership organization in September.

Meanwhile, in August 1947, the American, British, and French partisans of PWC met in Montreux at the Congress of Federalists, which endorsed the project as one possible means of attaining world government. Among the participants was a Tennessee lawyer, Fyke Farmer, who was stirred to new enthusiasm by Henry Usborne during the latter's autumn visit to America. Amid financial crises, interpersonal frictions, and even bitter recriminations, these and related endeavors led to a number of widely scattered but interrelated results. Organized support for the project developed in a score of countries, including India, Pakistan, Japan, and New Zealand. Unofficial "pilot" elections were held in June 1949, in the form of referenda on PWC and municipal "mondialization" in four selected cities: Chelmsford, England, where 3,500 persons participated, of whom 82 per cent voted affirmatively; Silkebord, Denmark (4,560 and 91 per cent); Nivelles, Belgium (5,870 and 92 per cent); and Kissingen, Germany (6,370 and 95 per cent). In March, 1950, on the initiative of Fyke Farmer and his co-workers, almost a hundred sympathizers from twenty countries assembled at Ghent and, amid much jurisdictional wrangling with the International Steering Committee, laid plans to insure a Convention at Geneva in December.

Supporters introduced bills for election of delegates into various legislatures—France, Italy, Belgium, Brazil, Turkey, and others. Only one such project was enacted into law. On April 7, 1949, Governor Gordon Browning of Tennessee signed a bill passed by the state Senate, 30-0, and by the House, 71-1. (The bill was repealed in January 1951.) Under its terms the voters of Tennessee on August 3, 1950, elected three delegates to PWC: state Senator William A. Harwell (173,196 votes); J. B. Avery, Jr. (129,151); and Fyke Farmer (113,081).

What followed was not without elements of comedy and tragedy. The Tennessee bill provided that the state would pay the expenses of the delegates only if fifteen other states of the U.S.A. took similar action. None did. Fyke Farmer appealed in vain, in letters of increasing bitterness, for twenty-five thousand dollars from the Foundation for World Government. Mr. Avery was unable to go to Geneva. The PWC met in the *Palais Electoral* on December 30, 1950. Some five hundred persons from 42 countries appeared. Henry Usborne presided. Lord Boyd Orr, president of WMWFG, sent greetings. Messrs. Farmer and Harwell turned out to be the only two elected delegates. Professor Eyo Ita of Nigeria claimed the same honor, but when it appeared that he had not been elected he was directed by Chairman Usborne to return to his seat in the audience. No less than eighteen resolutions asked that he be seated as a delegate. Delegates Farmer and Harwell, being charged with responsibility for a decision, held on January 4 that Professor Ita was entitled to be seated as a delegate—a conclusion he welcomed as "the most momentous decision at this Convention and a landmark in the history of mankind."

Messages of support were received from Nehru (who was passing through Geneva at the time), Einstein, and other notables. A parallel "Consultative Assembly" discussed sundry proposals for future action. Endorsement was given to a motion by Count Theodorico Wolkenstein Trostburg (Italy) to appeal to all governments to enact legislation similar to the Tennessee bill and to another by Gerry Kraus (England) urging a three-year world campaign to obtain a billion signatures for a PWC "directly elected by the peoples of the world." Acute controversy developed over the choice of a continuation committee. The Farmer-Kraus faction favored election of an executive by secret ballot in the Assembly and held that only elected delegates could pass on the credentials of others claiming to be delegates. "Nowhere," said Julian Snow, M.P., "outside of Bedlam, could such an idea be tolerated." The British participants, assembled in the Hotel Mirabeau, urged that the executive be selected by WMWFG, the International Secretariat of World Citizens, the International Steering Committee, the Ghent Committee, and the mondialized communities. A Committee of twenty-five was finally established under the name of "World Action Council," with five places left vacant for the Ghent (Farmer-Kraus) Committee—which, however, refused to co-operate. The session adjourned inconclusively, on January 5, 1951.

In the face of these dissensions, nothing significant came of the PWC movement during 1951—nor during 1952, as of the time of writing.[9] The "World Council" held its third meeting in Paris, December 8–9, 1951, and resolved to organize a "Preparatory Assembly" for PWC in 1953. But the prospects were scarcely inspiring. A creative idea appears to have been lost in the quarrels of its disciples. When those dedicated to the unity of the world show themselves incapable of overcoming disunity and suspicion among themselves, others may perhaps be forgiven for concluding that the brotherhood of man is a fantasy.

ROAD TO ROME—"The World Movement for World Federal Government" (WMWFG) was founded at a congress of federalists in Luxembourg, in October 1946, as a loose type of "federation" of, ultimately, some seventy groups in twenty countries. Lord Boyd Orr became its first president. At a second congress in September 1948, the purposes of its members were set forth in the "Luxembourg Declaration," which asserted *inter alia:*

> Modern technology has dramatically united a world community, but that community—unlike the national communities

[9] No one realizes more fully than this writer that the cursory account here presented of PWC and of other movements fails to "do justice" to any of the organizations and to the various factions and shadings of opinion within each. "Justice," however, would require many volumes if the intricacies and complexities of these disputes were to be unraveled and evaluated fairly. No one would have any interest in such volumes aside from the feudists themselves. In addition to my discussions with Fyke Farmer, Henry Usborne, John Fitzgerald, and others, the account here offered of PWC is chiefly based upon the following sources: *Peoples World Convention, 1950; The Plan in Outline*, International Steering Committee, 54 Baker Street, London; Fyke Farmer's article in *The Progressive* (Madison, Wisconsin), November 1950; *Le Monde* (Paris), September 30, 1950; *Peoples World Convention, Ghent Conference, March 10–12, 1950*, published jointly by "Across Frontiers," *Parlement*, and *Weltstaat* (1950); *The Nashville Tennessean*, November 26, 1950; "Reflections and Recommendations for the defense of the Peoples World Assembly," International Secretariat of World Citizens, Paris (December 9–10, 1950); "Peoples World Constituent Assembly, Geneva, December 30, 1950–January 5, 1951; *Chelmsford World Government Week* (Crusade for World Government, Chelmsford Office; 1949); *Humanity* (United World Publications, Glasgow), March and April issues, 1951; *Collection of Tennessee Bills*, Prepared by Gerry Kraus, Executive Committee on Arrangements for the PWC, "*Parlement*," Saethem Saint-Martin, Belgium; *Common Cause* (The Committee to Frame a World Constitution, University of Chicago Press), March and April issues, 1951; and sundry leaflets and pamphlets issued by the British "Crusade for World Government."

which compose it—has no common government. Without such government it cannot achieve either justice or peace or prosperity. Our generation demands the right to set its common house in order. It demands a government to serve the common welfare of all, to end hunger, and to protect the lives, liberties, and property of all men, which no national government can any longer protect. . . .

We believe that peace is not an accident or a freak of nature or circumstance. It has form and it has substance. It is the creation and operation of responsible authority. It is the existence of law. We believe that enforceable law requires government. We believe that the presiding fact of our time is the need for government on the world level—in time to avert the otherwise inevitable collision of nations not subject to law amongst themselves.[1]

The WMWFG champions a federal world constitution, with a bill of rights, providing for a global legislature, executive, and judiciary; world citizenship; world law enforceable on individuals; and reservation of residual powers to the members of the union. To this end WMWFG favors regional federations, U.N. reform, PWC, national political action, and all other steps likely to contribute toward the objective. In the "Montreux Declaration" of 1947, the peoples of the world were summoned to join forces "in solving the crucial problem of our time. Until it is solved, all other issues, whether national or international, will remain unsettled. It is not between free enterprise and planned economy or between capitalism and communism that peace lies, but between federalism and power politics."

At a third congress in Stockholm in September 1949, the 156 delegates, holding 245 votes, represented 35 organizations in 16 nations, including India and Japan. They gave serious consideration to constitutional questions, food and population, underdeveloped areas, atomic control, and the achievements and limitations of the U.N.

[1] Full text in Alan de Rusett, ibid., p. 72–5.

There is no peace. Men, women, and children are dying of hunger and disease. One child out of three is the victim of tuberculosis. In every country fear of another war, fear of hunger, fear of disease are in the saddle. The peoples of the world, whose faith once looked to the U.N., no longer dare to hope that it can assure peace. Yet . . . we believe it indispensable that the U.N. should be preserved and strengthened into a true World Federal Government with power to act.

At Stockholm Stringfellow Barr, Scott Buchanan, Clifford Dancer, and Stephen Benedict urged that the Movement embark upon a program of food distribution in poverty-stricken areas and set up other "functional" units to aid the peoples of backward regions. This proposal was opposed by Cord Meyer, Jr., Mortimer Adler, G. A. Borgese, and Raymond Swing and was rejected in favor of educational and political activities. A new statute, drafted by Elizabeth Mann Borgese, gave larger voting strength to the organizations, notably UWF, with the largest dues-paying membership. Peter Hunot and Pierre Hovelaque became co-secretaries-general.

The fourth congress in Rome, April 2–9, 1951, was more a comedy of errors and a semitragedy of European confusion and American hysteria than a forward step toward the strengthening of the Movement. Mrs. Borgese planned the meeting with loving care, but was finally unable to come from Chicago to Rome because of illness. Foreign Minister Count Sforza agreed to accept the honorary chairmanship and to deliver the opening address. The Italian government offered the Barberini Palace as a meeting-place, though in the end the two hundred delegates met in an art gallery. Preparations were made, chiefly by Pierre Hovelaque, for a simultaneous World Congress of Organizations interested in peace and global unity. Among those invited to participate as "observers" were the Communist-inspired "Partisans of Peace" —who probably, in any case, would have refused to take part. But the invitation itself was soon a source of furor.

The U. S. Embassy in Rome hinted darkly that any group

which would invite the "Partisans of Peace" must itself be Red-tainted. The Italian Cabinet displayed sympathetic anxiety. Count Sforza indicated that he could not address the gathering. Finally the large UWF delegation, with a wary eye on Senator McCarthy and the Un-American Committee, flatly refused to attend unless the invitation were revoked. The Executive Council thereupon voted 12 to 5, and the delegates on the floor 72 to 11, to withdraw it. In protest Pierre Hovelaque resigned as secretary-general and was joined in resignations from the Executive Council by Alexandre Marc, Jean Diedesheim, Gustav Malan, and Abbé Groués-Pierre. Dean Paul Shipman Andrews of Syracuse University Law School, a member of the UWF delegation, asserted, for reasons not immediately apparent, that this episode had strengthened the Movement and made the Rome gathering "the finest congress yet." The "World Congress of Organizations" never materialized. Hovelaque was replaced as secretary-general in September by an American, Maclean McLean.

Meanwhile, having thus demonstrated that in its quest for One World it would run no risks of contagion by any contact, however slight, with that half of the world addicted to Red Sin, WMWFG was suitably rewarded: Sforza spoke; the Italian government donated two million lira (about three thousand dollars) for expenses; and the Pope sympathetically received and addressed the delegates, thereby giving the congress far wider publicity than it would otherwise have received. Since Lord Boyd Orr had resigned for reasons of health, the Rome congress elected as President of WMWFG General Hjalmar Riisen-Larsen, naval commander, Arctic explorer, and chief of the Norwegian Air Forces in World War II.[2]

THE PHILOSOPHER-KINGS—A week after the vaporization of

[2] This brief account of WMWFG is based upon the publications of the Movement, interviews with J. Keith Killby, Pierre Hovelaque, and other participants in the Rome Congress, and on a "Report Back" meeting of delegates to Rome held at Caxton Hall, London, April 14, 1951. See also *The Federalist*, journal of UWF (May 1951).

Hiroshima, Chancellor Robert M. Hutchins, speaking on the University of Chicago Round Table program, declared that the atomic bomb "may frighten the peoples of the earth into taking the positive steps necessary to the creation of one world government, not 1,000 or 500 years hence, but now." Soon afterwards Dean Richard P. McKeon and Professor G. A. Borgese made proposals to the Chancellor which led to the establishment of the "Committee to Frame a World Constitution." This group in its final form consisted of eleven members: Hutchins as president, Borgese as secretary, Mortimer J. Adler, Rexford Guy Tugwell, Robert Redfield, Wilbur G. Katz (all from the University of Chicago faculty), Eric Kahler, Harold A. Innis, Charles H. McIlwain, Albert Guérard, and Stringfellow Barr. These scholars held various meetings from November 1945 to March 1948, and prepared, with the aid of other collaborators, 150 learned memoranda. They also launched a scholarly monthly journal, *Common Cause*. In its first issue, June 1947, Chancellor Hutchins wrote:

> If we wish to be saved, we shall have to practice justice and love, however humiliating it may be to do so. These practices have long been commended to us by the very highest authority; they now appear to be our only alternative to beggary and annihilation. . . . The universal brotherhood which alone will save us must be sought under law. . . . We do not think, of course, that our preliminary draft will be the law of the united world. The federal convention in Geneva, or wherever else it may be, will not have to break through a wilderness of immature and contradictory proposals. A pattern will be available. We do not think it will be adopted; we dare to hope it will not be ignored.

The Preliminary Draft of a World Constitution was presented in the March 1948 issue of *Common Cause* and later published in book form by the University of Chicago Press. Following Chancellor Hutchins's resignation to assume his post with the new Ford Foundation, *Common Cause* was discontinued with the June 1951 issue, thus depriving the

English-reading world of its most erudite, brilliant, and provocative journal devoted to world government. Its articles, taken together with the mimeographed memoranda of the Committee, and G. A. Borgese's book, *Foundations of the World Republic* (University of Chicago Press; 1952), constitute a searching analysis of the premises and implications of the "Preliminary Draft."

This "proposal to history" is a document of forty-seven articles devised with affectionate consideration and a high degree of ingenuity. Since peace, democracy, and justice are envisaged as inseparable, the constitution provides not for a "minimalist" but for a "maximalist" government of the world —linked, however, with an elaborate "separation of powers" and a liberal Declaration of Duties and Rights to insure that the generous authority granted shall not be abused. Sovereignty resides in the people of the world. Residual powers rest with the member States. Powers delegated to the federation are vested, to begin with, in a federal convention, consisting of popularly elected delegates, one for each million people, and divided into nine regional electoral colleges. The convention, meeting for one month every three years, shall by two-thirds vote and secret ballot, on the basis of three nominations made by each electoral college, elect a president for a six-year term, with limited veto-power over legislation and liability to impeachment. Each electoral college then nominates twenty-seven candidates from its region for the world council or unicameral legislature. The convention by secret and proportional ballot chooses nine councilmen from each list, plus eighteen additional members nominated by international organizations, making a total of ninety-nine. The world council, with a three-year term, shall establish various advisory and consultative bodies: a House of Nationalities and States, a Syndical Senate, an Institute of Science, Education, and Culture, and a Planning Agency.

Executive power rests with the president, who appoints a chancellor and cabinet-members, none of whom, however, may be a member of the council, though they must resign when the president so decides or when the council, in two successive votes, indicates "no confidence" by an absolute majority. Judicial power rests in a grand tribunal of sixty justices, divided into five benches, with the federal president as chief justice and the chairman of the world council as vice-chairman. The grand tribunal elects a supreme court of seven members and establishes lower federal courts. The federal convention also elects a Tribune of the People "as a spokesman for the minorities, this office being vested in the candidate obtaining the second largest vote among the eligible candidates." His function is "to defend the natural and civil rights of individuals and groups against violation or neglect by the World Government or any of its component units. . . ." Control of federal armed forces is vested in a Chamber of Guardians, consisting of the federal president and six councilmen elected by the council and the grand tribunal in congress assembled.

Ratification of the constitution is to be by majority vote of the founding convention followed by "collective majorities within as many delegations of States and nations as represent two thirds of the population of the earth." Amendments require concurrent recommendations by a two-thirds majority of the council and the grand tribunal, and ratification by a two-thirds majority in the federal convention.

World citizenship is not explicitly provided for in the Draft. The supremacy of federal over national law, and its enforcement on individuals, are implied in provisions for judicial review of legislation, but nowhere expressly stated. In other respects the proposal plainly contemplates a global federal union with sweeping powers to promote peace, justice, and welfare. Bicameralism is avoided and the awkward problem of representation of States and/or peoples is solved by the device of the electoral colleges.[3] While a few features

[3] See Maurice Parmelee: *Geo-Economic Regionalism and World Federation* (Exposition Press; 1949) for a highly suggestive and all too neglected analysis of these problems. Fremont Rider's *The Great Dilemma of World Organization* (Reynal & Hitchcock; 1946) is an interesting example of the "White Man's Burden"—meaning, here, an attempt to devise a system of

are reminiscent of the Roman Republic, the structure of the projected world government, while perhaps unduly cumbersome and complex, is clearly a synthesis of European parliamentary practices and the "Presidential" system of the U.S.A. This circumstance *per se* would not necessarily insure rejection of the scheme by the Communist nations, since their constitutions, on paper if not in practice, embody many similar features. Not soon nor easily will other men devise a more thoughtful and thought-provoking draft of a possible basic law for all mankind. As to the acceptability of such a proposal, the committee, imbued with faith in Reason and confidence in Man, is content to say: "It is necessary; therefore it is possible."

MISCELLANY—Our enumeration of organizations committed to world government is far from complete and, in the nature of the case, can never be complete. The Chicago Committee, as early as January 1947, was able to list (document No. 120) almost half a hundred such groups in fifteen countries. As these words are written, Colonel Thomas Tchou's "World Citizenship Movement" at Oberlin College; "World Republic"—a youth group originating at Northwestern University to promote PWC; and the Emergency Committee of Atomic Scientists are all still active in their several ways. One of the areas in which the Ford Foundation (with almost half a billion dollars at its disposal) proposes to support activities is "world peace and the establishment of a world order of law and justice."

The "Parliamentary Committee on World Government" has long functioned as a formal committee of the House of Commons, with Mr. Patrick Armstrong as Secretary. The larger, affiliated organization known as the "Parliamentary Association for World Government" (of which Clement Davies, M.P., and Gilbert McAllister, M.P., were leaders in 1951) was instrumental in calling together in London in

---

representation in a world parliament whereby the illiterate, miserable, and poverty-stricken two thirds of mankind in Asia, Africa, and Latin America will be deprived of a majority in the Parliament of Man.

September 1951 an international conference of legislators. Here it was resolved to establish a "World Association of Parliamentarians for World Government," [4] for the purpose of preparing a constitution for a global supranational federal union and working for alteration of the U.N. Charter in this direction. In these various ways, and many others, the work thus goes on for the uniting of mankind, though no man yet knows what its end will be.

---

3. HALF-WORLDS

> A day will come when these two immense groups, the United States of America and the United States of Europe, shall be seen placed in the presence of each other, extending the hand of fellowship across the ocean. . . . In our ancient Europe, England took the first step, and by her example declared to the people "You are free!" France took the second step, and announced to the people "You are sovereigns!" Let us now take the third step, and all simultaneously, France, England, Germany, Italy, Europe, America—let us proclaim to all nations "You are brethren!"
>
> —VICTOR HUGO, "The United States of Europe," Presidential Address at the International Peace Congress, Paris, August 22, 1849.

ONE WORLD sundered into two warring camps is ill suited to the early fulfillment of the hopes of the "universalists" among the advocates of international federation. All such schemes have been repeatedly denounced by spokesmen of the Scarlet Empire—now the world's most ardent disciples of unlimited national sovereignty—as devilish devices of "decadent capi-

[4] For background and details, see the address by Henry Usborne in the House of Commons, July 28, 1950; Gilbert McAllister, "Towards World Government," *The Fortnightly* (September 1951); *Federal News*, Special Conference Report Number (November 1951); and *The Times* (London; September 25 f., 1951).

talism" and fiendish plots of "Wall Street" to enslave mankind. The Kremlin and its converts, despite early talk of a World Soviet Republic, have taken no steps toward federating the Red realms into a larger union, nor have they need to, since a *de facto* union has been achieved through central direction and co-ordination of all the ruling Communist parties. In the West, however, pleas for a federation of democracies have been numerous and eloquent. All have in common the plausible contention that any effective federation —if it is to be democratic rather than totalitarian in its values, form and functioning—presupposes some minimum common standards of civil liberties, the rule of law, and representative institutions. Such practices are to be found only in Western Europe (with the exception of Spain and Portugal), the British Commonwealth, the U.S.A., and, more doubtfully, Latin America. Ergo, it is widely argued, these States, or some of them, should form a federal union as a step toward, or a "nucleus" of, or a substitute for, a federation of the world.

ULTIMA THULE—Federal Union, Inc., unlike its British namesake, was from the outset unsympathetic to the universalist ideal, deeming it impracticable or, at best, a possible development of the far future if, as, and when all the nations of earth should embrace the tenets of Western liberal democracy. Clarence K. Streit, who founded FU as a membership organization in July 1939—originally under the name of "Inter-Democracy Federal Unionists" or IFU—is at once leader, mentor, and Savior-with-the-Book. His first work, *Union Now* (1938) sold over 300,000 copies by 1940. His second, *Union Now with Britain*, appeared in 1941. A postwar edition of *Union Now*, with five new chapters, was published in 1949. In July of 1950 appeared *The New Federalist*, a compilation of articles from *Freedom and Union* by Streit, Owen J. Roberts, and John F. Schmidt, with an introduction by John Foster Dulles. The federation here proposed was originally envisaged as a Union limited to fifteen "Founder Democracies": the U.S.A., Britain, Ireland, Canada,

Australia, New Zealand, South Africa, France, Belgium, The Netherlands, Switzerland, Denmark, Norway, Sweden, and Finland. Definitions of geographical scope have shifted with changing circumstances—e.g., South Africa has ceased to be a democracy; Finland, albeit still a democracy, has become a protectorate of the U.S.S.R.; Italy and West Germany have acquired democratic regimes, *et cetera.* The gist of the argument is best put in Mr. Streit's own original words, as republished in *The Essence of Union Now* (New York: Union Press; 1940), pages 3–4:

This Union would be designed (a) to provide effective common government in our democratic world in those fields where such common government will clearly serve man's freedom better than separate governments, (b) to maintain independent national governments in all other fields where such government will best serve man's freedom, and (c) to create by its constitution a nucleus world government capable of growing into universal world government peacefully and as rapidly as such growth will best serve man's freedom.

By (a) I mean the Union of the North Atlantic democracies in these five fields: a union government and citizenship; a union defense force; a union customs-free economy; a union money; a union postal and communications system.

By (b) I mean the Union Government shall guarantee against all enemies, foreign and domestic, not only those rights of man that are common to all democracies but every existing national or local right that is not clearly incompatible with effective union government in the five named fields. The Union would guarantee the right of each democracy in it to govern independently all its home affairs and practice democracy at home in its own tongue, according to its own customs and in its own way, whether by republic or kingdom, presidential, cabinet or other form of government, capitalist, socialist or other economic system.

By (c) I mean the founder democracies shall so constitute The Union as to encourage the nations outside it and the colonies inside it to seek to unite with it instead of against it. Admission to The Union and to all its tremendous advantages for the individual man and woman would from the outset be open equally to every democracy, now or to come, that guarantees its citizens The Union's minimum Bill of Rights.

The Great Republic would be organized with a view to its spreading peacefully round the earth as nations grow ripe for it. Its Constitution would aim clearly at achieving eventually by this peaceful, ripening, natural method the goal millions have dreamed of individually, but never sought to get by deliberately planning and patiently working together to achieve it. That goal would be achieved by Union when every individual of our species would be a citizen of it, a citizen of a disarmed world enjoying world free trade, a world money and a world communications system. Then Man's vast future would begin.

With the advent of the North Atlantic Treaty, Mr. Streit became co-founder and a member of the board of governors of the Atlantic Union Committee, with Owen J. Roberts as president, Robert P. Patterson and Will L. Clayton as vice-presidents, and Hugh Moore as chairman of the executive committee. AUC, which is distinct from FU but works closely with it, held its first national convention in Memphis, Tennessee, early in November 1951. Federal Union, Ltd., has endorsed the committee's purpose, with Professor George Catlin (an able advocate of Atlantic Federation since 1923) working actively for the cause. Similar endorsement was given early by the International Committee for the Study of European Questions, whose leaders include Paul Reynaud, Maurice Schuman, Lord Vansittart, and Lord Brabazon.

The objective is a Federal Union of the sponsors of the North Atlantic Treaty, with these States to decide what other nations shall be invited to participate. The chief means to the end, aside from publications, meetings, and other modes of persuasion, is the Atlantic Union Resolution, introduced into the House and Senate on July 26, 1949, subsequently supported by more than a score of Senators and almost three score Representatives, opposed by the State Department, and, as of 1952, not yet acted upon favorably by Congress. After seven "whereases," the Resolution—described by Justice Roberts as offering "a minimum of commitment with a maximum of hope"—asserts:

That the President is requested to invite the democracies which sponsored the North Atlantic Treaty to name delegates, representing their principal political parties, to meet this year with delegates of the United States in a Federal Convention to explore how far their peoples, and the peoples of such other democracies as the convention may invite to send delegates, can apply among them, within the framework of the United Nations, the principle of free federal union.[5]

EUROPA—In October 1946, federalists from various Western European lands met in Luxembourg and decided to establish an organization to co-ordinate their efforts. On December 15, 1946, was born the *Union Européenne des Fédéralistes* (European Union of Federalists or EUF) with its Secretariat General, as of 1951–2, at 39 Blvd. Malesherbes, Paris *VIIIe*, and its Executive Bureau headed by Henri Frenay. EUF is itself a kind of federation of federalist groups. While its central purpose is clear and simple, the complexity of its structure is equaled only by the number and variety of its pronouncements and proposals.

The "bureaucracy" of EUF, if the term be permissible, comprises an international council, a general committee, an executive bureau, four "commissions," a secretariat, a department of federalist youth, and so on. Its first Annual Congress was held in Montreux in late August 1947; its second in Rome in November 1948; and its third in Strasbourg in mid-

[5] For details of these developments and news of continuing activities, see *Freedom and Union*, edited by Clarence K. Streit and published monthly by F.U., 700 9th Street NW, Washington, D.C., and *Atlantic Union News*, published monthly by the Committee, 537 5th Ave., New York City. See also Congressional Hearings on the Resolution; Owen J. Roberts: "The World Needs A Cop on the Corner," *The Saturday Evening Post* (March 24, 1951); Owen J. Roberts: "Background for Atlantic Union," *Bulletin of the American Association of University Professors* (Winter 1950); interview with Will L. Clayton in *The Houston Press*, April 4, 1949; letters by George Catlin, Robert Boothby, and the present writer in *The Sunday Times* (London: April 22, April 29, and May 6, 1951); and Jane Perry Clark Carey: "Western European Union and the Atlantic Community," *Foreign Policy Reports* (June 15, 1950).

November 1950, apart from an "Extraordinary General Assembly" in Paris in late October 1949, sundry other gatherings, and a Conference at Lugano in April 1951. The groups here linked together had among them (as of 1951) perhaps as many as 150,000 members throughout Western Europe, organized into no less than seven societies in France, four in Western Germany, two in The Netherlands, and one each in Britain (Federal Union, Ltd.), Belgium, Denmark, Italy, Luxembourg, Switzerland, and Yugoslavia—in addition to other groups among exiles and émigrés from Bulgaria, Czechoslovakia, Hungary, Poland, and Rumania. Among the better-known names of persons playing an active part in EUF in recent years are Henri Brugmans, Keith Killby, Henri Koch, Eugen Kogon, Alexandre Marc, Denis de Rougement, Raymond Silva, and Guglielmo Usellini.

The central drift and purport of all these activities are suggested by the "Final Documents" of the Lugano Conference of 1951. One was a "Draft Statute of the European Federal Constituent Assembly," summoning European governments to convene a constitutional convention made up of parliamentarians. Another was a "Memorandum on the Main Provisions of a Future Pact of Federal Union," suggesting in general terms the need for guarantees of the Rights of Man, common defense, economic union, common diplomatic representation and foreign policy, a European citizenship, and the establishment of federal legislative, executive, and judicial authorities. But "federal unification should not mean the creation of a single European State." Still another document appealed to all Federalists "to undertake a vast campaign to convince the responsible authorities in each country of the necessity of taking, at the earliest possible moment, the initiatives which the decisions (of the Conference) require for their early fulfillment." A general proclamation concluded:

If the urgent objective put forward here is a federated Europe, it is not done through any contempt for the principle of sovereignty. On the contrary, we insist that no true society can exist which does not wield the instruments of its own sovereignty. It is because the national States of Europe have in fact lost their sovereignty that they must recover it together in a new community. The legal possession of sovereignty without the real power which should go with it is the most dangerous of delusions, because it hides from the people the road to their enslavement.

The set-backs of the recent past, the hard and urgent necessities of the present, teach us that the federal way is the only way to union. It does not in any way prejudge the content of the Europe of the future. Placed above and outside all ideologies, it leaves this to be settled by the free play of the forces of democracy.

The countries of the Old World are at the cross-roads. They must make up their minds, for time waits for no man. They must realize that for them the choice is no longer between the status quo and union. There cannot be a status quo. The best informed observers affirm—and they are right—that to preserve the national structures and frameworks is to condemn each country to economic depression, to social and political crises, becoming ever more acute. There is only one alternative: divided we fall, united we face a new future.[6]

Such ardent words and dedicated deeds have been supplemented, duplicated, and often confounded and confused in late years by comparable utterances and activities on the part of other groups, ranging from the European Parliamentary Union (secretary-general, Count Coudenhove-Kalergi) and the "European Movement" to the "Socialist Movement for the United States of Europe." That attainment of the goal is deemed imperative by American policy-makers, and that progress toward it has been slow, was affirmed before the English-speaking Union in London (July 3, 1951) by General Dwight Eisenhower:

It would be difficult indeed to overstate the benefits, in these years of stress and tension, that would accrue to NATO if

[6] This sketch of E.U.F. is based upon a voluminous dossier of reports, pamphlets, addresses, and other documents assembled, with the gracious and generous aid of M. Henri Frenay, at the Paris Office, 39 Boulevard Malesherbes.

the free nations of Europe were truly a unit. But in that vital region, history, custom, language and prejudice have combined to hamper integration. Progress has been and is hobbled by a web of customs barriers interlaced with bilateral agreements, multilateral cartels, local shortages, and economic monstrosities. How tragic! Free men, facing the spectre of political bondage, are crippled by artificial bonds that they themselves have forged, and they alone can loosen! . . . Europe cannot attain the towering material stature possible to its peoples' skills and spirit so long as it is divided by patchwork territorial fences. . . . Unity would mean early independence of aid from America and other Atlantic countries. . . . The establishment of a workable European federation would go far to create confidence among people everywhere that Europe was doing its full and vital share in giving cooperation. . . . The project faces the deadly danger of procrastination, timid measures, slow steps and cautious stages. Granted that the bars of tradition and habit are numerous and stout, the greatest bars to this, as any human enterprise, lie in the minds of men themselves.

STRASBOURG—That the road to a United States of Europe is long, the way hard, the gate strait, and the goal remote are best attested by the origins and development of the Council of Europe, established in the new "House of Europe" in the northeast quarter of the chief city of Alsace. Here French and German mingle on many tongues in a mediæval metropolis dominated by one of the most magnificent of cathedrals. Here skilled and sturdy burghers have lived long and created much on their oval, urban island formed by the division and reunion of the waters of the little River Ill as it flows toward the Rhine. Prior to the aggression of Louis XIV in 1681, the Strasbourgers were neither German nor French but European. For Strasbourg was originally a "Free City" of the Sacred Empire.

In Europe's House dwells a secretariat of some 200 members. Here since 1950 meets in public twice a year, each time for a fortnight, a Consultative Assembly of 127 representatives, almost all members of national parliaments: 18 each from France, West Germany, Italy and Britain; 10 from Turkey;

6 each from Belgium, Greece, The Netherlands, and Sweden; 4 each from Denmark, Norway, and Eire; and 3 each from Iceland, Luxembourg, and the Saar. Here meets in private thrice a year a Committee of Ministers, consisting of the foreign ministers of the member States, or their alternates. All of Western Europe speaks here, save Switzerland, Austria, Spain, Portugal, and Yugoslavia—with the first too "neutral" to join, the second still "occupied," and the remaining three presumably not eligible for membership since they do not accept, as required by Art. 3 of the Statute, "the principles of the rule of law and of the enjoyment by all persons within their jurisdiction of human rights and fundamental freedoms."

The Council of Europe as a dream is centuries old. The Council of Europe as a reality, whatever else it may be, is not a fulfillment of the dream, is not a European federal government and, indeed, is not a government at all. It is another forum, albeit a useful one, where parliamentarians may consult, study, speak, and resolve, and where foreign ministers may, if they choose, negotiate and pay such heed as they wish to the Assembly's advice. The consultations and recommendations are more meaningful than they seem to many critics to be. They bring "good Europeans" together on a legislative and executive level. They serve common human needs, however haltingly, throughout the now truncated Continent. But the Council cannot pass laws, execute programs, or decide anything vital apart from its own agenda and procedure. Its sole authority is to recommend common action to national governments in the form of resolutions and declarations—which the member States are free to adopt or ignore. And this power it shares ambiguously with other entities—e.g., OEEC, NATO, the Brussels Treaty Organization, and various U.N. agencies.[7]

[7] For a detailed and fully documented account, see the present writer's article, "The Council of Europe," *The American Polical Science Review* (September 1951). For subsequent developments, see *Europe Today and Tomorrow: International Bulletin of the European Movement* (25 rue de Spa, Brussels), distributed, along with a *News Letter*, by the American Committee for a United Europe (William J. Donovan, Chairman), 537 5th Avenue, New York City; Council of Europe, Consultative Assembly:

Far more than this was once imagined by many and is still hoped for by some. Churchill championed "Union Now" with France in the black days of June 1940. He bespoke a United States of Europe, in March 1943, and September 1946, though without British participation—a qualification overlooked or misunderstood by not a few Continentals. During 1948 and 1949 the American State Department and Congress both urged the unification of Europe. Following a "Congress of Europe" at The Hague in May 1948—unofficial but most distinguished in personnel—there came into being the "European Movement," with Churchill, Léon Blum, Alcide de Gasperi, and Paul-Henri Spaak as honorary presidents. Its effective propaganda, coupled with repeated appeals from federalist circles and American pressure for "integration," led the Council of the Brussels Treaty Powers to act, after Robert Schuman visited Bevin on January 21, 1949, and secured his assent to an assembly provided it should be merely consultative. Subsequent discussions culminated on May 5, 1949, in St. James Palace, London, in the signature by ten foreign ministers of the "Statute of the Council of Europe," a multilateral treaty of forty-two articles subsequently ratified by all the signatories.

At the first meeting of the Assembly, held in September 1949, at the University of Strasbourg, Mr. R. W. G. Mackay, M.P., seconded by André Philip, moved that "this Assembly considers that its aim and goal is the creation of a European political authority with limited functions but real powers." The representatives approved, 88 to 2, thus seeming to commit themselves to European federation. But agreement on "real powers" was not forthcoming. A year later it was evident

---

Speech delivered by Lord Layton, November 27, 1951; and *The Union of Europe; Its Progress, Problems, Prospects, and Place in the Western World* —Report of the Meetings Between a Delegation Appointed by the United States Congress as Authorized by S. Con. Res. 36 and Representatives Appointed by the Consultative Assembly of the Council of Europe, November, 1951, 82nd Congress, 2nd session, Senate Document No. 90 (Washington, D.C.: U.S. Government Printing Office; 1952). See also Karl Loewenstein: "The Union of Western Europe: Illusion and Reality," *Columbia Law Review,* Jan.–Feb., 1952.

that Britain, the Scandinavian States, and even the Beneluxers were unwilling to join a federal union, and that Paris, Bonn, and Rome had no heart for a purely French-German-Italian federation. On November 23, 1950, the assembly, 82 to 19 with 16 abstentions, endorsed "functionalism" rather than federalism as the way to unity. The "Mackay Plan" sought to achieve federation by small steps through the device of having the Committee and Assembly become chambers of a bicameral parliament empowered to legislate in whatever fields might be agreed upon. This having failed of adoption, a modified "Mackay Plan" of 1951 proposed a new statute under which the two bodies (with the Committee acting by unanimity and the Assembly by a two-thirds vote) could prepare draft conventions which the member States would be bound to submit to their national parliaments for ratification.[8] Even this modest proposal had not been approved by mid-1952, nor did it seem likely to command general support.

On December 30, 1951, the foreign ministers of France, Italy, West Germany, and the Benelux States, meeting in Paris, tentatively agreed (with no mention of the Council of Europe) that the projected treaty to establish a European Army should provide for a joint-defense board, a council of ministers, and an assembly from the six parliaments to criticize the board and perhaps have power to dismiss it. The assembly, moreover, would draw up proposals for a European federal parliament, presumably to be directly elected, to be bicameral, and to have authority to administer the European Army and the Schuman plan—with power to tax and a common defense budget. Hope was expressed that the contemplated parliament might be established by January 1, 1955. The treaty for a European Defence Community signed in Paris, May 27, 1952, contained no such ambitious provisions. Its

[8] See Council of Europe, Consultative Assembly: *Special Report* (submitted by Mr. Mackay and Messrs. Bastanietto, Bohy, Jakobsen, Kapani, Mommer, and Carlo Schmid) *of the Committee on General Affairs*, October 16, 1951, and Third Ordinary Session, Second Part: *Report on Constitutional Questions for the Committee on General Affairs*, containing the text of the proposed new Statute (Strasbourg: 1951).

purpose was not a United States of Europe but the rearmament of a reluctant Germany on terms acceptable to a worried France. That a European federation will emerge from a European Army in the years to come is altogether unlikely.

If we ask ourselves, as querulous American Congressmen are wont to do, why the age-old goal of a federation of Europe has even in our time, under the double impetus of American exhortation and the Red Menace, gone glimmering into limbo, several answers suggest themselves, apart from mere inertia, lethargy, local loyalties, and pride of sovereignty on the part of the nations of the Old World. The most obvious is British refusal to join—out of doubts of the Continent's future, unwillingness to transfer even small powers of decision-making and legislation from Westminster to Strasbourg, and a conviction that the United Kingdom's special ties with the Commonwealth and the U.S.A. are irreconcilable with British membership in a European Union. Less obvious, but no less real, is the ancient feud of Frenchmen and Germans, which now, as always, transmutes every scheme for union into a suspect device for the domination of the one nation by the other or into a source of anxiety lest each suffer, directly or by involvement in the other's quarrels, from the *revanchard* and irredentist ambitions of its neighbor. Both peoples are weary of the centuries of bloodshed between them, but plainly not enough so to renounce forever the possibility of its recurrence (and therewith their own sovereignty and their "interest" as "Powers") by restoring some semblance of the realm of Charlemagne in which both were one people and one polity.

But the root reason, usually unspoken, for the failure thus far of European federalism to attain its goal is this: informed Europeans of the 1950's, regardless of nationality or party, do not accept the American premise that Western Europe is threatened by Russian invasion and conquest, nor the American corollary that it can be rendered secure by federation or by rearmament, nor the American conclusion that, at worst, Europe can be "liberated" and restored by American arms after being overrun by the hosts of the Scarlet Empire.

On the contrary, despite lip-service and gestures to insure continued American aid, they believe almost unanimously that the menace of Communism is ideological, economic, and social rather than military; that massive rearmament at the expense of living standards will not contain or deter but will promote the spread of Communism; and that World War III means a death-sentence for European civilization. Given these attitudes and beliefs, federation appears to most Europeans (save for the few passionate federalists) to be neither necessary, possible, nor relevant to the problems and perils before them.

From these considerations it would seem to follow that in their assessment of world politics at midcentury, either Americans or Europeans must manifestly be mad. Who is madder than whom in these matters we have considered earlier and need not here decide. The best answer to the question is still that given to Alice by the Cheshire Cat.

---

4. THE FEDERALIST DILEMMA

> How can Satan cast out Satan? And if a kingdom be divided against itself, that kingdom cannot stand. And if a house be divided against itself, that house cannot stand. And if Satan rise up against himself and be divided, he cannot stand, but hath an end.
>
> —Mark iii, 22–26.

A MANKIND that spurns deliverance from evil confronts its Savior with no choice but to sacrifice his life in the hope that his death may yet move his disciples to redeem the world. In the pseudoscience and trial-and-error of modern politics, federalism is the most promising formula of salvation thus far offered to a world society disordered by virtue of the fragmentation of power among rival local units. The human race displays little desire to accept the prescription. Federalists are scarcely prepared to die on the cross for their Vision—nor, in all conscience, would such a procedure seem likely to make their dream come true.

The ancient question—What shall I do to be saved?—admits of no neat answer among the federalists of the mid-twentieth century. They have labored mightily and devotedly to convince people and politicians of the desirability and necessity of salvation and of the relevance of the federal formula to what the world obviously needs and ought to want. As these words are written, the fruits of their efforts have by no means sufficed to evoke effective public action in the direction proposed. And since nothing fails like failure, the result has been a waning of initial enthusiasm, a decline of membership, and the slow descent of the converts into boredom and fatalism.[9]

This melancholy muddle and drift toward apathy is attributable in part to the effect on public attitudes of the counter-propaganda of antifederalists, some of it the product of xenophobia and some the result of responsible reflection and analysis. In a special category are the Communist assaults on all proposals for international federation as devices to mask the

[9] Membership figures in the various federalist organizations are, of necessity, ephemeral, fluctuating, and unreliable. There can be little doubt, however, that in Western Europe, the British Isles, and the U.S.A., membership in such groups declined appreciably in the period 1949–52. In England, Federal Union Ltd. claimed a dues-paying membership (5 shillings annually) of over 10,000 in 1939, of 3,000 in 1947, and of something less than this in 1951, although almost 100,000 Britons during these years were members at one time or another. In the autumn of 1951 (see *The New York Times*, September 21, 1951) the Atlantic Union Committee asserted in its annual report that membership in the United World Federalists had declined in the preceding year from 40,000 to 27,000, with an $18,000 deficit "despite a greatly reduced budget" and with only 16 out of an original group of 117 members of the House of Representatives still supporting its proposals. UWF promptly denied these allegations. Walden Moore of the Atlantic Union Committee conceded that "the past year has been a difficult one" for all such organizations, including the American Association for the United Nations, and that WMWFG showed "signs of disintegration." By the spring of 1952, sixteen of the twenty-three state legislatures in the U.S.A. which had, in earlier years, passed "world government" resolutions, had reconsidered their decision and repealed the resolutions. On criticisms of UWF as "subversive," see John Hersey: "The Attacks on World Government," *U.S. Naval Institute Proceedings*, Vol. LXXVII, No. 11 (November 1951).

plots of "American imperialists," to destroy national sovereignty, and to deliver all the world into bondage to the "warmongers." While having appreciable effects on the Continent, such attacks have no influence in Britain and America save perhaps the negative one of attracting some persons to the federalist cause only because Communists are against it. The conservative antifederalist offensive is far more formidable. In its more frenetic form it is well exemplified in America by the D.A.R., the American Legion, the Veterans of Foreign Wars (whose slogan in 1952 was "World Government means World Communism"!), Merwin K. Hart (see, e.g., his *Economic Council Letter*, No. 231, January 15, 1950, seeking to smear UWF as "Red"), and, on a somewhat more amusing level, *The Chicago Daily Tribune*. The tone and direction of such invective can best be suggested by excerpts from typical *Tribune* editorials:

The United World Federalists, an outfit dedicated to the extinction of the American Republic, recently trotted out a retreaded New Deal wartime propagandist as its new president and mouthpiece: Alan Cranston. . . . These enthusiasts would have their countrymen buy a pig in a poke on the gamble that the sacrifice might offer peace. The notion that universalism of any sort can either achieve or maintain peace is old in history. . . . Attempts to establish world dominion have been repeatedly made both by empires and by religions. No one has ever worked. . . . Judging from the record of the past, world government is more likely to promote wars than to end them forever. Eternal vigilance is still the price of liberty and it should be exercised equally against political herbmen and potential foreign enemies. The destruction of the Republic is the goal of both. (November 9, 1949.)

When 27 Senators espouse the Atlantic Union scheme to merge America with the military, political, economic, and social destinies of Europe, Americans can well believe that intelligence at the center of government has reached a nadir. . . . The Atlantic Union is a device for America to fight everybody's wars and pay everybody's bills for the privilege of being dictated to by anybody but Americans. (January 18, 1951.)

What is termed a strategy conference was held last week in Washington by the Atlantic Union Committee. . . . The attitude of some of these anti-Americans is easily explained. Kefauver has a Scotch wife, for example, and Fulbright is a Rhodes Scholar. It is as simple to explain their attachment to England as it is that of Secretary of State Acheson or Lewis W. Douglas, Truman's former Ambassador to England, whose fathers were British subjects. (May 24, 1951.)

The preliminary draft of a world constitution was stillborn, but we occasionally get it out of the files when in need of a laugh. The persistence of efforts to draft global pronunciamentos of this sort demonstrates that the spirit of the high school fraternity will never die. We cling to the belief, however, that it was a lot more fun to dig a cave, build a shack over it, and prescribe entry only by secret password. . . . The companionship achieved was limited, but it had a valid existence, and that is more than can be said for any world government yet projected. (October 1, 1951.)

Doubtless less influential, but worthy of more consideration by thoughtful federalists, are the sober criticisms of thinkers and writers who challenge the premises of the federalist position. Thus Crane Brinton:

It would seem probable in international affairs, as in other kinds of human relations, that over ambitious, premature and "unrealistic" planning and chartering is bound to lead to failure. It is because I believe that international relations can be improved, that we can get longer breathing spells of peace, that we may even in some ways regulate wars, that we shall almost certainly get increasing political integration among hitherto "independent" states, that I am against an attempt *now* to create a true world government or a true world-state. . . . If you think of the human passions, the human habits, all of what Mark Twain called the "damned human race," lying behind these concrete difficulties, I think you will not have the temerity to call them ephemeral difficulties. They, and their like, are in our times permanent difficulties. They, and their like, in our times make the attainment of a world-state by the method of federal union impossible.[1]

[1] Crane Brinton: *From Many One*, pp. 8–9 and 106.

Similar voices are many. "We cannot secure peace for ourselves," writes Merle Kling, "by evading the real issues and migrating to the never-never land of a world state."[2] Harold Nicolson comments in like vein:

> I cannot but feel that these schemes of world-government are an escape from reality; the danger is so imminent that we have no time to snuff the cocaine of illusion. It would be delightful if we could avoid rearming, not have military service, and live in a world composed of handsome men and women, as benevolent, as gentle and as intelligent as Clarence Streit. We live in no such world. We live in a world threatened with war; the only way to prevent that war is to convince any aggressor that he is bound to lose it; to do that we must be very united and extremely strong. It is dangerous to evade the necessity of rearmament, or our irksome and perhaps humiliating dependence upon the United States, by inventing cloud worlds where gods and goddesses bask in the sunshine of blissful indolence, and where no thunderbolts can fall. For *Union Now* is some such cloud world. The impossible sometimes happens, but it takes many years; and we, poor generation, have only got a handful of months.[3]

Mr. Nicolson's method of "preventing war," we may note parenthetically, is as old as the pyramids and far less successful. Indeed its only results have been armament races between rival Powers invariably culminating in hostilities. The fallacy was never better put than by the English maiden-lady who is alleged to have said, during the Anglo-German arms race of the first decade of this century: "We ought to build our Navy up to the point which they say they're going to build theirs up to if we build ours up!" In a more penetrating commentary, Reinhold Niebuhr observes:

> American liberalism refuses to face the fact that there is a tremendous difference between the problem of community on the national and global level, a difference which no constitu-

[2] Dr. Merle Kling, Professor of Political Science at Washington University, St. Louis, Missouri: "World Government—A World of False Premises," *Social Education* (April 1950).

[3] Harold Nicolson: "Marginal Comment," *The Spectator* (London: April 27, 1951).

tional magic can overcome. National and imperial communities all have ethnic, linguistic, geographic, historical, and other forces of social unity. The universal community, however, has no common language or common culture—nothing to create the consciousness of "we." Modern democratic communities may be culturally and ethnically pluralistic, but they all possess a core of common spiritual possessions which the world community lacks. . . .

These are tragic facts, and one could wish that they were not true; but it is hardly mature to deny what is so obvious. The world community lacks, in short, the potent elements of "togetherness" which national communities boast. Neither law nor police power can supply this defect. If one trusted to police power alone, the amount required by a universal state to maintain order in a community which did not cohere naturally and organically would be so great as to amount to tyranny. This was Thomas Hobbes' answer to the problem of community; the similarity between his answer and that of many of our modern constitutional idealists is instructive. Fortunately, national communities had a more organic unity than Hobbes supposed. Unfortunately, the international community corresponds at least partly to his picture. These simple lessons must be spelled out to American idealists, not to induce a mood of defeatism, but to get them to direct the impulses of their idealism to real rather than imaginary objectives. . . . It would be intolerable if we again presented the world with a case of American schizophrenia, allowing our idealists to dream up pure answers for difficult problems while our cynics make our name odious by the irresponsible exercise of our power.[4]

Instances need not be further multiplied. The antifederalist case, reduced to bare bones, holds that world government, federal or otherwise, is either undesirable or unnecessary or irrelevant or impossible, or all four together. Those who deem it undesirable comprise a weirdly mixed company—in which, as usual, bedfellows make strange politics—including superpatriots, xenophobes, neo-Hegelians, Fascists, Communists,

[4] Reinhold Niebuhr: "The Myth of World Government," *The Nation* (March 16, 1946).

Nietzschean worshippers of war, and nihilists eager that the race should put itself out of its misery as soon as possible. Since this shared response, set off by a variety of stimuli impinging upon a multiplicity of differently conditioned organisms, is visceral, not cerebral, discussion of its merits would be futile.

As for the question of necessity, it admits of no answer save in terms of guesses about the most probable alternatives. If these are held to be a negotiated global peace of long duration among the Powers, or even an indefinite, armed truce, this prospect is doubtless more attractive to more people than the perplexities of agreement in establishing a Parliament of Man. But if the alternative, as is far more probable in terms of all the history and logic of power, is to be an atomic World War or a series of such—and if world government be deemed a feasible method of averting these disasters, or at any rate minimizing their probability and thus postponing the vaporization of civilization—then the question of necessity answers itself.

The contention of irrelevancy comes to this: either that federalists are wasting their time working for an unattainable goal and neglecting actual issues threatening peace—e.g., the East-West struggle, the revolt of Asia, the cry for bread—or that world government, if attainable, would not keep the peace. The latter plea is plausible if taken to mean that no arrangements, short of universal death or the transmutation of all humans into saints, can offer any hundred-per-cent guarantee of perpetual peace among men. But if the plea be a denial that world government offers greater promise of peace than other "solutions," then it is historically untenable. The World-States or universal empires of the past kept the peace remarkably well throughout vast and populous areas for centuries on end. The first form of the argument of irrelevancy is indeed applicable to some breeds of federalists, a few of whom (e.g., Edgar Ansel Mowrer) are so ardent in their Russophobia as to approximate the position of the advocates of peace by war. But it bears no relationship to the actual concerns and activities of the majority of Continental and British federalists and of American world federalists.

The argument of impossibility is more ambiguous and elusive and at the same time more cogent. In one of its shapes, it was well put by Herbert V. Evatt, Australian Foreign Minister, speaking in New York, November 27, 1945:

> It should be clearly understood that such a proposal [as world government] is quite impossible of acceptance. The plain fact is that the nations and peoples of the world are not yet prepared to surrender the rights of self-government in order to be governed by a central executive and a central legislature in which most of them would have a tiny and very insignificant representation.

As a statement of fact regarding popular attitudes and public policies, such an observation is unexceptionable. But the appointed task of all revolutionists is to change attitudes and policies. To assert that no such change as federalists strive for is conceivable is to ignore the record of all the great revolutions of time gone by.

"Impossible" is a term of various meanings in this context. World government is plainly impossible in the face of ever-mounting tension in the War between East and West. Only with the termination or mitigation of the struggle would the political preconditions of effective action toward the goal become realities—although in this case, paradoxically, many might deem world government no longer necessary, since the only present threat of more world war would have disappeared. Lesser and local wars are inevitable concomitants of every system of separate sovereignties. They can be endured by the rest of mankind with relative equanimity and with no need of world government to halt them, provided that the common sense of the species is capable of restraining the fanatics of "collective security" from trying to universalize every petty conflict in arms.

If "impossible" be taken to imply that the governance of all mankind is beyond men's capacity for organizing and exercising public power, the proposition is clearly false. What Pharaohs, God-Kings, Cæsars, Caliphs, Khans, and Sultans, lacking modern science and technology, succeeded in doing effectively in the smaller "worlds" of past civilizations, the men of today can assuredly do now, if they choose to, in the larger world of the Great Society. If it be objected that all past world-States were tyrannies and that what is now striven for is a democratic world-republic, the answer is that if enough of humankind desires to establish a global federal union on the basis of individual liberty, the rule of law, and representative institutions, there is available a vast reservoir of ancient and modern experience in constitution-making, in electoral devices, in policy-formulation, and in legislation, adjudication, and administration to make the enterprise entirely feasible. It is in this sense, though perhaps only in this sense, that the Chicago Committee spoke truly in contending that "world government is necessary, and therefore possible."

Finally (although finality is lacking in these matters), the appeal to the nonunity of the human community as an insuperable obstacle to global government may be briefly disposed of, despite its apparent validity. With all due respect, Reinhold Niebuhr is in error in saying (ibid.) that "all human communities had a long history of organic cohesion before they ever began explicitly and consciously to extend it." The reverse is more nearly the truth. Without exception, all the World-States of the past ruled over vast and diverse societies among which organic cohesion and unity were the slow consequence and gradual result of common government, not its source or prerequisite. In each case, to be sure, common government was not the outcome of contractual agreement but a beneficence initially imposed by the might of conquering armies.

It is arguable that among diverse local units the type of voluntary contract that is the essence of federalism does indeed presuppose a larger measure of consensus in the way of common values, folkways, mores, and other components of culture than the world community, made up of many different cultures, does in truth possess. But the argument cannot be pressed by responsible participant-observers to the point of minimizing or overlooking two crucial considerations. One is the circumstance that all of contemporary mankind, under the impact through recent centuries of the globe-girdling Western or Atlantic civilization, shares a greater store of common purposes, practices, and aspirations than ever before in the experience of the species. It is pleasing to politicians and professional warriors to dramatize and exaggerate differences—between East and West, Orient and Occident, Democracy and Communism, white men and colored men, metropole and colony. The fact remains that the revolt of Asia and Africa is the product of the yearning of yellow men, brown men, and black men to translate into reality the vision of independence and a more abundant life which they have acquired from the white men of the West. The Communism that is the religion of the rulers of Russia and China is a fusion of the ways of the Mongols with a dogma conceived in the brain of a German Jew, exiled from France and Belgium, working in the Library of the British Museum, and sending occasional articles to the New York *Tribune*. The oneness of our world may be daily denied by demagogues and may indeed be inadequate as the basis of federation. Yet it is a reality.

The second consideration here not to be ignored is that constitutions and governments promote unity quite as much and as often as they reflect unity. In the words of Robert M. Hutchins:

> Mr. Niebuhr exaggerates the state of perfection which world community must achieve before world government can be considered. Before the atomic bomb we could take world government or leave it. We could rely on the long process of evolution to bring world community and world government hand in hand. Any such program today means another war, and another war means the end of civilization. . . .
>
> Those who oppose discussion of world government on the ground that a world community must precede a world government seem to me to overlook the interaction between the two.

This is what the Greeks had in mind when they said that law was an educational force and that the city educates the man. The Constitution of the United States has educated the people of this country to believe in and support the Constitution of the United States. We are so used to thinking of law as repressive and constitutions as the embodiment of pre-existing agreement that we neglect the tremendous force which any constitution and any system of law exerts in behalf of its own acceptance and perpetuation. Anybody who has studied the relation between the political institution of a state and its educational system, for example, must agree with Aristotle that politics is the architectonic science. One of the reasons Aristotle gives for this conclusion is that politics determines what is studied in the state.

The way to promote world community is to have world government. But since we, as private citizens, cannot establish a world government, the next best thing we can do to promote world community is to talk about world government. World discussion of world government, far from disrupting the world, may have some chance of uniting it; for the consideration of what is necessary to unite the world, the discussion of a common problem of overwhelming importance, should lead to a growing sense of community among all peoples.[5]

The premises, and therefore the conclusions, of the new federalists are open to a possibly valid line of criticism on grounds, albeit seldom mentioned or even hinted at, quite other than those yet suggested. The counterargument here envisaged is not absolute but relative, not conclusive but tentative, since it stems in part from speculative and unverifiable hypotheses. To begin with the least intangible portion of the doubts here in mind, it has earlier been argued in these pages that every viable and enduring World-State must rest upon Myth, Authority, Adaptation, and Elite. Every functioning federal government, by its very nature, possesses adequate authority for its tasks. And if this be lacking, it can commonly be acquired through judicial reinterpretation or

[5] Robert M. Hutchins in *Foundations for World Order* (University of Denver Press; 1949), pp. 105–6.

constitutional amendment. A federal government, moreover, by its very structure and principle, is more adaptable to changing needs and expectations than most other forms of polity. These same qualities, we may assume, would be manifested in a world federation—if, as, and when established. The difficulty resides in the first and last prerequisites.

The federalist faith *per se* has never served as a political Myth capable, on its own, of moving masses of men to action and binding them together in unity. The fervor of many contemporary federalists is no exception to the rule. They are few. Their ranks are split into feuding factions. Thus far all federations that have come to birth as living schemes of governance have not been the offspring of any process of political parthenogenesis but have been the polygamously conceived progeny of the coupling of the federal concept with ardent local loyalties and the dynamic, mass cult of national patriotism. French Swiss, German Swiss, Italian Swiss, and Romansh Swiss united their Alpine cantons in a federal Switzerland less because they loved federalism than because they were ambivalently inspired with a common nationalism and with local allegiances that could best be reconciled by the federal formula. The American leviathan was born as a nation out of revolution unleashed in the minds and acts of men by the intoxicating ferments of nationalism, liberalism, and republicanism. Federalism was not the incentive to union but rather an inescapable condition of uniting the separate states into one nation. The troops of the Grand Army of the Republic fought through four bitter years, ostensibly as federalists to "save the union," but actually as patriots to preserve "one nation indivisible, with liberty and justice for all." Their gallant Confederate foes were less devotees of any such bloodless abstraction as "confederation" than ardent patriots of Dixie. All other federalisms are compromises between national and local loyalties, fused in a common patriotism. The pseudo-federalisms of the U.S.S.R. and Yugoslavia, where federal principles are allegedly married to Marxism, display this same characteristic.

Until the cause of world federation is intimately linked in the loyalties of men with some transcendant faith whose fulfillment appears to require the establishment of the Parliament of Man, there is little reason for supposing that any decisive portion of mankind will embrace the cause or that there will emerge in requisite measure that unity of spirit and purpose among citizens without which no federal union can function or endure. Nationalism, obviously, cannot play this role. Its effect is to unite nations but to divide the community of nations against itself. "Internationalism," "cosmopolitanism," "universalism," or "humanism," however defined, still lack sufficient appeal to sufficient numbers of people to serve as the stuff of Myth. Fear of war and love of peace are irrelevant. All men cherish some values more than peace and are prepared to kill and be killed in their service if no other way toward their realization appears available—even when they know in their minds and hearts that all they desire, and much else besides, will be lost in a welter of violence. Most federalists have assumed, tacitly or expressly, that the liberal-democratic ideology of the Atlantic societies is the Great Faith or Sacred Myth whose enrichment and indeed very survival require among the nations that degree of pacific collaboration in common tasks which can be had only through the federation of the Great Society. The assumption is correct enough. But the Myth of Freedom, in its Western form at least, has no meaning to the vast multitudes, comprising two-thirds of mankind, who live out their cramped and precarious lives throughout Eurasia, the Near and Far East, and the Dark Continent. Hence this Myth is inadequate to the task in hand. And no other is on the horizon.

An effective Myth for a time of transition, moreover, must be so devised that men, in embracing it, are led to believe that they are thereby conserving all that they worship in the past and achieving all that they most desire from the future. Such was the superlative accomplishment of Octavian and, in lesser measure but with equal efficacy, of Alexander the God-King and of the later Caliphs, Sultans, Khans, and

Commissars. The federal formula possesses much of this quality, for it appeals to a mankind that desires passionately to preserve national identities and loyalties and yet somehow attain order and peace all over the earth. But federalism, however diluted or disguised, presupposes that the States of the union will at the very least yield up those prerogatives of sovereignty, infinitely precious to all patriots, which are preconditions of conducting diplomacy and waging war. Augustus Cæsar found the means of creating an imperial *Pax Romana* within the forms of the Roman Republic. Not yet have the new federalists, for all their ardor and ingenuity, devised the symbols whereby men can be persuaded to accept the substance of peace through world government while still venerating the shadow of global anarchy.

Equally problematical is the nature of the Elite in the type of World-State dear to federalist hearts. Is it conceivable that the fluid, fluctuating, and amorphous "ruling classes" characteristic of the Atlantic democracies could carry on their tasks in a global federal union in co-operation with the feudal aristocrats of the Islamic world, the *caudillos* of Latin America, the governors of colonies, and the disciplined fanatics of the Scarlet Empire? Perhaps. It is possible, once the constitutional foundations of the new order are laid, that a new type of cosmopolitan intelligentsia or managerial bureaucracy may gradually emerge with an *esprit de corps* and a sense of dedication all its own. But who the "guardians" are to be, and who is to guard the guardians, in the federation of the world is not now clear, nor have many federalists faced this inescapable issue.

The most crucial of all questions posed by federalism, however, lies in the deepest places of the heart and in the very bowels of political man. It is the ancient question of the nature and purpose of the State in the literate cultures of mankind. Modern federalism is inseparable from the "social contract" theory of the origin and function of government, first propounded by the spokesmen of the medieval Conciliar Movement, later by the Monarchomachs, and more recently by the philosophers of the liberal-democratic bourgeois revolution. In the words of the American Declaration of Independence: "We hold these truths to be self-evident: that all men are created equal; that they are endowed by their Creator with inherent and inalienable rights; that among these are life, liberty, and the pursuit of happiness; that to secure these rights governments are instituted among men, deriving their just powers from the consent of the governed. . . ." Men, by an act of will and by discussion and compromise and solemn compacts one with another, create government by contract to serve the general welfare and give communities the blessings of peace through law and justice. Having done these things on a national scale, it follows in the federalist logic that as much can be done, if men so will, on a world scale, to the end that the human community as a whole may similarly benefit.

It is nevertheless arguable—and has been argued from Thrasymachus and Machiavelli to Friedrich Engels and Franz Oppenheimer—that all of this is illusion and that the State in its genesis and social role is an institution of a wholly different and far darker character. From this somber perspective, government is the product of violence and conquest. It is an organization of force, fraud, and favors to enable the victors to rule and rob the vanquished. It is a set of devices whereby elites hold masses in subjection. The initial and ultimate functions of the State are here deemed to be the exploitation of the lower classes for the advantage of the upper classes, and the waging of war abroad to promote obedience at home, to defend privileges against outer threats, and to expand the areas within which the processes of exploitation may profitably be carried on. If these premises be granted, then it follows that peace among peoples and social justice within communities can never be furthered by any imaginable expansion of the scope or functions of the State but are attainable only by the final achievement (in the jargon of anarchism and of the Marxist revelation, though the view referred to is by no means restricted to these sects) of a "classless society" with a resultant "withering away of the State." By this analysis, all government is evil. National government is worse than local government. World government would be worse than national government. Mankind is to be saved not by the extension of government but by its abolition.

This evaluation of the State, at least in its assumptions regarding the sources and social role of government, if not in its nihilistic prescription for salvation, is not to be dissolved by scorn or dismissed with epithets. Most arrangements for the governance of men by men throughout the recorded experience of the race do in truth resemble the grim image here delineated far more closely than they resemble that model covenant of each with all for the common good which is postulated in the federalist dispensation. Nor are the ranks of federalists lacking in those whose prime consideration is the more effective mobilization of part of the world for the waging of war against another part—always, to be sure, in the name of the age-old fallacy of "peace through strength." Federal unions are no less addicted to hostilities with foreign foes than unitary States or confederations or coalitions. A federated half-world confronting its counterpart across a potential line of mortal combat offers no greater guarantee of peace than an unfederated half-world—and, quite possibly, much less. If the very essence of the State is war, then a World-State is a contradiction in terms (in the absence of interplanetary warfare) and any new regional federation, whether called "nuclear" or "ideological" or "etaoin shrdlu," aggravates rather than reduces the likelihood of global bloodshed and devastation.

Although federalists and other peace-seekers ignore these considerations at their peril, we are happily not here called upon to choose irrevocably between the alternative portraits of government here painted. Governments, like other ways of men, have many functions and facets. The political animal is both Dr. Jekyll and Mr. Hyde. Oscar Wilde's *Picture of Dorian Gray* is sometimes as applicable to institutions as to individuals. Unlimited "free will" is a fantasy. Yet men, within limits, can make of their social and political arrangements what they will, and use them to serve such ends as they choose.

The faith of federalists may indeed be a misplaced and feckless faith, though this writer does not believe that it must needs be so. If it proves at worst futile, it remains at best a ringing reaffirmation of the dignity and rationality of Man, and a summons to men to take thought together, to love one another, and in common concord to make themselves captains of their souls and masters of their fate. The cause is thus akin to that of the creative empire-builders and the religious prophets of far lands and distant days. Such a faith, whatever its fruits, is its own justification and a beacon-light in the gloom—so long as some men always and all men sometimes continue to believe that mankind is capable of survival and worthy of salvation.

EPILOGUE:

WHEN THE SLEEPER WAKES

The hungry dream of food, the thirsty of drink, and the sick of health. Where all suffer uncertainty amid the mazes and muddles of a world they never made, everyone dreams of security. In pursuit of this good, men and women often escape from fear through work or play or love or religion. But success in the quest is ever jeopardized by the knowledge that each such private world, thus patiently pieced together, is always subject to swift destruction by the unpredictable confusions and convulsions of an all-embracing public universe, resistant of comprehension and defiant of control.

Bitter is the fate that decrees that human lives, carefully contrived to afford surcease from loneliness and some semblance of comradeship, may at any moment be inexplicably crushed, as men squash bugs, by unseen powers bred of the disorders of human society. Old are the efforts to transcend this dismal destiny. High among them in order of priority and persistence is the search for government—imagined, at worst, to be a new form of magic and, at best, to be a device whereby men can attain together what they cannot separately achieve.

This hope is not unwarranted. The manmade artifacts by which men wield power over men do in fact afford the warm glow of brotherhood, the boon of reassurance (even if only of danger shared, which is exciting and far more bearable than terror faced alone), and the shadow, if not always the substance, of common striving for the commonweal. It is doubtless true that most people, whether they trust or mistrust politicians, are prone to magnify the efficacy of government in shaping human fortunes. Political man is but a part of Man. Not even the most authoritarian of States can truly transcend or much modify the society and the culture from which it stems. The efforts of statesmen to perform this miracle are commonly more productive of misery than of amelioration. It is none the less beyond dispute, as the Greeks perceived, that the political community is the Great Community that includes all others. For the mass of men in the literate cultures of mankind, political means are the most effective means toward the safety and welfare of all.

But the politics of the *polis* or of the nation-State or even of the far-flung imperium no longer serve these needs in an age when nothing short of the governance of all mankind offers promise of protecting men from the evils of anarchy. The road toward a world polity is long and tortuous. The foggy horizon is remote. Meanwhile the need of the race is for qualities rare in times of chronic crisis: patience, perseverance, and perspective. Rash preoccupation with immediate purposes may well bring about in the atomic era an irreparable rending of the whole fabric of civilized living.

Precepts of moderation and self-restraint are unwelcome in a Great Society long addicted to dynamic action and currently beset with rival fanaticisms. Yet it has become commonplace to point out that Homo sapiens in this century, by virtue of his obsession with technology and warfare, has devised modes of collective murder that are wholly disproportionate to his "progress" in morals—i.e., in the discovery and enjoyment of truth, beauty, and goodness and in the gentle skills of living together as brethren. Unlike the new gadgets of death, the arts of life cannot be produced in laboratories and factories. They flow only from men's long-shared experience in dwelling with one another in peace—a blessing our generation has denied itself precisely when it is most in need of it. A renascence of these arts is possible, we may fairly assume, only through the mutual practice of a politics of prevention, accommodation, and co-existence, and through firm rejection of all crusades to vindicate moral values or save the world from sin.

The barriers in men's minds which block the path of those who see this need are lying all about, almost in a visible and tangible form. The earthlings who have achieved television, atomic fission, and stratospheric flight are still "barbarians" devoted to the ways of the clan and the gods of the tribe. The new cults of nationalism among the Asiatic and African peoples are but twisted reflections in a broken mirror of the older Atlantic worship of jealous local deities. Humankind, even in its most sophisticated societies, has moved but a short step from the mysticism and blood-sacrifices of savagery. Everywhere in our world, even as in ancient days, those most highly honored as "heroes" are still those who have killed or been killed in the service of tribal creeds. The bright light of science has promoted creature-comforts and perfected the arts of death. It has not as yet enabled the species to live together in virtue and in peace. In the most prosperous and productive community of our time, popular "news" and entertainment are almost wholly preoccupied with crimes of violence—a circumstance that we might well regard as auguring ill for sanity and self-control.

The postulates of democracy make Reason the guide to the good life, to the good society, and to political beliefs and acts. Inspiring is the vision of the self-determined intelligence of Man, enabling him to make all the earth a garden and to reach out among the stars. But humans are commonly self-defeated by their atavistic values, and by nonrational patterns of response as old as protoplasm, and by the dark, irrational forces of the mind as ancient as the psyche. The "political animal" inherits a brain capable of sharp analysis, subtle distinctions, and complex problem-solving quite beyond the talents of other mammals. He also inherits, from an earlier ancestry, the powers of blood and glands and viscera driving him to meet challenges in ways that are often the negation of rational judgment. Even the most civilized of men and women live the larger segment of their lives by magic and myth, superstition and stereotype, conditioned reflex and nonlogical inference. The *credenda* and *miranda* of all politics consist chiefly of clichés and rituals evoking behavior in which Reason plays no role.

Skepticism of the instrument is reinforced by contemplation of that which is more frightening than Man's nonreason—i.e., his frequent disintegration into unreason and madness under the stress of outer frustrations and inner conflicts. Our nature-knowledge far exceeds our self-knowledge. Despite the best efforts of artists, theologians, and psychiatrists, the Hominid who knows all about the nucleus of the atom and the temperature of distant suns knows little of the mysteries of his own heart. He knows only that from time to time, under circumstances and for reasons always puzzling, men and women find balm for spiritual torment by reverting to childishness or savagery and surrendering their wills to satanic powers, bred of forgotten grief or pain, and beyond conscious awareness or control.

The beast who would be a god then walks sightlessly through the valley of the shadow, as if acting out a nightmare. In single cases he can be sometimes helped by those skilled in fighting fear. But when whole communities find their souls by losing their minds, lunacy is crowned king, while the sane are jailed or silenced or slain. The tensions and anxieties statesmen are called upon to cure then pass the point of no return. Such epidemics yield to no panacea save bloodletting—a remedy that destroys patients and physicians alike.

This nemesis looms ominously over the Great Society of our time. The obscenities of Auschwitz, Buchenwald, and Maidenek are symptoms of this putrescence of the human spirit, as are the horrors of blood-purges and slave camps, of lynchings and witch-hunts, of the senseless butcheries of war for peace, and of all the degradations and indecencies of our age. Long before such things were deemed again conceivable, Matthew Arnold—perhaps sensing their possibility and despairing of Man's capacity to keep faith with himself and his God—wrote in *Dover Beach* (1867) that "the world, which seems to lie before us like a land of dreams, so various, so beautiful, so new, hath really neither joy, nor love, nor light, nor certitude, nor peace, nor help for pain; and we are here as on a darkling plain, swept with confused alarms of struggle and flight, where ignorant armies clash by night."

To despair of the human adventure is the easiest course of all for any of us to pursue. To assume, with Mr. Micawber, that "something will turn up" and all will somehow come right is, in our time, less easy and yet perhaps more justified, since the species is tough. Its most intricate and delicately poised civilizations have shown amazing resilience in surviving attempts at suicide. What is difficult is to analyze, with some conviction of correctness in premises and conclusions, how the needs of mankind in our current time of troubles can best be served through political action. What is more difficult is to translate any prescriptions that may emerge from such analysis into a living faith capable of moving men to creative deeds.

The disciples of world government have not solved these problems, nor is it reasonable to expect them, unaided, to do so. Today's generation is no longer to be saved by any Savior-with-a-Book nor yet by any Savior-with-a-Sword or Savior-with-a-Time-Machine. The mankind of the twentieth century will be saved, if at all, from the fruits of its follies only by divine intervention or by its own spiritual and intellectual resources, expressed in revolutionary political imagination. The former contingency will be an Act of God and thus beyond any prediction or evaluation by merely human agents. The latter hope presupposes a possibility at once human and godlike—i.e., that Man, challenged to rescue his future from the dark forces of his past, still possesses the attributes of mind and spirit requisite for salvation.

The immortal glory of all the apostles of the unity of mankind, whatever the results of their own works, is their faith in Man's potentiality for brotherhood, in his ultimate rationality, and in his talents for finding ways to realize his fairest dreams. Such faith is futile when it fails to touch men's daily lives, for it is then the concern only of monks or mystics or lonely scholars. But in our era the Vision of Man is interwoven with the fortunes of all humankind—all the more so wherever men and women are unaware of its import and are bound blindly to the altars of fear and hate. The aspiration toward a united humanity is again large with life. The child may be aborted or die aborning or survive as a misfit or, *Deo volente*, grow to healthy maturity.

The contemporary advocates of world government who would fain be the midwives of this blessed delivery are not only the custodians of the ancient ideal of the brotherhood of man. They are also—if we may pursue a medical metaphor in different form—the diagnosticians of the disease of the Great Society. The remedy they propose may be quite unacceptable to the patient. But the essential correctness of the prescription is no longer in doubt. The mounting fever and ever-more-alarming symptoms of the body politic, convulsed with violent and possibly fatal paroxysms, daily offer new evidence that the disorder corresponds in its cause and course to the prognosis of those who contend that its source lies in the political anarchy of separate sovereignties.

Men who live without government live inescapably by the way of violence. In a war of each against all, every man must distrust his neighbor and, in the last extremity, slay or be slain by his fellows. For mankind has entered this vale of tears not trailing clouds of glory from some pristine age of innocence but smeared with the blood-lust of an animal and cannibal ancestry. The bestiality of his forbears is oft compounded with deviltry, engendered by resentments and guilts at the restraints of social life. Most other gregarious species know nothing of rage and cruelty against their own kind. But our time-binding, word-using, culture-creating Primates—by the very process of lifting themselves from beasts to men and aspiring to become as gods—have suffered new tensions and frustrations, driving them either to a Research Magnificent for spiritual atonement and apotheosis, or to depths of brutishness more appalling than any displayed by the most ferocious hellcats of the jungle. Man's ability in his saner moments to distinguish clearly between these ultimates of his own responses to his problems is evidence of the existence in the secret places of his heart of some heavenly spark, human or divine, lighting his way to redemption.

But the way leads nowhere without brotherhood and without the experience of justice under law which the best minds of the race have always hoped would be the ultimate meaning of "government." Through the worship of totem-ghosts and local gods, men long ago found fraternity in their little sibs and narrow clans and selfish tribes. For the past three millennia men have sought universal brotherhood in One God, apparently arriving at this striving through their political experience as members of the earliest "World-State" and transmitting their memories and their hopes through Israel to later generations. Never yet has this aspiration come to fulfillment for all the human family, though we have seen it come to partial fruition for many peoples over many centuries in the universal empires of olden times.

In our day the global anarchy of contending States menaces the welfare, and the very survival, of the civilization of the West whose emissaries, on the wings of science, have flown to the ends of the earth and all unwittingly made all men neighbors. That this is a truism makes it no less true. Those who would deny it must ignore the recurrent miseries of most of mankind since 1914, and question the probability that like causes will produce like results tomorrow as yesterday. During the century between Waterloo and Sarajevo all the earth-dwellers moved perceptibly, with no one charting the route, toward the destiny implicit in the systematic application of scientific knowledge to the service of human needs. A world economy assumed visible form, however amorphous and incomplete, within the matrix of free travel, free trade, and the international gold standard. A world polity, or at least the preconditions thereof, seemed about to emerge out of the practices of neutrality, nonintervention, and localization of armed conflicts, and out of growing participation by the nation-States in the processes of mediation, arbitration, and international organization. A world society, whether or not possessed of the ingredients of a genuine "community," came into being. Our ancestors equated these developments with "progress."

Most of these hopes now lie in ruin all about us, like the broken shards and shattered temples of a civilization that has already passed away. The calamities we have endured, and the worse disasters looming before us, admit of innumerable explanations, naïve and subtle, open and recondite. But the common source of our woes, whatever other meanings may be read into them, is the manifest incompatibility of two "worlds" at war in the beliefs and acts of men. Contrary to vulgar opinion, the two worlds in conflict are not the Western "world" of democracy and the Eastern "world" of totalitarianism. This struggle is as real as the long-forgotten conflicts between Athens and Sparta, Rome and Carthage, Popes and Emperors—and as irrelevant to the exigencies of our age.

The dichotomy we are here concerned with is not between Sin and Virtue, Truth and Falsehood, Love and Hate, Piety and Godlessness, Jehovah and Lucifer, or even Freedom and Tyranny. Such schisms are with us always. The soul-searchings to which they lead are as old as civilization. The issue of life or death for the Great Society hangs upon a dualism of a different order. Its essence is a mortal struggle between warring loyalties, between clashing orientations toward humankind, between alternative and irreconcilable ways of striving for virtue and for escape from fear. Each protagonist is the legitimate progeny of our common cultural heritage. Both have long co-existed in many climes and times. But there is no good ground for supposing that they can much longer co-exist within the body and soul of the contemporary Great Society without bringing the body to destruction and the soul to damnation.

The contestants in this age-old strife, now in its final phase in our own culture, are Ethnocentrism and Universalism. Preliterate man seeks peace and brotherhood through his totem-gods. Literate man pursues the same goals through his various pantheons and through the sacred symbols of the nation-State. In each instance fraternity among neighbors is bought at the cost of shared contempt and hostility toward other human groups across some invisible barrier of power or belief. Nationalism is ethnocentrism writ large. So also is every dedication to a belief-system whose devotees find spiritual solace only through hatred of heretics and infidels.

From the record of human acts through historic time, it might seem that our species has found no better way to satisfy its huge desire to love and be loved in some comradeship of souls larger than the family. But from the record of human aspirations, it is evident that Man, at least since the days of Aton and Yahweh, has never found this way a true way or a good way. For he has been ever searching among the stars and in the recesses of his soul for a vision of the universal fraternity of all mankind. During the past thirty centuries and more, many men and women occasionally, and a few always, have seen the glory and achieved transfiguration from bestiality to godliness. This is the common meaning (and if not this, then nothing) of the messages of Ikhnaton and the Hebrew Prophets, of Confucius and Gautama the Buddha, of Jesus of Nazareth, of Marcus Aurelius and Saint Augustine, of Mohammed and Saint Thomas, of Martin Luther and George Fox, of Leo Tolstoy and Mahatma Gandhi. That these and other seers are revered by millions as holy men and as spokesmen of the divine will is sufficient testimony to the longing of all peoples everywhere for a god-given faith in the common humanity of all mankind.

This yearning has over and again been frustrated by the

disposition of men to transmute their soaring universalisms into new versions of ethnocentrism even more intolerant than the old. Persecutions, holy wars, and sanctified genocide for the salvation of souls have ever marked the course of the efforts of men to win other men to the one true faith. Caliban in uniform, or in priestly vestments, or in evening clothes, is still Caliban, son of Sycorax. Whether he mouths words of "peace" and promises the liberation of the proletariat, or shrieks of "freedom" and brandishes atomic bombs, he is still the incarnation of fear and force and evil magic as old as the Neanderthalers and as new as Commissars, Gauleiters, and the impassioned apostles of "preventive war." Behind a mask of humanism and religiosity, the cannibal within still sneers at the dignity of Man and drools expectantly at the prospect of new anthropophagies.

The global community of our time cannot reasonably be expected to survive much longer the self-destructive violence of ethnocentrists and of universalists turned inquisitors and crusaders. A choice must be made. In its making, it is quite possible that the way of the savage may triumph. Our common civilization will then disintegrate into a new barbarism, threatening the very life of our species. It is equally possible, though the available margin for error is ever narrower, that Man's faith in reason and brotherhood may prevail. The Great Society may then endure and devise the values and practices requisite for the transformation of disorder and violence into some semblance of political unity in diversity, and mutual forbearance among divergent ways of life.

"World government" has become for this generation the central symbol of Man's will to survive, and of his moral abhorrence of collective murder and suicide. Some of the movements devoted to this cause have already been corrupted by age-old evil. Others have displayed invincible ignorance toward the realities of power and the facts of life. Yet the only universalism of our epoch which proposes to give effective political expression to the timeless words of righteousness and wisdom is the universalism of the prophets of a global polity. This is clearly the case regardless of whether these endeavors come to something or to nothing, and regardless of whether the debauched universalists of "proletarian world revolution" and of the "American Century" succeed or fail in their adventures in competitive paranoia and mutual annihilation. A Saturnalia of homicidal madness, to be sure, will defer to the Greek kalends any possibility of a reign of reason. But far from altering the terms of the central problem of humankind, such a debacle will merely vindicate, however hideously, those who have long contended that all the race must either achieve common government or suffer death on the bloodstained altars of the false gods.

This is not to say that all is lost unless world government can be achieved tomorrow. Quite obviously it cannot be. Those who would promote its attainment by portraying the alternative in inevitably catastrophic terms do a disservice to the cause. Fear, often uniting some men against others, can scarcely serve to unite all in a common purpose rooted in shared loves and hopes. It is at least arguable that total disaster is not necessarily the most probable alternative to global government in our time. The uneasy equipoise of the super-Powers may continue indefinitely without recourse to wholesale violence. The makers of high policy are, at best, befuddled and confused by the immensity of problems beyond the grasp of their imaginations and by the constant pressures upon them of the self-seeking, the ignorant, or the demented. But so long as those who wield great power are not incurably madmen, some calculation of consequences is possible, and indeed probable, in hidden reservoirs of cerebration. The fruits of irresponsible fanatacism are likely to be lethal to all concerned. Even fanatics and barbarians shrink from meaningless self-immolation. A long period of unstable rivalry and balance is hence quite as conceivable as an abrupt descent into Avernus.

Such a prospect, let us grant, is no basis for complacency. Its effects may be such as to generate tensions that ultimately must either explode in a new Armageddon or lead to "One World" on the ugly model of Orwell's *1984*. Conversely, its effects under the spell of the New Machiavelli may finally promote prudent moderation and foster a creative *Realpolitik* characterized by mutual toleration bred of the impracticality of reciprocal violence.

But if there be any logic in the cosmos and any order in the fortunes of the civilizations of mankind, then it is altogether likely that the era in which we find ourselves will terminate either in a breakdown of the Great Society and a new Dark Age, or in the building of a Global Polity within which most of humankind, by sharing a common destiny and accepting common duties of citizenship, will arrive at some tolerable reality of justice and self-fulfillment. This hope came to partial realization in the limited and local World-States of times gone by. Our own task is at once simpler and more formidable: we are summoned to unite all humanity in a truly planetary polity. We possess in abundance the skills of science, technology, and administration which make such as enterprise materially feasible. If we lack the spiritual and intellectual resources requisite to the enterprise, we may well lose the future.

The means most appropriate to the attainment of the end will necessarily remain matters of disputation and experimentation for years to come. Questions of method, as we have seen, have divided honest and enlightened spirits against one another in often-bitter controversies, sometimes productive of new insights and sometimes self-defeating. Our analysis is more conducive to certitude on the negative than on the affirmative side of the issue. It is far easier to say how world government will not be achieved than how it will be or might be.

World government is unattainable in our time by conquest. Unity by the sword presupposes the suppression of anarchy through the subjugation of the weak by the strong. In a bipolar world of delicately balanced and equally gigantic aggregations of power, both possessed of atomic weapons, a conqueror's peace can only be the peace of the grave for all.

World government in our generation is equally impossible

through treason, subversion, and conspiracy. Policemen in well-administered communities will always prove more effective than traitors and enemy agents. World government is likewise not to be had through "functionalist" planning, however useful in the service of human needs such activities may be. World government will never conceivably be arrived at through "collective security," since this device, currently so popular in the West, is a fallacy and a fantasy.

If the burden of the preceding pages has seemed to be more negative than affirmative, this has been due less to pessimism over the enterprise than to the fondness of men for roads that have no destinations. In the search for world government, as in the practice of all government, politics is still the art of the possible.

We are left with the possibility of world government through a voluntary extension of the principles of federalism to the whole society of nations. Here also, despite devoted efforts by many people in many lands, nothing may seem to the so-called "realists" less likely of accomplishment during the decades looming before us. Inertia, fatalism, and national and ideological ethnocentrism may appear to many to be insuperable obstacles. Regional adventures in federalism fare scarcely better, and may even prove antithetical to the larger purpose.

Yet it would be wholly premature to conclude from these considerations that the Parliament of Man and the Federation of the World are beyond attainment. Arrival at the goal may not be indispensable to the survival of contemporary civilization. But it would appear to be necessary if appalling risks are to be avoided. Human beings, so long as they do not become hopelessly aberrated in the face of their frustrations, are capable of acting together in the service of their needs.

This capacity of the animal who would be divine offers no certainty of relevant action, or of the success of such action as may be taken. All that is offered is an opportunity. In Spengler's words: "We have not the freedom to reach to this or to that, but the freedom to do the necessary or to do nothing."

If the opportunity is wasted, all is not irretrievably lost. If seized upon, no Millennial Golden Age will dawn. Those who imply that world government will solve all problems and resolve all conflicts serve the cause no better than those who cry havoc if their advice is ignored. If the Temple of Man can slowly be reared on foundations of swords beaten into plowshares, the result will not be Paradise, even if the structure is finally completed. Men will not thereby become saints nor be magically liberated from unreason. They will still struggle with themselves and with one another for goals ignoble and noble, and find many of their conflicts desperately difficult of resolution. But the result, we may reasonably believe, will be an escape from an Inferno wherein men like devils torture one another to death in a vain quest for salvation. And without such escape, none can sensibly hope for betterment of our common lot or for a chance for human self-realization.

Further speculation as to the forms in which such aspirations and efforts may express themselves would, as of now, be idle. If Caliban triumphs, as well he may, nothing will come of any of these activities. If the gospel of the Unknown God prevails, as Saint Paul hoped would be the case when he came upon a strange altar in Athens, then limitless vistas of future achievement are open to a united mankind. The creation of a *Pax Orbis* will constitute only a negative blessing of times to come—yet one invaluable, since it will spell escape from fear and surcease from most of the anxieties and agonies that have plagued humanity in our tragic century. For a *Pax Orbis*, as the experience of the past has shown, is the precondition in all times of troubles for a new flowering of the human spirit.

Is such a vision of the human community utopian? Perhaps. If so, mankind must be judged to be not seriously concerned about its own salvation, or the meaning of Man to himself. Is the vision attainable, or at least imaginable? Assuredly, since a generation that has achieved the means of self-destruction has also thereby achieved, if the will to live is still alive, the means of self-preservation and of a more abundant life for most of humanity than any of our ancestors ever knew. Are we free to choose? Undoubtedly, if we cease to cling fearfully to the ways of darkness and raise our eyes to the sunlit heights where we can finally banish savagery and unreason and live, if we will, as men like gods. As to whether we shall choose wisely and in time, each must answer for himself.

INDEX & GLOSSARY

A GUIDE TO THE BEWILDERED: Ships and shoes and sealing wax and cabbages and kings are not all of equal importance in the study of power politics and world government. The first four items have therefore been omitted from the entries that follow. All kings (and queens) mentioned in the text are included, however, along with bishops, knights, and pawns—though not castles. Indeed in a work of this kind it has seemed to me not only permissible but desirable to avoid, as dull and pointless, any indexing of places, wars, religions, treaties, ideologies, abstractions, and other items of miscellany. All of these can readily be located if the reader will but consult the entries under the name of the individuals and organizations connected with them.

This Index includes every mention of every person (living or dead, mortal or divine) quoted or cited or referred to in the text and Preface; every movement or association, public or private, connected with the matters here in hand; and every quoted publication of anonymous or collective authorship.

The notes in the text comprise a select bibliography of the various problems touched upon. Where no other place of publication is mentioned, the place is New York City. Every author named is here indexed. Other useful bibliographies on world government will be found in Gerard J. Mangone: *The Idea and Practice of World Government* (Columbia U. Press; 1951), pp. 241–59; Gertrude S. Hooker: *Outline of a Basic Bibliography on World Government* (Document #110, Committee to Frame a World Constitution, Chicago, 1946, 17 pp., Mimeographed); Alexander D. Mebane: *Whither Must I Fly?* (The Author; 1949, Mimeographed), pp. 90–4; Hornell Hart, Director of the Consensus Project: *Toward Consensus for World Law and Order* (Durham, N. C.: Duke University; 1950); and Alan De Rusett: *Strengthening the Framework of Peace* (London: Royal Institute of International Affairs; 1950), pp. 219–21.

The symbols here employed have these meanings: q. = quoted; c. = cited as to published writings or oral statements to this writer; n. = footnote; f. = and pages immediately following.—F. L. S.

A NOTE ON THE TYPE

This book was set on the Linotype in Janson, a recutting made direct from the type cast from matrices (now in possession of the Stempel foundry, Frankfurt am Main) made by Anton Janson some time between 1660 and 1687.

Of Janson's origin nothing is known. He may have been a relative of Justus Janson, a printer of Danish birth who practiced in Leipzig from 1614 to 1635. Some time between 1657 and 1668 Anton Janson, a punch-cutter and type-founder, bought from the Leipzig printer Johann Erich Hahn the type-foundry which had formerly been a part of the printing house of M. Friedrich Lankisch. Janson's types were first shown in a specimen sheet issued at Leipzig about 1675. Janson's successor, and perhaps his son-in-law, Johann Karl Edling, issued a specimen sheet of Janson types in 1689. His heirs sold the Janson matrices in Holland to Wolffgang Dietrich Erhardt, of Leipzig.

COMPOSED, PRINTED, AND BOUND BY H. WOLFF, NEW YORK